THE CASE FILES OF JEWELER RICHARD

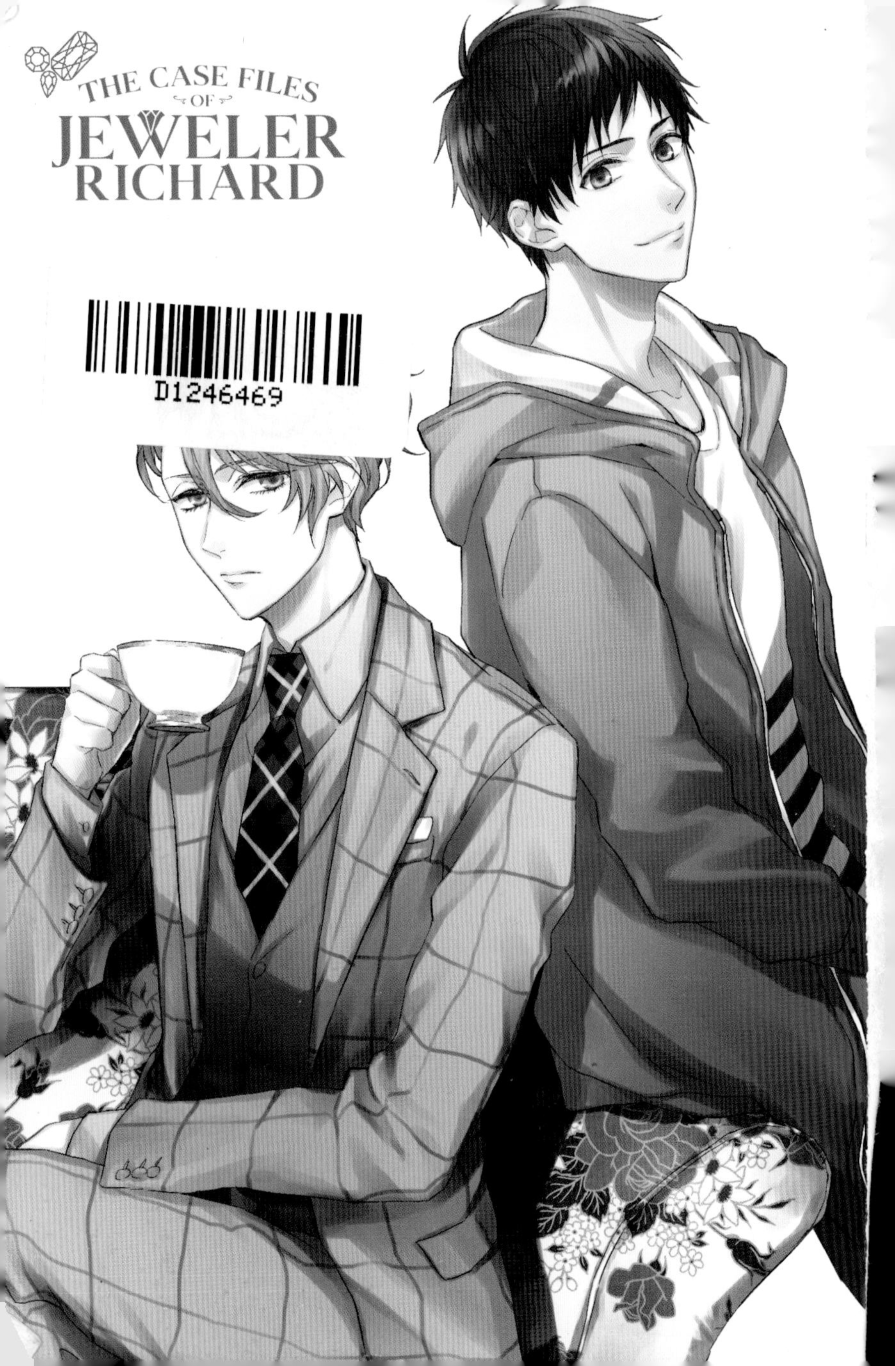

Contents

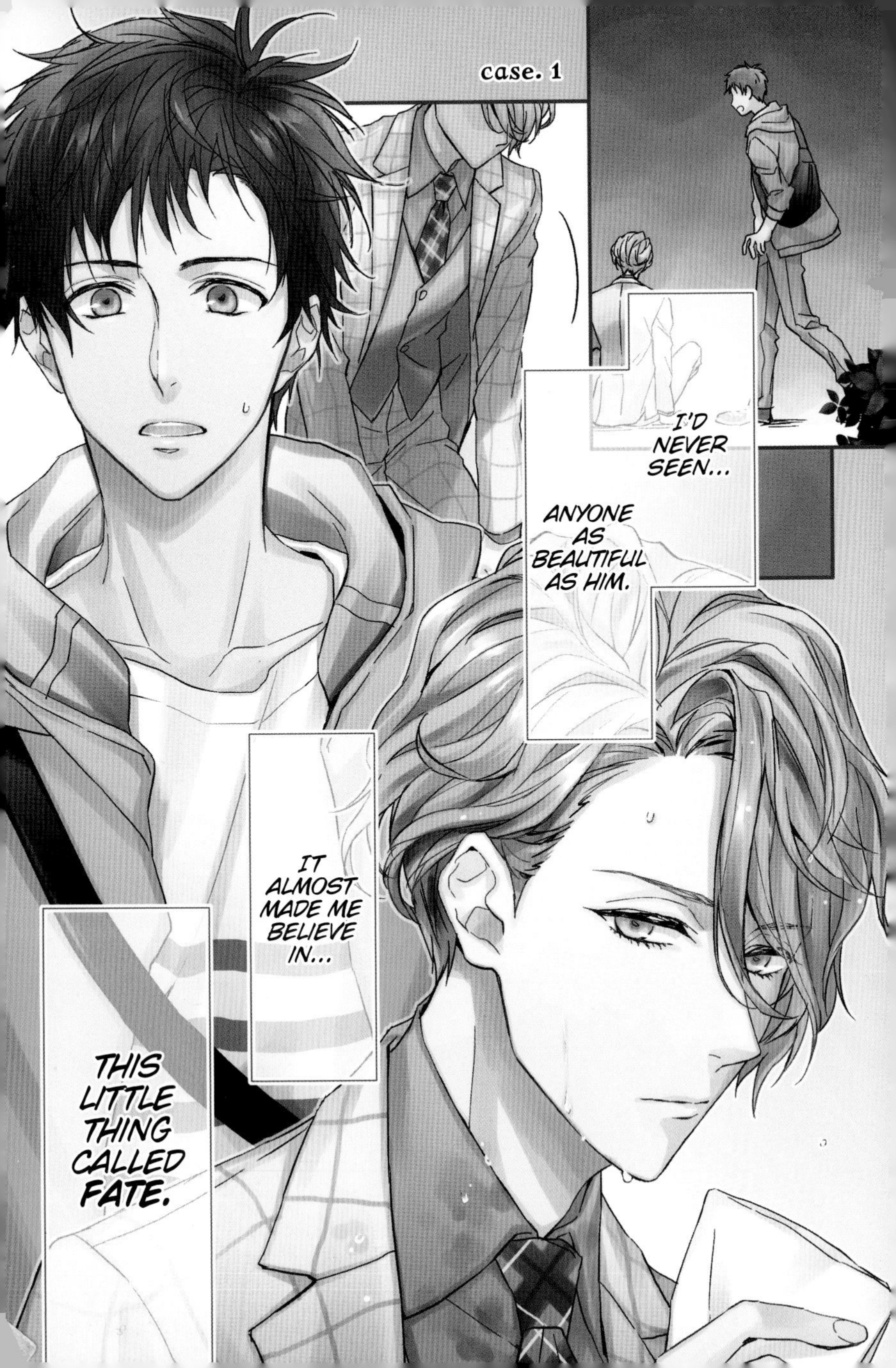
case. 1
I'D NEVER SEEN...
ANYONE AS BEAUTIFUL AS HIM.
IT ALMOST MADE ME BELIEVE IN...
THIS LITTLE THING CALLED FATE.

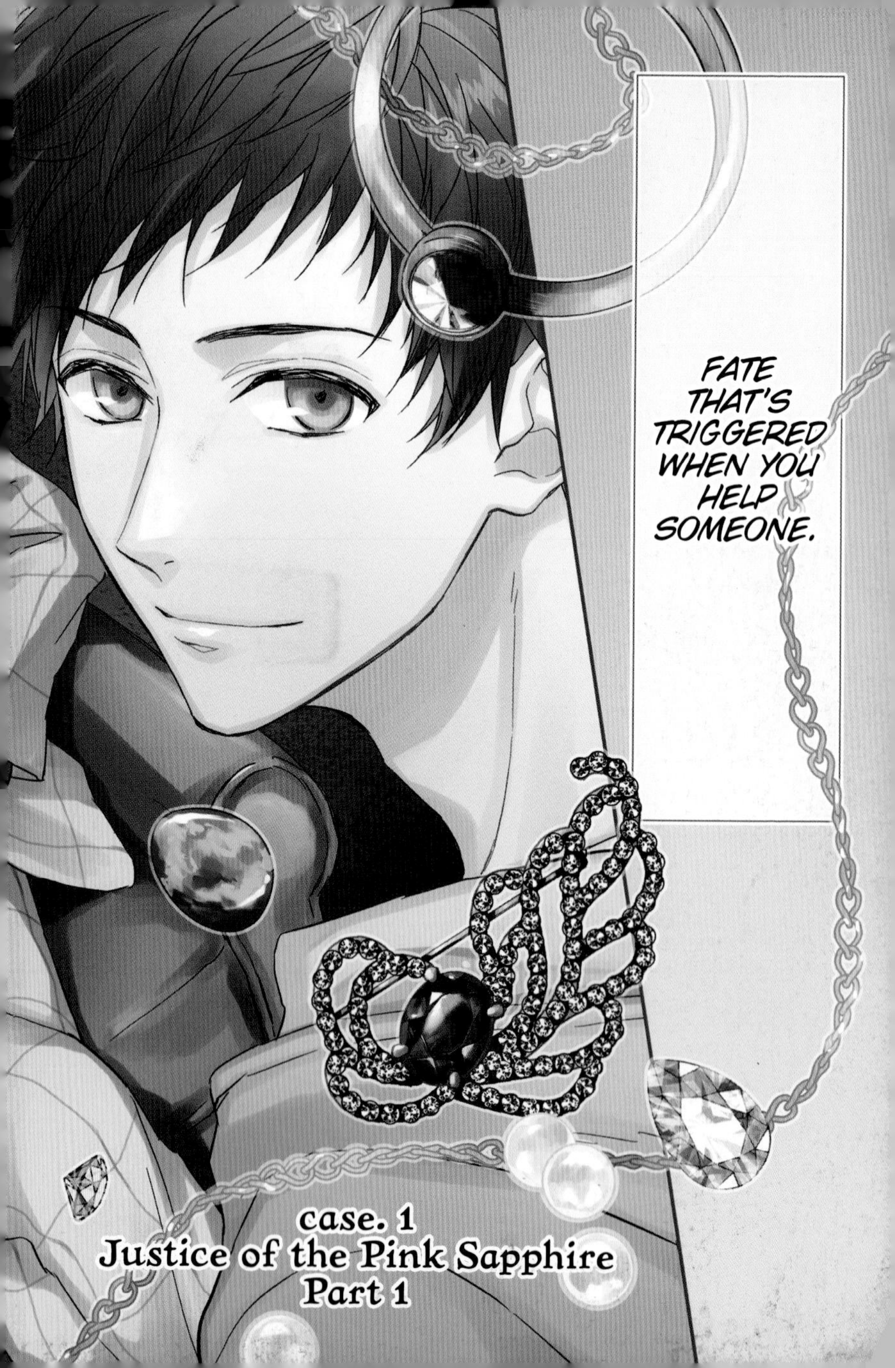
FATE THAT'S TRIGGERED WHEN YOU HELP SOMEONE.
case. 1
Justice of the Pink Sapphire
Part 1

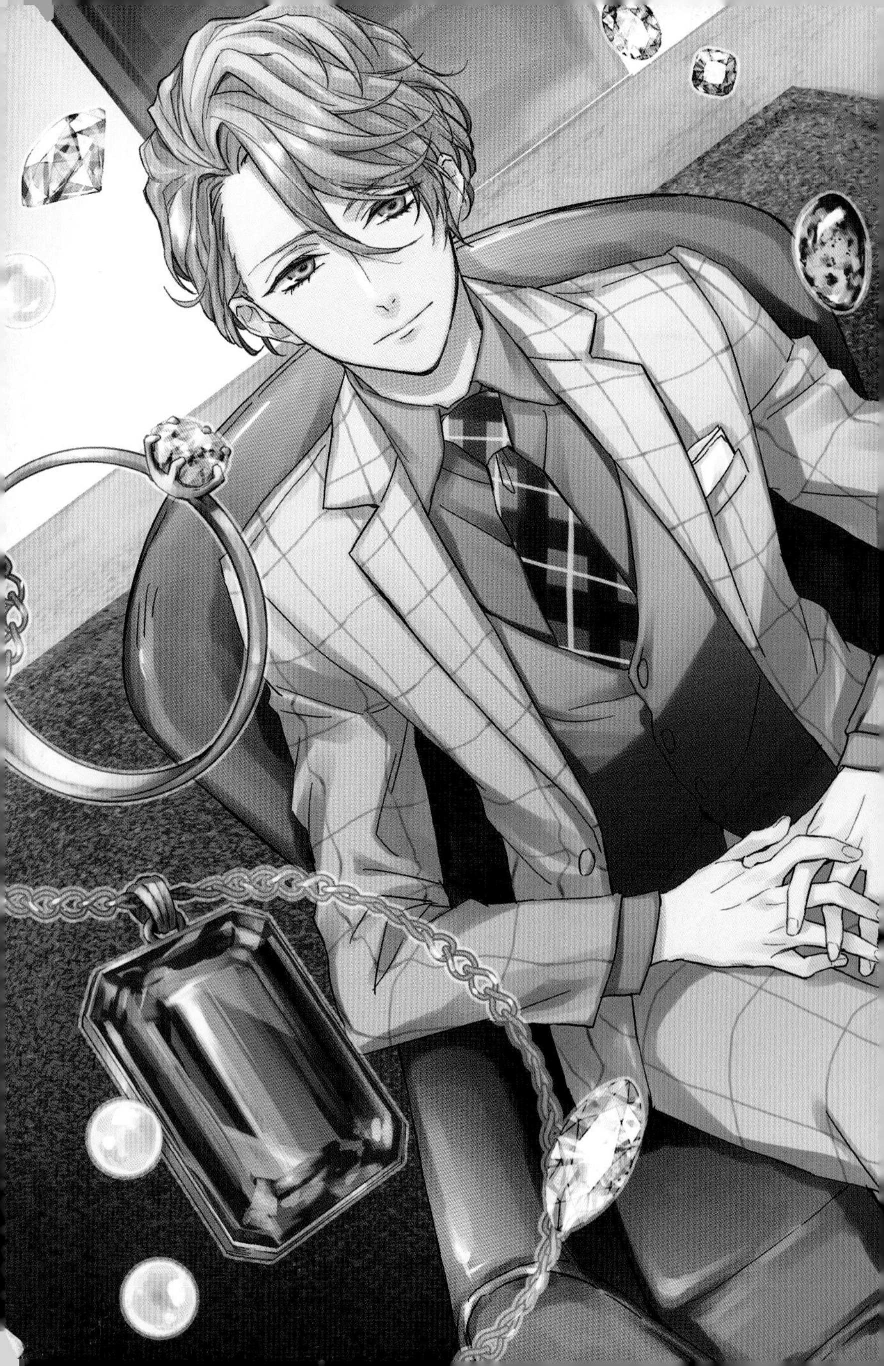

THE CASE FILES
OF
JEWELER
RICHARD

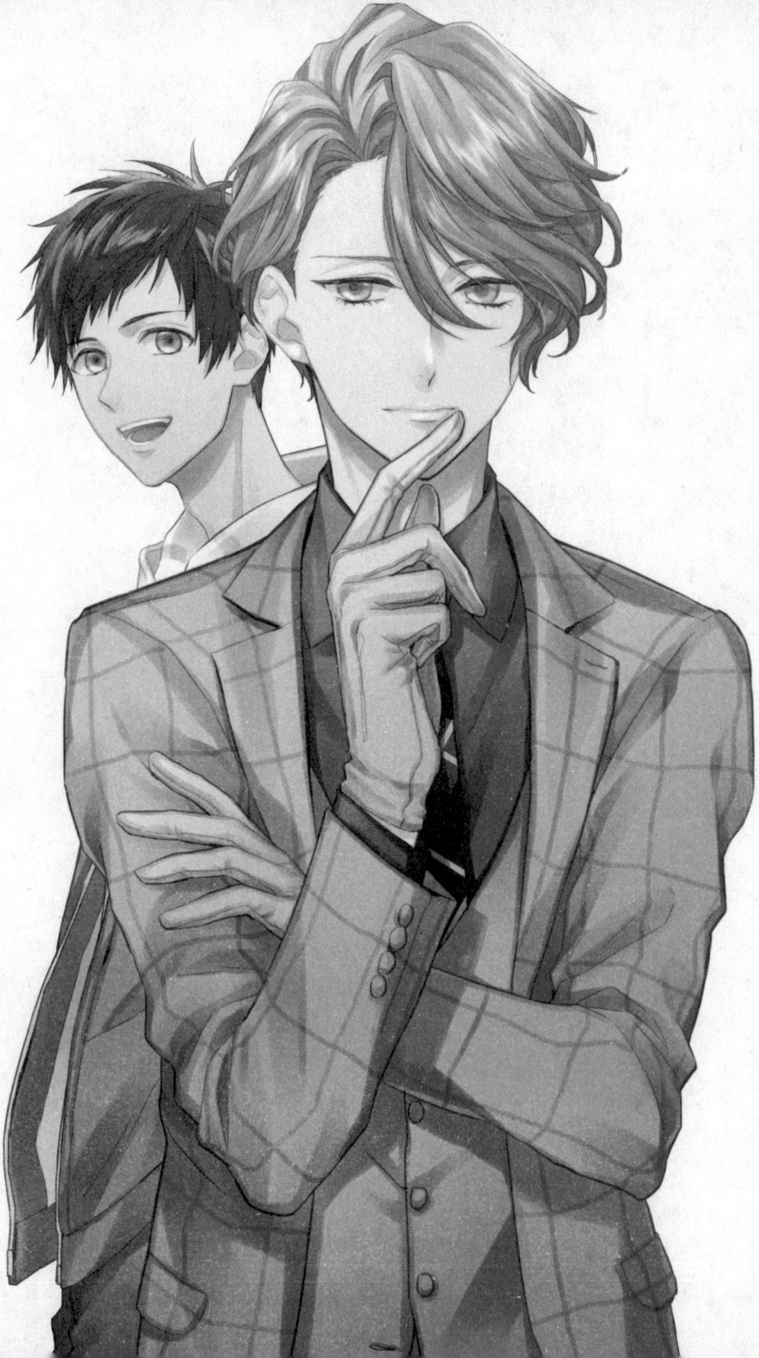

THE CASE FILES OF JEWELER RICHARD

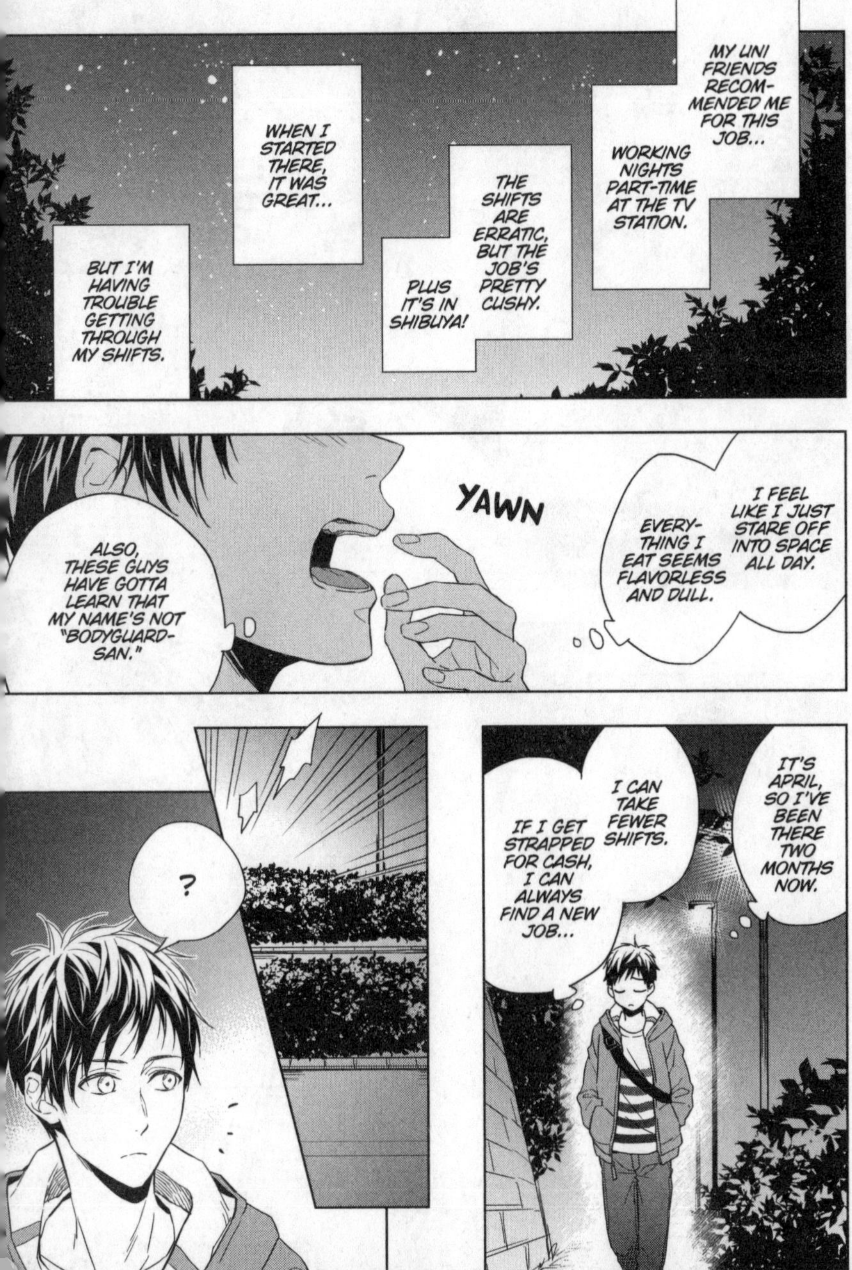

MY UNI FRIENDS RECOMMENDED ME FOR THIS JOB...
WORKING NIGHTS PART-TIME AT THE TV STATION.
THE SHIFTS ARE ERRATIC, BUT THE JOB'S PRETTY CUSHY.
PLUS IT'S IN SHIBUYA!
WHEN I STARTED THERE, IT WAS GREAT...
BUT I'M HAVING TROUBLE GETTING THROUGH MY SHIFTS.
I FEEL LIKE I JUST STARE OFF INTO SPACE ALL DAY.
EVERYTHING I EAT SEEMS FLAVORLESS AND DULL.
YAWN
ALSO, THESE GUYS HAVE GOTTA LEARN THAT MY NAME'S NOT "BODYGUARD-SAN."
IT'S APRIL, SO I'VE BEEN THERE TWO MONTHS NOW.
I CAN TAKE FEWER SHIFTS.
IF I GET STRAPPED FOR CASH, I CAN ALWAYS FIND A NEW JOB...
?

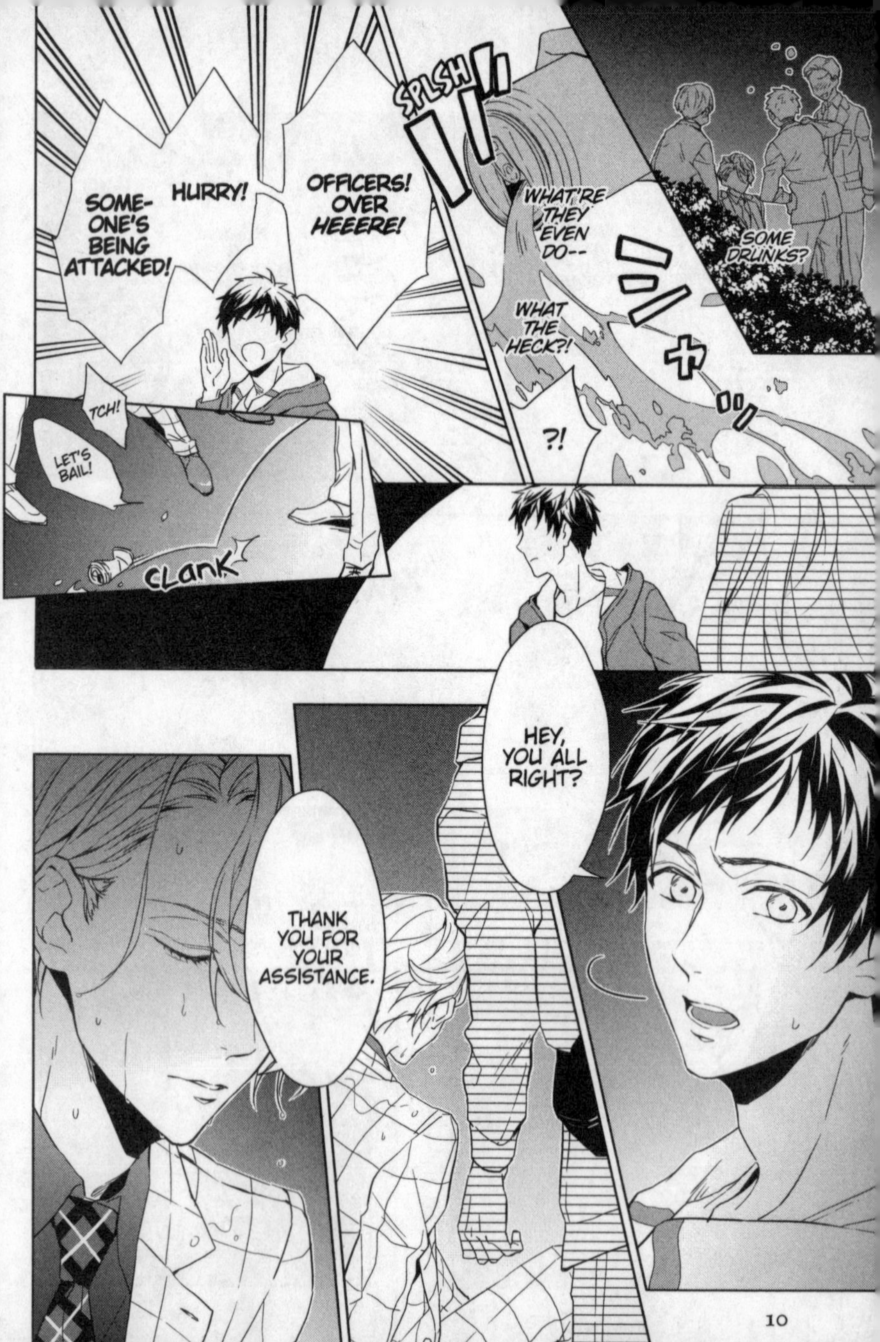
SOME DRUNKS?
SPLSH
WHAT'RE THEY EVEN DO--
WHAT THE HECK?!
?!
OFFICERS! OVER HEEERE!
HURRY!
SOME-ONE'S BEING ATTACKED!
TCH!
LET'S BAIL!
CLANK
HEY, YOU ALL RIGHT?
THANK YOU FOR YOUR ASSISTANCE.

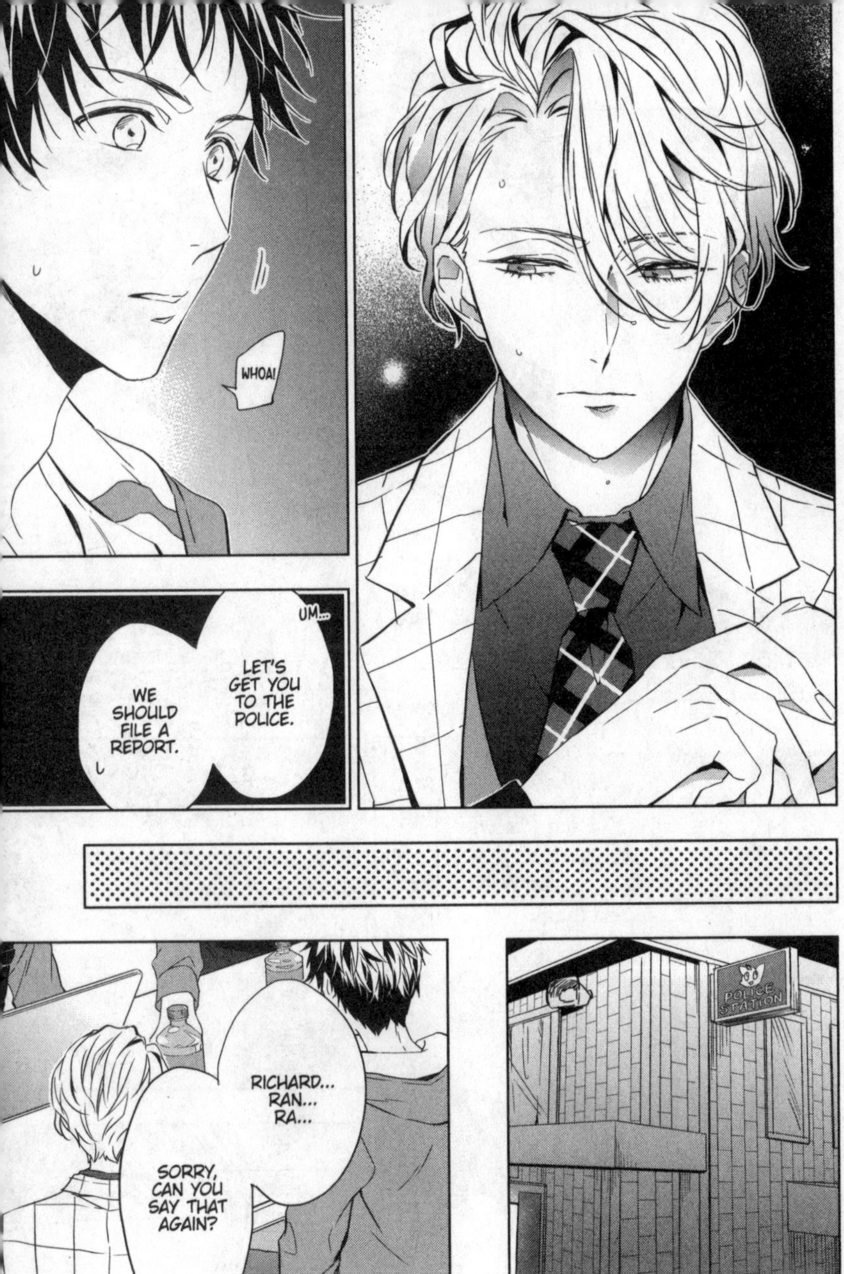
WHOA!
UM...
LET'S GET YOU TO THE POLICE.
WE SHOULD FILE A REPORT.
POLICE STATION
RICHARD... RAN... RA...
SORRY, CAN YOU SAY THAT AGAIN?

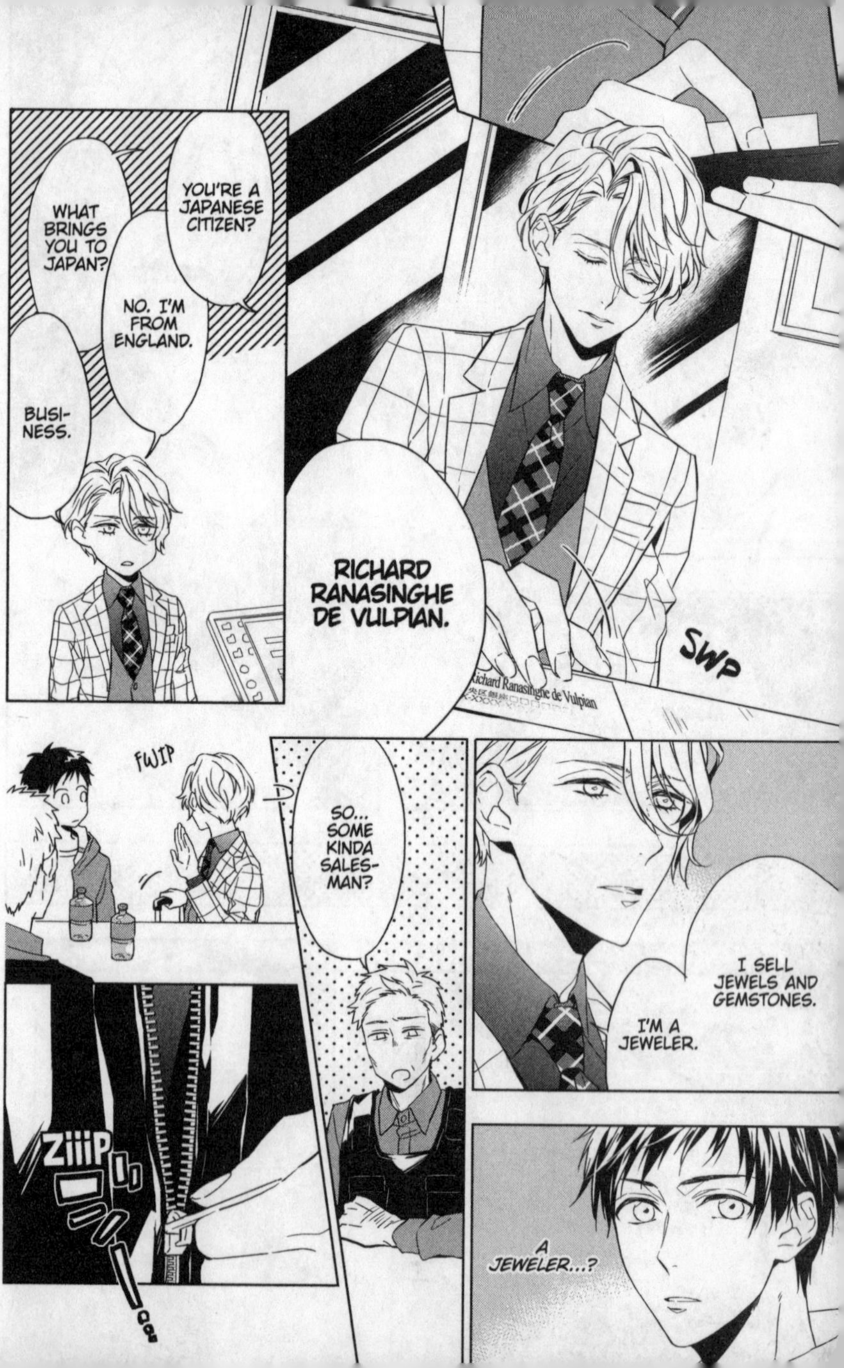
RICHARD RANASINGHE DE VULPIAN.
SWP
Richard Ranasinghe de Vulpian
YOU'RE A JAPANESE CITIZEN?
NO. I'M FROM ENGLAND.
WHAT BRINGS YOU TO JAPAN?
BUSINESS.
SO... SOME KINDA SALES-MAN?
I SELL JEWELS AND GEMSTONES.
I'M A JEWELER.
A JEWELER...?
FWIP
ZiiiP

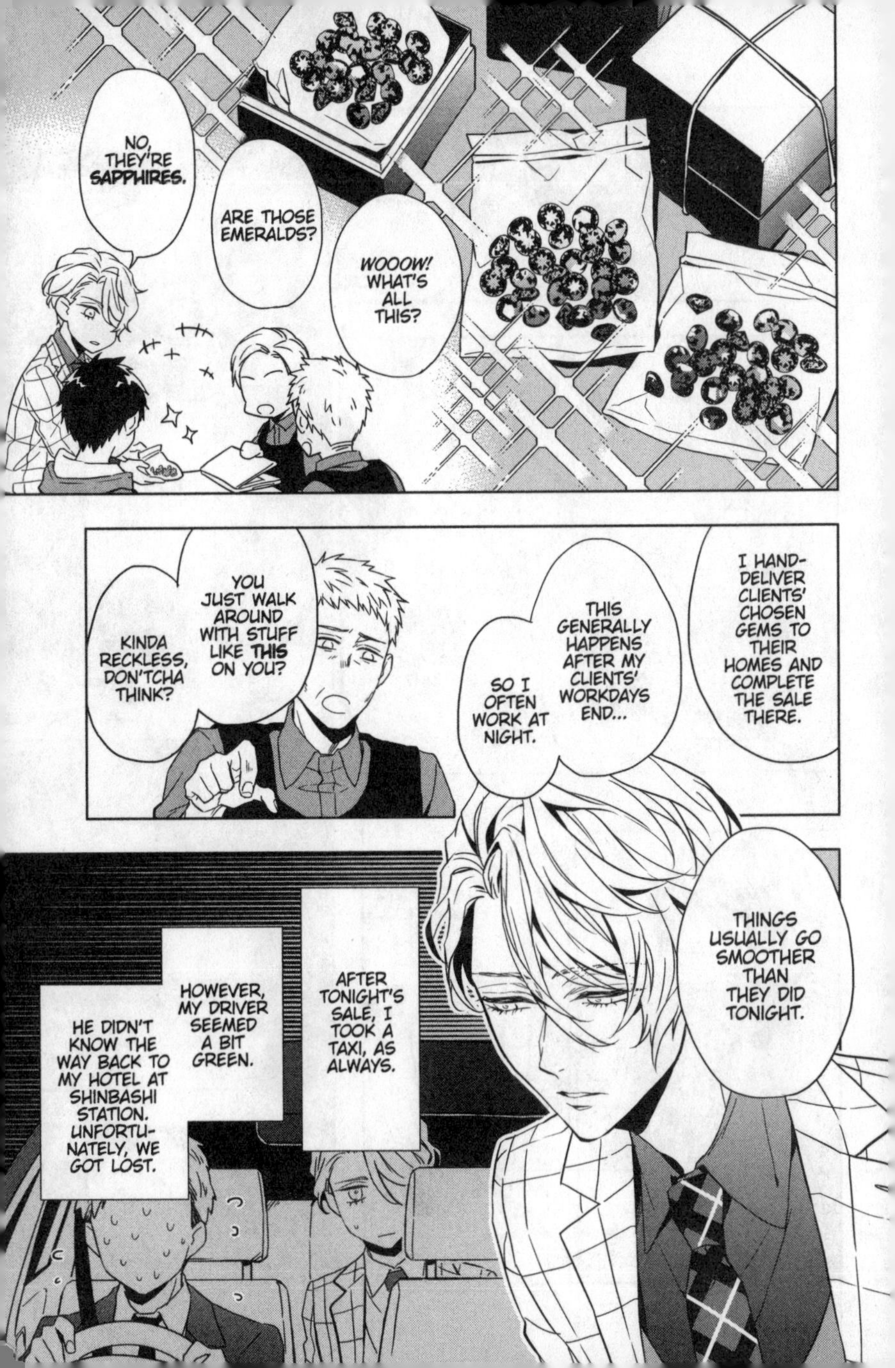
WOOOW! WHAT'S ALL THIS?
ARE THOSE EMERALDS?
NO, THEY'RE SAPPHIRES.
I HAND-DELIVER CLIENTS' CHOSEN GEMS TO THEIR HOMES AND COMPLETE THE SALE THERE.
THIS GENERALLY HAPPENS AFTER MY CLIENTS' WORKDAYS END...
SO I OFTEN WORK AT NIGHT.
YOU JUST WALK AROUND WITH STUFF LIKE THIS ON YOU?
KINDA RECKLESS, DON'TCHA THINK?
THINGS USUALLY GO SMOOTHER THAN THEY DID TONIGHT.
AFTER TONIGHT'S SALE, I TOOK A TAXI, AS ALWAYS.
HOWEVER, MY DRIVER SEEMED A BIT GREEN.
HE DIDN'T KNOW THE WAY BACK TO MY HOTEL AT SHINBASHI STATION. UNFORTUNATELY, WE GOT LOST.

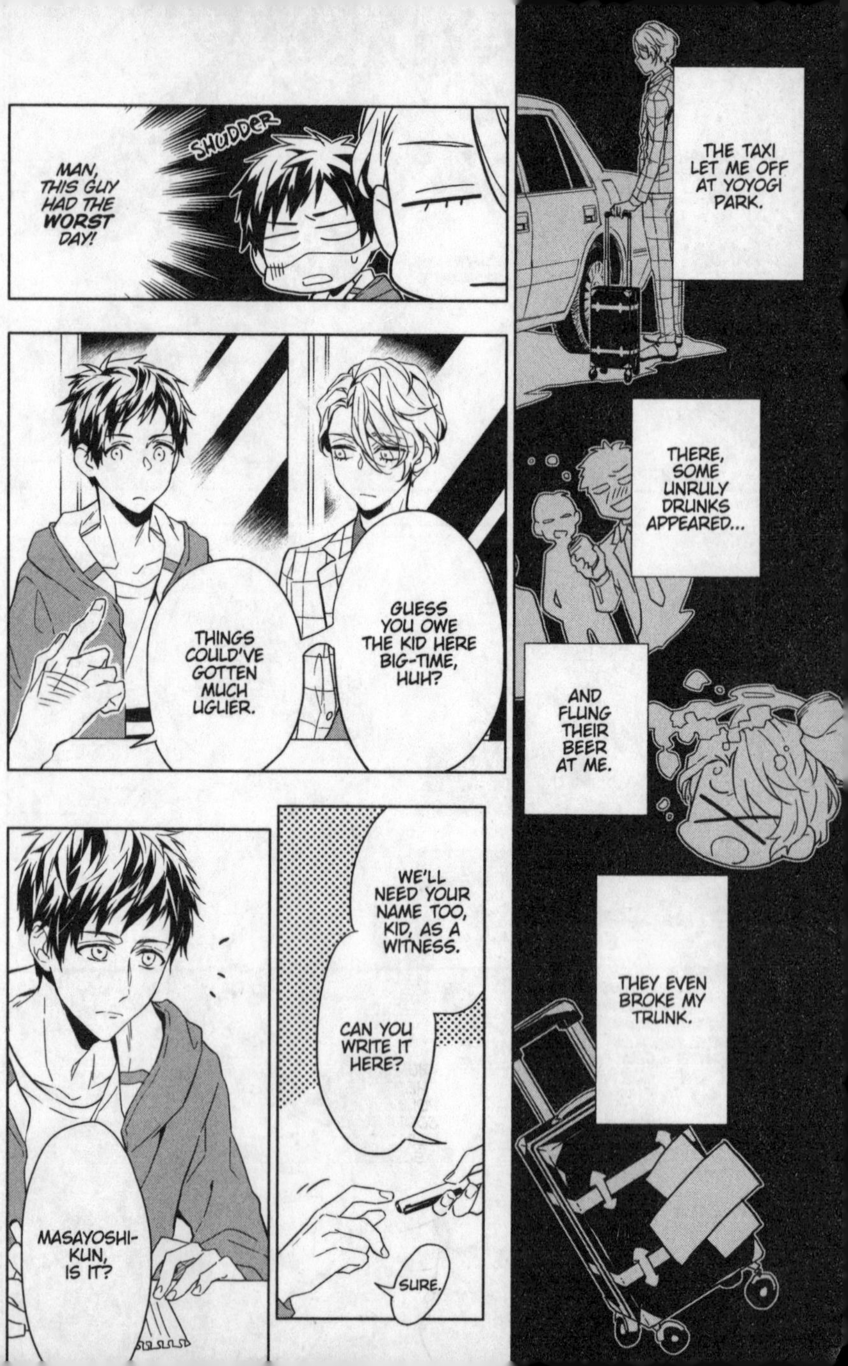
THE TAXI LET ME OFF AT YOYOGI PARK.
THERE, SOME UNRULY DRUNKS APPEARED...
AND FLUNG THEIR BEER AT ME.
THEY EVEN BROKE MY TRUNK.
SHUDDER
MAN, THIS GUY HAD THE WORST DAY!
GUESS YOU OWE THE KID HERE BIG-TIME, HUH?
THINGS COULD'VE GOTTEN MUCH UGLIER.
WE'LL NEED YOUR NAME TOO, KID, AS A WITNESS.
CAN YOU WRITE IT HERE?
SURE.
MASAYOSHI-KUN, IS IT?

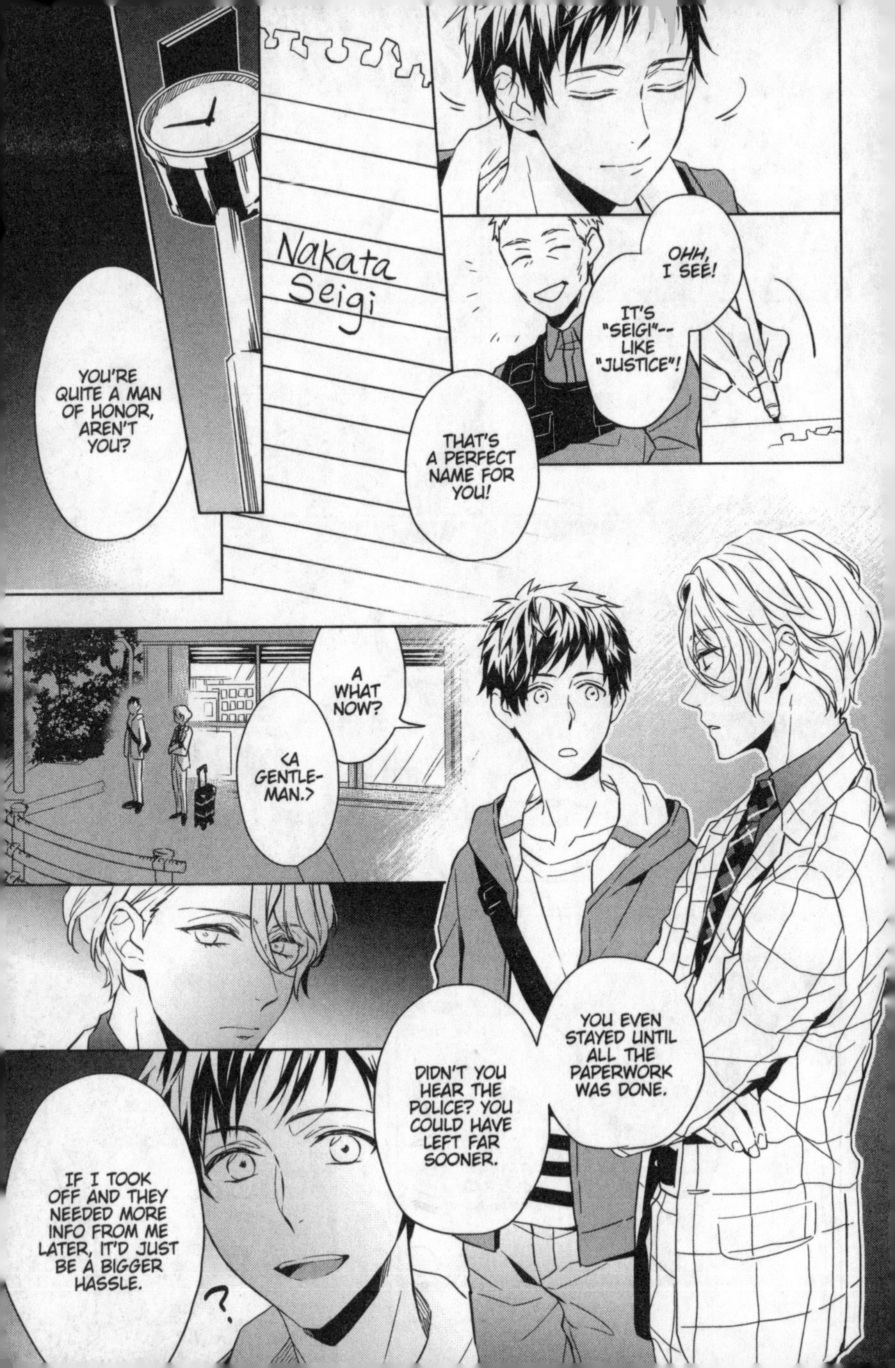
Nakata Seigi
OHH, I SEE!
IT'S "SEIGI"--LIKE "JUSTICE"!
THAT'S A PERFECT NAME FOR YOU!
YOU'RE QUITE A MAN OF HONOR, AREN'T YOU?
A WHAT NOW?
<A GENTLE-MAN.>
YOU EVEN STAYED UNTIL ALL THE PAPERWORK WAS DONE.
DIDN'T YOU HEAR THE POLICE? YOU COULD HAVE LEFT FAR SOONER.
IF I TOOK OFF AND THEY NEEDED MORE INFO FROM ME LATER, IT'D JUST BE A BIGGER HASSLE.
?

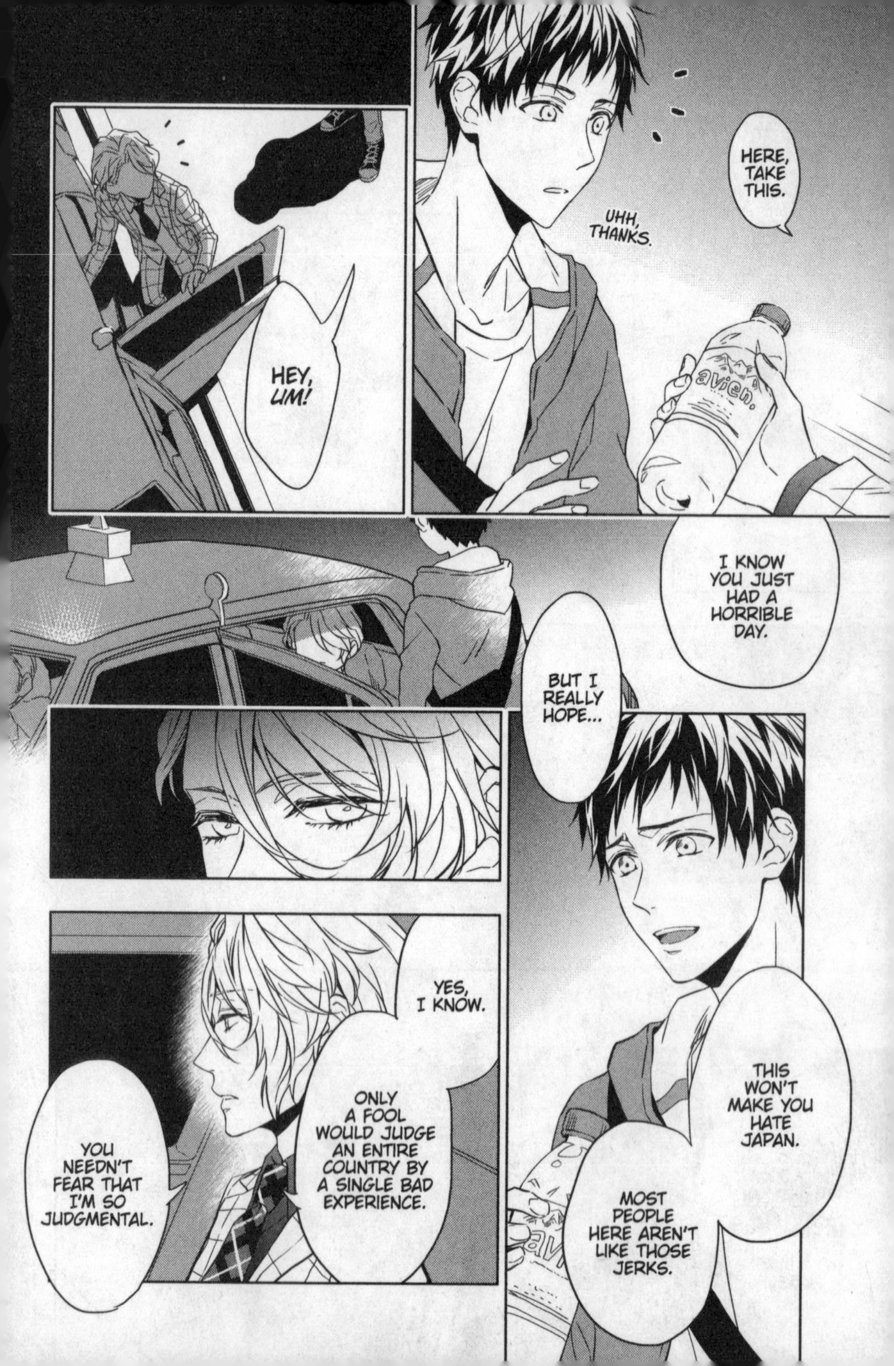
HERE, TAKE THIS.
UHH, THANKS.
HEY, UM!
I KNOW YOU JUST HAD A HORRIBLE DAY.
BUT I REALLY HOPE...
THIS WON'T MAKE YOU HATE JAPAN.
MOST PEOPLE HERE AREN'T LIKE THOSE JERKS.
YES, I KNOW.
ONLY A FOOL WOULD JUDGE AN ENTIRE COUNTRY BY A SINGLE BAD EXPERIENCE.
YOU NEEDN'T FEAR THAT I'M SO JUDGMENTAL.

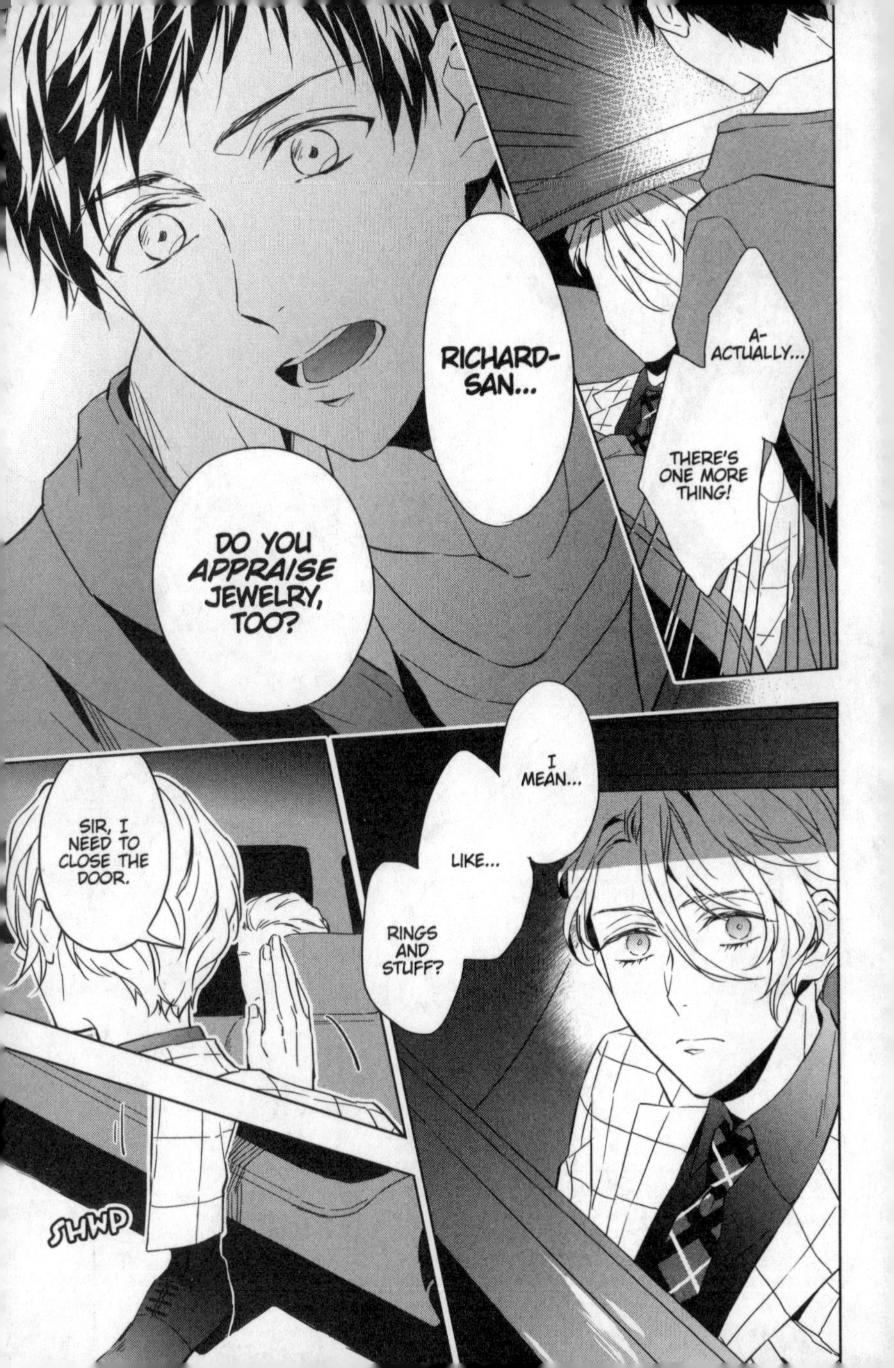
A-
ACTUALLY...
THERE'S ONE MORE THING!
RICHARD-SAN...
DO YOU *APPRAISE* JEWELRY, TOO?
I MEAN...
LIKE...
RINGS AND STUFF?
SIR, I NEED TO CLOSE THE DOOR.
SHWP

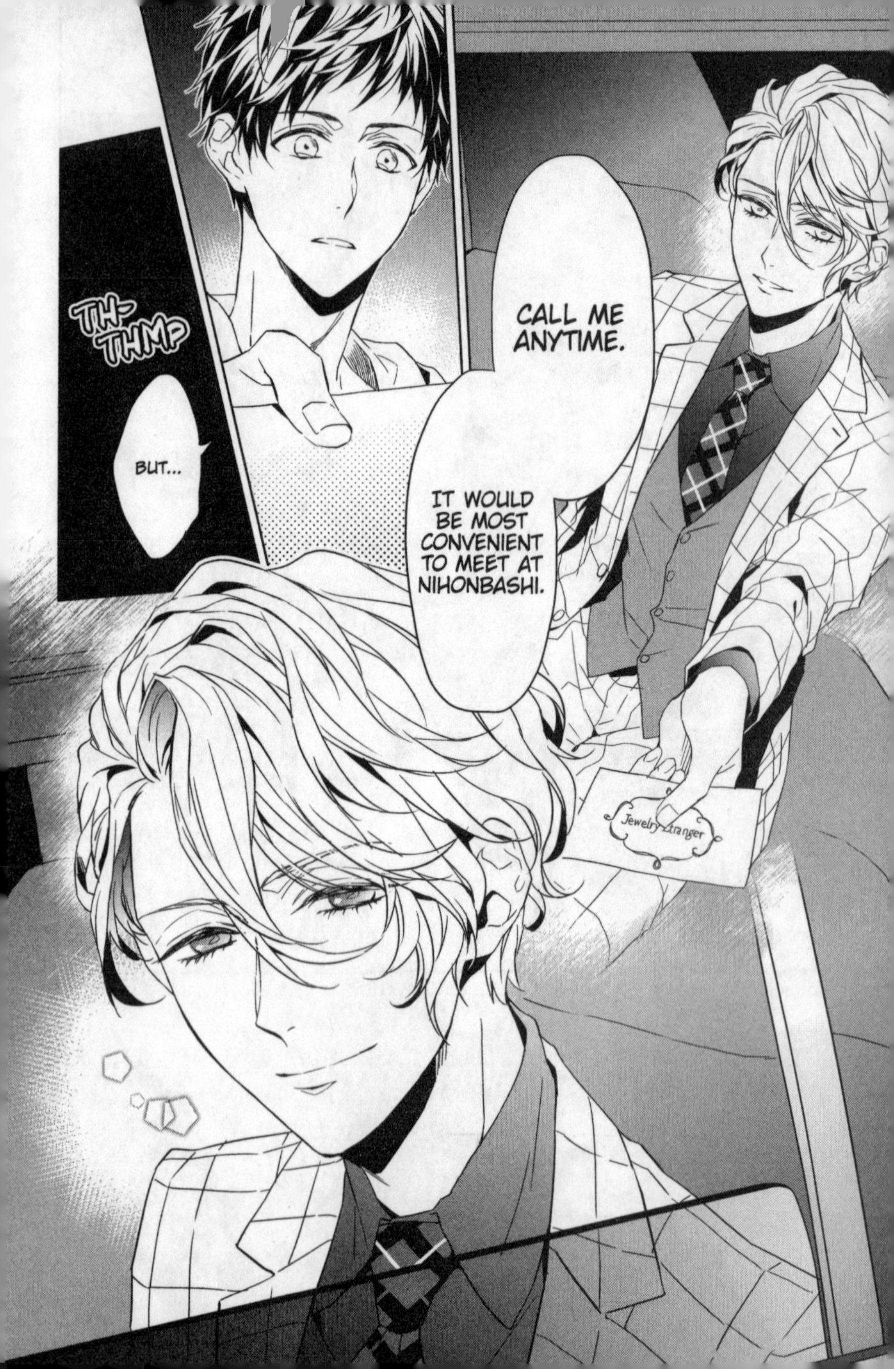
CALL ME ANYTIME.
IT WOULD BE MOST CONVENIENT TO MEET AT NIHONBASHI.
Jewelry Etranger
TH-THMP
BUT...

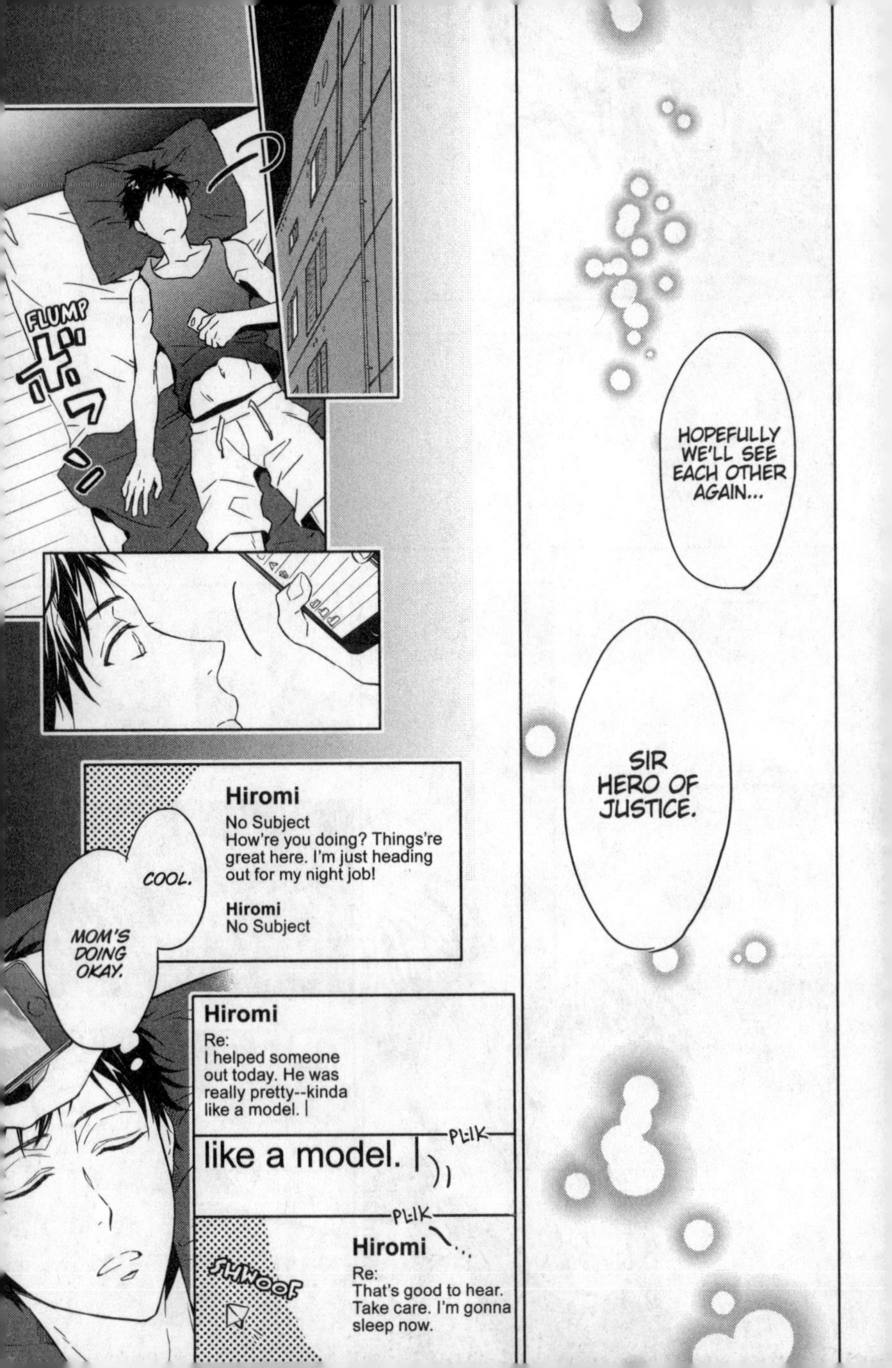
HOPEFULLY WE'LL SEE EACH OTHER AGAIN...
SIR HERO OF JUSTICE.
FLUMP
Hiromi
No Subject
How're you doing? Things're great here. I'm just heading out for my night job!
Hiromi
No Subject
COOL.
MOM'S DOING OKAY.
Hiromi
Re:
I helped someone out today. He was really pretty--kinda like a model.
like a model.
PLIK
PLIK
Hiromi
Re:
That's good to hear. Take care. I'm gonna sleep now.
SHWOOF

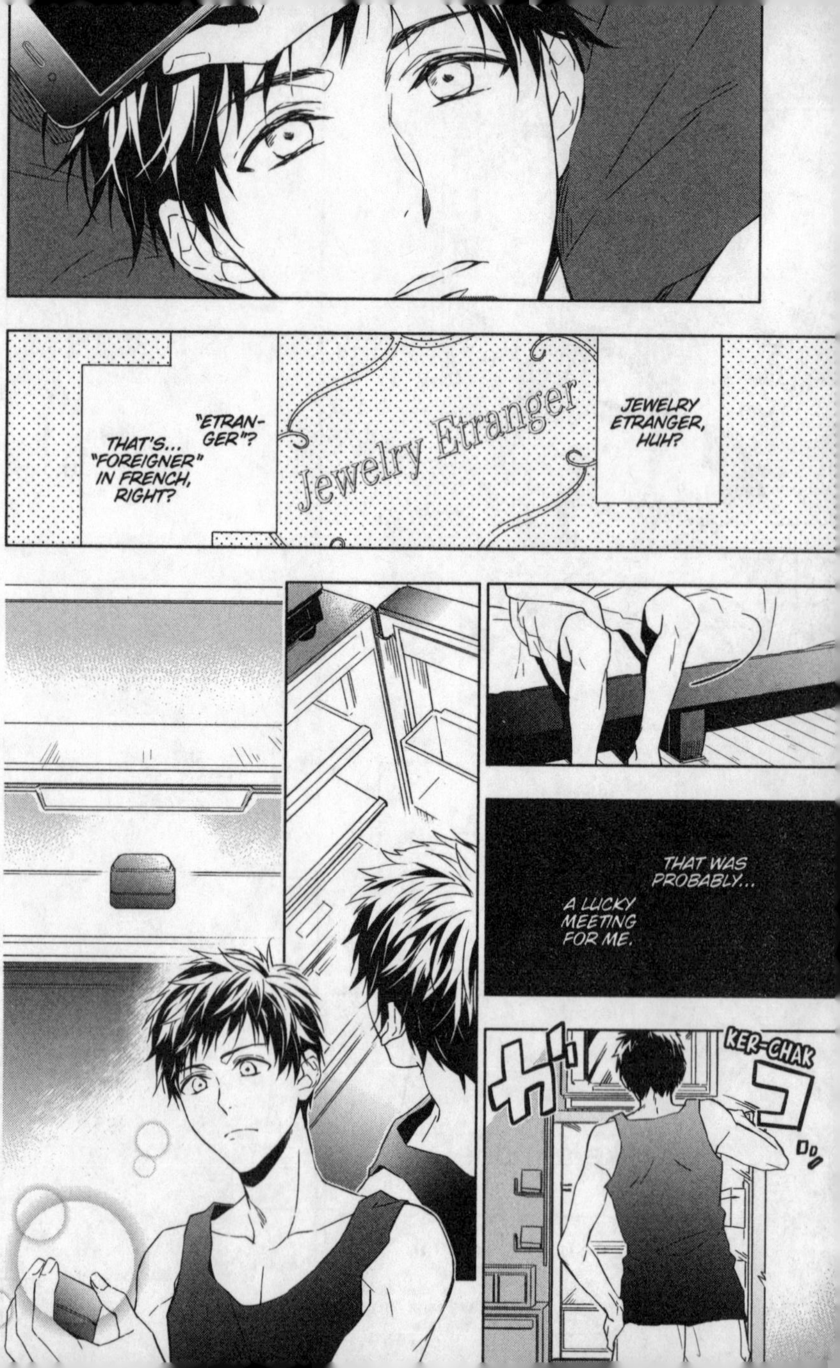
JEWELRY ETRANGER, HUH?
Jewelry Etranger
"ETRANGER"?
THAT'S... "FOREIGNER" IN FRENCH, RIGHT?
THAT WAS PROBABLY...
A LUCKY MEETING FOR ME.
KER-CHAK

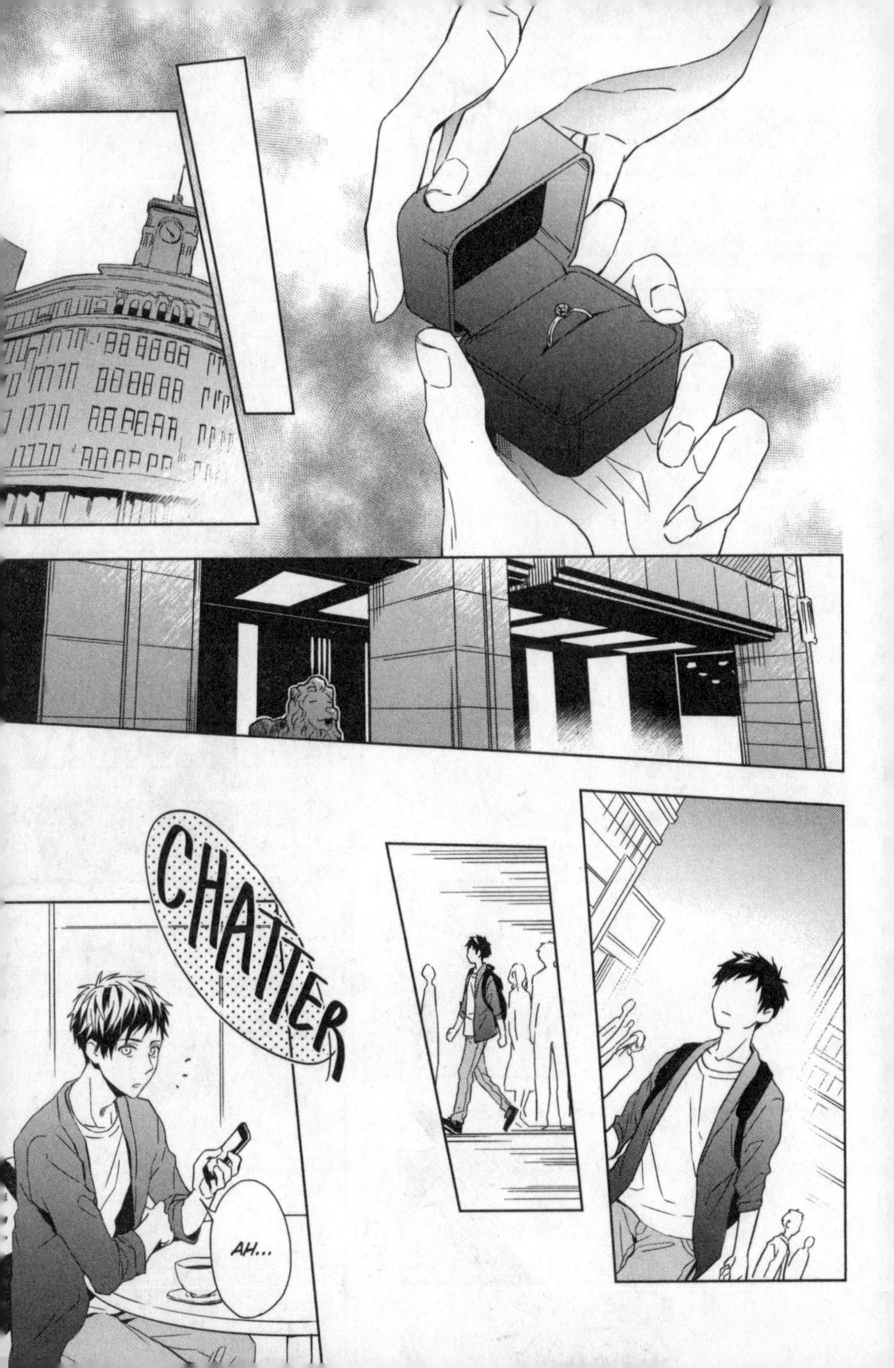
CHATTER
AH...

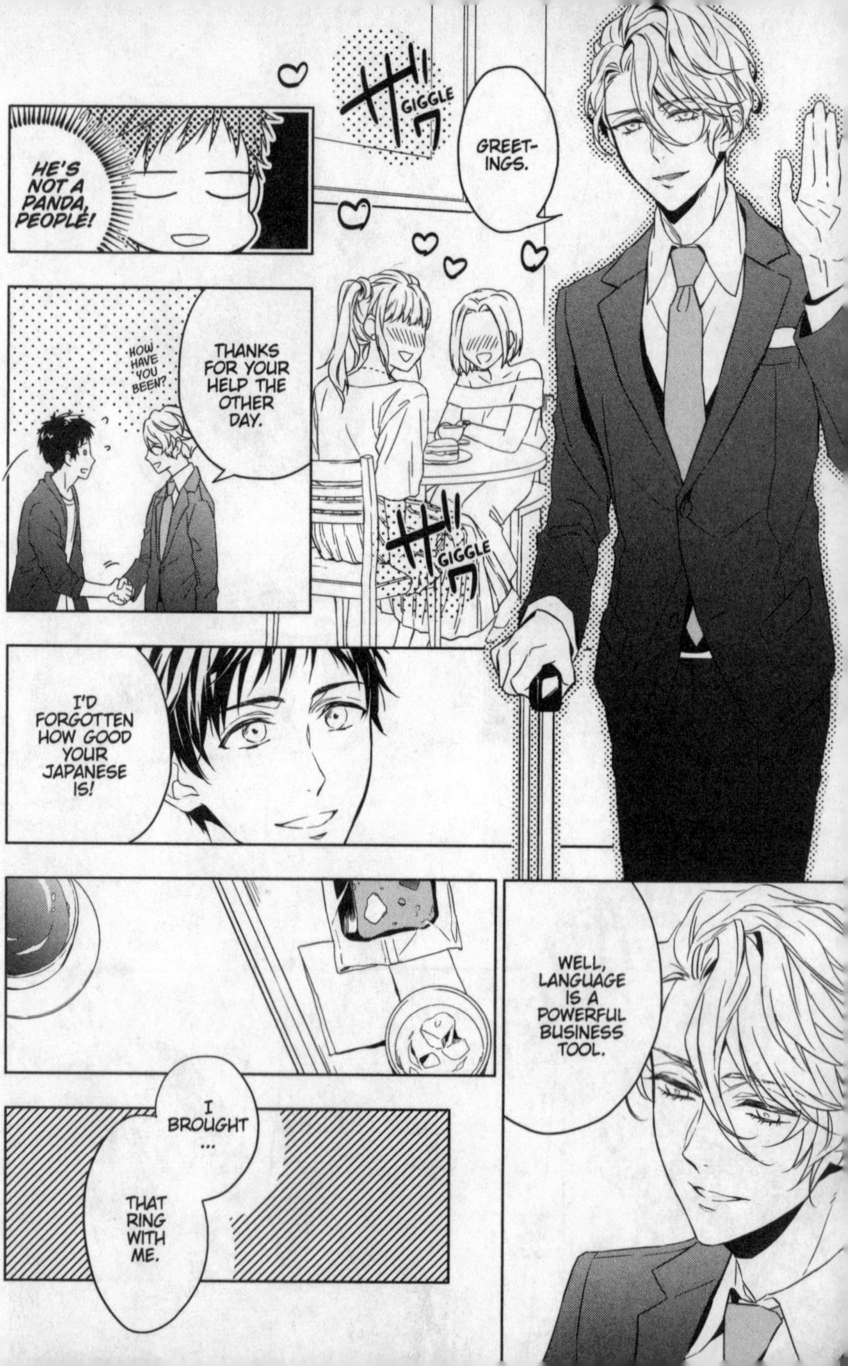
GREET-INGS.
GIGGLE
GIGGLE
HE'S NOT A PANDA, PEOPLE!
THANKS FOR YOUR HELP THE OTHER DAY.
HOW HAVE YOU BEEN?
I'D FORGOTTEN HOW GOOD YOUR JAPANESE IS!
WELL, LANGUAGE IS A POWERFUL BUSINESS TOOL.
I BROUGHT ...
THAT RING WITH ME.

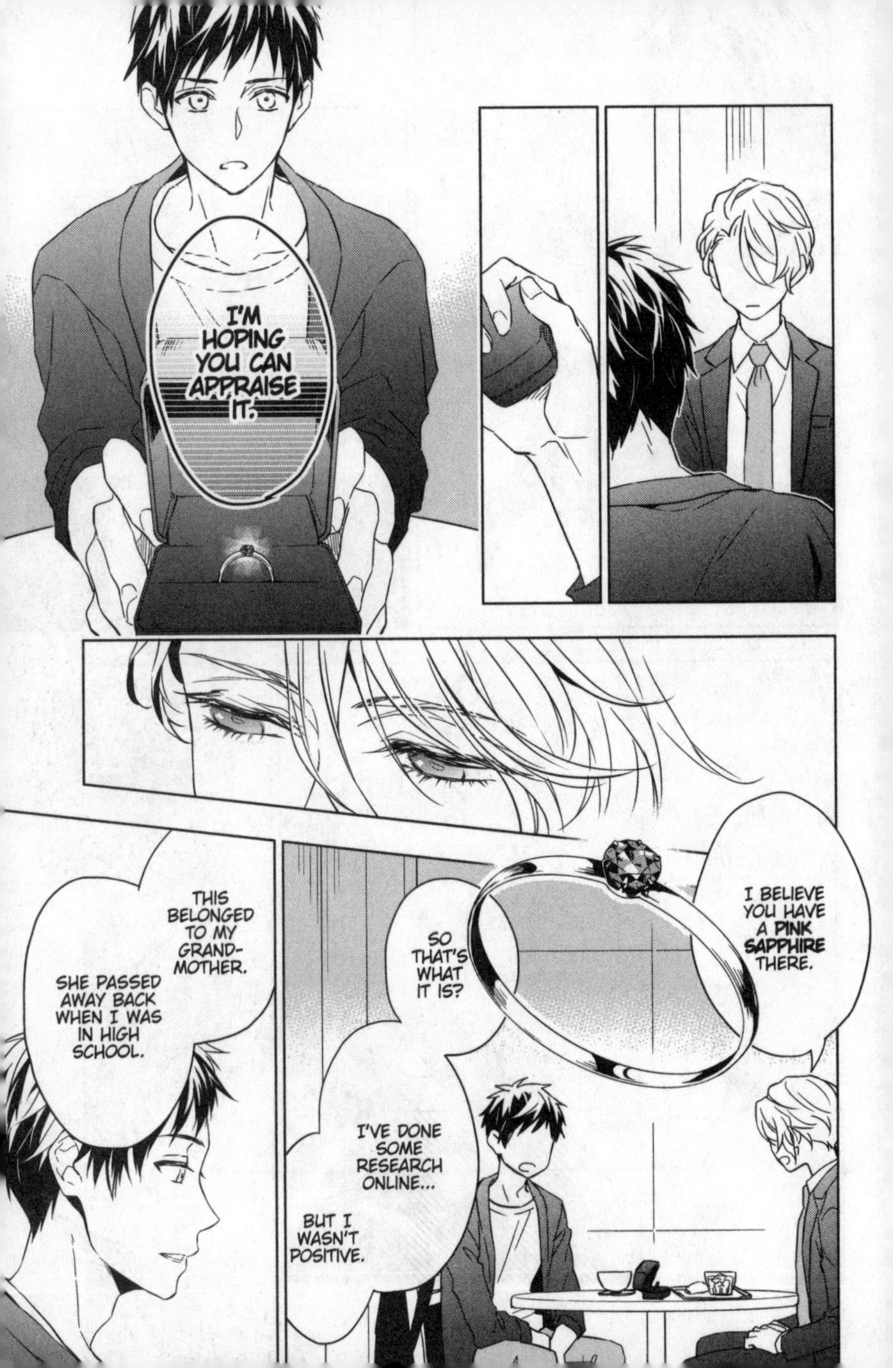
I'M HOPING YOU CAN APPRAISE IT.
I BELIEVE YOU HAVE A PINK SAPPHIRE THERE.
SO THAT'S WHAT IT IS?
I'VE DONE SOME RESEARCH ONLINE...
BUT I WASN'T POSITIVE.
THIS BELONGED TO MY GRAND-MOTHER.
SHE PASSED AWAY BACK WHEN I WAS IN HIGH SCHOOL.

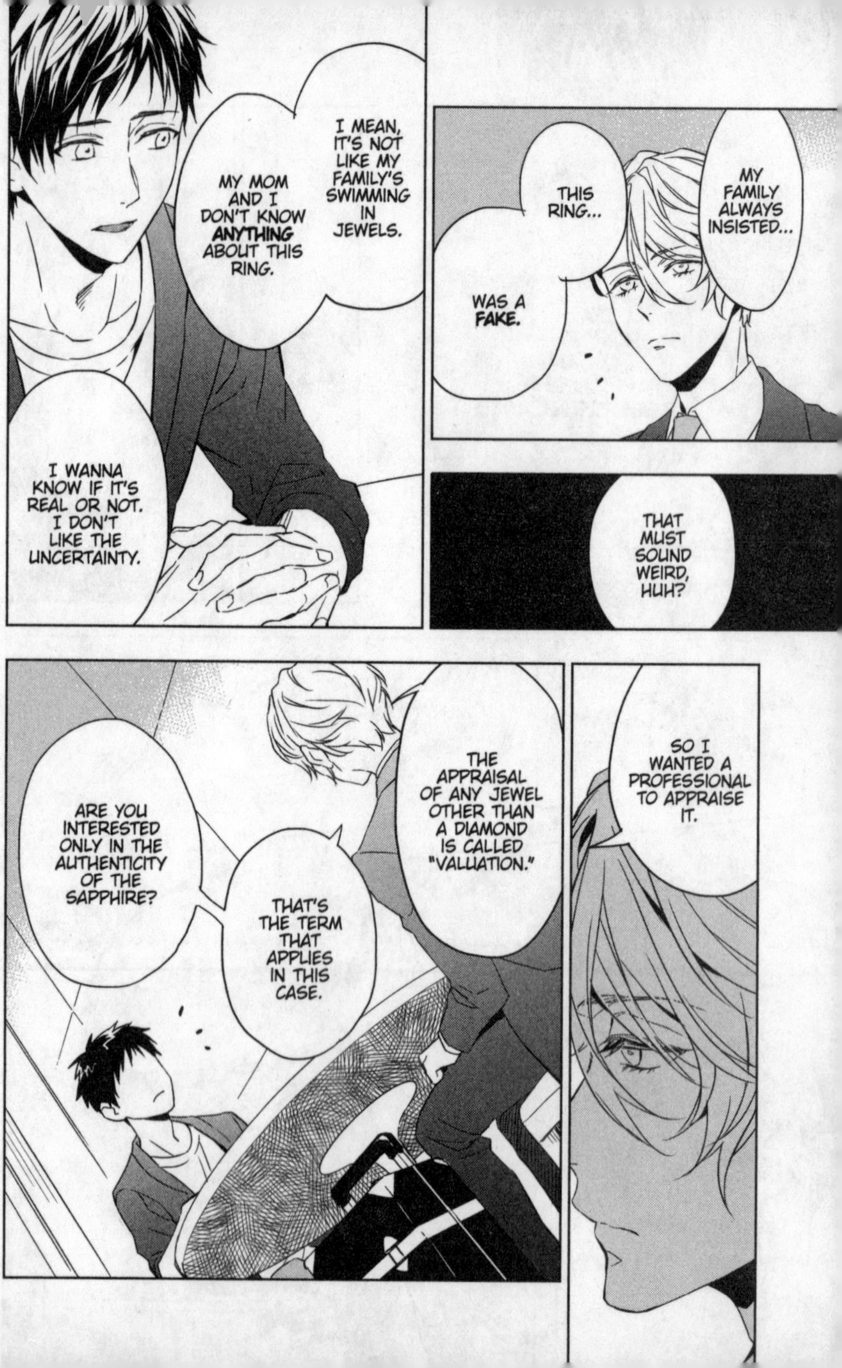
MY FAMILY ALWAYS INSISTED...
THIS RING...
WAS A FAKE.
THAT MUST SOUND WEIRD, HUH?
I MEAN, IT'S NOT LIKE MY FAMILY'S SWIMMING IN JEWELS.
MY MOM AND I DON'T KNOW **ANYTHING** ABOUT THIS RING.
I WANNA KNOW IF IT'S REAL OR NOT. I DON'T LIKE THE UNCERTAINTY.
SO I WANTED A PROFESSIONAL TO APPRAISE IT.
THE APPRAISAL OF ANY JEWEL OTHER THAN A DIAMOND IS CALLED "VALUATION."
THAT'S THE TERM THAT APPLIES IN THIS CASE.
ARE YOU INTERESTED ONLY IN THE AUTHENTICITY OF THE SAPPHIRE?

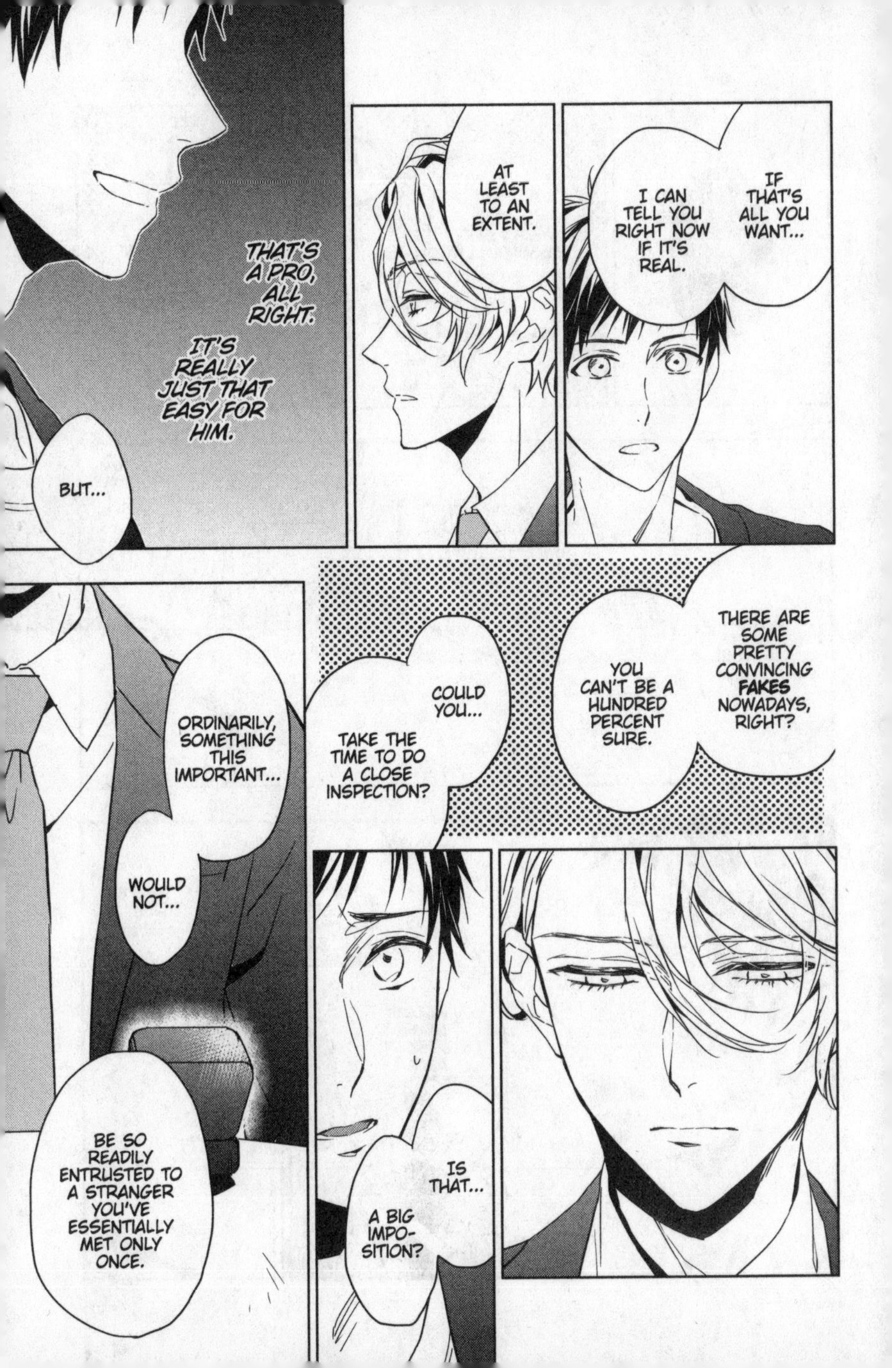
IF THAT'S ALL YOU WANT...
I CAN TELL YOU RIGHT NOW IF IT'S REAL.
AT LEAST TO AN EXTENT.
THAT'S A PRO, ALL RIGHT.
IT'S REALLY JUST THAT EASY FOR HIM.
BUT...
THERE ARE SOME PRETTY CONVINCING **FAKES** NOWADAYS, RIGHT?
YOU CAN'T BE A HUNDRED PERCENT SURE.
COULD YOU...
TAKE THE TIME TO DO A CLOSE INSPECTION?
IS THAT...
A BIG IMPOSITION?
ORDINARILY, SOMETHING THIS IMPORTANT...
WOULD NOT...
BE SO READILY ENTRUSTED TO A STRANGER YOU'VE ESSENTIALLY MET ONLY ONCE.

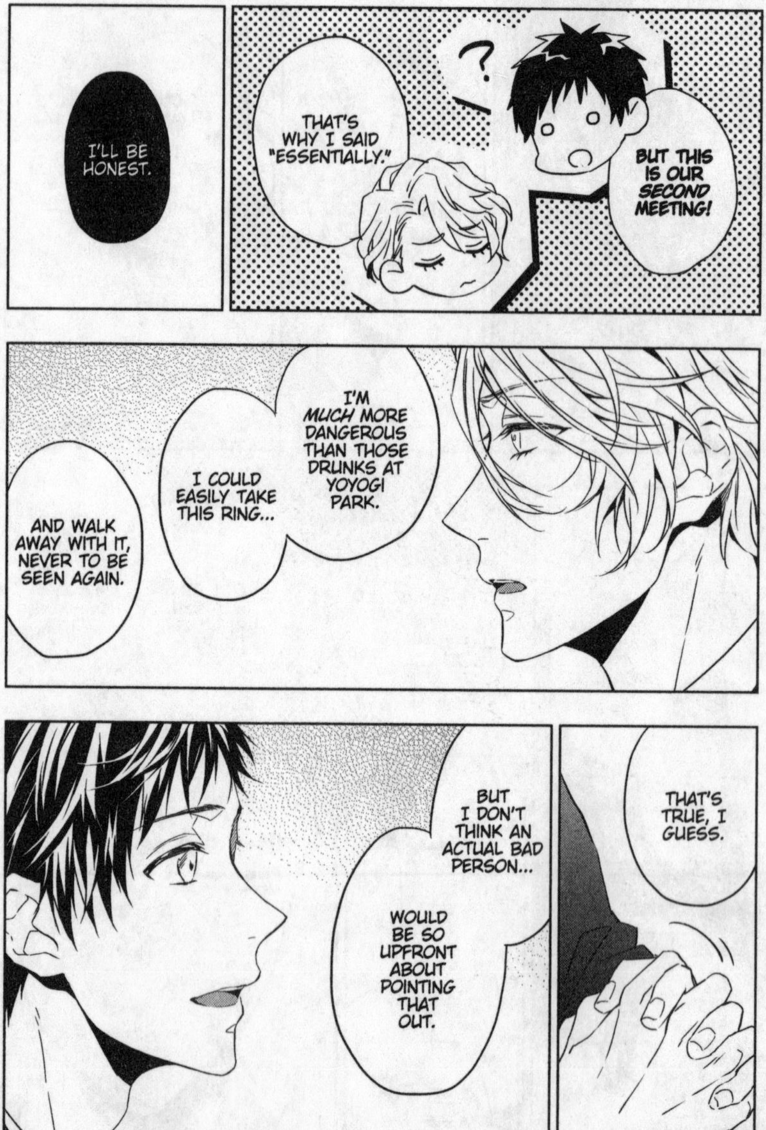
BUT THIS IS OUR *SECOND* MEETING!
?
THAT'S WHY I SAID "ESSENTIALLY."
I'LL BE HONEST.
I'M *MUCH* MORE DANGEROUS THAN THOSE DRUNKS AT YOYOGI PARK.
I COULD EASILY TAKE THIS RING...
AND WALK AWAY WITH IT, NEVER TO BE SEEN AGAIN.
THAT'S TRUE, I GUESS.
BUT I DON'T THINK AN ACTUAL BAD PERSON...
WOULD BE SO UPFRONT ABOUT POINTING THAT OUT.

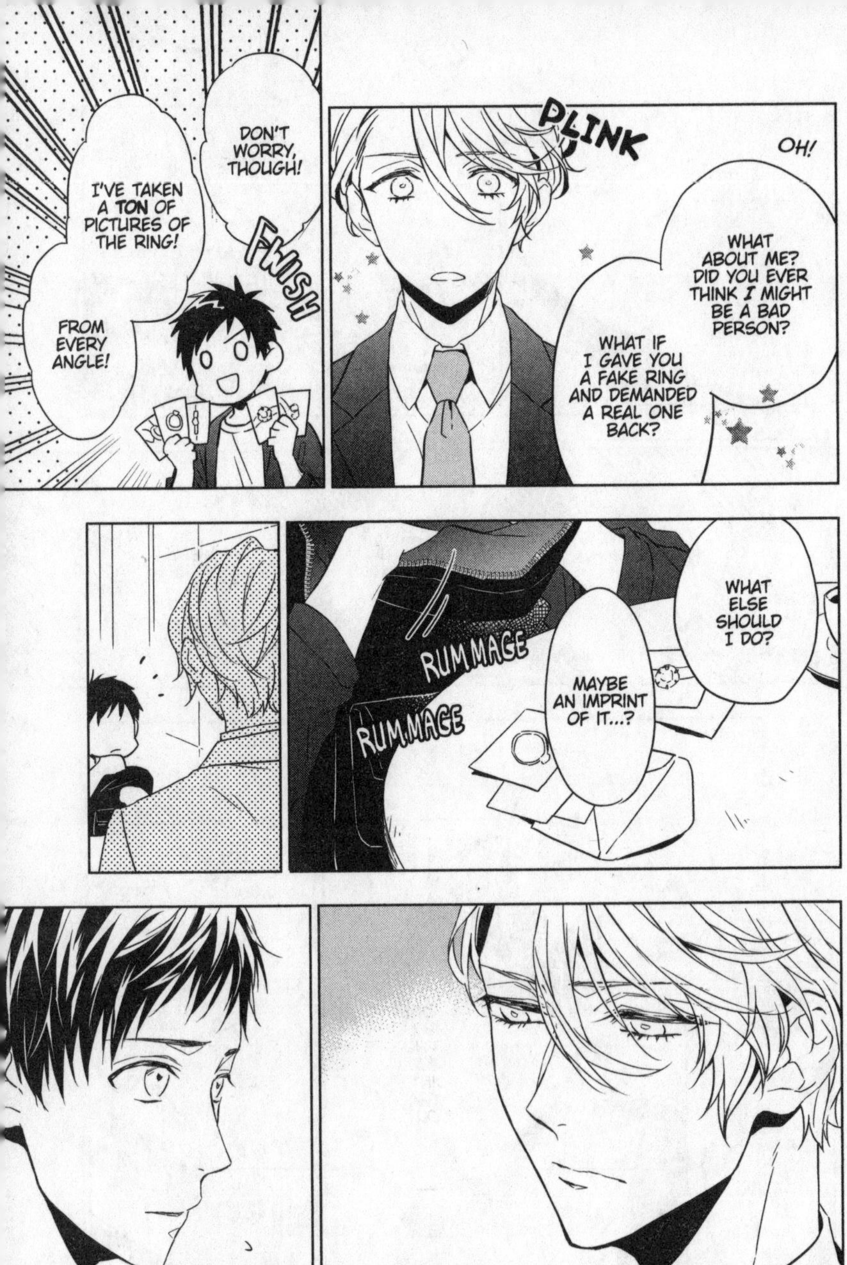
PLINK
OH!
WHAT ABOUT ME? DID YOU EVER THINK *I* MIGHT BE A BAD PERSON?
WHAT IF I GAVE YOU A FAKE RING AND DEMANDED A REAL ONE BACK?
DON'T WORRY, THOUGH!
I'VE TAKEN A **TON** OF PICTURES OF THE RING!
FWISH
FROM EVERY ANGLE!
WHAT ELSE SHOULD I DO?
MAYBE AN IMPRINT OF IT...?
RUMMAGE
RUMMAGE

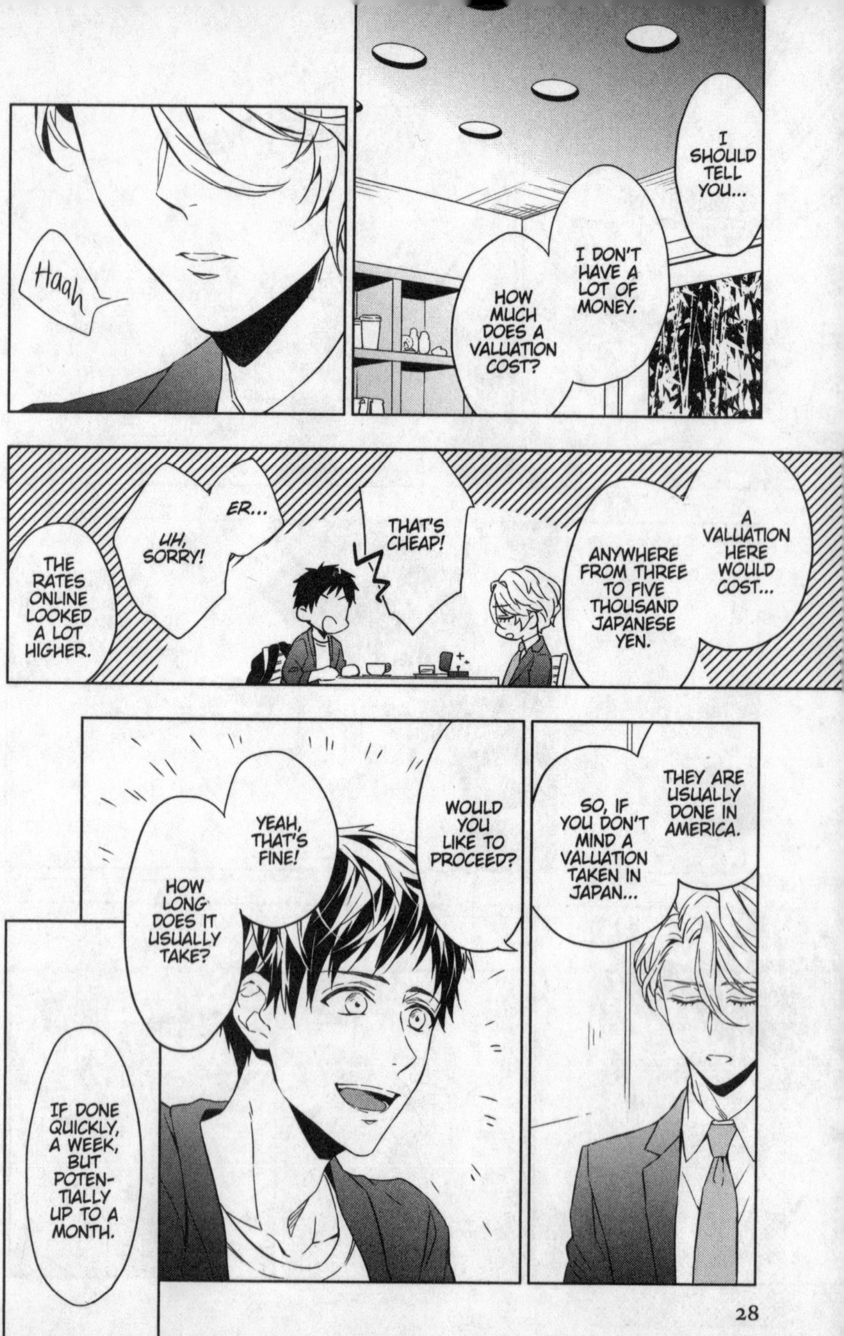

I SHOULD TELL YOU...
I DON'T HAVE A LOT OF MONEY.
HOW MUCH DOES A VALUATION COST?
Haah
A VALUATION HERE WOULD COST...
ANYWHERE FROM THREE TO FIVE THOUSAND JAPANESE YEN.
THAT'S CHEAP!
ER...
UH, SORRY!
THE RATES ONLINE LOOKED A LOT HIGHER.
THEY ARE USUALLY DONE IN AMERICA.
SO, IF YOU DON'T MIND A VALUATION TAKEN IN JAPAN...
WOULD YOU LIKE TO PROCEED?
YEAH, THAT'S FINE!
HOW LONG DOES IT USUALLY TAKE?
IF DONE QUICKLY, A WEEK, BUT POTEN-TIALLY UP TO A MONTH.

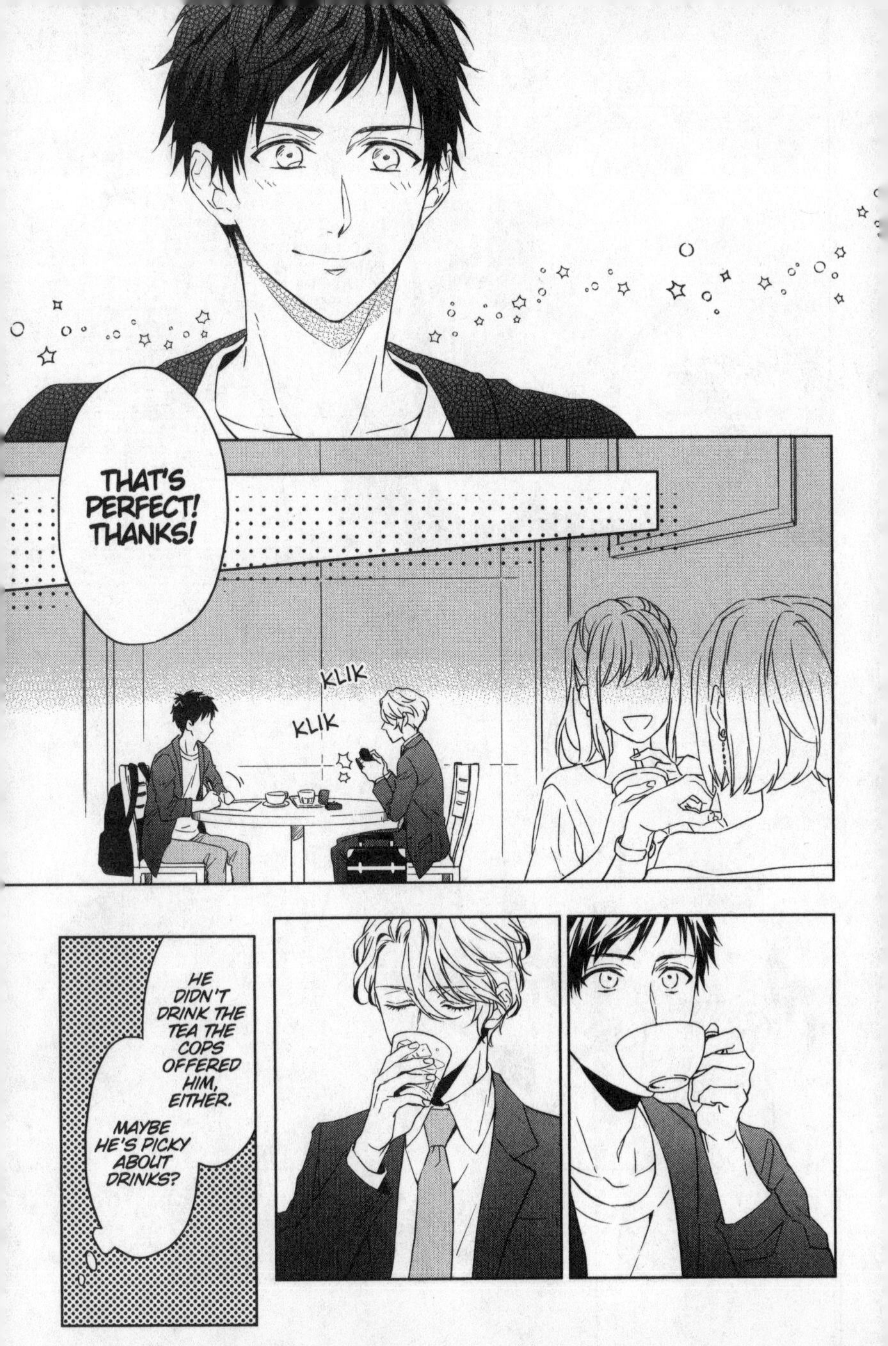
THAT'S PERFECT! THANKS!
KLIK
KLIK
HE DIDN'T DRINK THE TEA THE COPS OFFERED HIM, EITHER.
MAYBE HE'S PICKY ABOUT DRINKS?

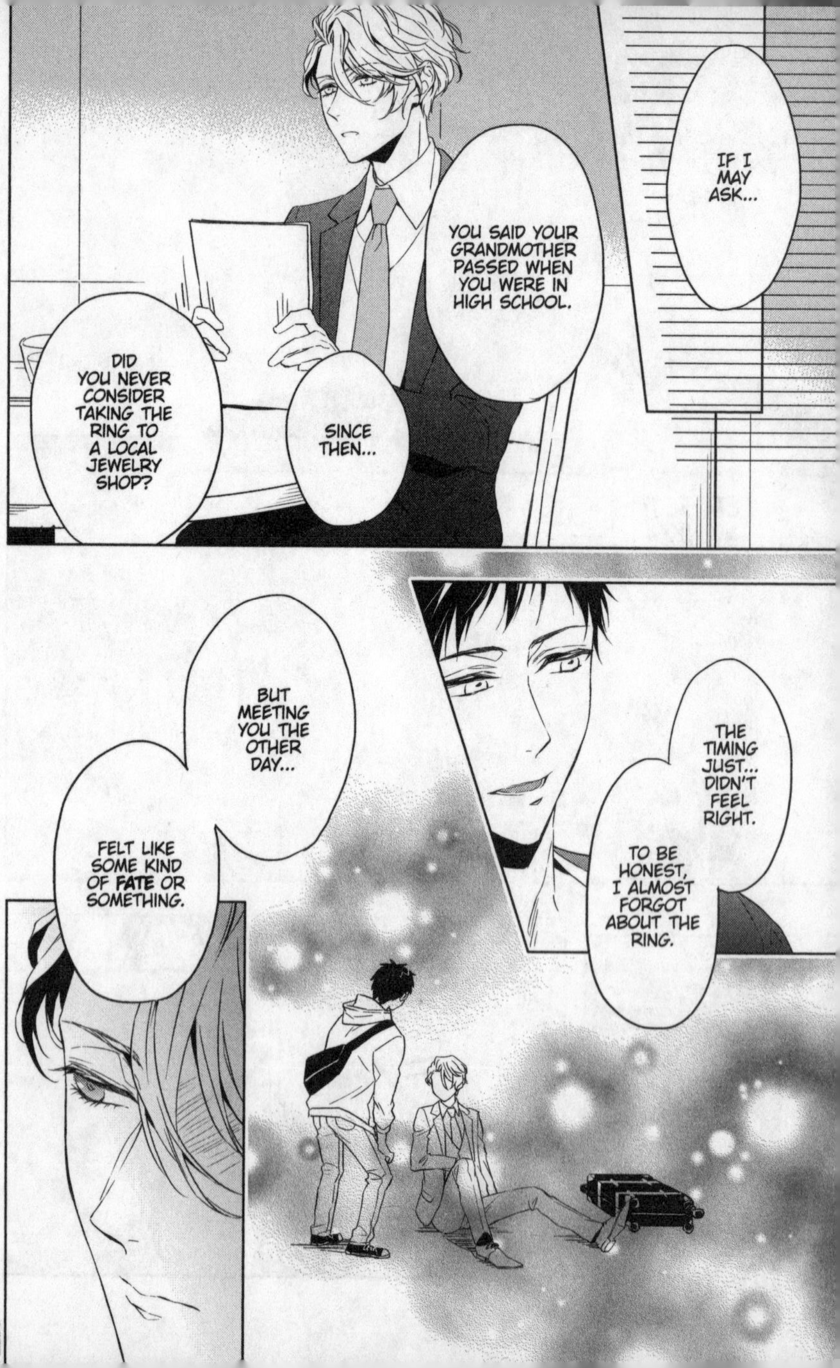
IF I MAY ASK...
YOU SAID YOUR GRANDMOTHER PASSED WHEN YOU WERE IN HIGH SCHOOL.
SINCE THEN...
DID YOU NEVER CONSIDER TAKING THE RING TO A LOCAL JEWELRY SHOP?
THE TIMING JUST... DIDN'T FEEL RIGHT.
TO BE HONEST, I ALMOST FORGOT ABOUT THE RING.
BUT MEETING YOU THE OTHER DAY...
FELT LIKE SOME KIND OF FATE OR SOMETHING.

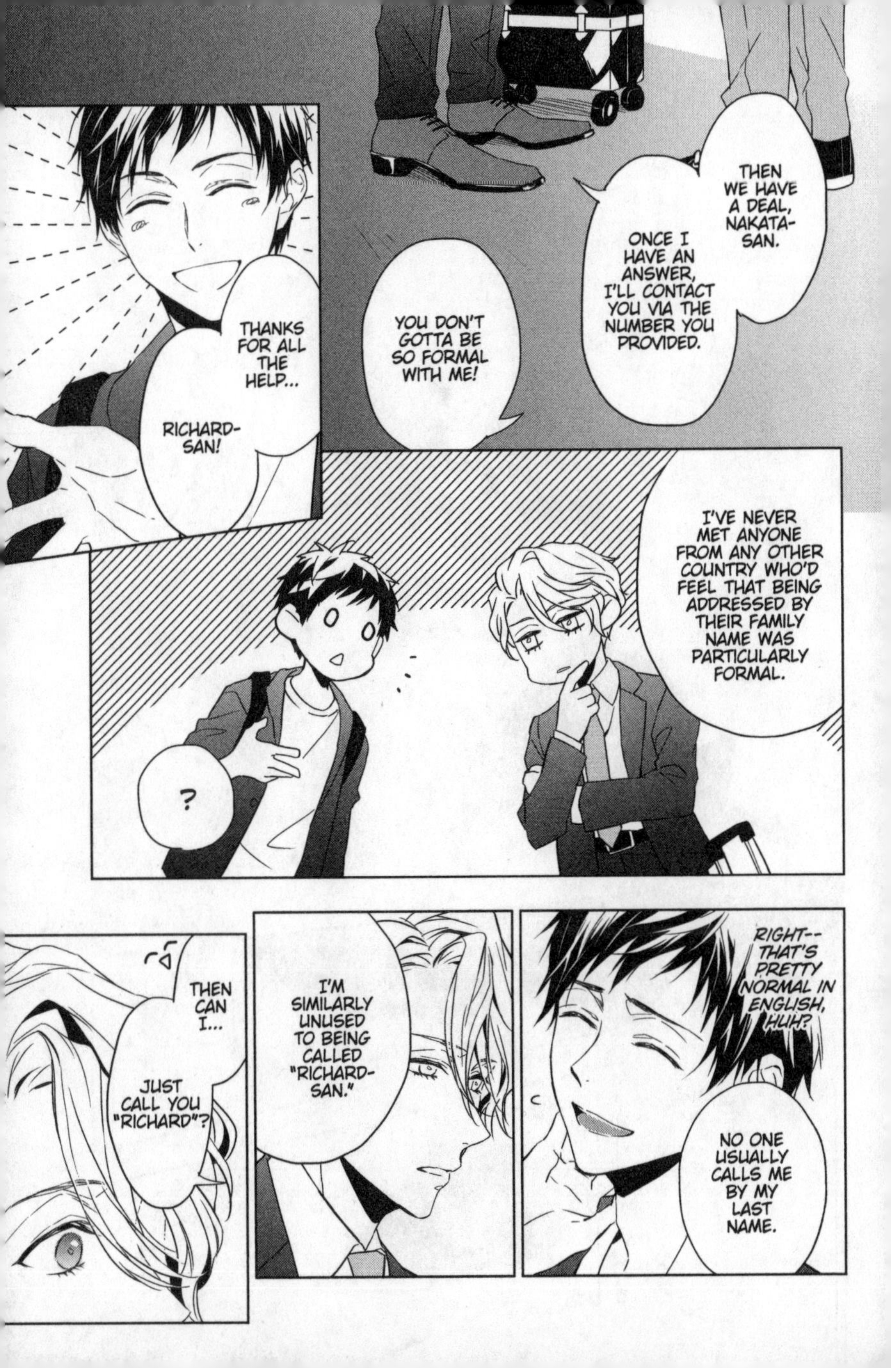
THEN WE HAVE A DEAL, NAKATA-SAN.
ONCE I HAVE AN ANSWER, I'LL CONTACT YOU VIA THE NUMBER YOU PROVIDED.
YOU DON'T GOTTA BE SO FORMAL WITH ME!
THANKS FOR ALL THE HELP...
RICHARD-SAN!
I'VE NEVER MET ANYONE FROM ANY OTHER COUNTRY WHO'D FEEL THAT BEING ADDRESSED BY THEIR FAMILY NAME WAS PARTICULARLY FORMAL.
?
RIGHT--THAT'S PRETTY NORMAL IN ENGLISH, HUH?
NO ONE USUALLY CALLS ME BY MY LAST NAME.
I'M SIMILARLY UNUSED TO BEING CALLED "RICHARD-SAN."
THEN CAN I...
JUST CALL YOU "RICHARD"?

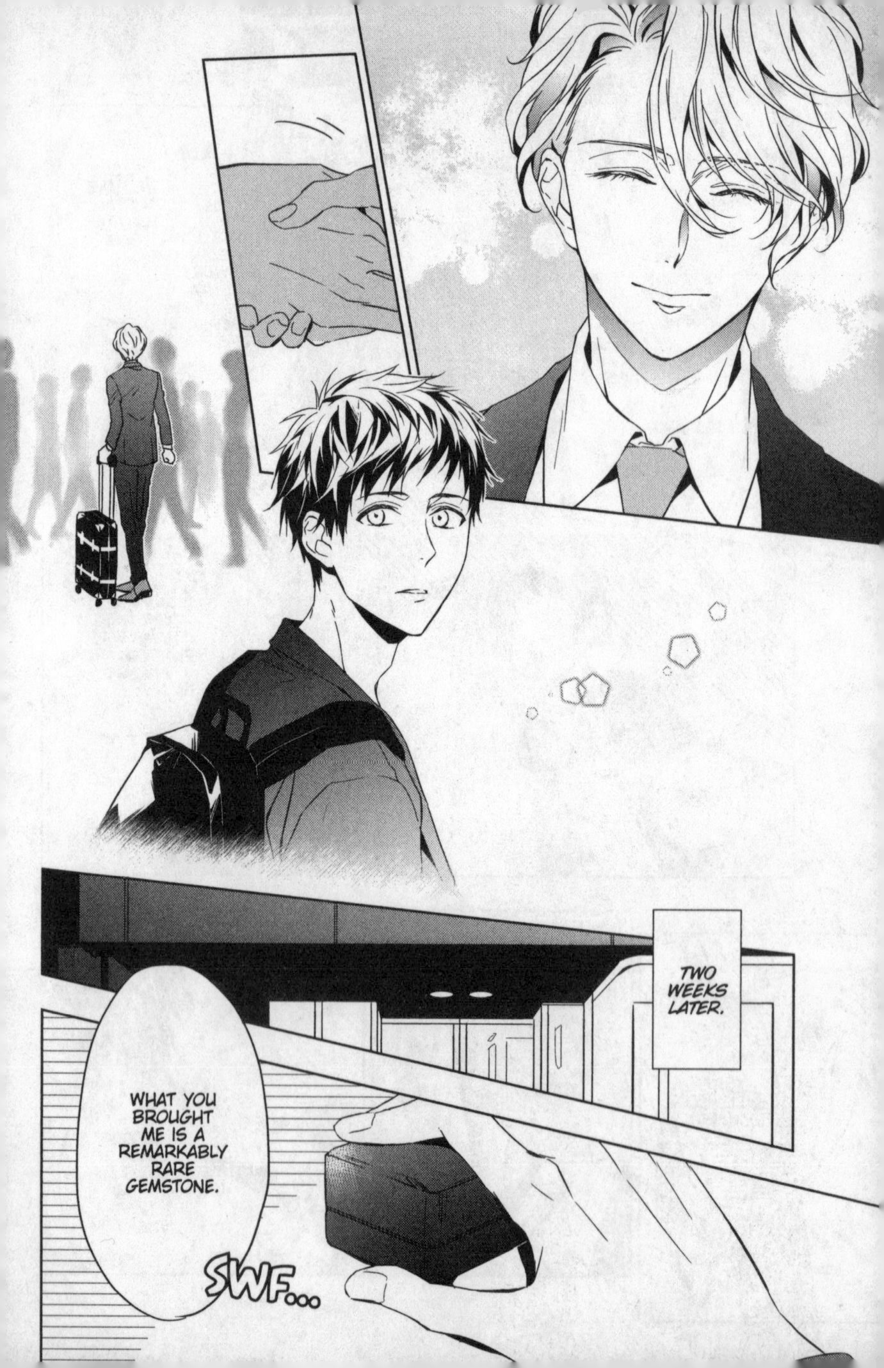
TWO WEEKS LATER.
WHAT YOU BROUGHT ME IS A REMARKABLY RARE GEMSTONE.
SWF...

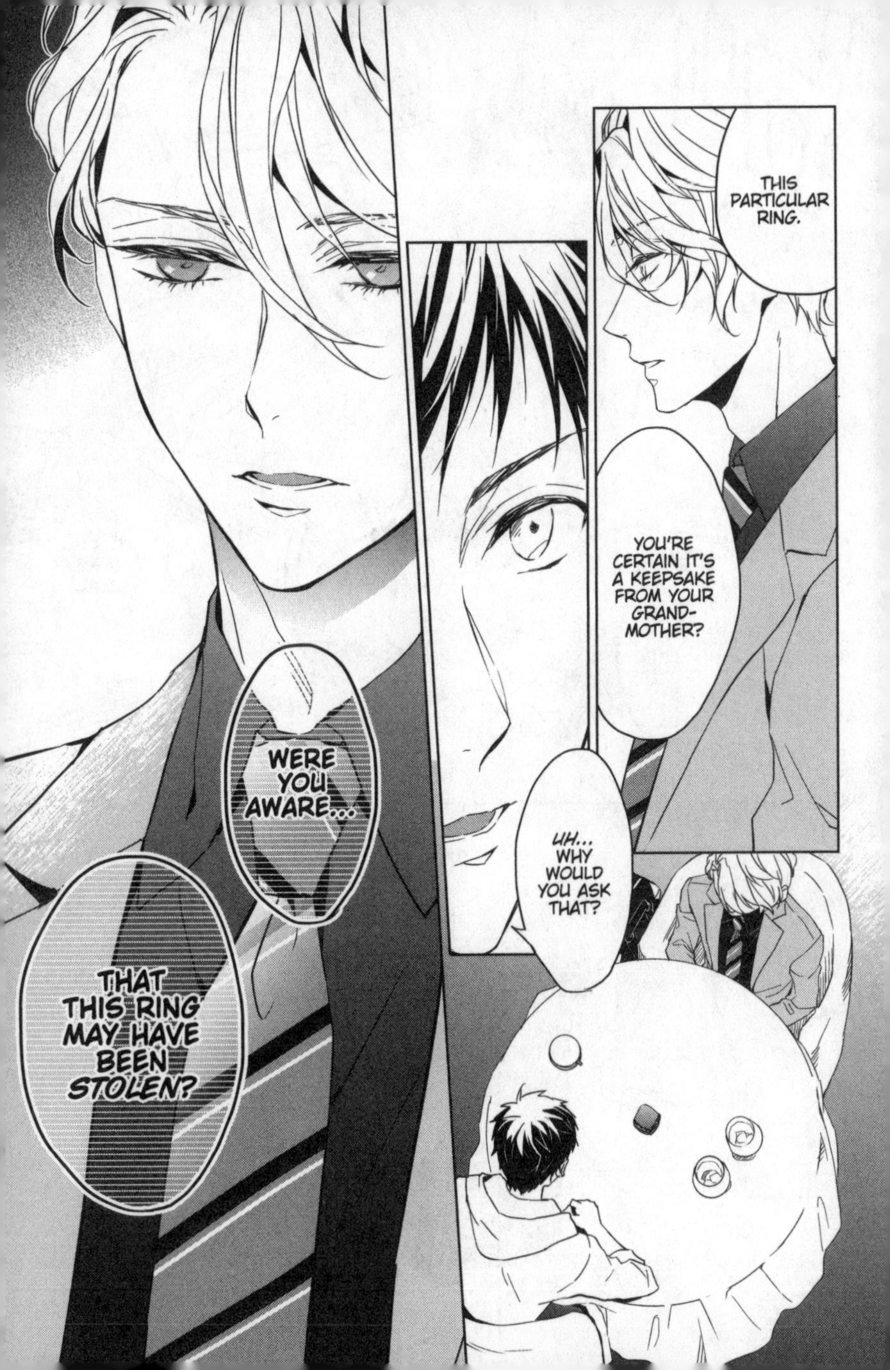
THIS PARTICULAR RING.
YOU'RE CERTAIN IT'S A KEEPSAKE FROM YOUR GRAND-MOTHER?
UH... WHY WOULD YOU ASK THAT?
WERE YOU AWARE...
THAT THIS RING MAY HAVE BEEN STOLEN?

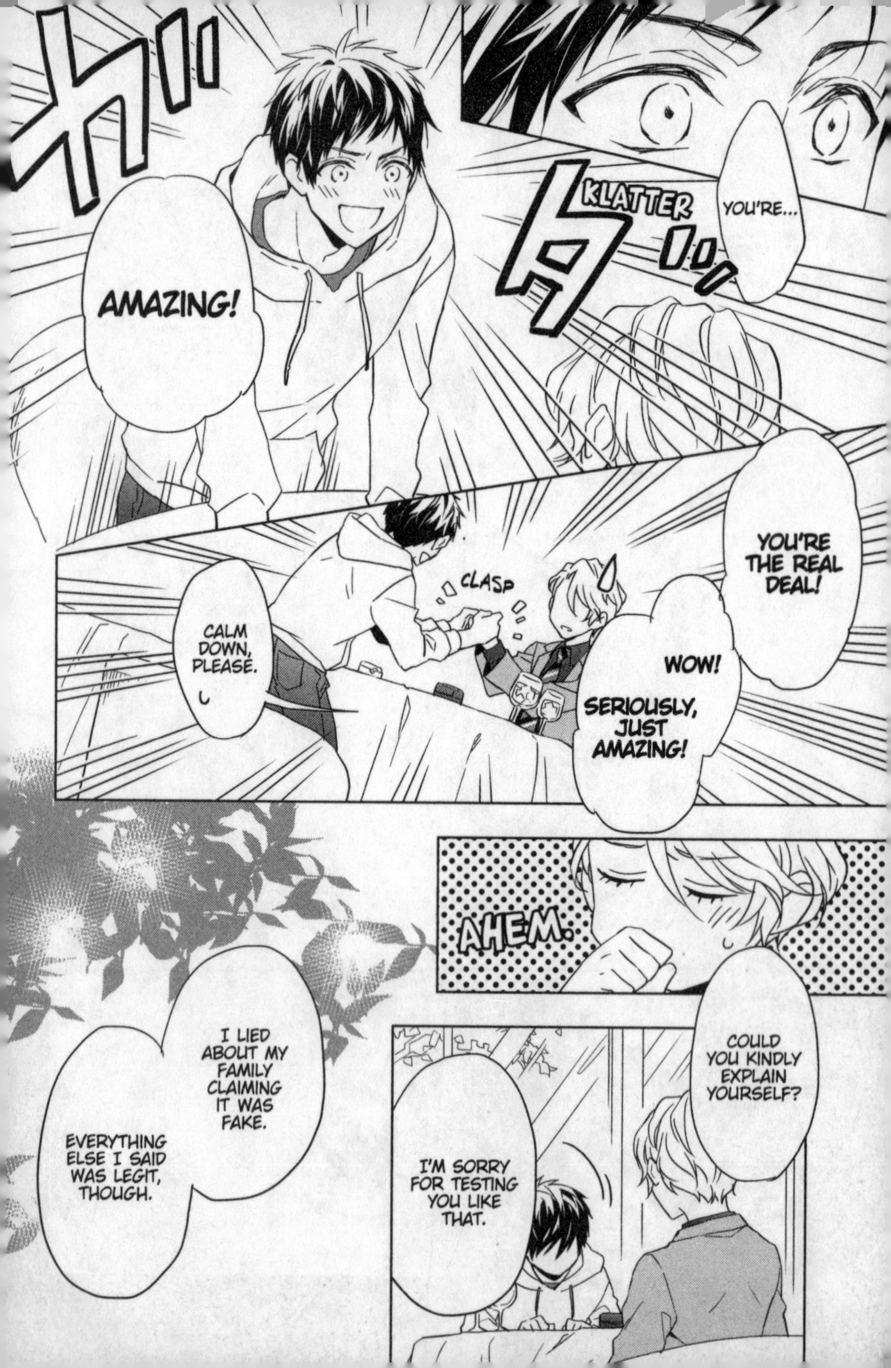
YOU'RE...
KLATTER
AMAZING!
YOU'RE THE REAL DEAL!
WOW!
SERIOUSLY, JUST AMAZING!
CLASP
CALM DOWN, PLEASE.
AHEM.
COULD YOU KINDLY EXPLAIN YOURSELF?
I'M SORRY FOR TESTING YOU LIKE THAT.
I LIED ABOUT MY FAMILY CLAIMING IT WAS FAKE.
EVERYTHING ELSE I SAID WAS LEGIT, THOUGH.

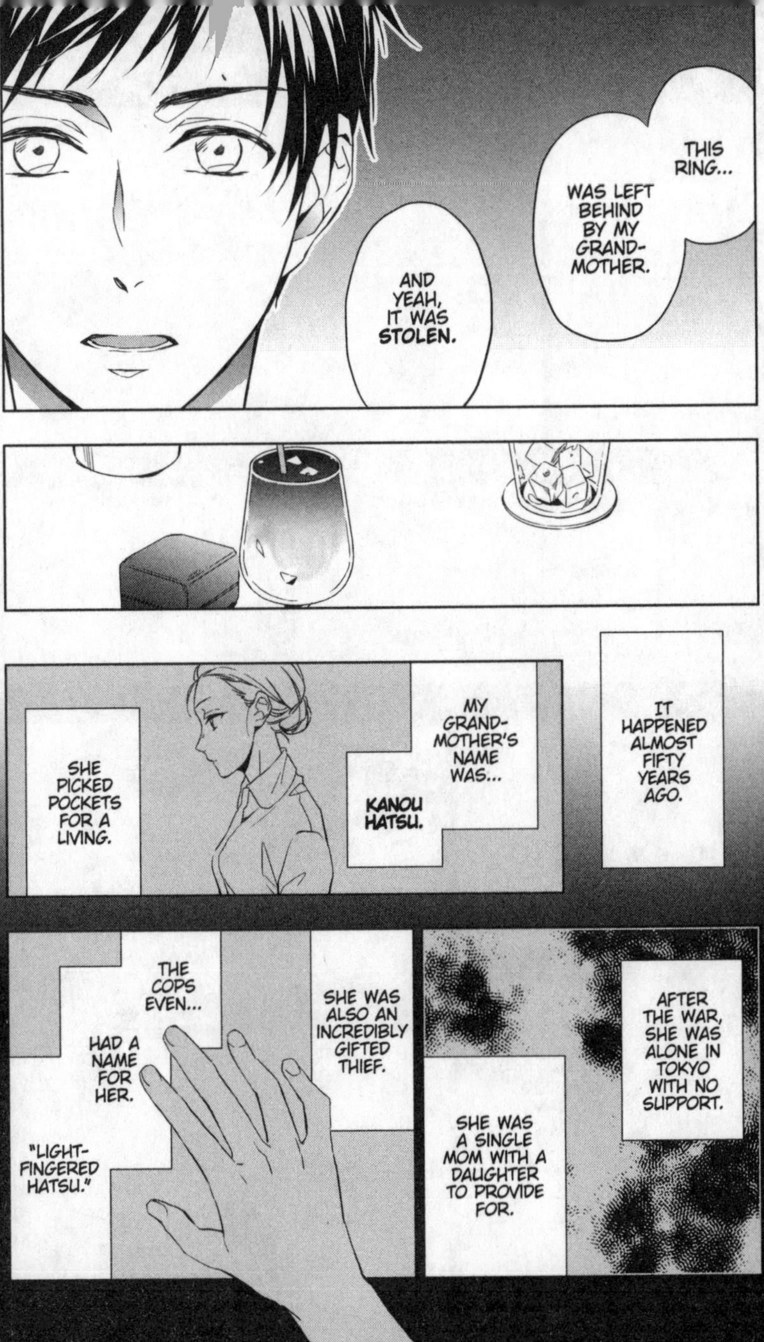
THIS RING...
WAS LEFT BEHIND BY MY GRANDMOTHER.
AND YEAH, IT WAS STOLEN.
IT HAPPENED ALMOST FIFTY YEARS AGO.
MY GRANDMOTHER'S NAME WAS...
KANOU HATSU.
SHE PICKED POCKETS FOR A LIVING.
AFTER THE WAR, SHE WAS ALONE IN TOKYO WITH NO SUPPORT.
SHE WAS A SINGLE MOM WITH A DAUGHTER TO PROVIDE FOR.
SHE WAS ALSO AN INCREDIBLY GIFTED THIEF.
THE COPS EVEN...
HAD A NAME FOR HER.
"LIGHT-FINGERED HATSU."

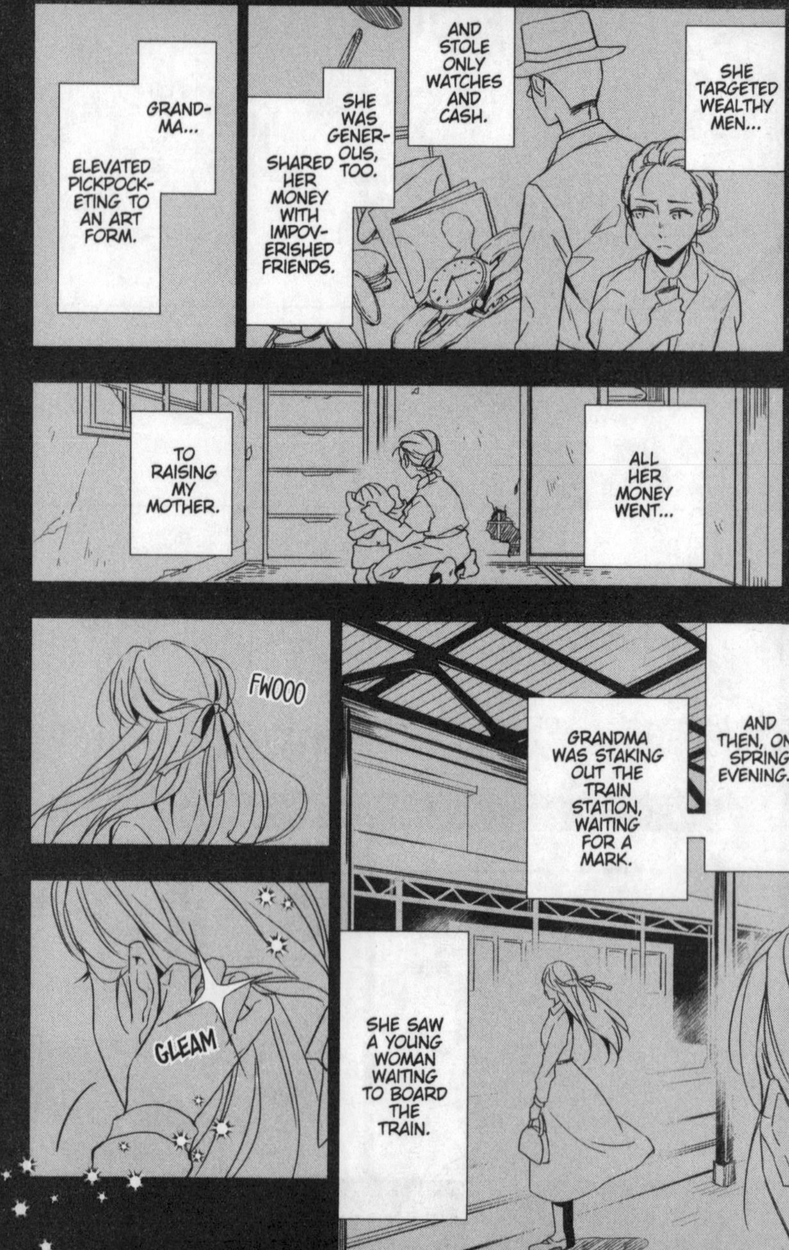
SHE TARGETED WEALTHY MEN...
AND STOLE ONLY WATCHES AND CASH.
SHE WAS GENEROUS, TOO.
SHARED HER MONEY WITH IMPOVERISHED FRIENDS.
GRANDMA...
ELEVATED PICKPOCKETING TO AN ART FORM.
ALL HER MONEY WENT...
TO RAISING MY MOTHER.
AND THEN, ONE SPRING EVENING...
GRANDMA WAS STAKING OUT THE TRAIN STATION, WAITING FOR A MARK.
SHE SAW A YOUNG WOMAN WAITING TO BOARD THE TRAIN.
FWOOO
GLEAM

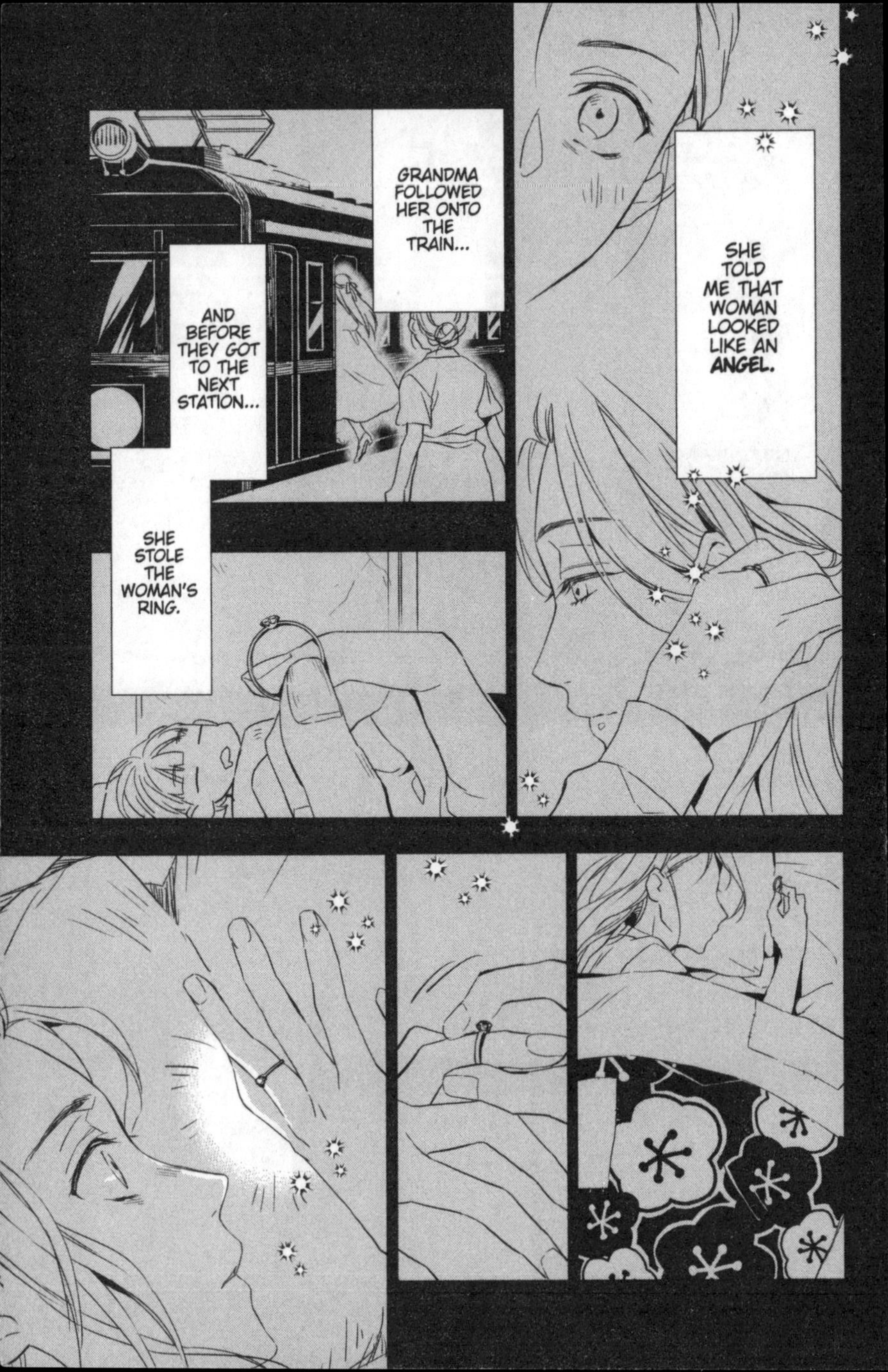
SHE TOLD ME THAT WOMAN LOOKED LIKE AN **ANGEL.**
GRANDMA FOLLOWED HER ONTO THE TRAIN...
AND BEFORE THEY GOT TO THE NEXT STATION...
SHE STOLE THE WOMAN'S RING.

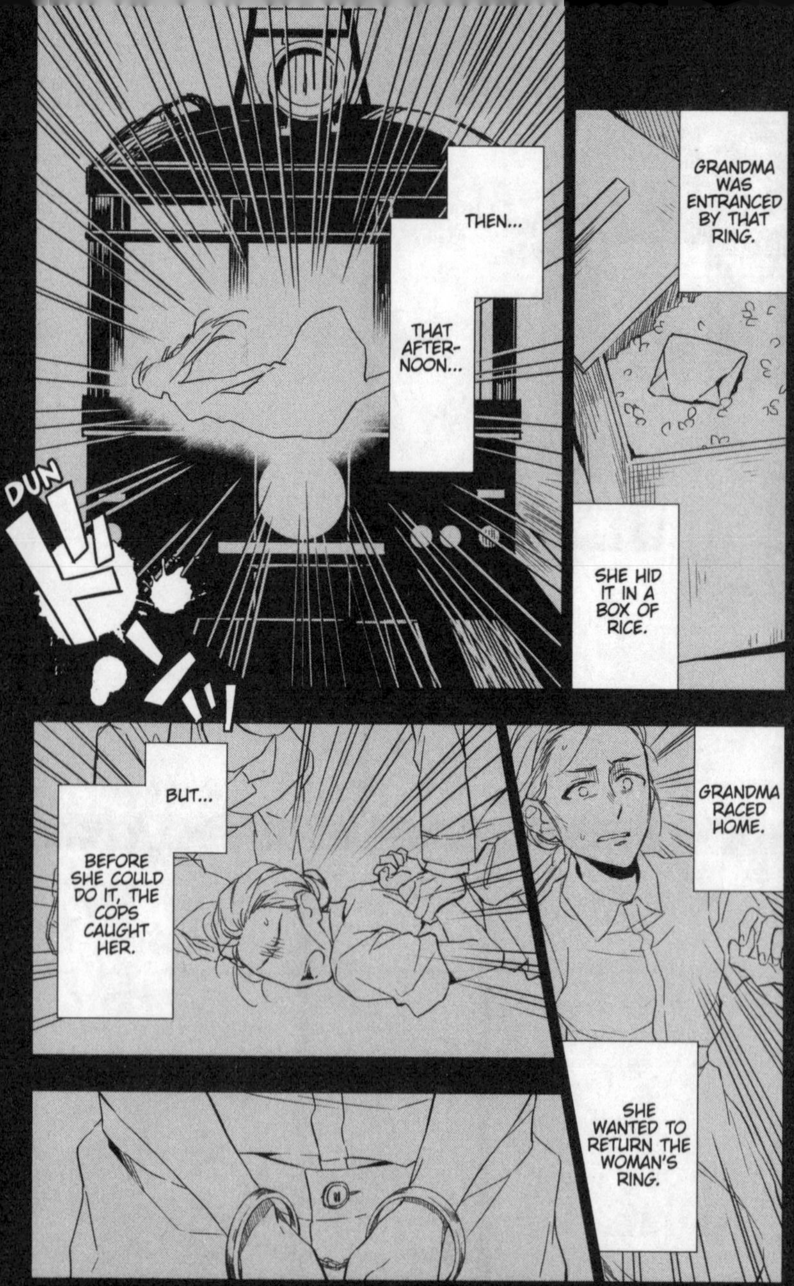
GRANDMA WAS ENTRANCED BY THAT RING.
SHE HID IT IN A BOX OF RICE.
THEN...
THAT AFTER-NOON...
DUN
GRANDMA RACED HOME.
SHE WANTED TO RETURN THE WOMAN'S RING.
BUT...
BEFORE SHE COULD DO IT, THE COPS CAUGHT HER.

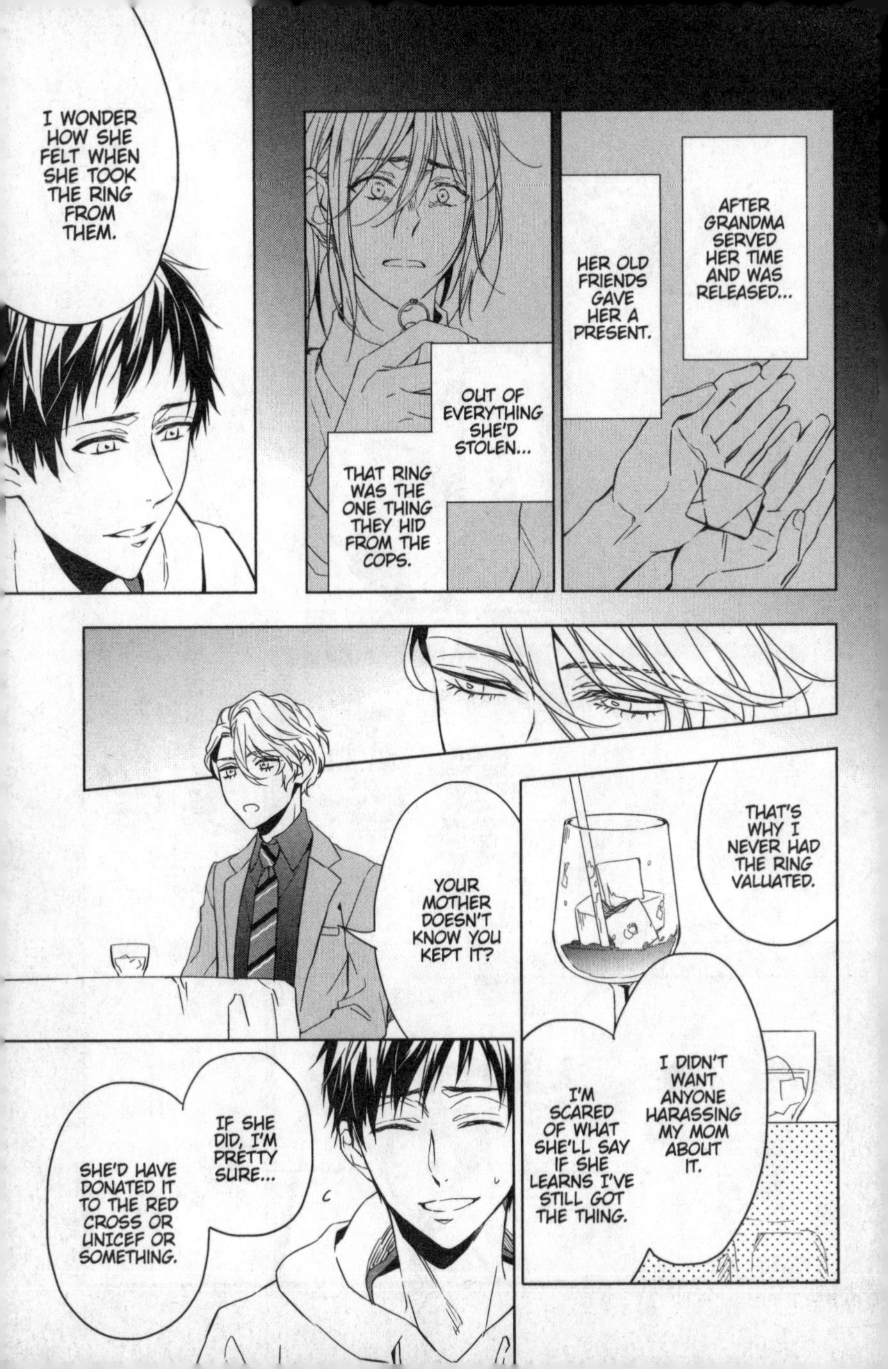
AFTER GRANDMA SERVED HER TIME AND WAS RELEASED...
HER OLD FRIENDS GAVE HER A PRESENT.
OUT OF EVERYTHING SHE'D STOLEN...
THAT RING WAS THE ONE THING THEY HID FROM THE COPS.
I WONDER HOW SHE FELT WHEN SHE TOOK THE RING FROM THEM.
THAT'S WHY I NEVER HAD THE RING VALUATED.
YOUR MOTHER DOESN'T KNOW YOU KEPT IT?
I DIDN'T WANT ANYONE HARASSING MY MOM ABOUT IT.
I'M SCARED OF WHAT SHE'LL SAY IF SHE LEARNS I'VE STILL GOT THE THING.
IF SHE DID, I'M PRETTY SURE...
SHE'D HAVE DONATED IT TO THE RED CROSS OR UNICEF OR SOMETHING.

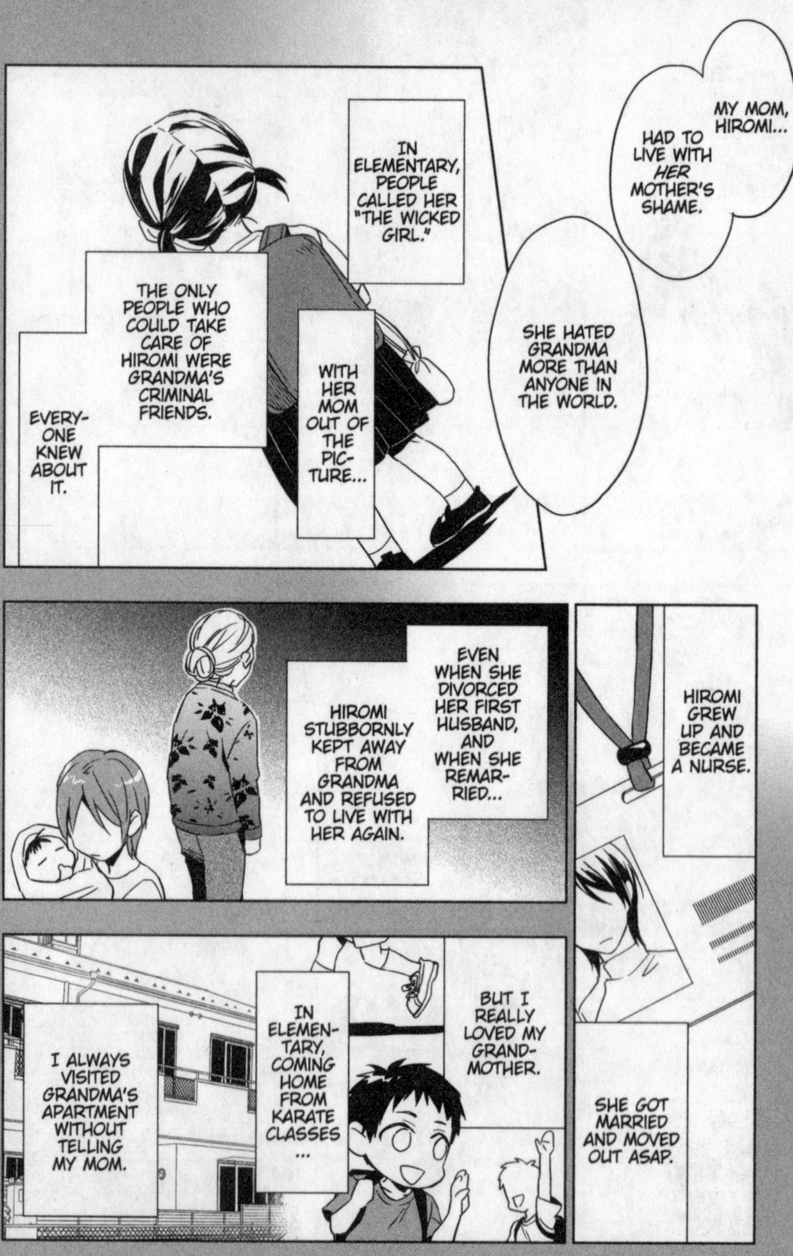

MY MOM, HIROMI...
HAD TO LIVE WITH *HER* MOTHER'S SHAME.
SHE HATED GRANDMA MORE THAN ANYONE IN THE WORLD.
IN ELEMENTARY, PEOPLE CALLED HER "THE WICKED GIRL."
WITH HER MOM OUT OF THE PICTURE...
THE ONLY PEOPLE WHO COULD TAKE CARE OF HIROMI WERE GRANDMA'S CRIMINAL FRIENDS.
EVERYONE KNEW ABOUT IT.
HIROMI GREW UP AND BECAME A NURSE.
SHE GOT MARRIED AND MOVED OUT ASAP.
EVEN WHEN SHE DIVORCED HER FIRST HUSBAND, AND WHEN SHE REMARRIED...
HIROMI STUBBORNLY KEPT AWAY FROM GRANDMA AND REFUSED TO LIVE WITH HER AGAIN.
BUT I REALLY LOVED MY GRANDMOTHER.
IN ELEMENTARY, COMING HOME FROM KARATE CLASSES...
I ALWAYS VISITED GRANDMA'S APARTMENT WITHOUT TELLING MY MOM.

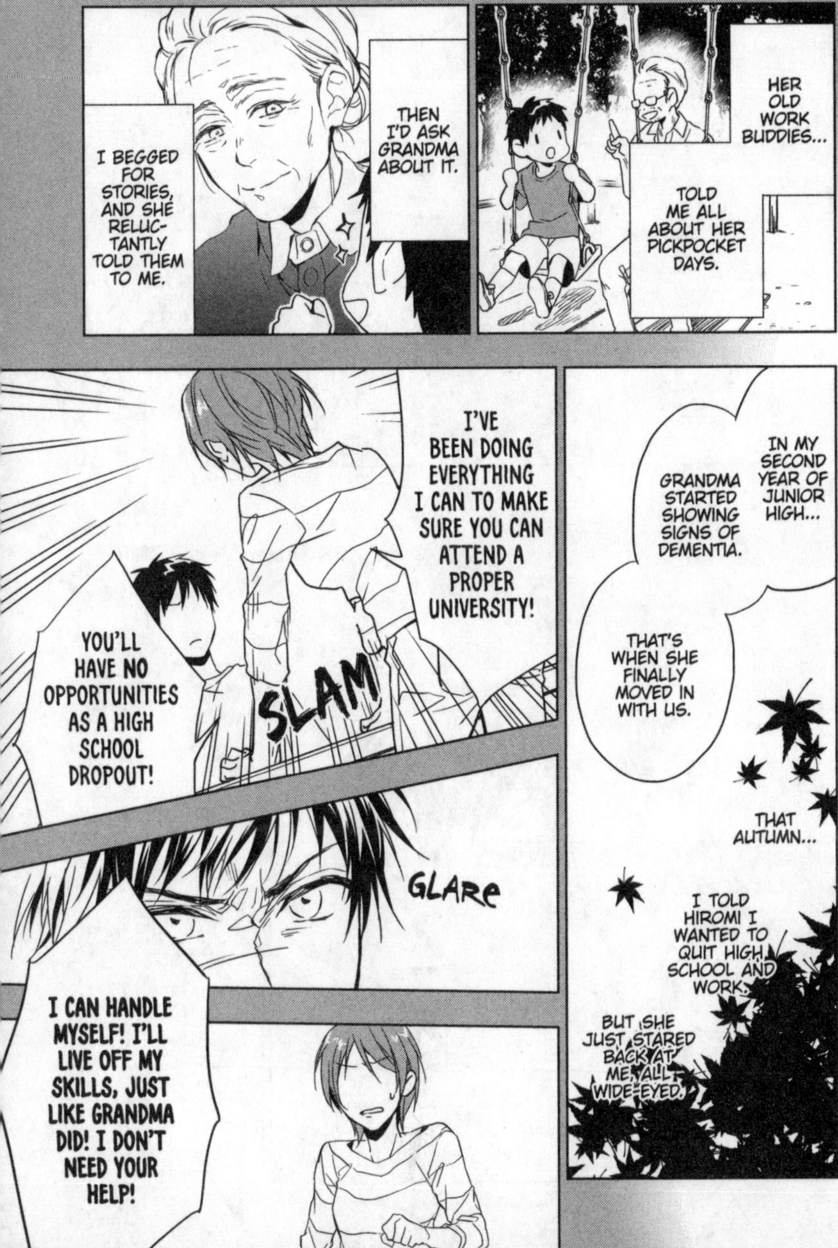
HER OLD WORK BUDDIES...
TOLD ME ALL ABOUT HER PICKPOCKET DAYS.
THEN I'D ASK GRANDMA ABOUT IT.
I BEGGED FOR STORIES, AND SHE RELUCTANTLY TOLD THEM TO ME.
IN MY SECOND YEAR OF JUNIOR HIGH...
GRANDMA STARTED SHOWING SIGNS OF DEMENTIA.
THAT'S WHEN SHE FINALLY MOVED IN WITH US.
THAT AUTUMN...
I TOLD HIROMI I WANTED TO QUIT HIGH SCHOOL AND WORK.
BUT SHE JUST STARED BACK AT ME, ALL WIDE-EYED.
I'VE BEEN DOING EVERYTHING I CAN TO MAKE SURE YOU CAN ATTEND A PROPER UNIVERSITY!
YOU'LL HAVE NO OPPORTUNITIES AS A HIGH SCHOOL DROPOUT!
SLAM
GLARE
I CAN HANDLE MYSELF! I'LL LIVE OFF MY SKILLS, JUST LIKE GRANDMA DID! I DON'T NEED YOUR HELP!

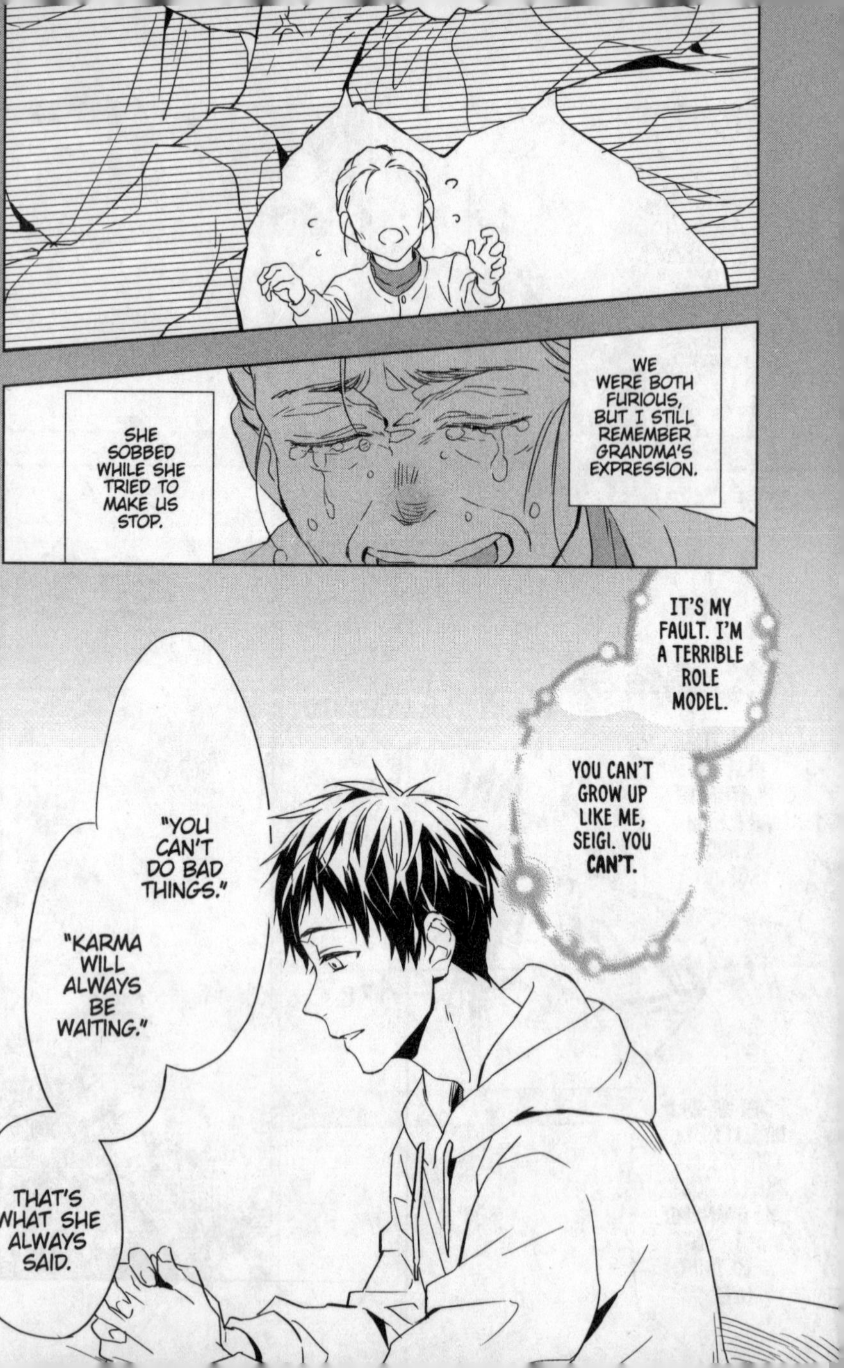
WE WERE BOTH FURIOUS, BUT I STILL REMEMBER GRANDMA'S EXPRESSION.
SHE SOBBED WHILE SHE TRIED TO MAKE US STOP.
IT'S MY FAULT. I'M A TERRIBLE ROLE MODEL.
YOU CAN'T GROW UP LIKE ME, SEIGI. YOU **CAN'T**.
"YOU CAN'T DO BAD THINGS."
"KARMA WILL ALWAYS BE WAITING."
THAT'S WHAT SHE ALWAYS SAID.

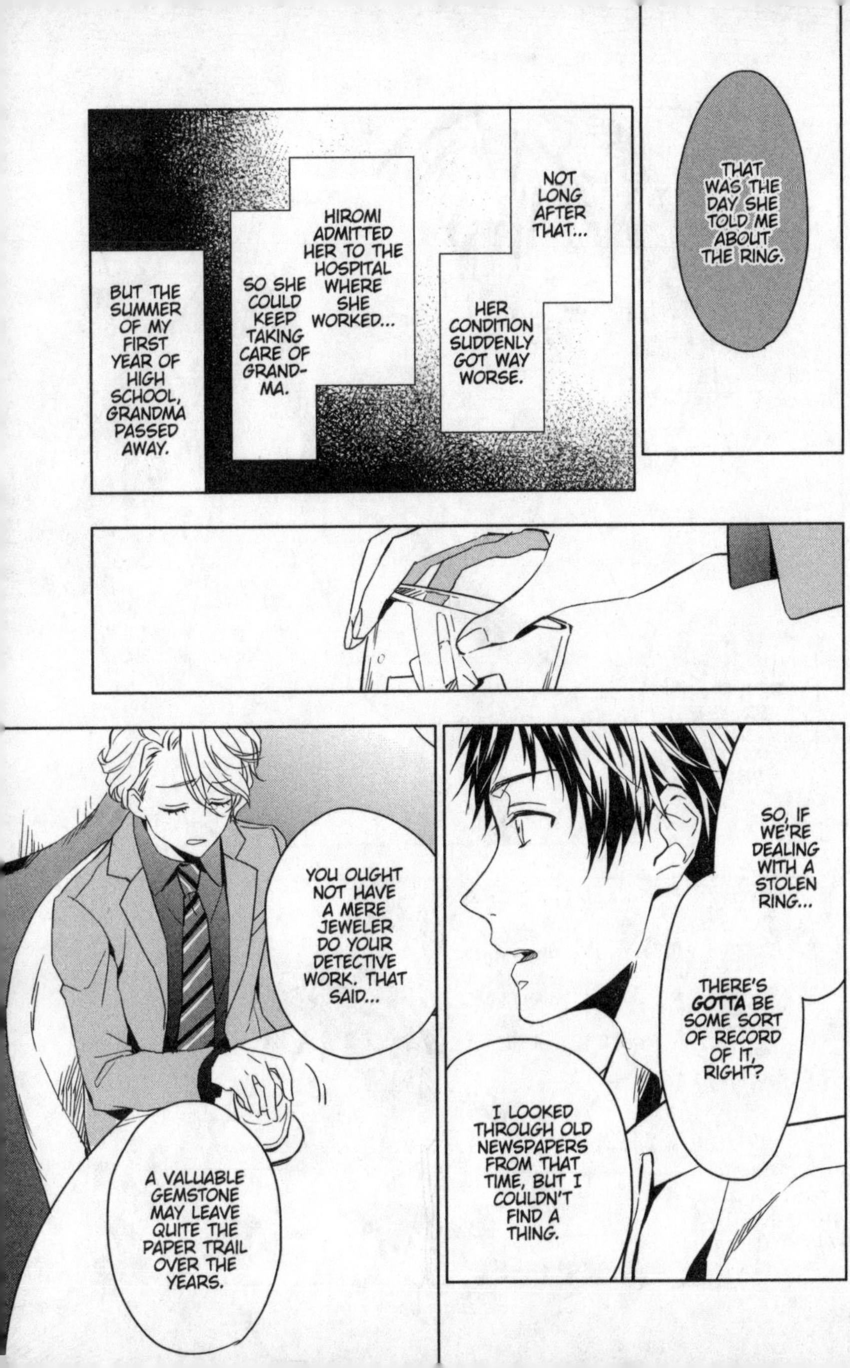
THAT WAS THE DAY SHE TOLD ME ABOUT THE RING.
NOT LONG AFTER THAT...
HER CONDITION SUDDENLY GOT WAY WORSE.
HIROMI ADMITTED HER TO THE HOSPITAL WHERE SHE WORKED...
SO SHE COULD KEEP TAKING CARE OF GRAND-MA.
BUT THE SUMMER OF MY FIRST YEAR OF HIGH SCHOOL, GRANDMA PASSED AWAY.
SO, IF WE'RE DEALING WITH A STOLEN RING...
THERE'S **GOTTA** BE SOME SORT OF RECORD OF IT, RIGHT?
I LOOKED THROUGH OLD NEWSPAPERS FROM THAT TIME, BUT I COULDN'T FIND A THING.
YOU OUGHT NOT HAVE A MERE JEWELER DO YOUR DETECTIVE WORK. THAT SAID...
A VALUABLE GEMSTONE MAY LEAVE QUITE THE PAPER TRAIL OVER THE YEARS.

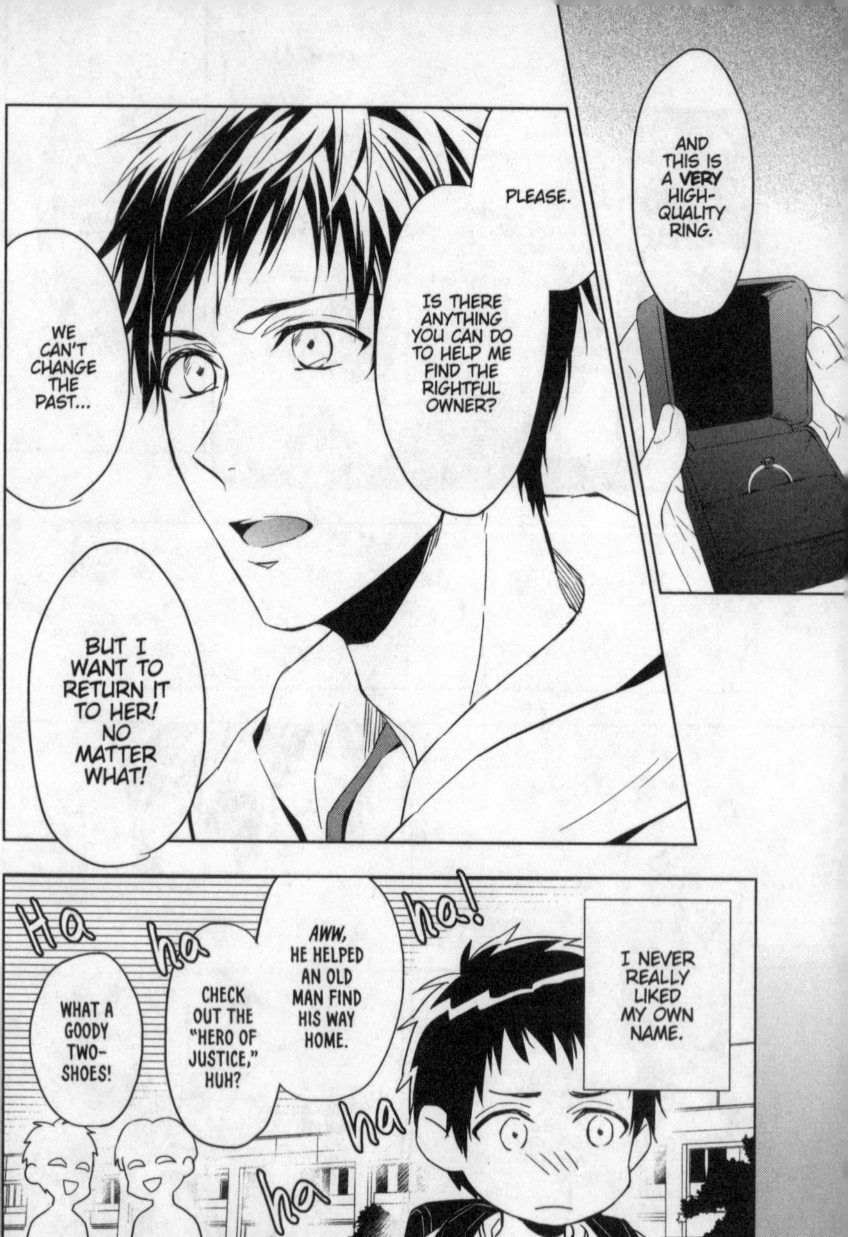
AND THIS IS A VERY HIGH-QUALITY RING.
PLEASE.
IS THERE ANYTHING YOU CAN DO TO HELP ME FIND THE RIGHTFUL OWNER?
WE CAN'T CHANGE THE PAST...
BUT I WANT TO RETURN IT TO HER! NO MATTER WHAT!
I NEVER REALLY LIKED MY OWN NAME.
Ha ha ha!
AWW, HE HELPED AN OLD MAN FIND HIS WAY HOME.
CHECK OUT THE "HERO OF JUSTICE," HUH?
WHAT A GOODY TWO-SHOES!
ha ha

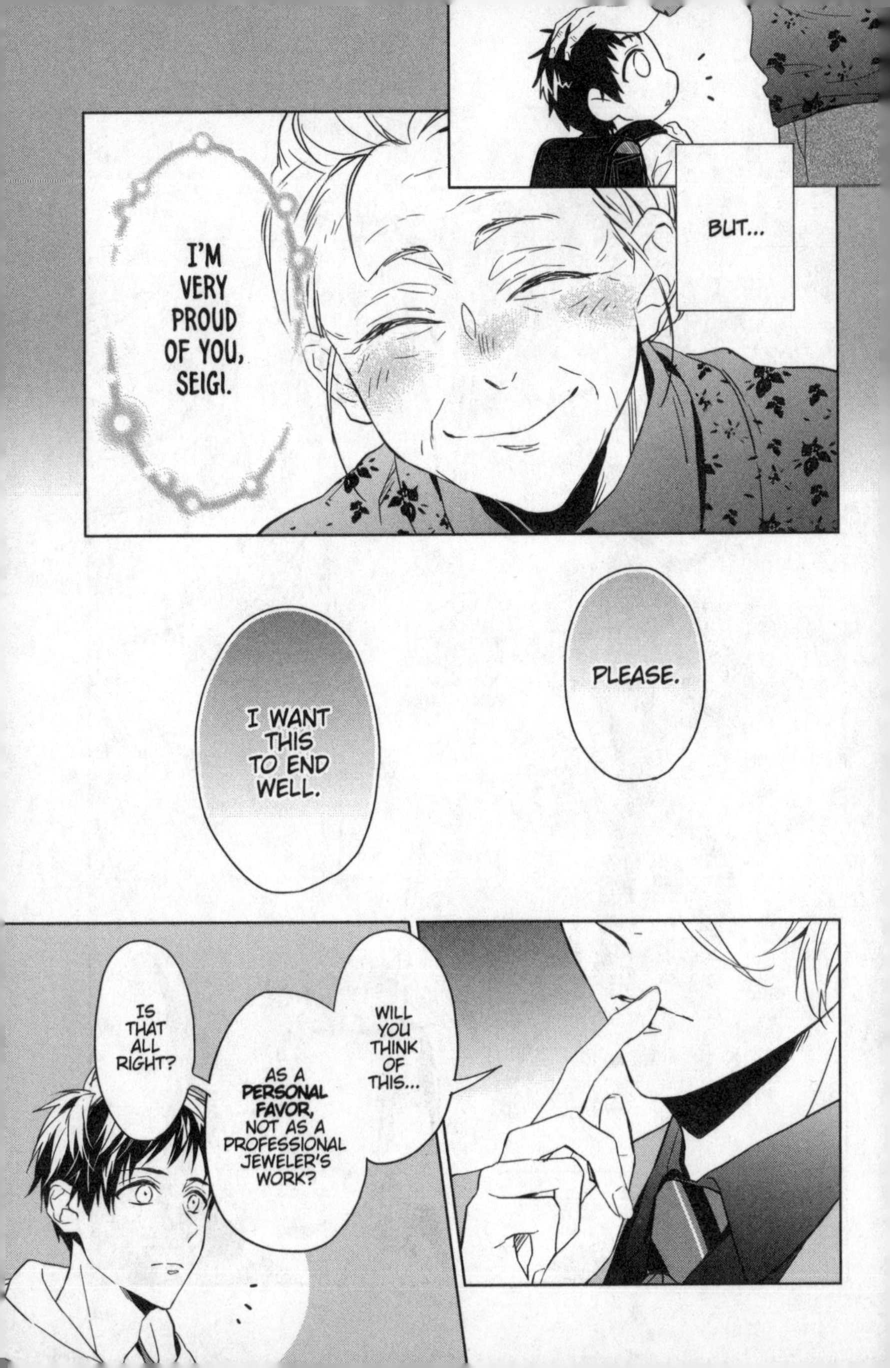
BUT...
I'M VERY PROUD OF YOU, SEIGI.
PLEASE.
I WANT THIS TO END WELL.
WILL YOU THINK OF THIS...
AS A **PERSONAL FAVOR,** NOT AS A PROFESSIONAL JEWELER'S WORK?
IS THAT ALL RIGHT?

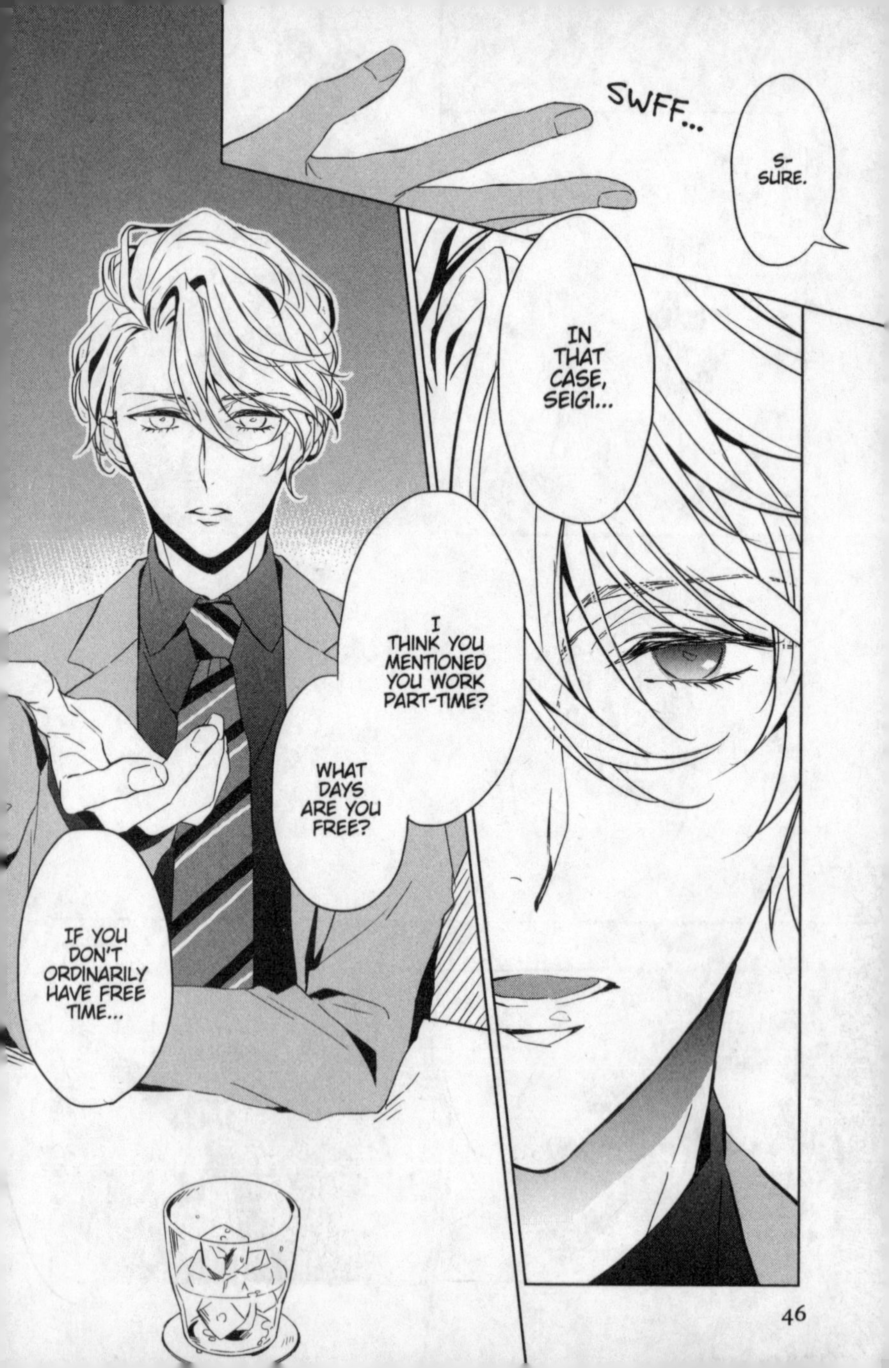
S-SURE.
SWFF...
IN THAT CASE, SEIGI...
I THINK YOU MENTIONED YOU WORK PART-TIME?
WHAT DAYS ARE YOU FREE?
IF YOU DON'T ORDINARILY HAVE FREE TIME...

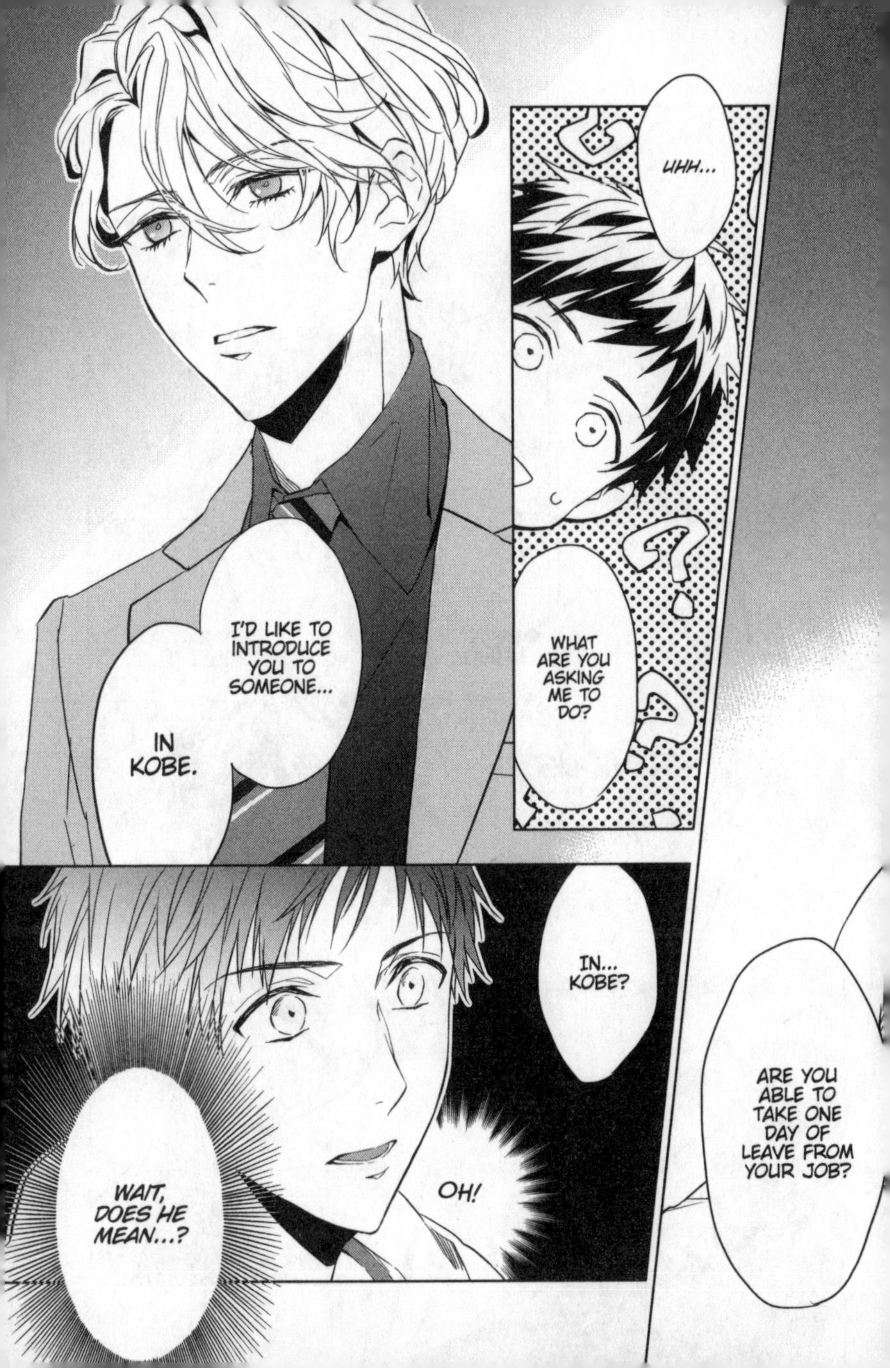

UHH...
WHAT ARE YOU ASKING ME TO DO?
I'D LIKE TO INTRODUCE YOU TO SOMEONE...
IN KOBE.
ARE YOU ABLE TO TAKE ONE DAY OF LEAVE FROM YOUR JOB?
IN... KOBE?
OH!
WAIT, DOES HE MEAN...?

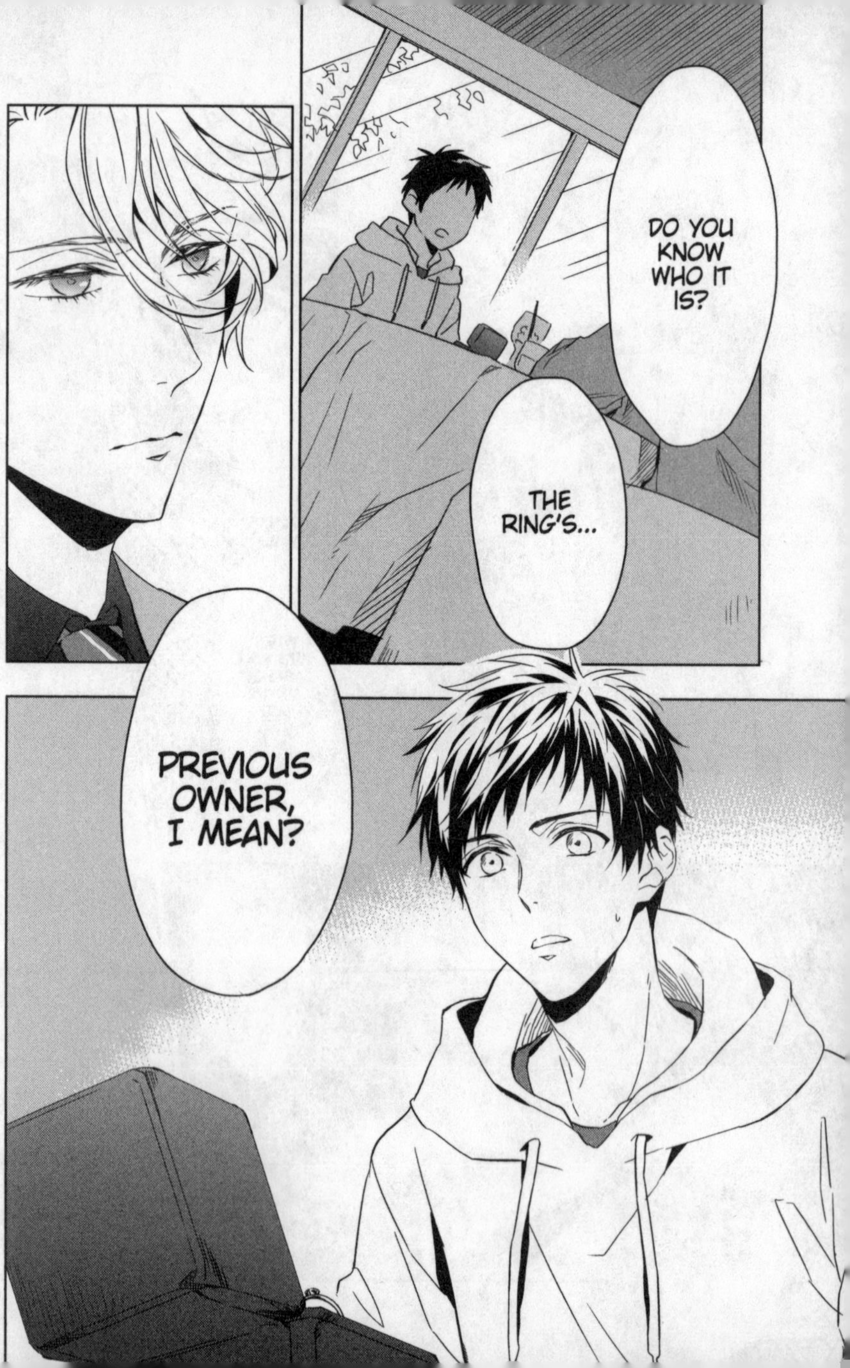
DO YOU KNOW WHO IT IS?
THE RING'S...
PREVIOUS OWNER, I MEAN?

THE CASE FILES
~ OF ~
JEWELER
RICHARD

THE CASE FILES OF JEWELER RICHARD

case. 2

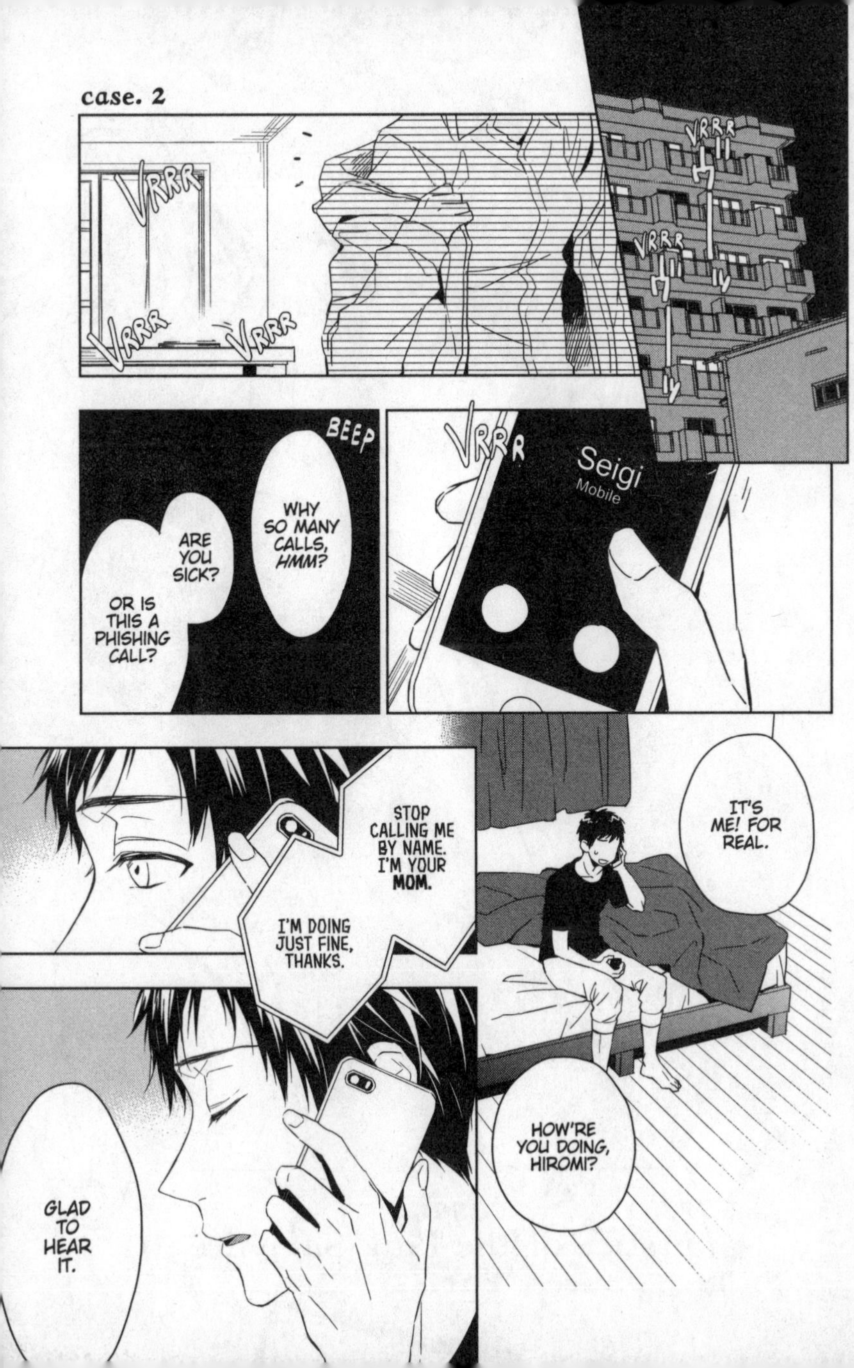
VRRR
VRRR
VRRR
VRRR
VRRR
VRRR
Seigi
Mobile
BEEP
WHY SO MANY CALLS, HMM?
ARE YOU SICK?
OR IS THIS A PHISHING CALL?
IT'S ME! FOR REAL.
HOW'RE YOU DOING, HIROMI?
STOP CALLING ME BY NAME. I'M YOUR MOM.
I'M DOING JUST FINE, THANKS.
GLAD TO HEAR IT.

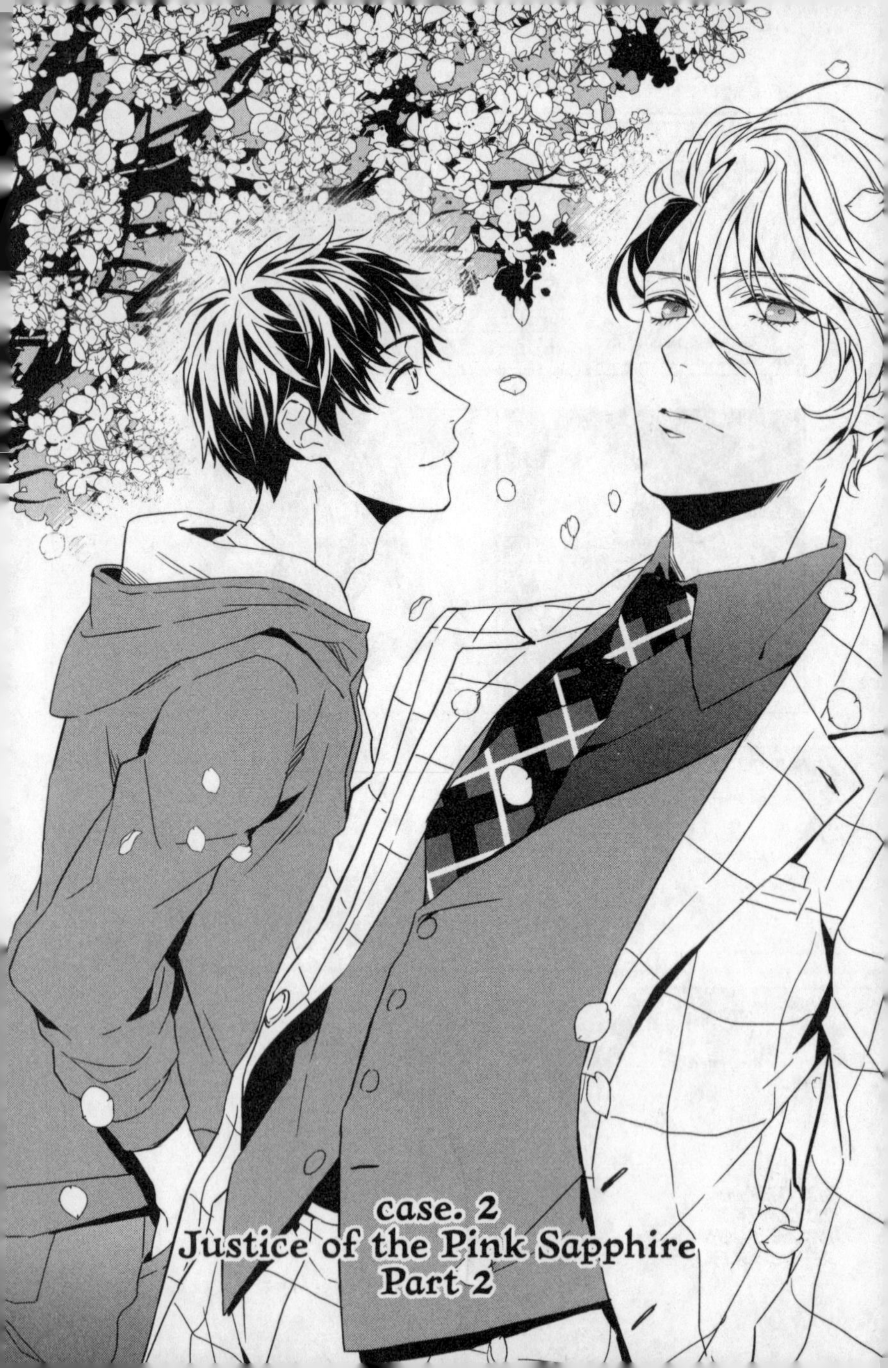
case. 2
Justice of the Pink Sapphire
Part 2

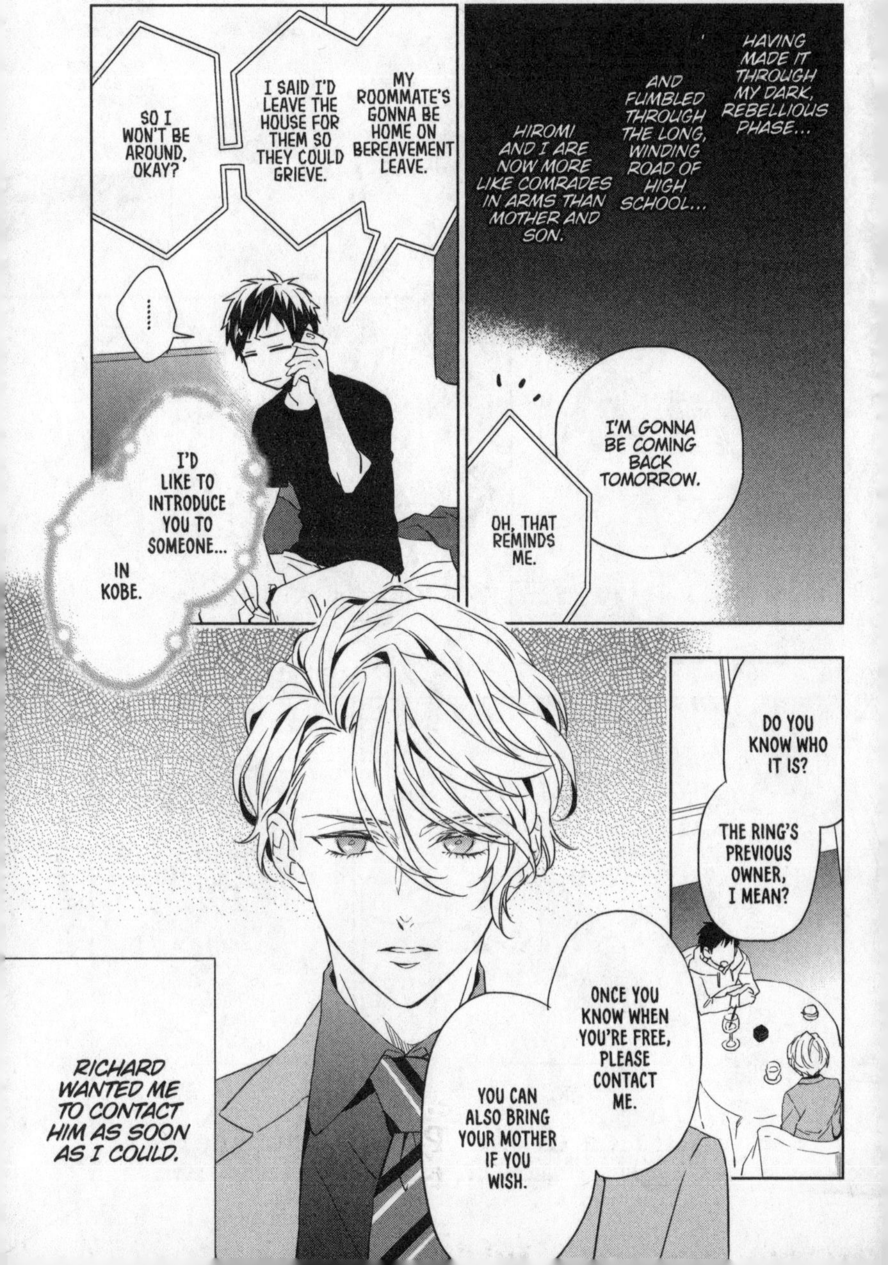
HAVING MADE IT THROUGH MY DARK, REBELLIOUS PHASE...
AND FUMBLED THROUGH THE LONG, WINDING ROAD OF HIGH SCHOOL...
HIROMI AND I ARE NOW MORE LIKE COMRADES IN ARMS THAN MOTHER AND SON.
I'M GONNA BE COMING BACK TOMORROW.
OH, THAT REMINDS ME.
MY ROOMMATE'S GONNA BE HOME ON BEREAVEMENT LEAVE.
I SAID I'D LEAVE THE HOUSE FOR THEM SO THEY COULD GRIEVE.
SO I WON'T BE AROUND, OKAY?
......
I'D LIKE TO INTRODUCE YOU TO SOMEONE...
IN KOBE.
DO YOU KNOW WHO IT IS?
THE RING'S PREVIOUS OWNER, I MEAN?
ONCE YOU KNOW WHEN YOU'RE FREE, PLEASE CONTACT ME.
YOU CAN ALSO BRING YOUR MOTHER IF YOU WISH.
RICHARD WANTED ME TO CONTACT HIM AS SOON AS I COULD.

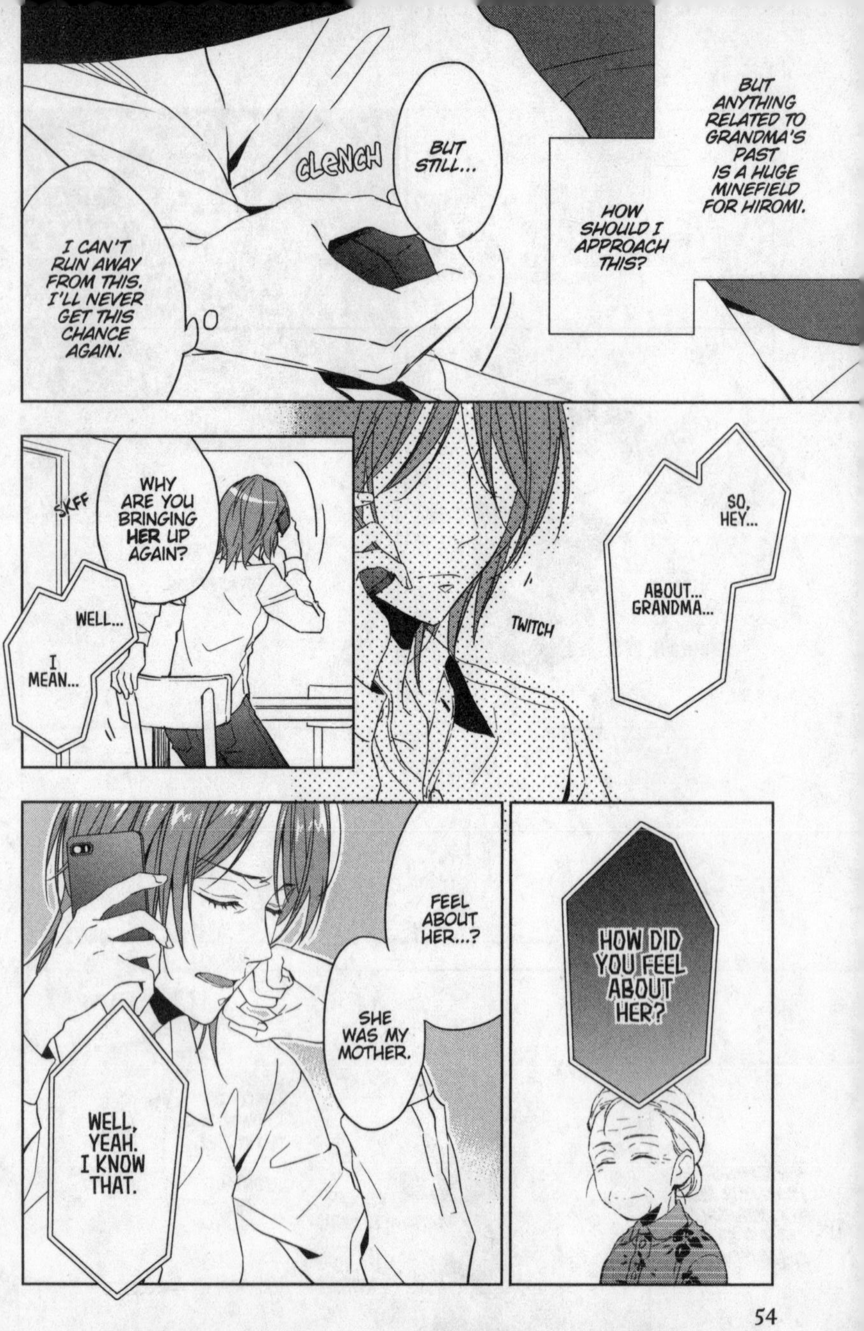
BUT ANYTHING RELATED TO GRANDMA'S PAST IS A HUGE MINEFIELD FOR HIROMI.
HOW SHOULD I APPROACH THIS?
BUT STILL...
CLENCH
I CAN'T RUN AWAY FROM THIS. I'LL NEVER GET THIS CHANCE AGAIN.
SO, HEY...
ABOUT... GRANDMA...
TWITCH
WHY ARE YOU BRINGING HER UP AGAIN?
SKFF
WELL...
I MEAN...
HOW DID YOU FEEL ABOUT HER?
FEEL ABOUT HER...?
SHE WAS MY MOTHER.
WELL, YEAH. I KNOW THAT.

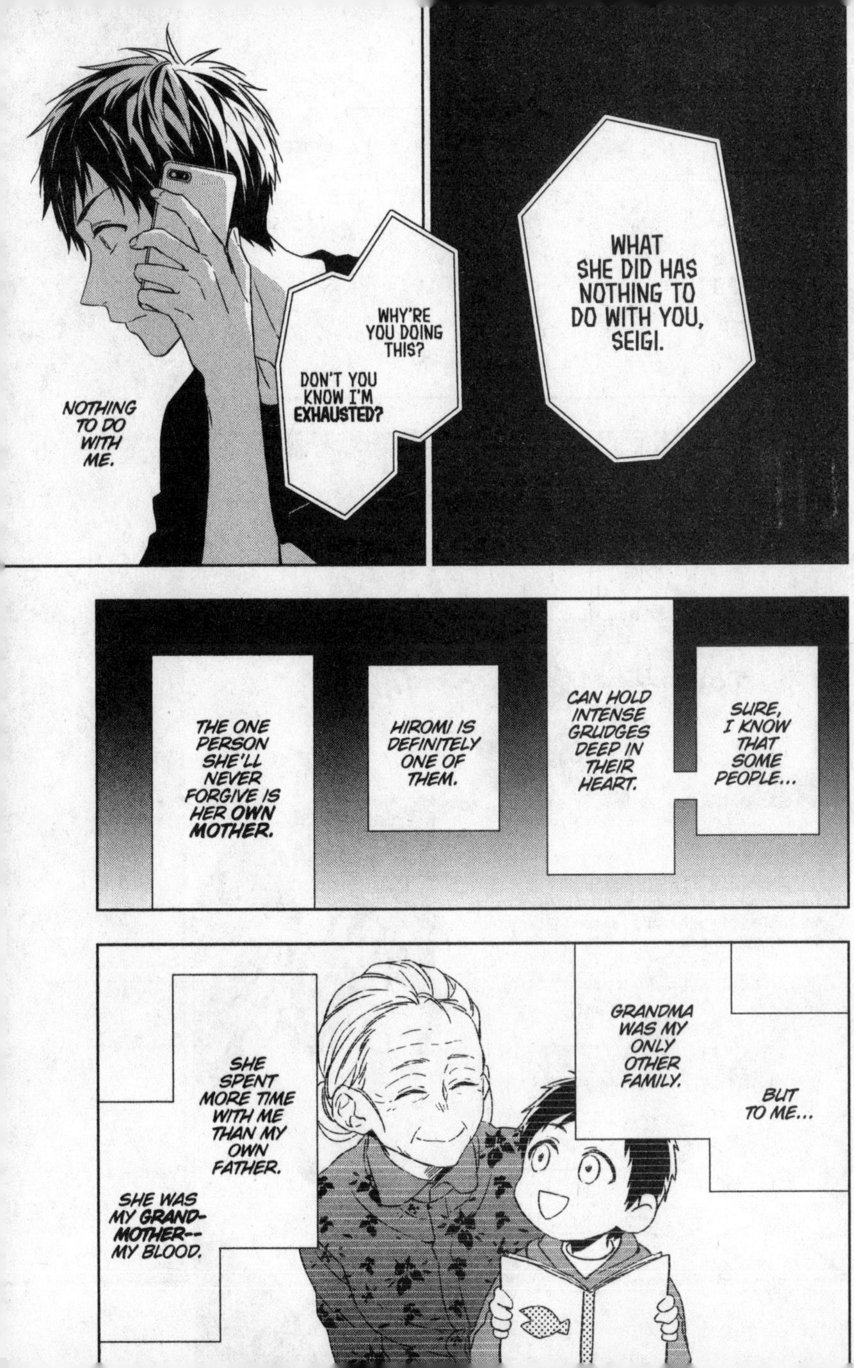
WHAT SHE DID HAS NOTHING TO DO WITH YOU, SEIGI.
WHY'RE YOU DOING THIS?
DON'T YOU KNOW I'M EXHAUSTED?
NOTHING TO DO WITH ME.
SURE, I KNOW THAT SOME PEOPLE...
CAN HOLD INTENSE GRUDGES DEEP IN THEIR HEART.
HIROMI IS DEFINITELY ONE OF THEM.
THE ONE PERSON SHE'LL NEVER FORGIVE IS HER OWN MOTHER.
BUT TO ME...
GRANDMA WAS MY ONLY OTHER FAMILY.
SHE SPENT MORE TIME WITH ME THAN MY OWN FATHER.
SHE WAS MY GRAND-MOTHER-- MY BLOOD.

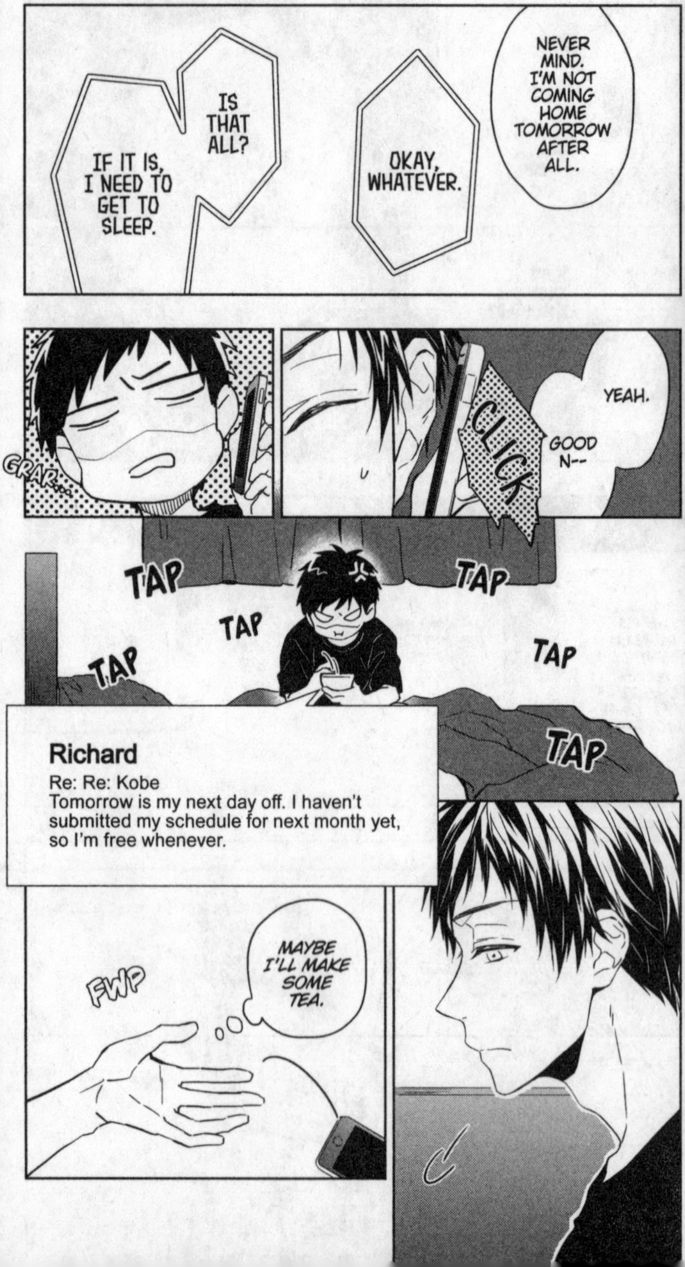
NEVER MIND. I'M NOT COMING HOME TOMORROW AFTER ALL.
OKAY, WHATEVER.
IS THAT ALL?
IF IT IS, I NEED TO GET TO SLEEP.
YEAH.
GOOD N--
CLICK
GRAR...
TAP
TAP
TAP
TAP
TAP
TAP
Richard
Re: Re: Kobe
Tomorrow is my next day off. I haven't submitted my schedule for next month yet, so I'm free whenever.
FWP
MAYBE I'LL MAKE SOME TEA.

HOW DOES THAT HAVE "NOTHING TO DO WITH ME"?!

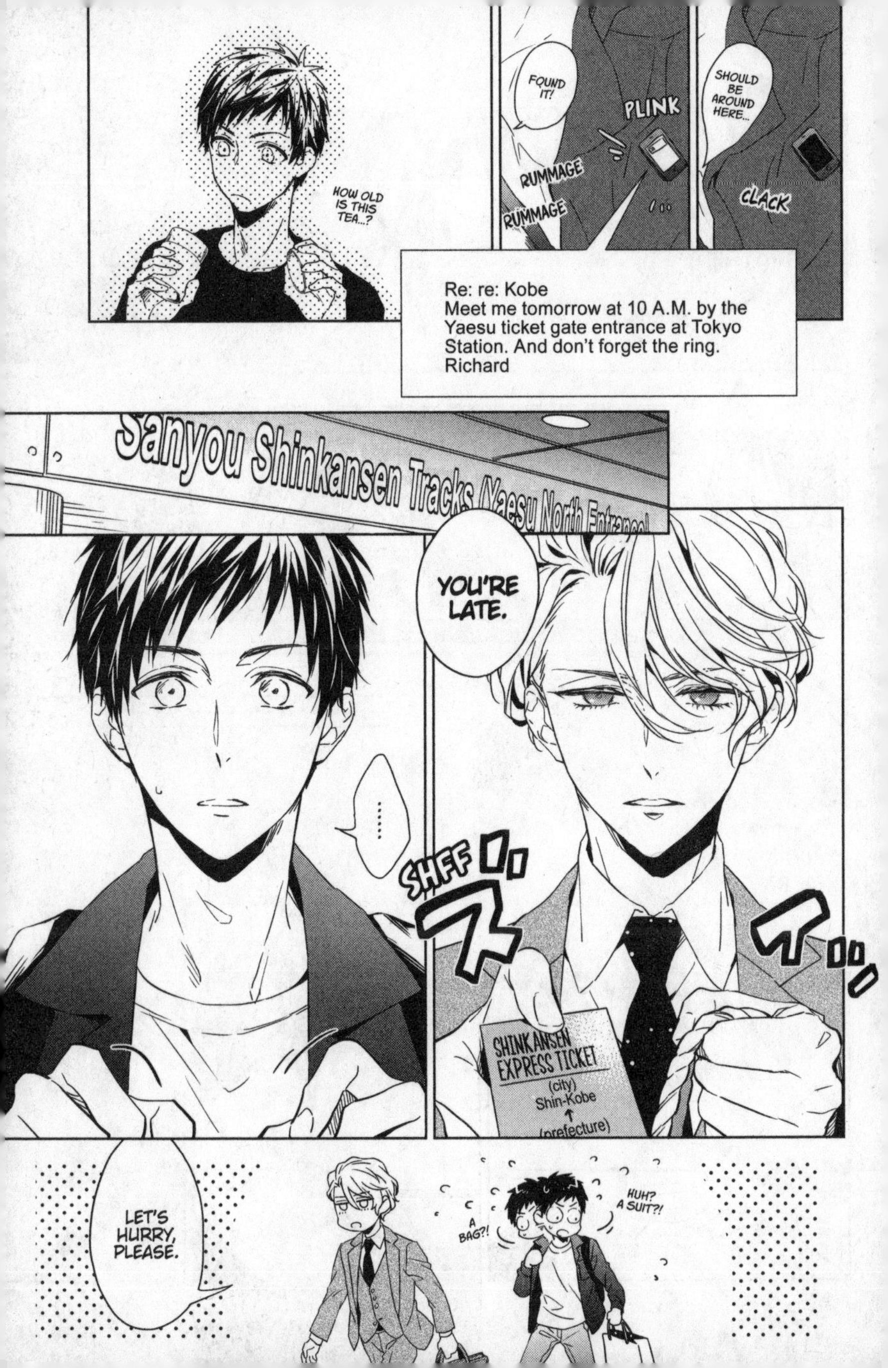

SHOULD BE AROUND HERE...
CLACK
FOUND IT!
PLINK
RUMMAGE
RUMMAGE
Re: re: Kobe
Meet me tomorrow at 10 A.M. by the Yaesu ticket gate entrance at Tokyo Station. And don't forget the ring.
Richard
HOW OLD IS THIS TEA...?
Sanyou Shinkansen Tracks (Yaesu North Entrance
YOU'RE LATE.
SHFF
SHINKANSEN EXPRESS TICKET
(city)
Shin-Kobe
↑
(prefecture)
......
HUH? A SUIT?!
A BAG?!
LET'S HURRY, PLEASE.

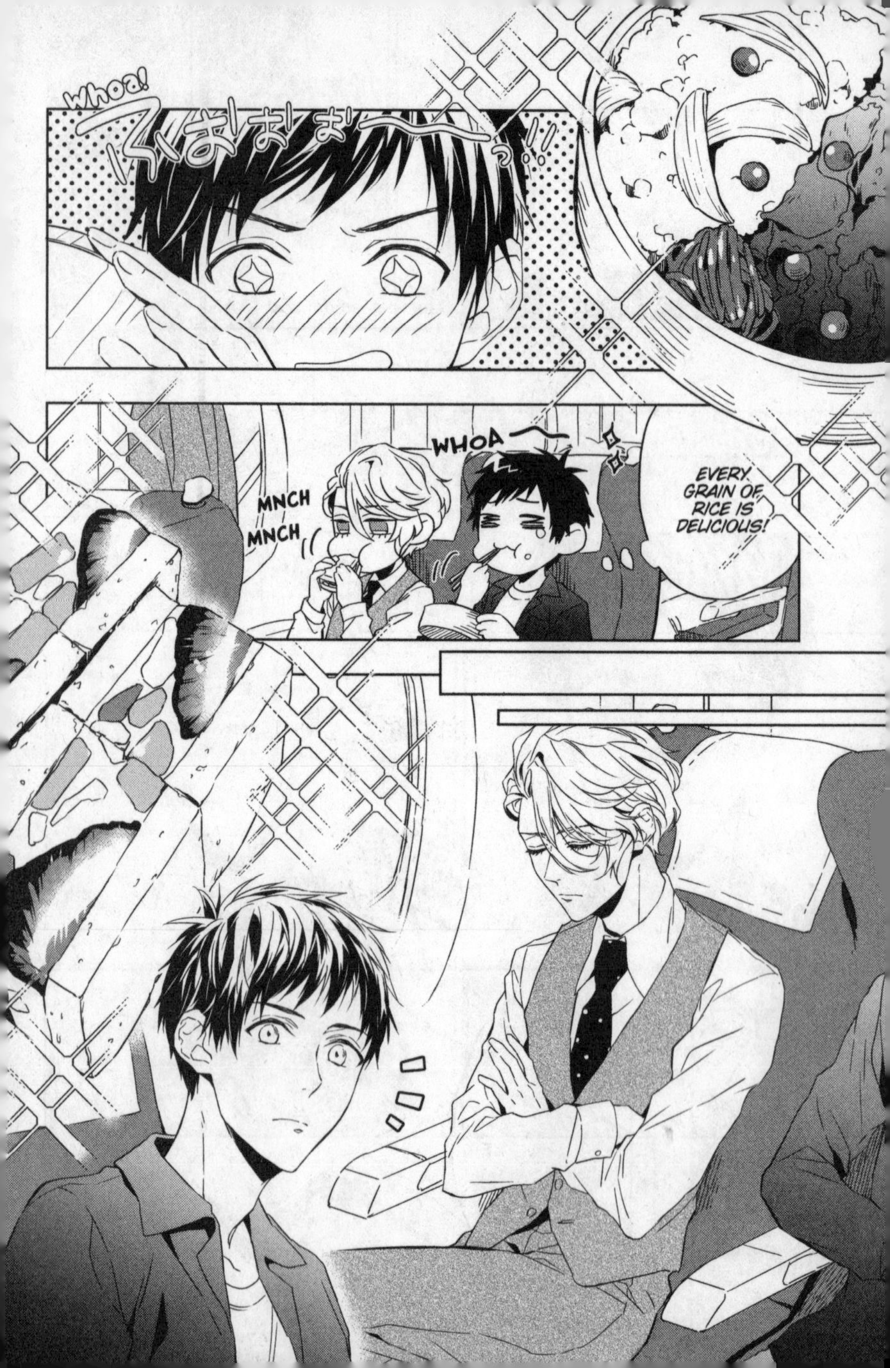
Whoa!
EVERY GRAIN OF RICE IS DELICIOUS!
WHOA
MNCH MNCH

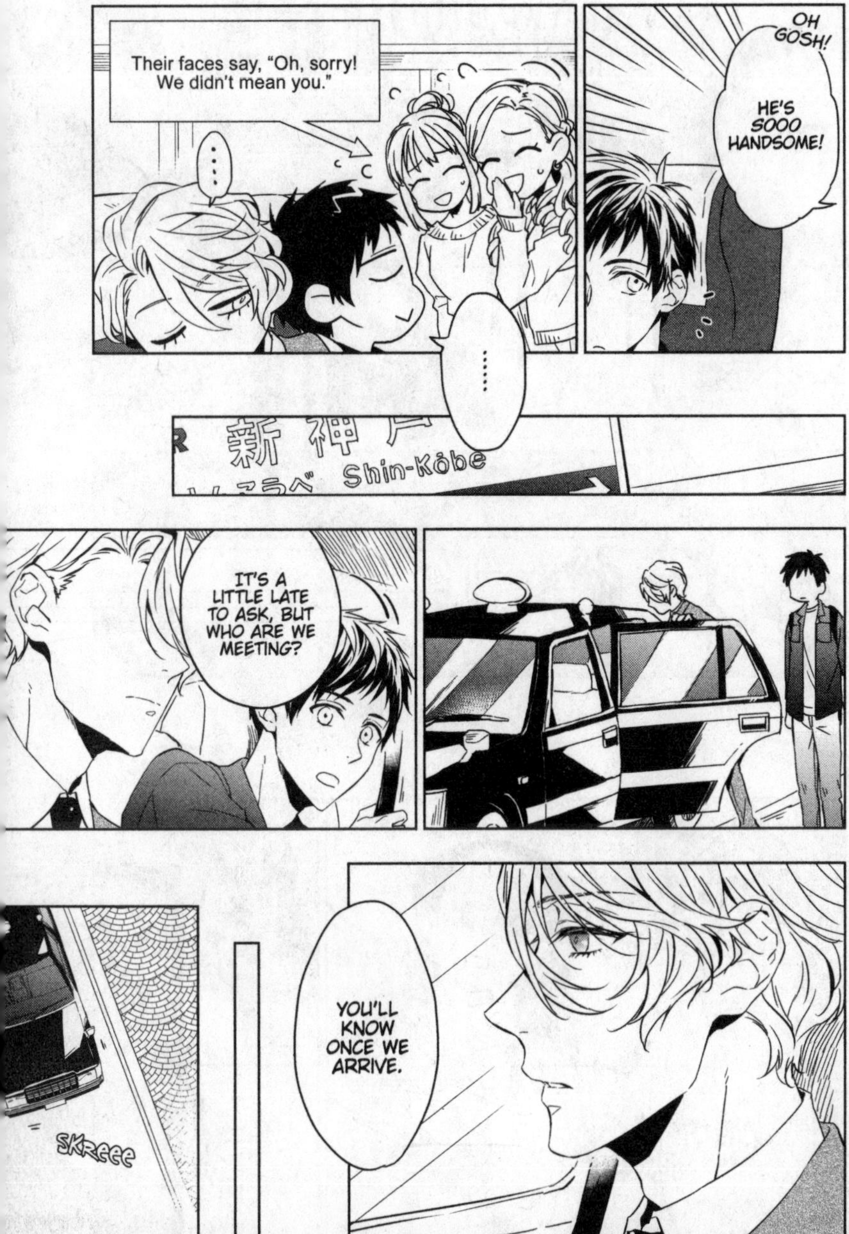
OH GOSH!
HE'S SOOO HANDSOME!
Their faces say, "Oh, sorry! We didn't mean you."
.....
......
新神戸
Shin-Kôbe
IT'S A LITTLE LATE TO ASK, BUT WHO ARE WE MEETING?
YOU'LL KNOW ONCE WE ARRIVE.
SKreee

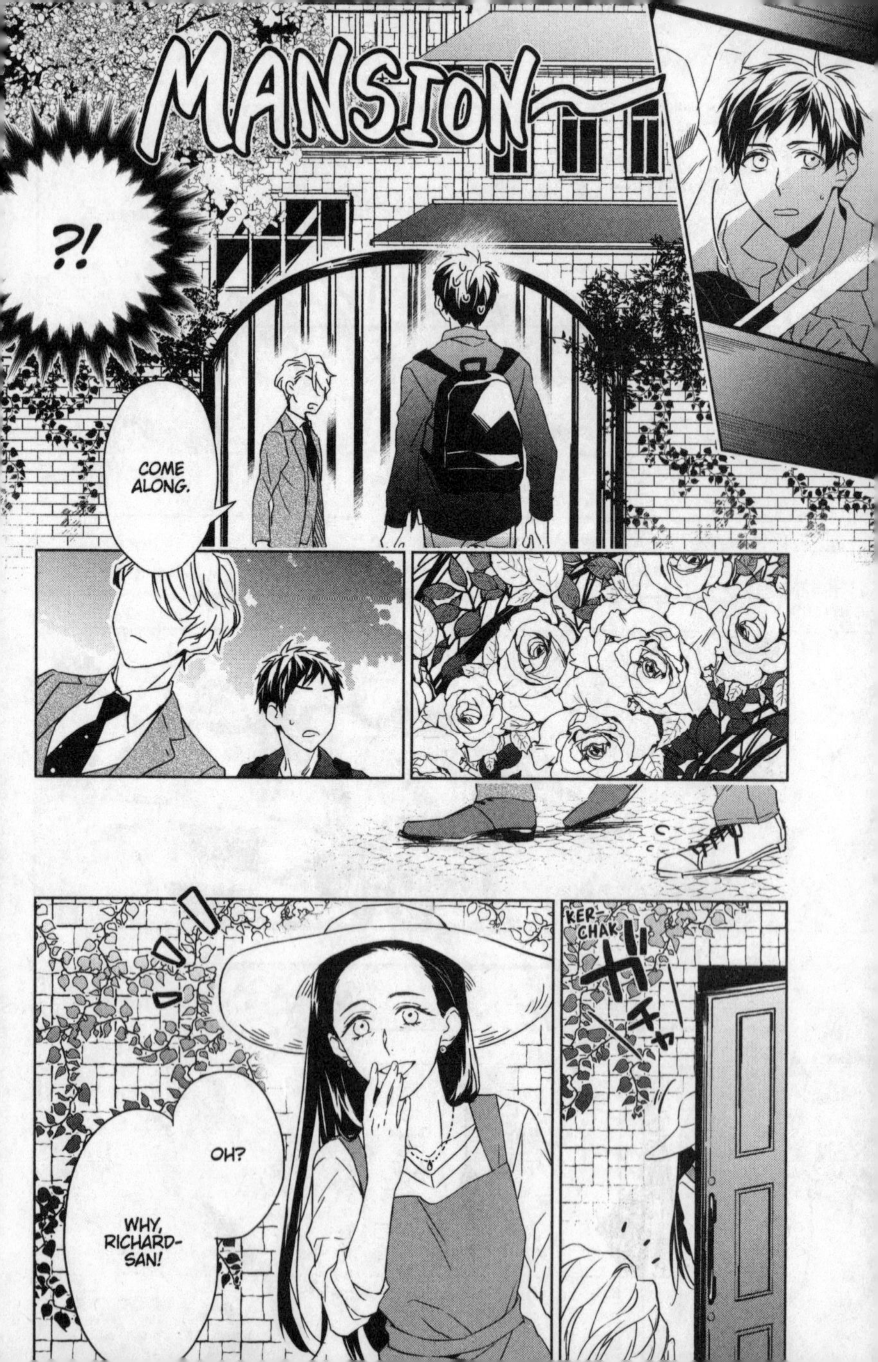
MANSION~
?!
COME ALONG.
KER-CHAK
ガチャ
OH?
WHY, RICHARD-SAN!

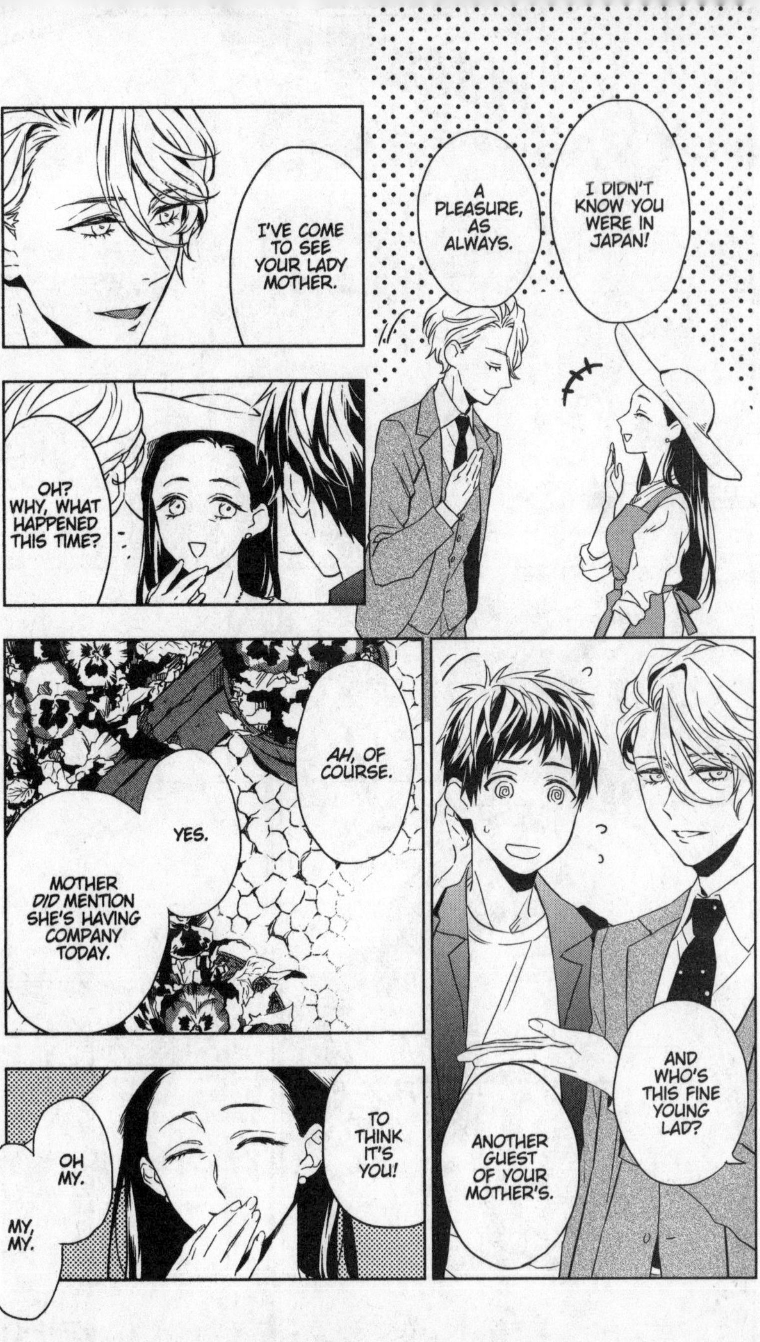
I DIDN'T KNOW YOU WERE IN JAPAN!
A PLEASURE, AS ALWAYS.
I'VE COME TO SEE YOUR LADY MOTHER.
OH? WHY, WHAT HAPPENED THIS TIME?
AND WHO'S THIS FINE YOUNG LAD?
ANOTHER GUEST OF YOUR MOTHER'S.
AH, OF COURSE.
YES.
MOTHER *DID* MENTION SHE'S HAVING COMPANY TODAY.
TO THINK IT'S YOU!
OH MY.
MY, MY.

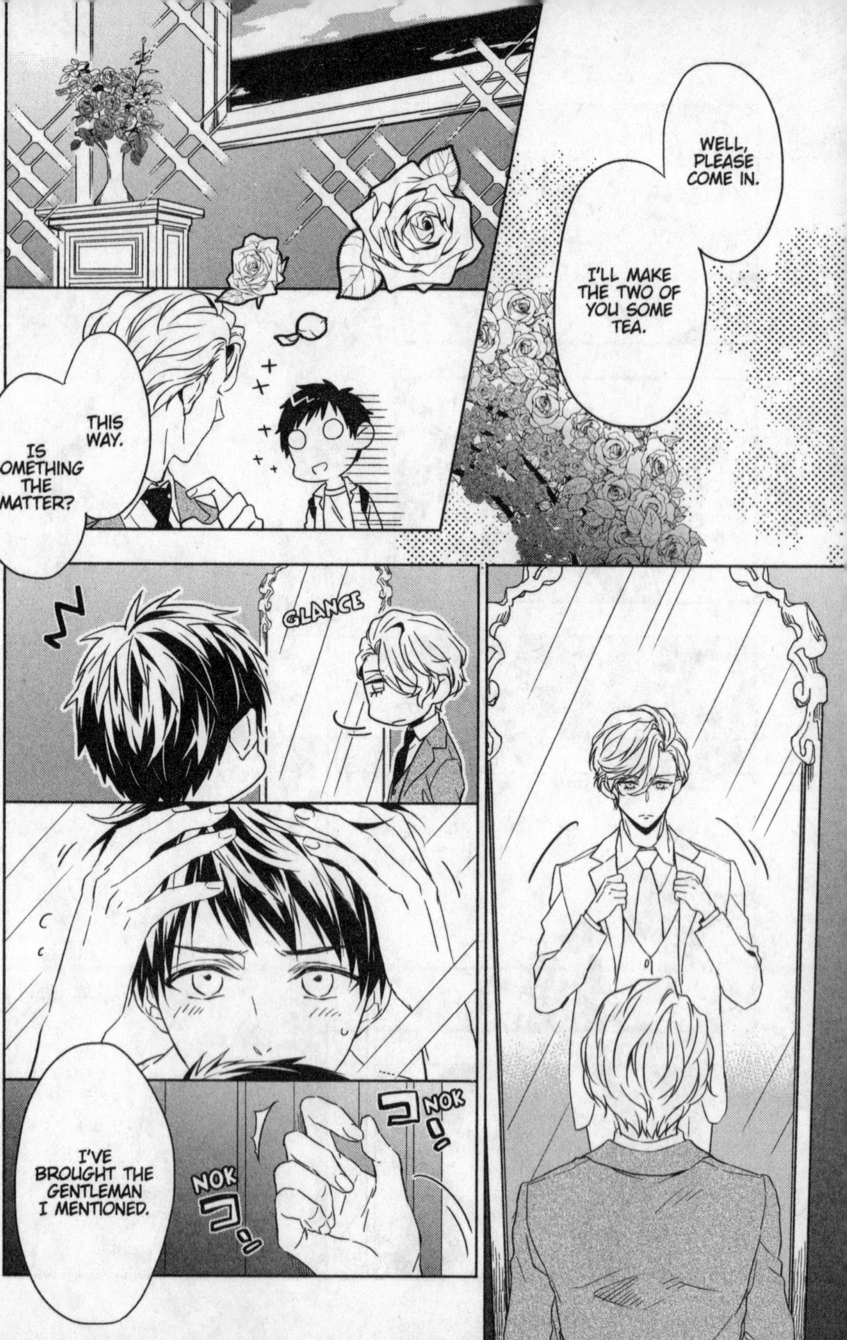
WELL, PLEASE COME IN.
I'LL MAKE THE TWO OF YOU SOME TEA.
THIS WAY.
IS SOMETHING THE MATTER?
GLANCE
NOK
I'VE BROUGHT THE GENTLEMAN I MENTIONED.
NOK

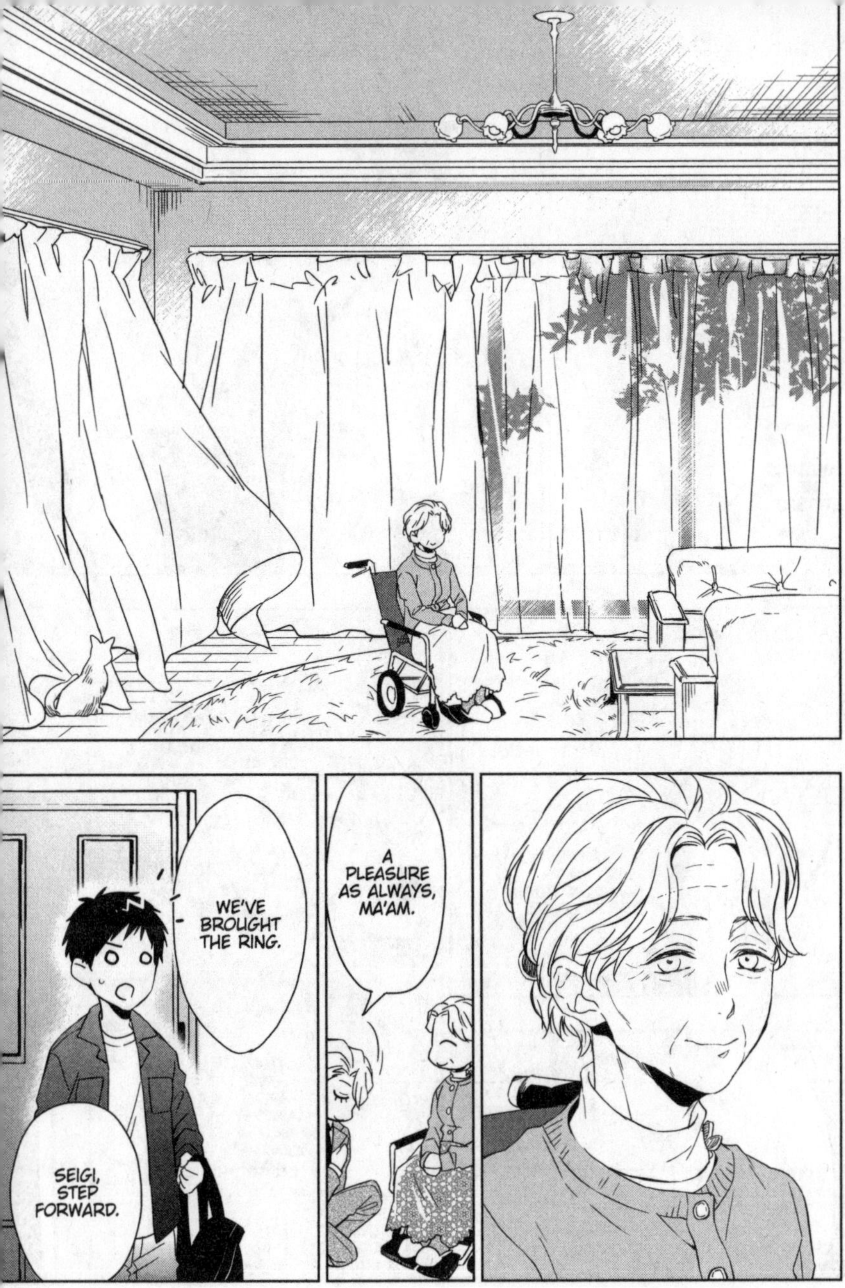
A PLEASURE AS ALWAYS, MA'AM.
WE'VE BROUGHT THE RING.
SEIGI, STEP FORWARD.

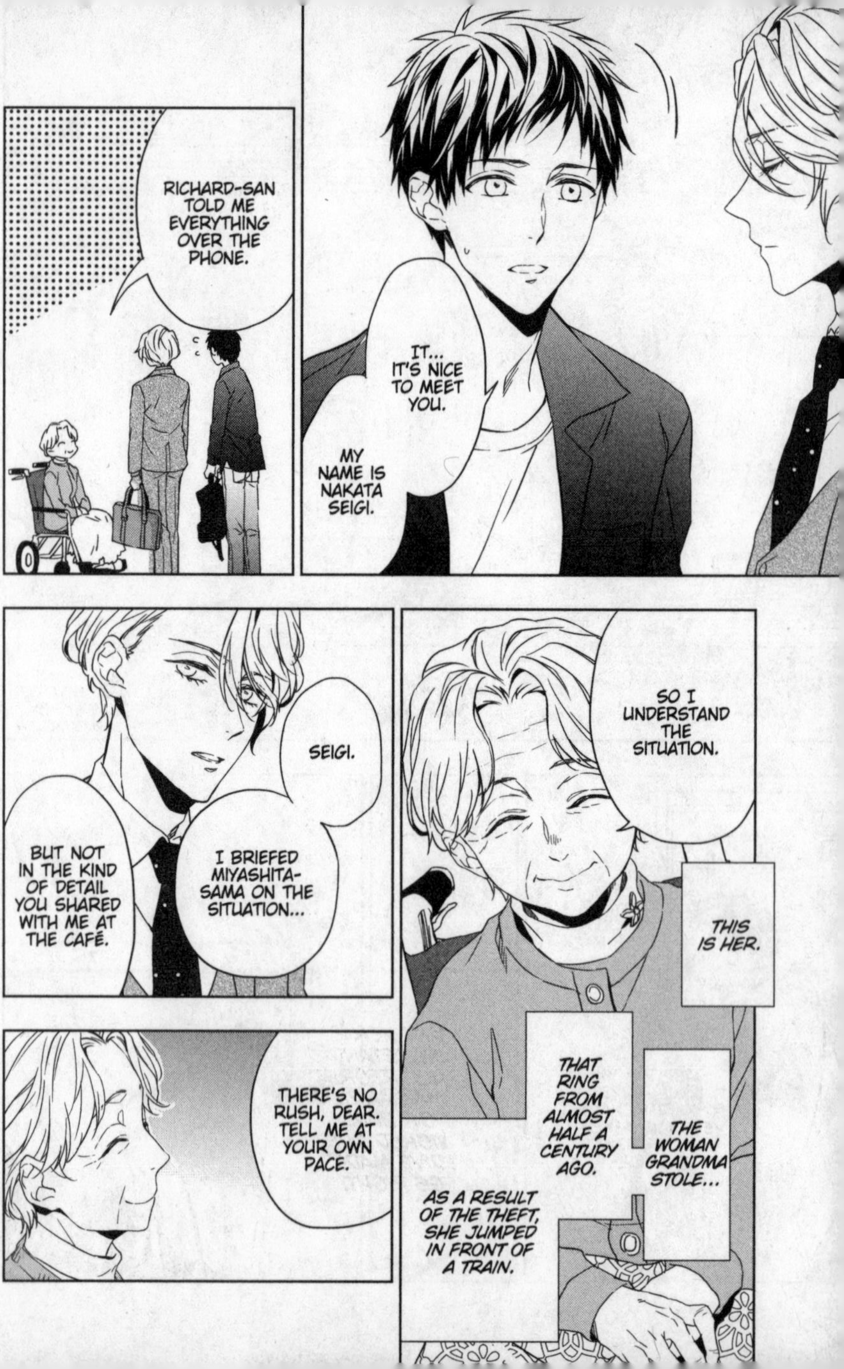
IT... IT'S NICE TO MEET YOU.
MY NAME IS NAKATA SEIGI.
RICHARD-SAN TOLD ME EVERYTHING OVER THE PHONE.
SO I UNDERSTAND THE SITUATION.
THIS IS HER.
THE WOMAN GRANDMA STOLE...
THAT RING FROM ALMOST HALF A CENTURY AGO.
AS A RESULT OF THE THEFT, SHE JUMPED IN FRONT OF A TRAIN.
SEIGI.
I BRIEFED MIYASHITA-SAMA ON THE SITUATION...
BUT NOT IN THE KIND OF DETAIL YOU SHARED WITH ME AT THE CAFÉ.
THERE'S NO RUSH, DEAR. TELL ME AT YOUR OWN PACE.

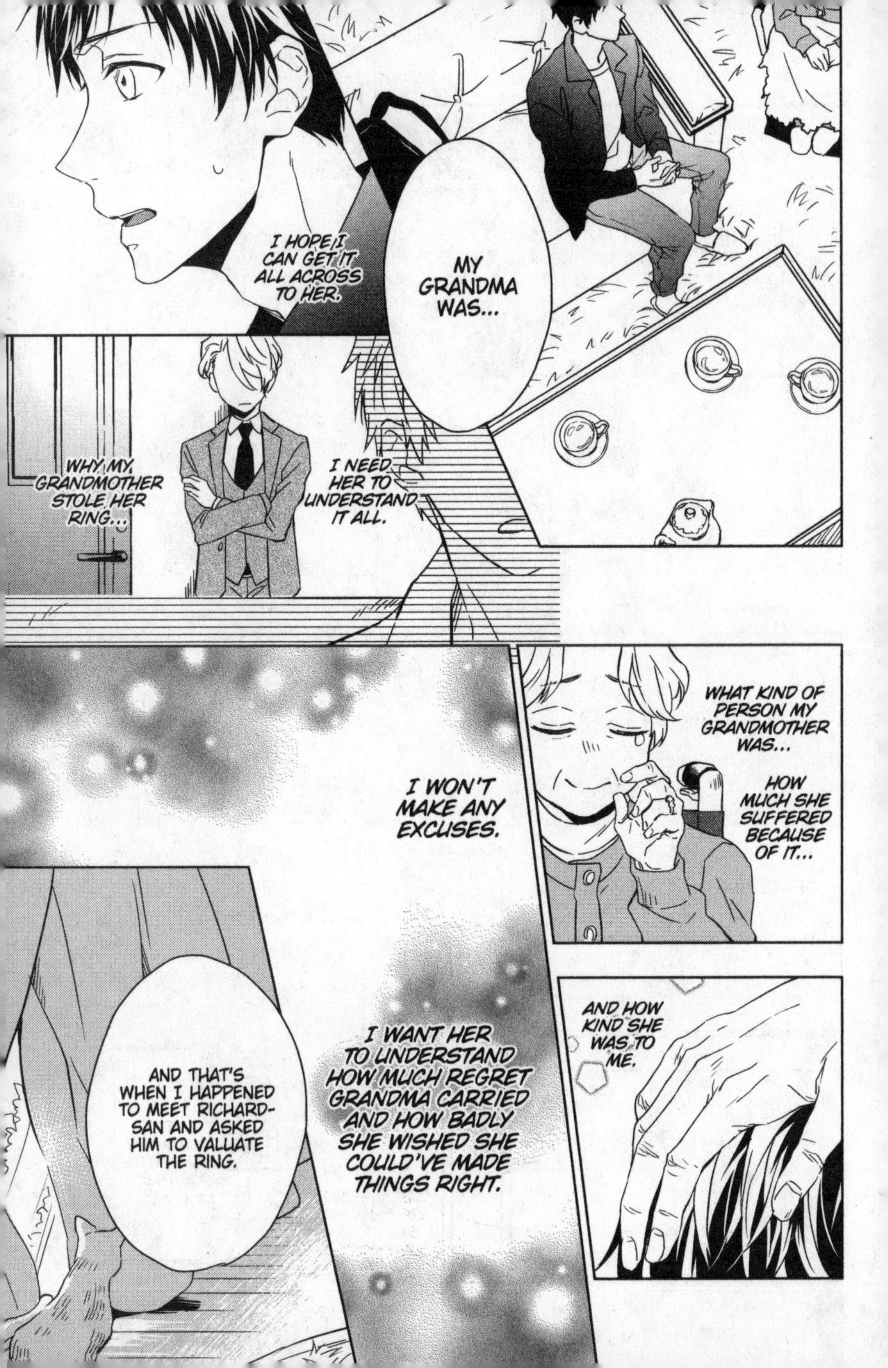
MY GRANDMA WAS...
I HOPE I CAN GET IT ALL ACROSS TO HER.
I NEED HER TO UNDERSTAND IT ALL.
WHY MY GRANDMOTHER STOLE HER RING...
WHAT KIND OF PERSON MY GRANDMOTHER WAS...
HOW MUCH SHE SUFFERED BECAUSE OF IT...
I WON'T MAKE ANY EXCUSES.
AND HOW KIND SHE WAS TO ME.
I WANT HER TO UNDERSTAND HOW MUCH REGRET GRANDMA CARRIED AND HOW BADLY SHE WISHED SHE COULD'VE MADE THINGS RIGHT.
AND THAT'S WHEN I HAPPENED TO MEET RICHARD-SAN AND ASKED HIM TO VALUATE THE RING.

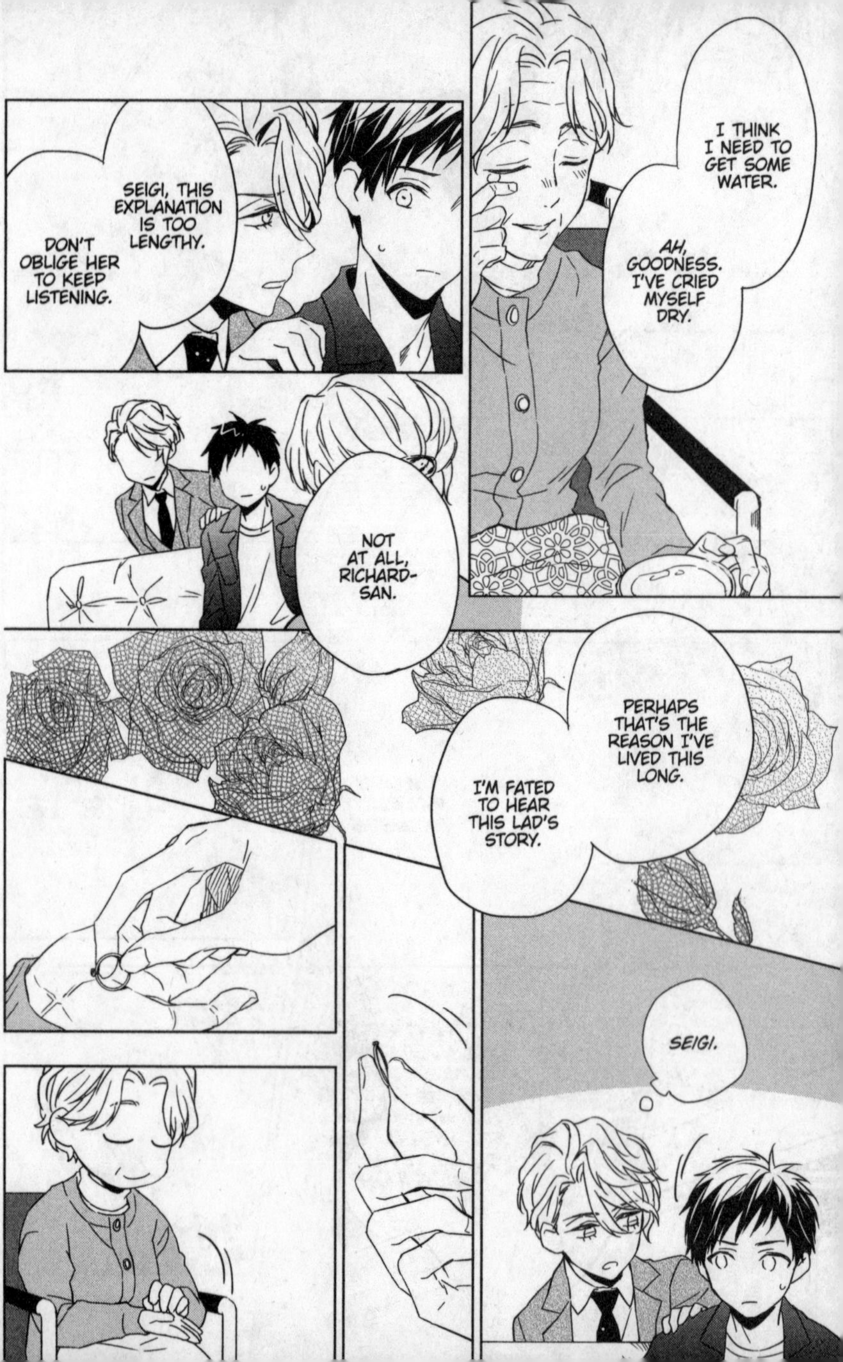
I THINK I NEED TO GET SOME WATER.
AH, GOODNESS. I'VE CRIED MYSELF DRY.
SEIGI, THIS EXPLANATION IS TOO LENGTHY.
DON'T OBLIGE HER TO KEEP LISTENING.
NOT AT ALL, RICHARD-SAN.
PERHAPS THAT'S THE REASON I'VE LIVED THIS LONG.
I'M FATED TO HEAR THIS LAD'S STORY.
SEIGI.

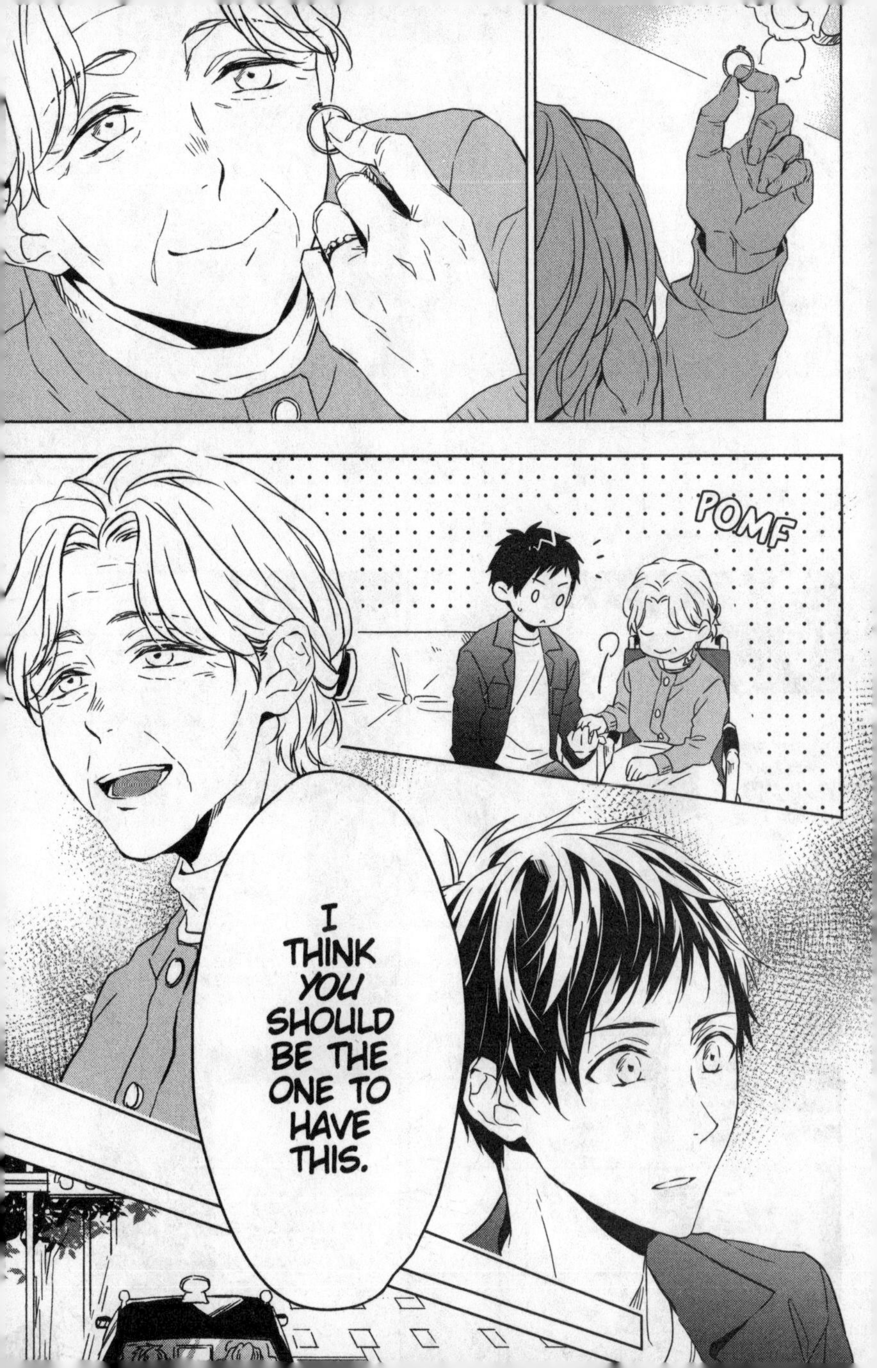
POMF
I THINK YOU SHOULD BE THE ONE TO HAVE THIS.

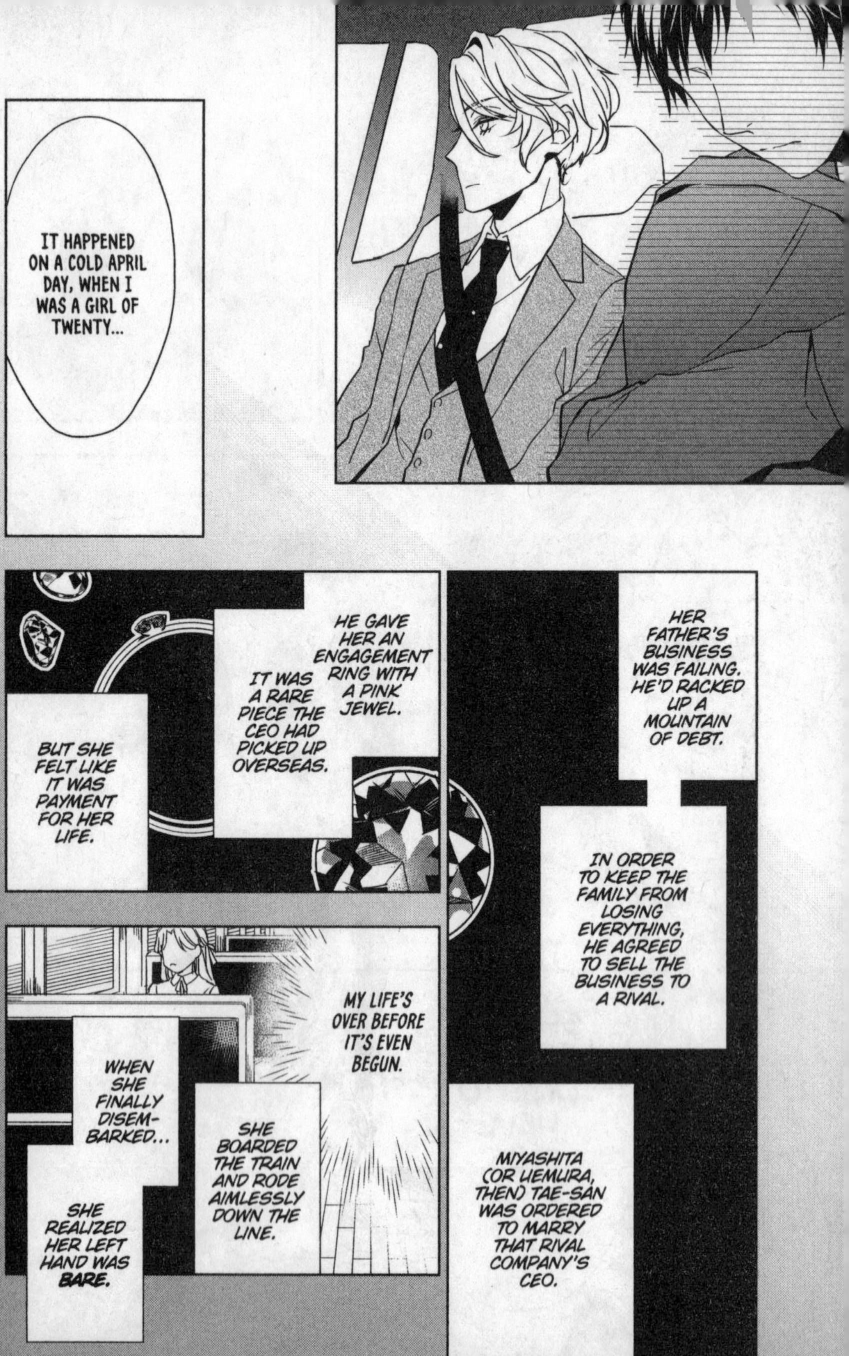
IT HAPPENED ON A COLD APRIL DAY, WHEN I WAS A GIRL OF TWENTY...
HER FATHER'S BUSINESS WAS FAILING. HE'D RACKED UP A MOUNTAIN OF DEBT.
IN ORDER TO KEEP THE FAMILY FROM LOSING EVERYTHING, HE AGREED TO SELL THE BUSINESS TO A RIVAL.
MIYASHITA (OR UEMURA, THEN) TAE-SAN WAS ORDERED TO MARRY THAT RIVAL COMPANY'S CEO.
HE GAVE HER AN ENGAGEMENT RING WITH A PINK JEWEL.
IT WAS A RARE PIECE THE CEO HAD PICKED UP OVERSEAS.
BUT SHE FELT LIKE IT WAS PAYMENT FOR HER LIFE.
MY LIFE'S OVER BEFORE IT'S EVEN BEGUN.
SHE BOARDED THE TRAIN AND RODE AIMLESSLY DOWN THE LINE.
WHEN SHE FINALLY DISEMBARKED...
SHE REALIZED HER LEFT HAND WAS BARE.

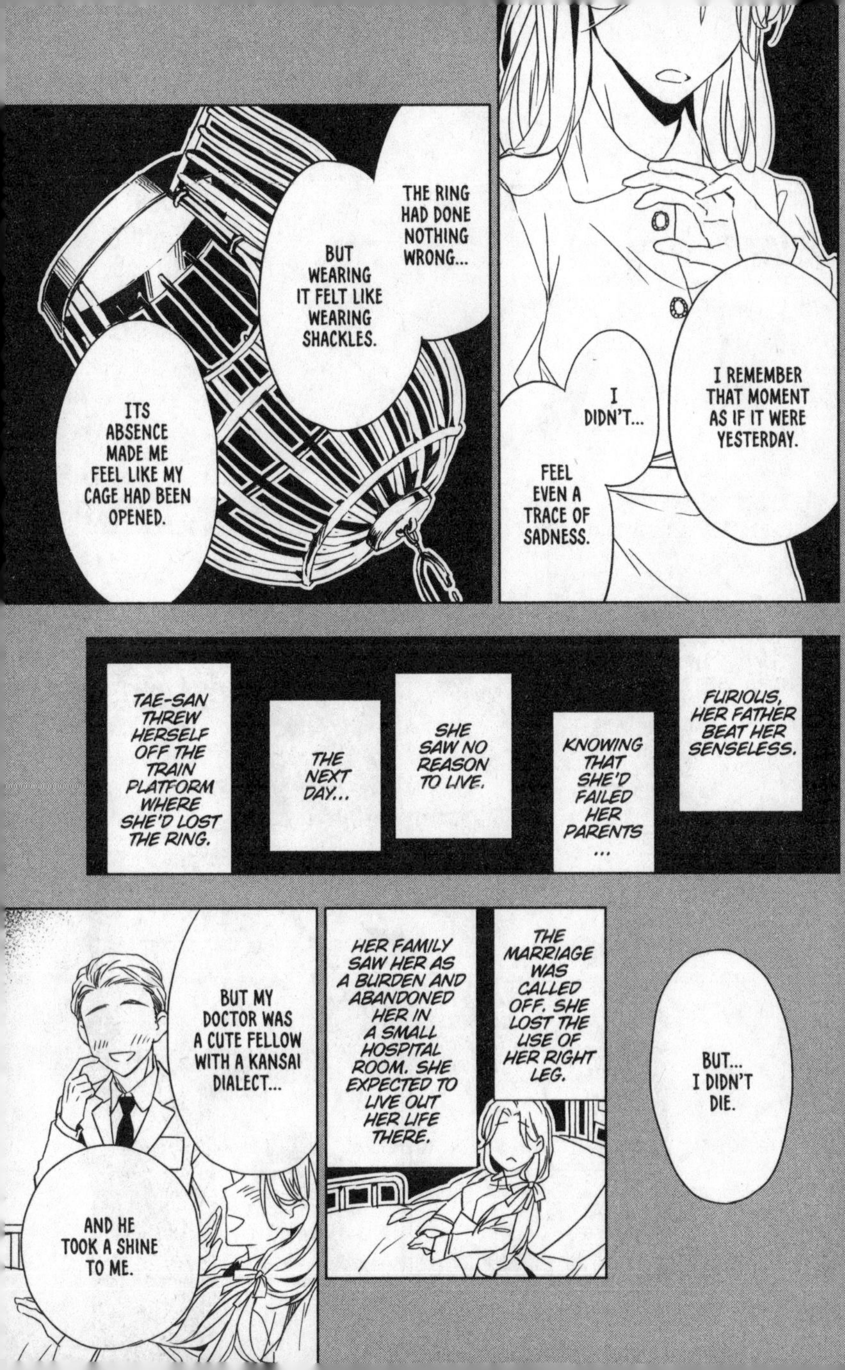
I REMEMBER THAT MOMENT AS IF IT WERE YESTERDAY.
I DIDN'T...
FEEL EVEN A TRACE OF SADNESS.
THE RING HAD DONE NOTHING WRONG...
BUT WEARING IT FELT LIKE WEARING SHACKLES.
ITS ABSENCE MADE ME FEEL LIKE MY CAGE HAD BEEN OPENED.
FURIOUS, HER FATHER BEAT HER SENSELESS.
KNOWING THAT SHE'D FAILED HER PARENTS...
SHE SAW NO REASON TO LIVE.
THE NEXT DAY...
TAE-SAN THREW HERSELF OFF THE TRAIN PLATFORM WHERE SHE'D LOST THE RING.
BUT... I DIDN'T DIE.
THE MARRIAGE WAS CALLED OFF. SHE LOST THE USE OF HER RIGHT LEG.
HER FAMILY SAW HER AS A BURDEN AND ABANDONED HER IN A SMALL HOSPITAL ROOM. SHE EXPECTED TO LIVE OUT HER LIFE THERE.
BUT MY DOCTOR WAS A CUTE FELLOW WITH A KANSAI DIALECT...
AND HE TOOK A SHINE TO ME.

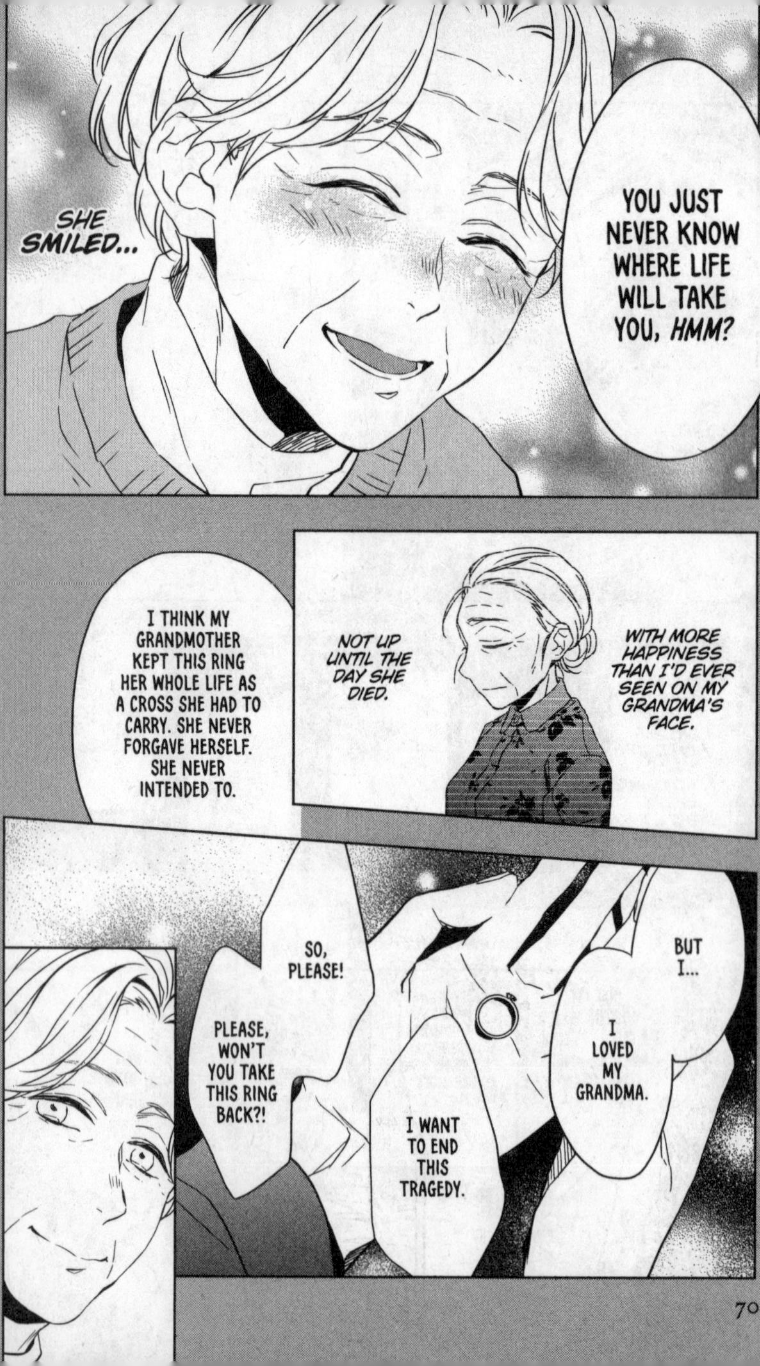
YOU JUST NEVER KNOW WHERE LIFE WILL TAKE YOU, *HMM?*
SHE SMILED...
WITH MORE HAPPINESS THAN I'D EVER SEEN ON MY GRANDMA'S FACE.
NOT UP UNTIL THE DAY SHE DIED.
I THINK MY GRANDMOTHER KEPT THIS RING HER WHOLE LIFE AS A CROSS SHE HAD TO CARRY. SHE NEVER FORGAVE HERSELF. SHE NEVER INTENDED TO.
BUT I...
I LOVED MY GRANDMA.
I WANT TO END THIS TRAGEDY.
SO, PLEASE!
PLEASE, WON'T YOU TAKE THIS RING BACK?!

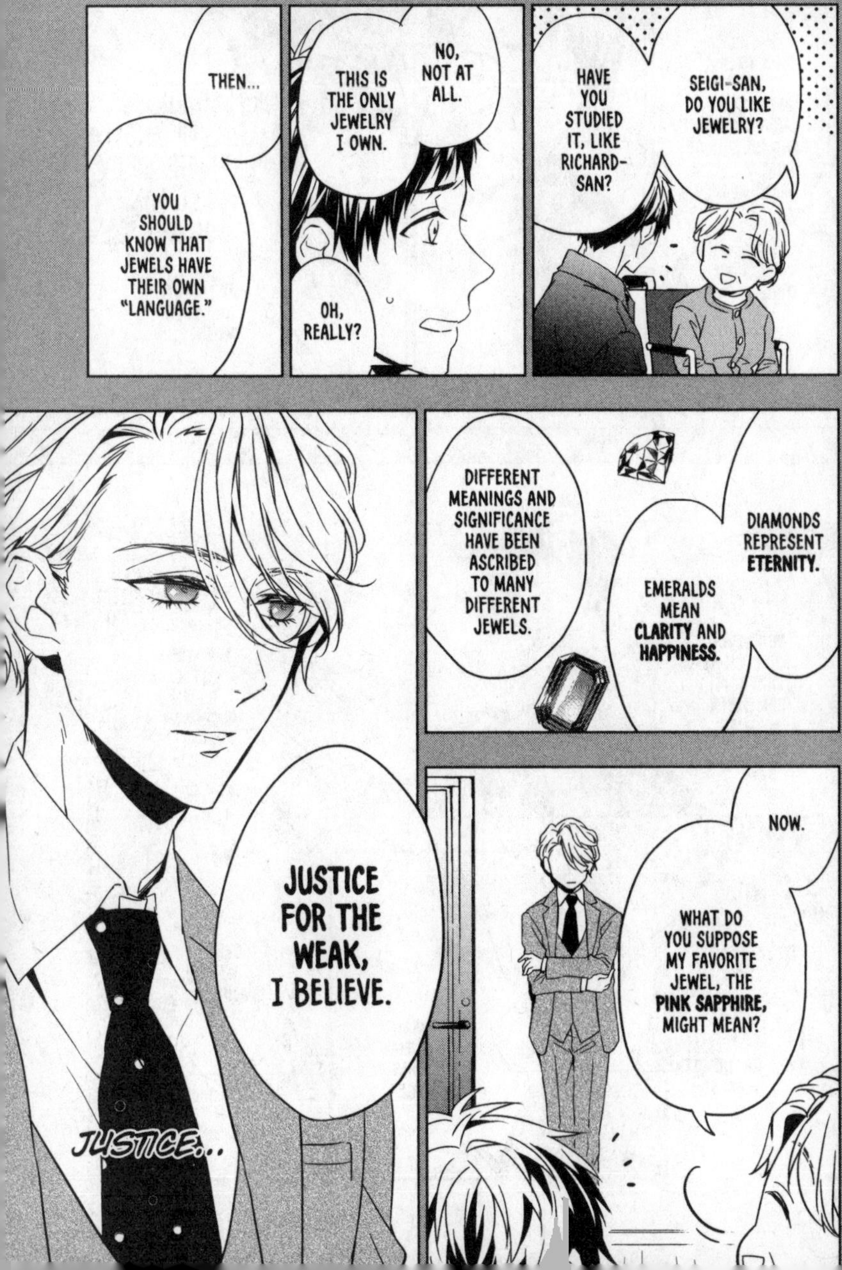
SEIGI-SAN, DO YOU LIKE JEWELRY?
HAVE YOU STUDIED IT, LIKE RICHARD-SAN?
NO, NOT AT ALL.
THIS IS THE ONLY JEWELRY I OWN.
OH, REALLY?
THEN...
YOU SHOULD KNOW THAT JEWELS HAVE THEIR OWN "LANGUAGE."
DIAMONDS REPRESENT **ETERNITY.**
EMERALDS MEAN **CLARITY** AND **HAPPINESS.**
DIFFERENT MEANINGS AND SIGNIFICANCE HAVE BEEN ASCRIBED TO MANY DIFFERENT JEWELS.
NOW.
WHAT DO YOU SUPPOSE MY FAVORITE JEWEL, THE **PINK SAPPHIRE,** MIGHT MEAN?
JUSTICE FOR THE WEAK, I BELIEVE.
JUSTICE...

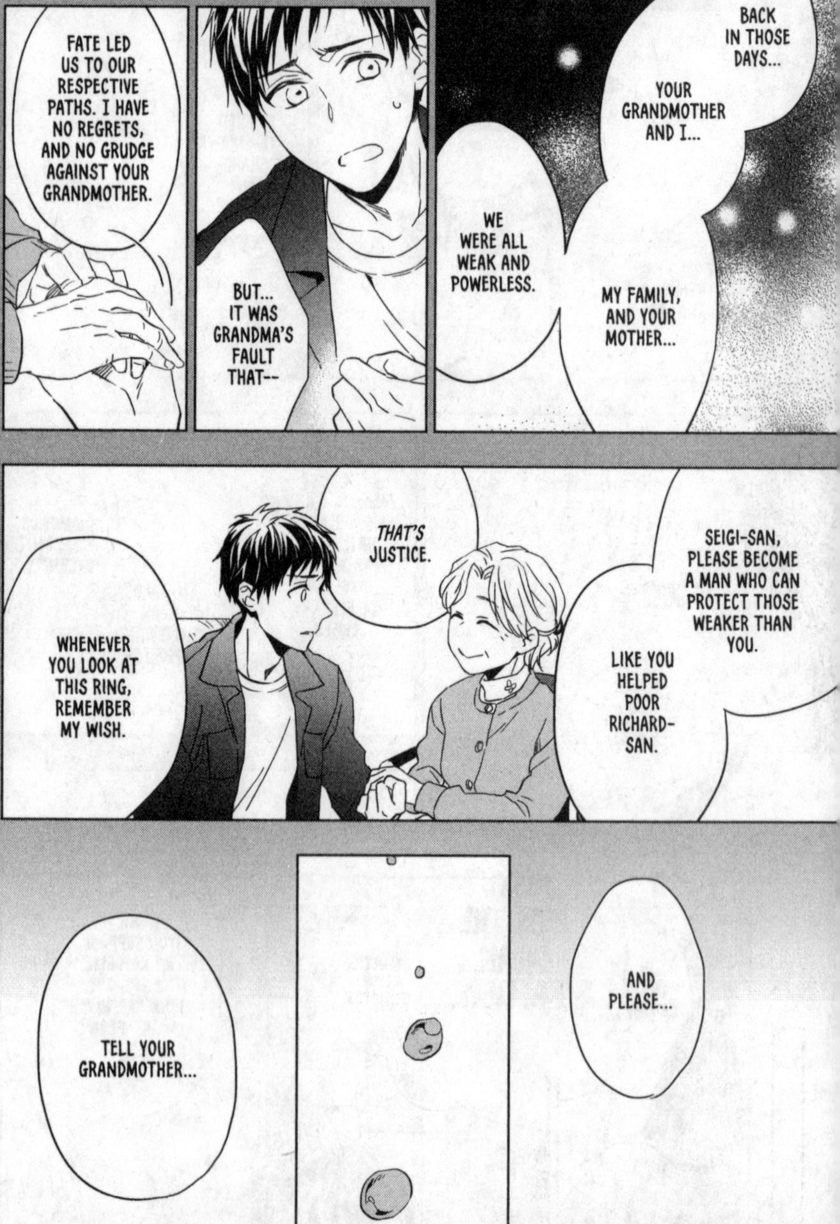
BACK IN THOSE DAYS...
YOUR GRANDMOTHER AND I...
MY FAMILY, AND YOUR MOTHER...
WE WERE ALL WEAK AND POWERLESS.
BUT... IT WAS GRANDMA'S FAULT THAT--
FATE LED US TO OUR RESPECTIVE PATHS. I HAVE NO REGRETS, AND NO GRUDGE AGAINST YOUR GRANDMOTHER.
SEIGI-SAN, PLEASE BECOME A MAN WHO CAN PROTECT THOSE WEAKER THAN YOU.
LIKE YOU HELPED POOR RICHARD-SAN.
THAT'S JUSTICE.
WHENEVER YOU LOOK AT THIS RING, REMEMBER MY WISH.
AND PLEASE...
TELL YOUR GRANDMOTHER...

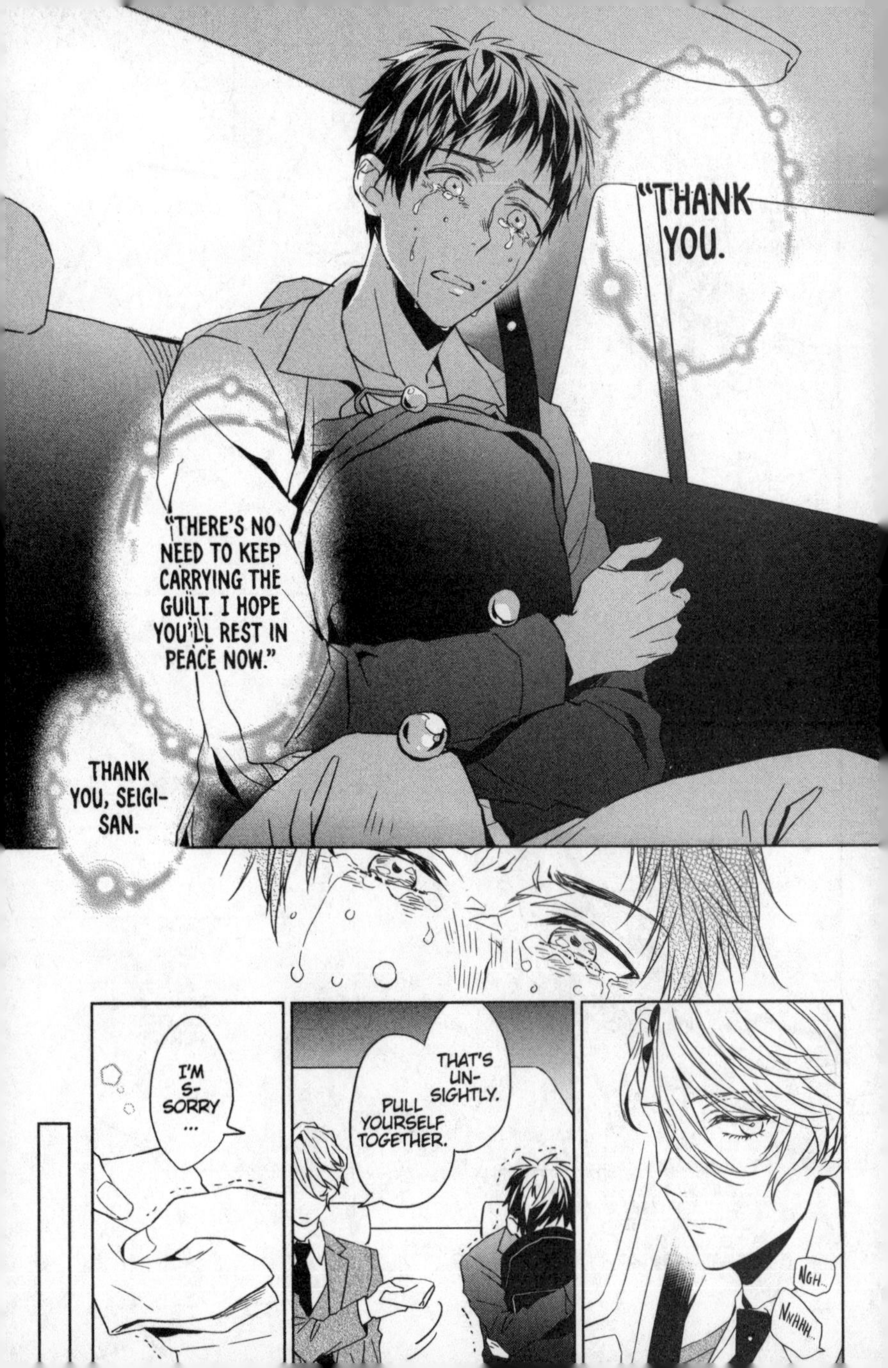
"THANK YOU.
"THERE'S NO NEED TO KEEP CARRYING THE GUILT. I HOPE YOU'LL REST IN PEACE NOW."
THANK YOU, SEIGI-SAN.
NGH...
NNHHH...
THAT'S UN-SIGHTLY.
PULL YOURSELF TOGETHER.
I'M S-SORRY ...

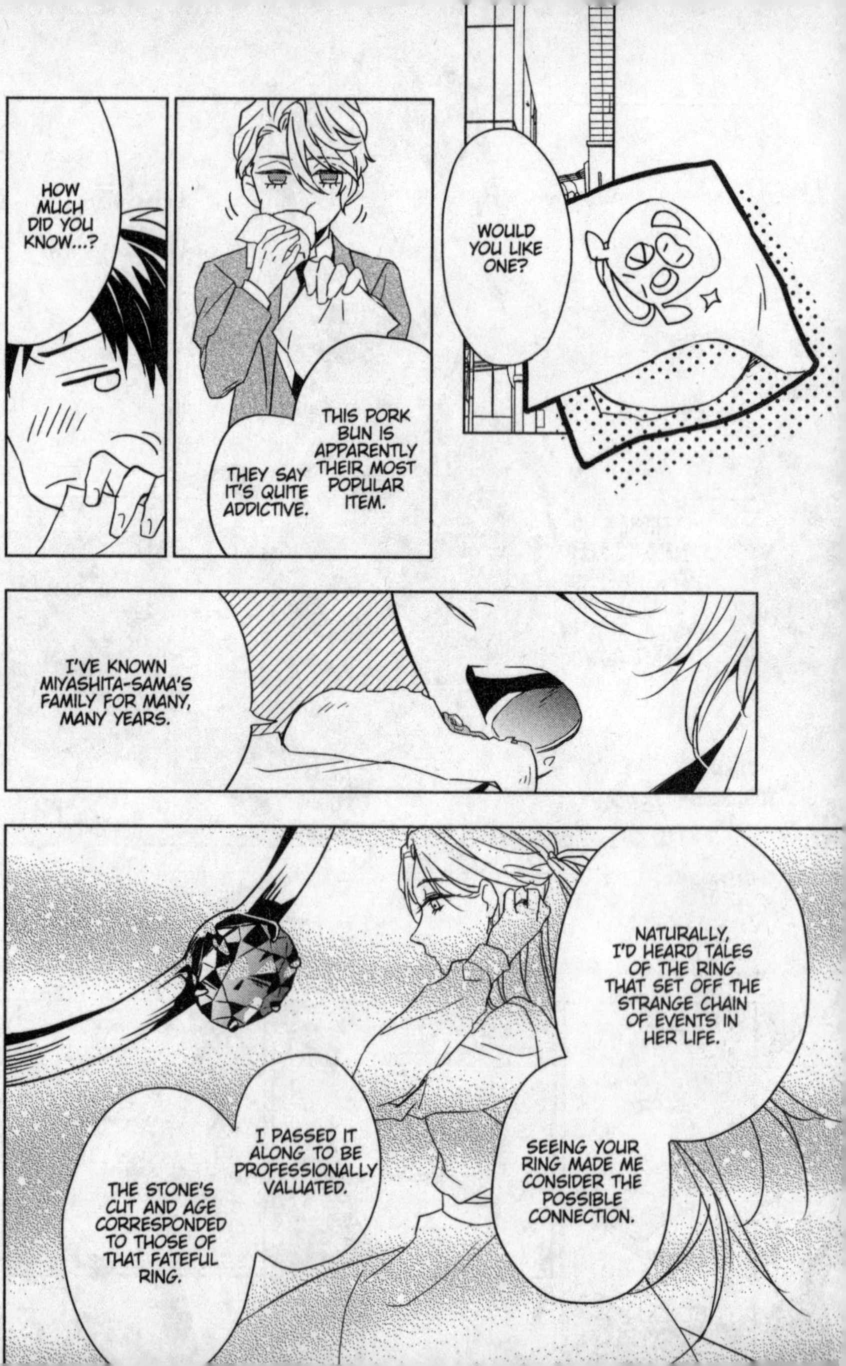
WOULD YOU LIKE ONE?
THIS PORK BUN IS APPARENTLY THEIR MOST POPULAR ITEM.
THEY SAY IT'S QUITE ADDICTIVE.
HOW MUCH DID YOU KNOW...?
I'VE KNOWN MIYASHITA-SAMA'S FAMILY FOR MANY, MANY YEARS.
NATURALLY, I'D HEARD TALES OF THE RING THAT SET OFF THE STRANGE CHAIN OF EVENTS IN HER LIFE.
SEEING YOUR RING MADE ME CONSIDER THE POSSIBLE CONNECTION.
I PASSED IT ALONG TO BE PROFESSIONALLY VALUATED.
THE STONE'S CUT AND AGE CORRESPONDED TO THOSE OF THAT FATEFUL RING.

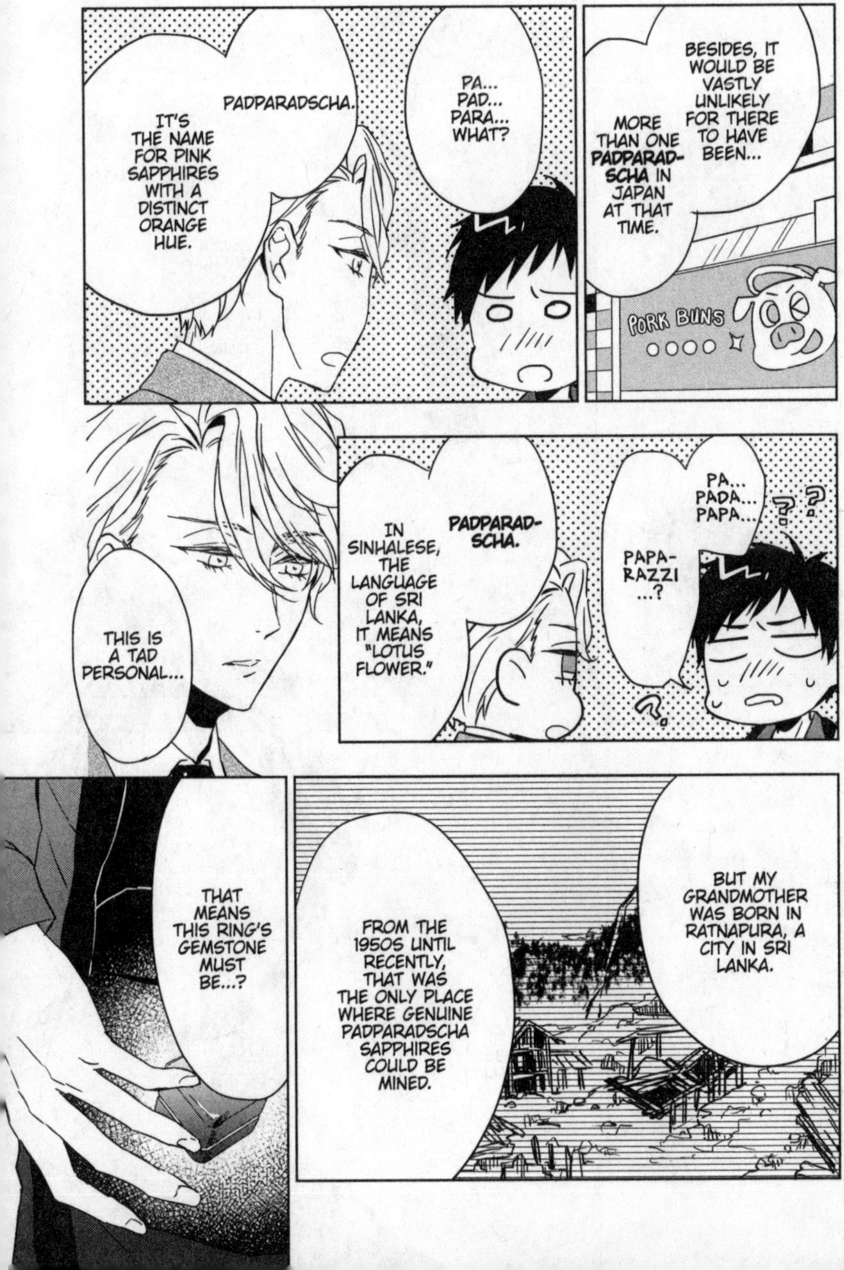
BESIDES, IT WOULD BE VASTLY UNLIKELY FOR THERE TO HAVE BEEN...
MORE THAN ONE PADPARADSCHA IN JAPAN AT THAT TIME.
PORK BUNS
PA... PAD... PARA... WHAT?
PADPARADSCHA.
IT'S THE NAME FOR PINK SAPPHIRES WITH A DISTINCT ORANGE HUE.
PA... PADA... PAPA...
PAPARAZZI ...?
PADPARADSCHA.
IN SINHALESE, THE LANGUAGE OF SRI LANKA, IT MEANS "LOTUS FLOWER."
THIS IS A TAD PERSONAL...
BUT MY GRANDMOTHER WAS BORN IN RATNAPURA, A CITY IN SRI LANKA.
FROM THE 1950S UNTIL RECENTLY, THAT WAS THE ONLY PLACE WHERE GENUINE PADPARADSCHA SAPPHIRES COULD BE MINED.
THAT MEANS THIS RING'S GEMSTONE MUST BE...?

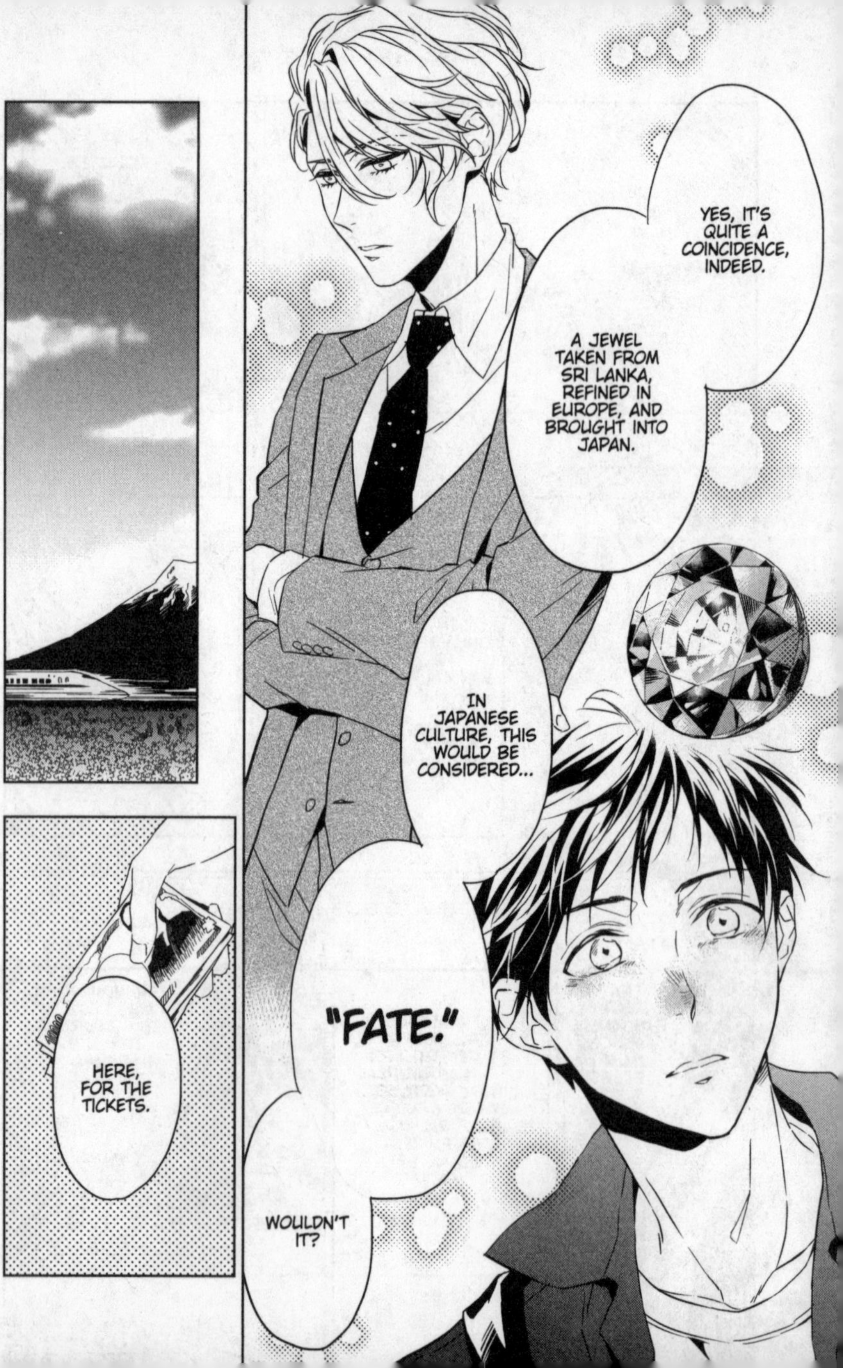
YES, IT'S QUITE A COINCIDENCE, INDEED.
A JEWEL TAKEN FROM SRI LANKA, REFINED IN EUROPE, AND BROUGHT INTO JAPAN.
IN JAPANESE CULTURE, THIS WOULD BE CONSIDERED...
"FATE."
WOULDN'T IT?
HERE, FOR THE TICKETS.

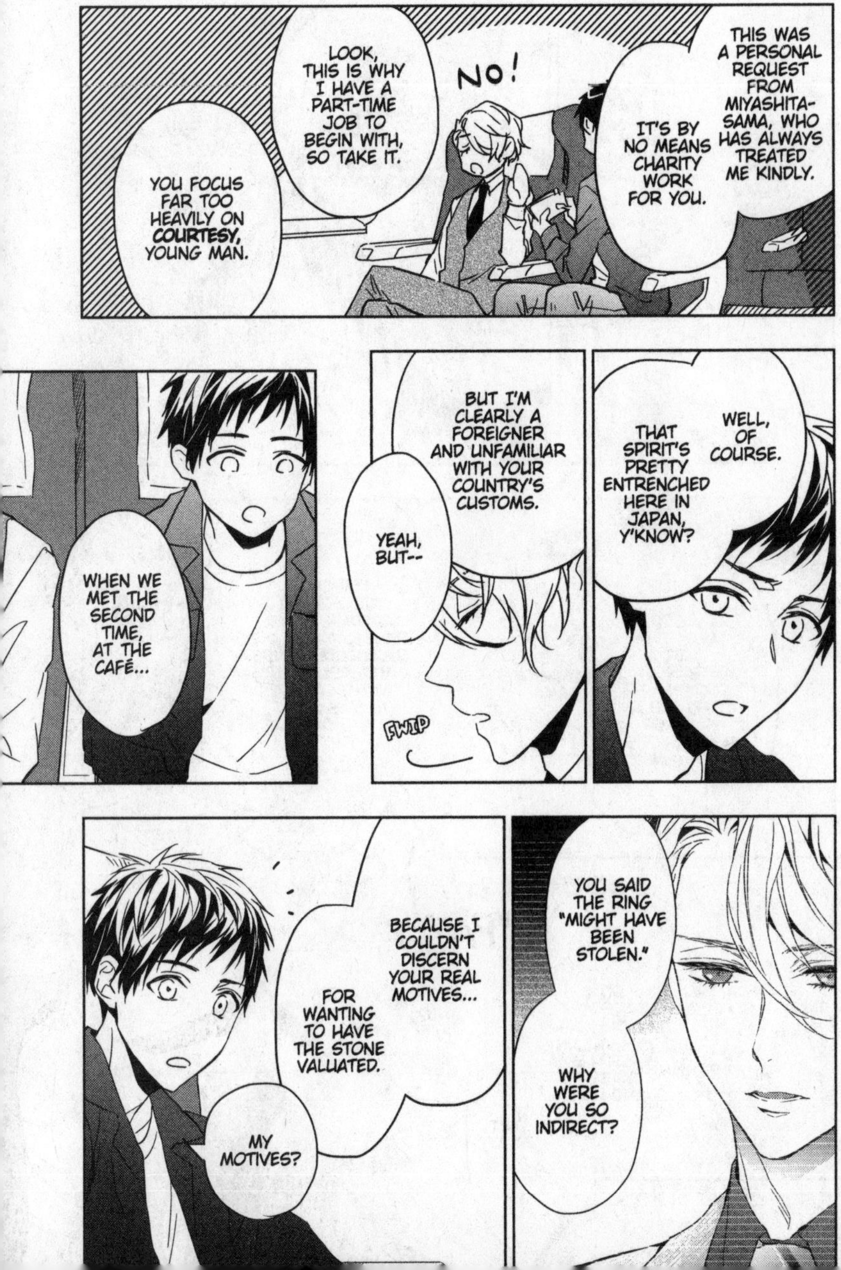
THIS WAS A PERSONAL REQUEST FROM MIYASHITA-SAMA, WHO HAS ALWAYS TREATED ME KINDLY.
IT'S BY NO MEANS CHARITY WORK FOR YOU.
NO!
LOOK, THIS IS WHY I HAVE A PART-TIME JOB TO BEGIN WITH, SO TAKE IT.
YOU FOCUS FAR TOO HEAVILY ON **COURTESY**, YOUNG MAN.
WELL, OF COURSE.
THAT SPIRIT'S PRETTY ENTRENCHED HERE IN JAPAN, Y'KNOW?
BUT I'M CLEARLY A FOREIGNER AND UNFAMILIAR WITH YOUR COUNTRY'S CUSTOMS.
YEAH, BUT--
FWIP
WHEN WE MET THE SECOND TIME, AT THE CAFÉ...
YOU SAID THE RING "MIGHT HAVE BEEN STOLEN."
WHY WERE YOU SO INDIRECT?
BECAUSE I COULDN'T DISCERN YOUR REAL MOTIVES...
FOR WANTING TO HAVE THE STONE VALUATED.
MY MOTIVES?

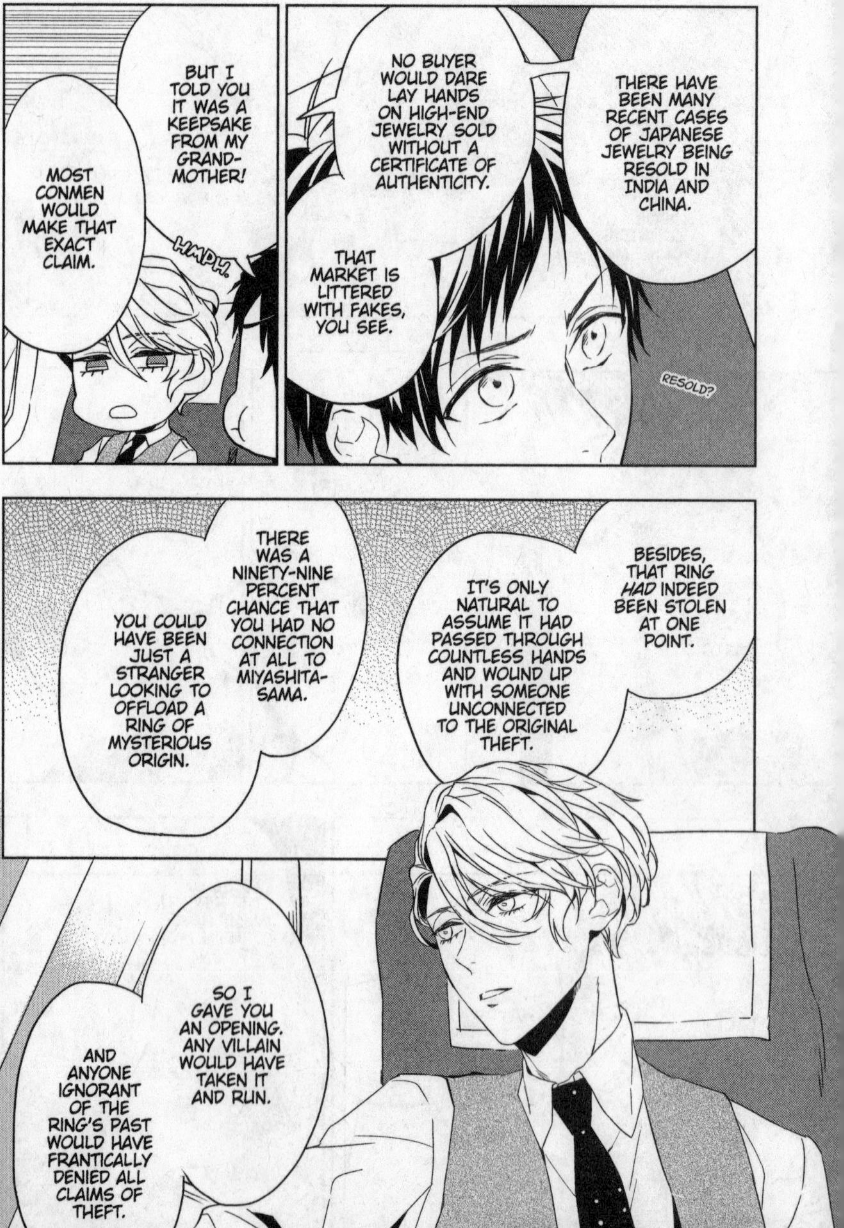
THERE HAVE BEEN MANY RECENT CASES OF JAPANESE JEWELRY BEING RESOLD IN INDIA AND CHINA.
NO BUYER WOULD DARE LAY HANDS ON HIGH-END JEWELRY SOLD WITHOUT A CERTIFICATE OF AUTHENTICITY.
THAT MARKET IS LITTERED WITH FAKES, YOU SEE.
RESOLD?
BUT I TOLD YOU IT WAS A KEEPSAKE FROM MY GRAND-MOTHER!
HMPH.
MOST CONMEN WOULD MAKE THAT EXACT CLAIM.
BESIDES, THAT RING *HAD* INDEED BEEN STOLEN AT ONE POINT.
IT'S ONLY NATURAL TO ASSUME IT HAD PASSED THROUGH COUNTLESS HANDS AND WOUND UP WITH SOMEONE UNCONNECTED TO THE ORIGINAL THEFT.
THERE WAS A NINETY-NINE PERCENT CHANCE THAT YOU HAD NO CONNECTION AT ALL TO MIYASHITA-SAMA.
YOU COULD HAVE BEEN JUST A STRANGER LOOKING TO OFFLOAD A RING OF MYSTERIOUS ORIGIN.
SO I GAVE YOU AN OPENING. ANY VILLAIN WOULD HAVE TAKEN IT AND RUN.
AND ANYONE IGNORANT OF THE RING'S PAST WOULD HAVE FRANTICALLY DENIED ALL CLAIMS OF THEFT.

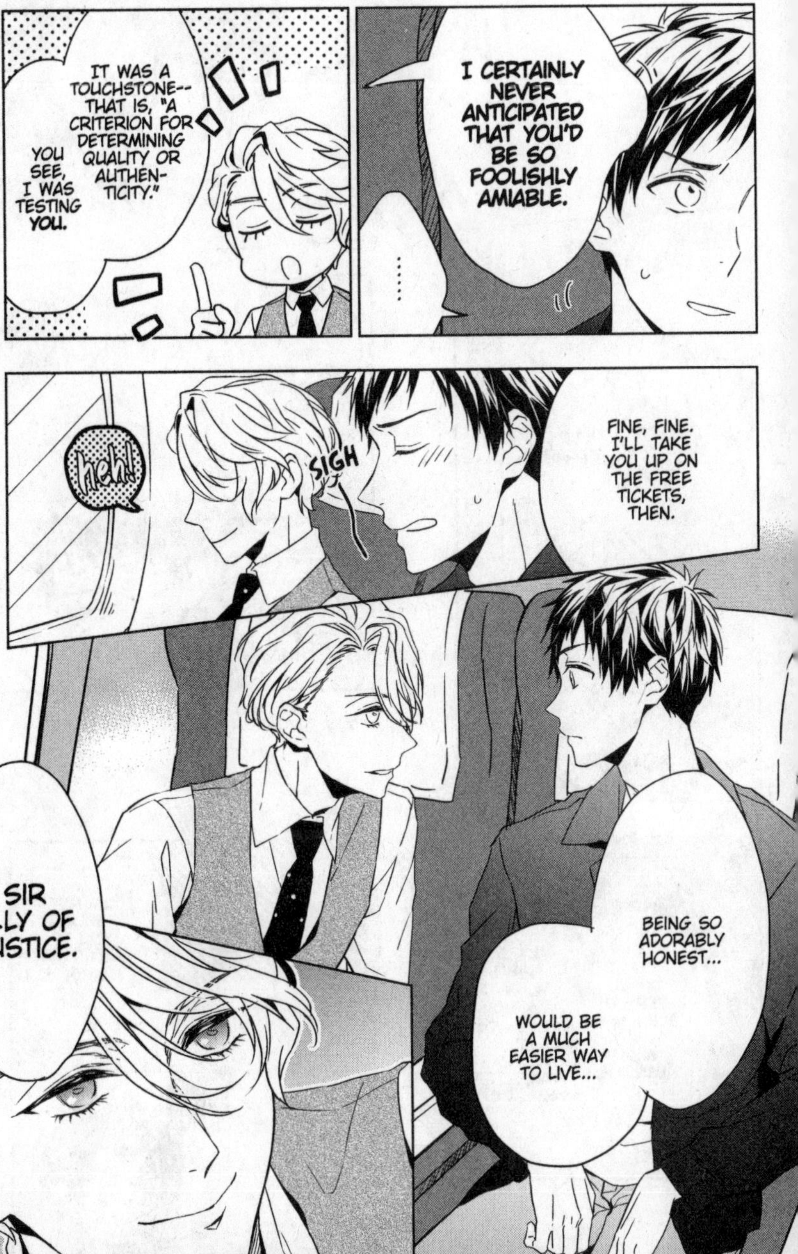
I CERTAINLY NEVER ANTICIPATED THAT YOU'D BE SO FOOLISHLY AMIABLE.
......
YOU SEE, I WAS TESTING YOU.
IT WAS A TOUCHSTONE-- THAT IS, "A CRITERION FOR DETERMINING QUALITY OR AUTHENTICITY."
FINE, FINE. I'LL TAKE YOU UP ON THE FREE TICKETS, THEN.
SIGH
heh!
BEING SO ADORABLY HONEST...
WOULD BE A MUCH EASIER WAY TO LIVE...
SIR ALLY OF JUSTICE.

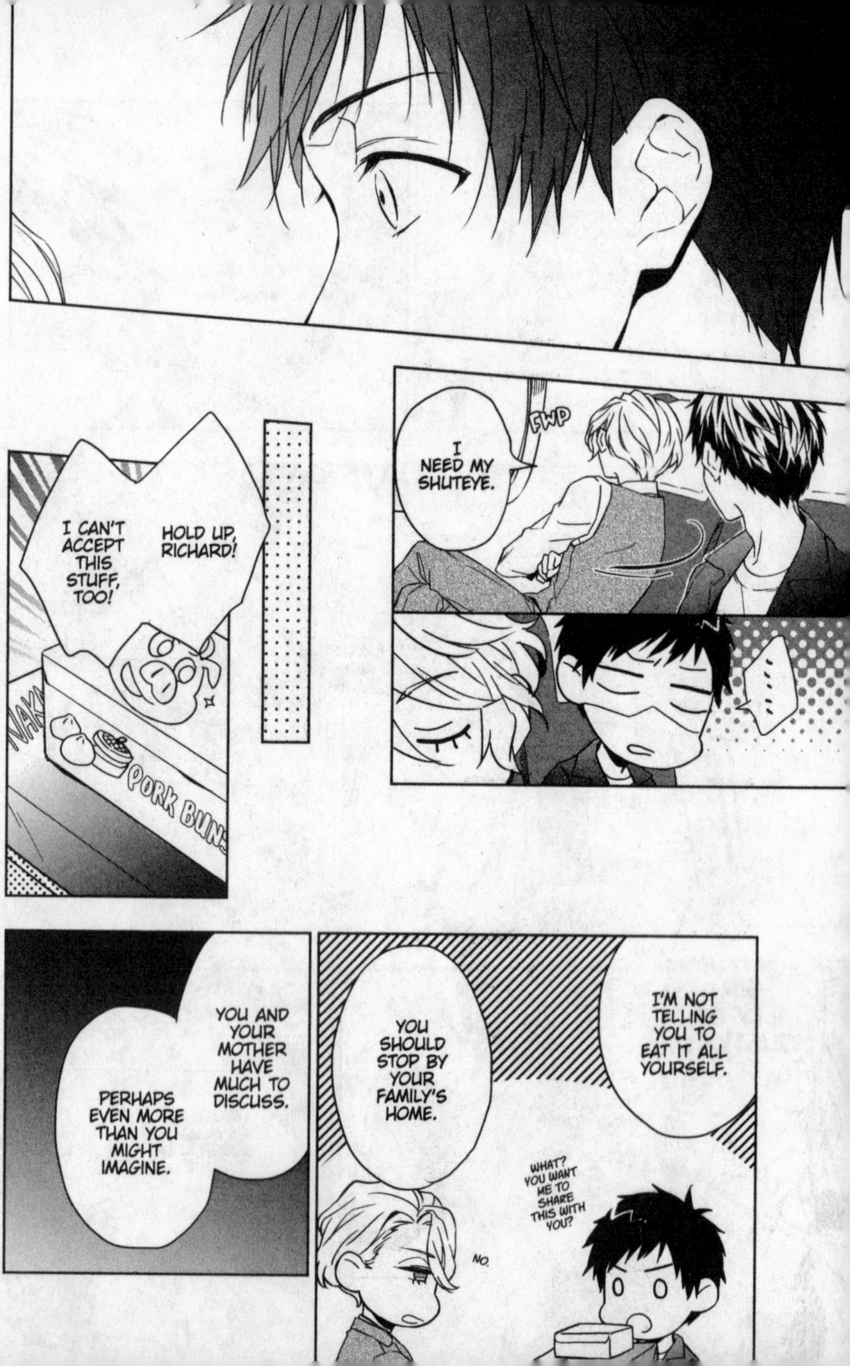

FWP
I NEED MY SHUTEYE.
...
HOLD UP, RICHARD!
I CAN'T ACCEPT THIS STUFF, TOO!
PORK BUNS
I'M NOT TELLING YOU TO EAT IT ALL YOURSELF.
YOU SHOULD STOP BY YOUR FAMILY'S HOME.
WHAT? YOU WANT ME TO SHARE THIS WITH YOU?
NO.
YOU AND YOUR MOTHER HAVE MUCH TO DISCUSS.
PERHAPS EVEN MORE THAN YOU MIGHT IMAGINE.

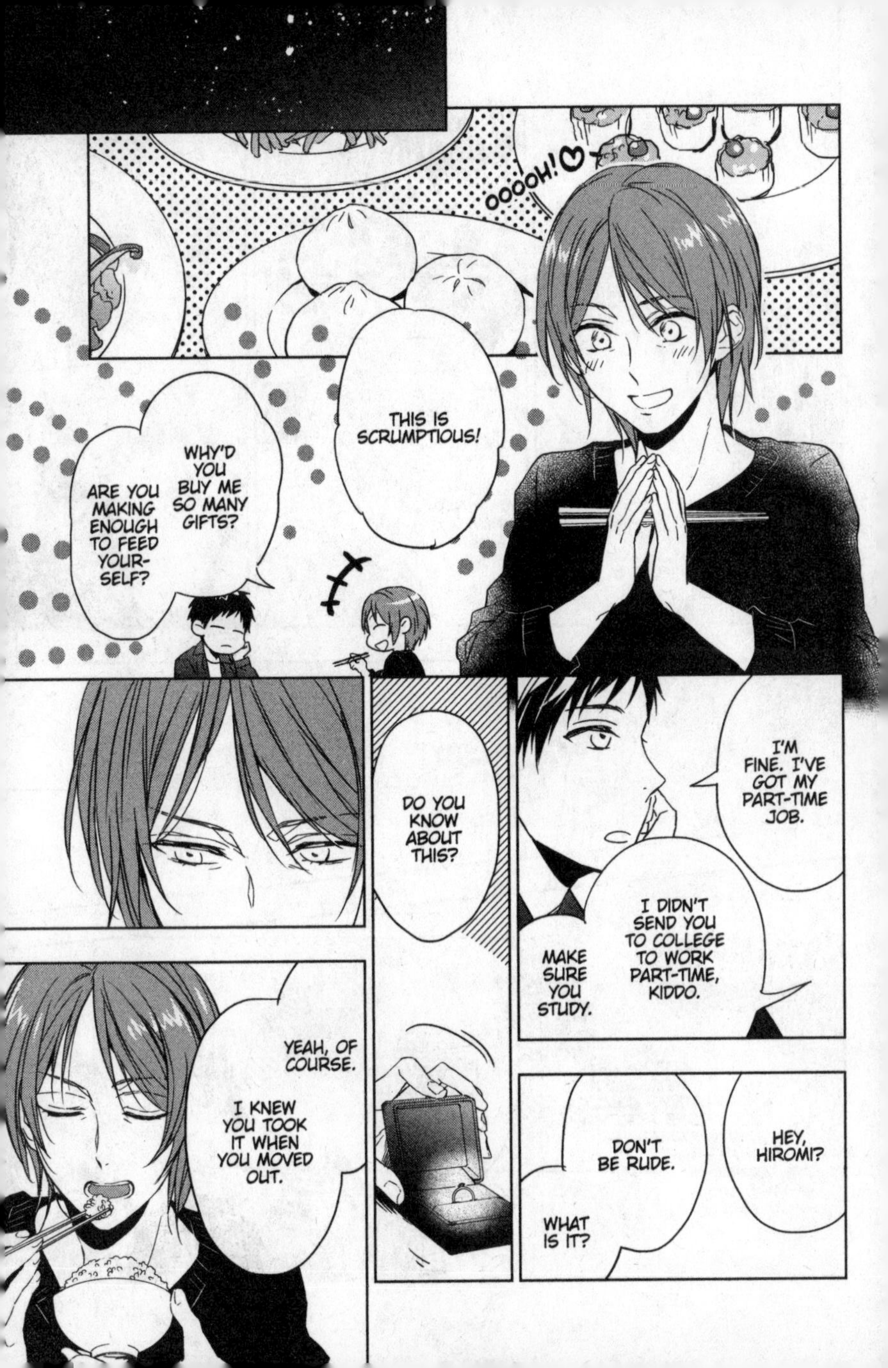
OOOOH! ♡
THIS IS SCRUMPTIOUS!
WHY'D YOU BUY ME SO MANY GIFTS?
ARE YOU MAKING ENOUGH TO FEED YOUR-SELF?
I'M FINE. I'VE GOT MY PART-TIME JOB.
I DIDN'T SEND YOU TO COLLEGE TO WORK PART-TIME, KIDDO.
MAKE SURE YOU STUDY.
HEY, HIROMI?
DON'T BE RUDE.
WHAT IS IT?
DO YOU KNOW ABOUT THIS?
YEAH, OF COURSE.
I KNEW YOU TOOK IT WHEN YOU MOVED OUT.

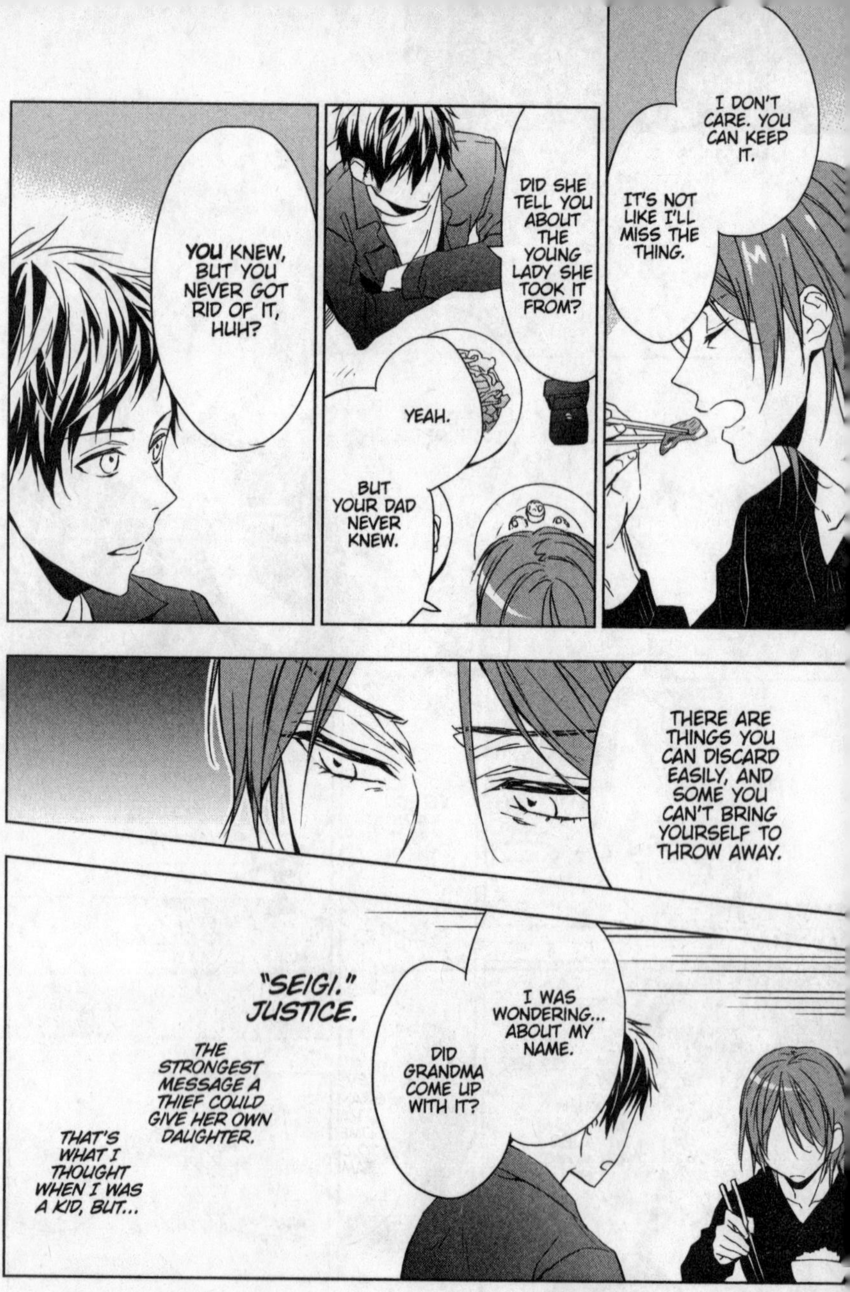
I DON'T CARE. YOU CAN KEEP IT.
IT'S NOT LIKE I'LL MISS THE THING.
DID SHE TELL YOU ABOUT THE YOUNG LADY SHE TOOK IT FROM?
YEAH.
BUT YOUR DAD NEVER KNEW.
YOU KNEW, BUT YOU NEVER GOT RID OF IT, HUH?
THERE ARE THINGS YOU CAN DISCARD EASILY, AND SOME YOU CAN'T BRING YOURSELF TO THROW AWAY.
I WAS WONDERING... ABOUT MY NAME.
DID GRANDMA COME UP WITH IT?
"SEIGI." JUSTICE.
THE STRONGEST MESSAGE A THIEF COULD GIVE HER OWN DAUGHTER.
THAT'S WHAT I THOUGHT WHEN I WAS A KID, BUT...

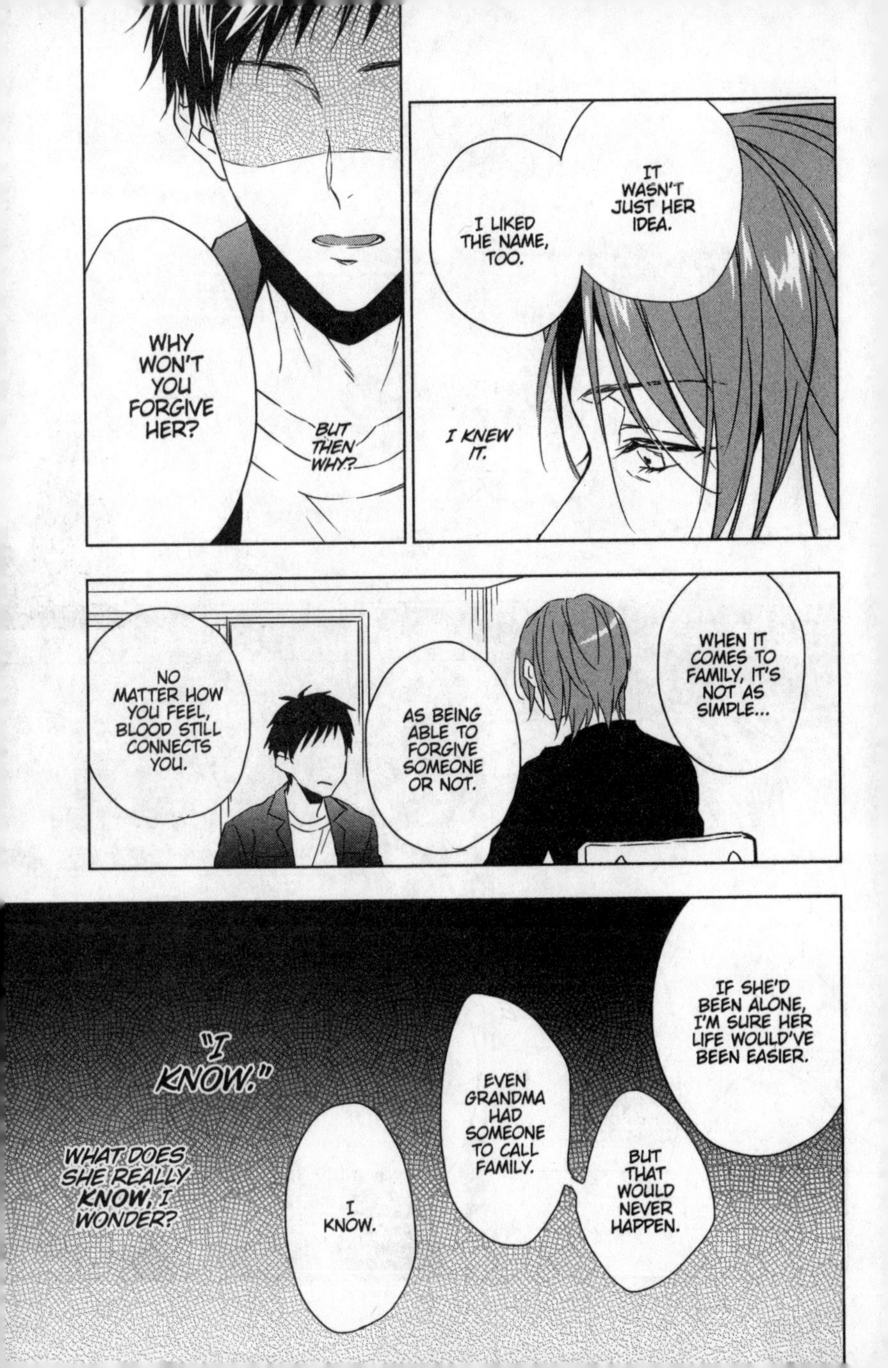
IT WASN'T JUST HER IDEA.
I LIKED THE NAME, TOO.
I KNEW IT.
BUT THEN WHY?
WHY WON'T YOU FORGIVE HER?
WHEN IT COMES TO FAMILY, IT'S NOT AS SIMPLE...
AS BEING ABLE TO FORGIVE SOMEONE OR NOT.
NO MATTER HOW YOU FEEL, BLOOD STILL CONNECTS YOU.
IF SHE'D BEEN ALONE, I'M SURE HER LIFE WOULD'VE BEEN EASIER.
BUT THAT WOULD NEVER HAPPEN.
EVEN GRANDMA HAD SOMEONE TO CALL FAMILY.
I KNOW.
"I KNOW."
WHAT DOES SHE REALLY KNOW, I WONDER?

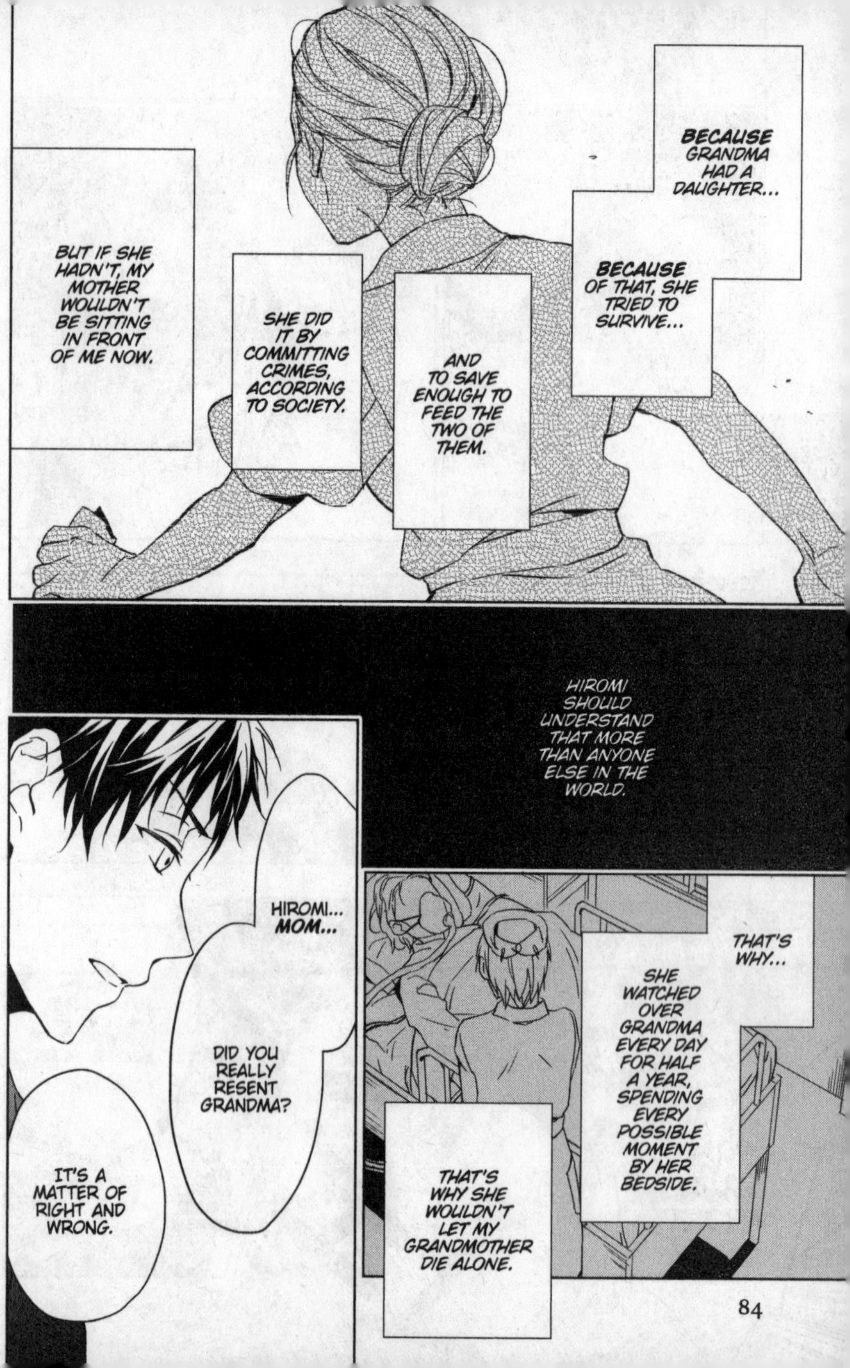
BECAUSE GRANDMA HAD A DAUGHTER...
BECAUSE OF THAT, SHE TRIED TO SURVIVE...
AND TO SAVE ENOUGH TO FEED THE TWO OF THEM.
SHE DID IT BY COMMITTING CRIMES, ACCORDING TO SOCIETY.
BUT IF SHE HADN'T, MY MOTHER WOULDN'T BE SITTING IN FRONT OF ME NOW.
HIROMI SHOULD UNDERSTAND THAT MORE THAN ANYONE ELSE IN THE WORLD.
THAT'S WHY...
SHE WATCHED OVER GRANDMA EVERY DAY FOR HALF A YEAR, SPENDING EVERY POSSIBLE MOMENT BY HER BEDSIDE.
THAT'S WHY SHE WOULDN'T LET MY GRANDMOTHER DIE ALONE.
HIROMI... MOM...
DID YOU REALLY RESENT GRANDMA?
IT'S A MATTER OF RIGHT AND WRONG.

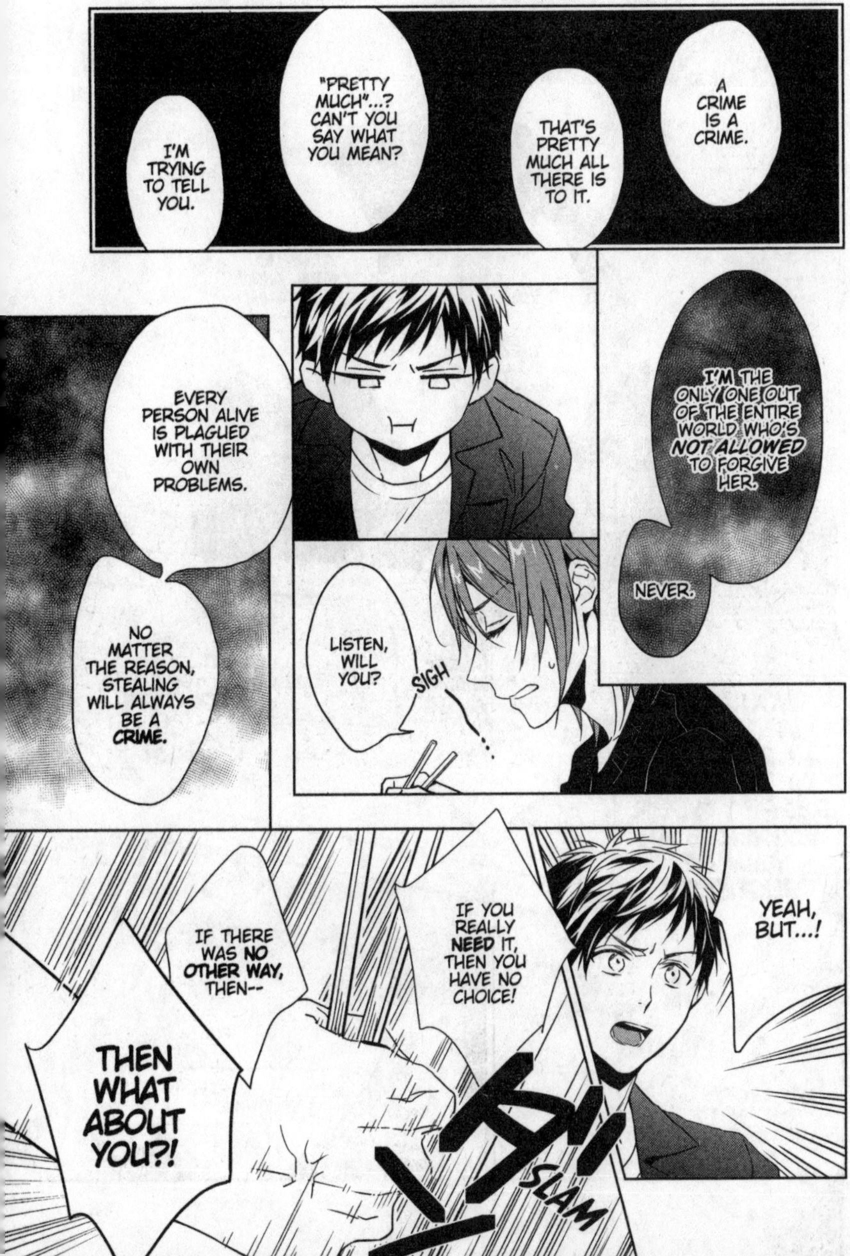
A CRIME IS A CRIME.
THAT'S PRETTY MUCH ALL THERE IS TO IT.
"PRETTY MUCH"...? CAN'T YOU SAY WHAT YOU MEAN?
I'M TRYING TO TELL YOU.
I'M THE ONLY ONE OUT OF THE ENTIRE WORLD WHO'S NOT ALLOWED TO FORGIVE HER.
NEVER.
LISTEN, WILL YOU?
SIGH
EVERY PERSON ALIVE IS PLAGUED WITH THEIR OWN PROBLEMS.
NO MATTER THE REASON, STEALING WILL ALWAYS BE A CRIME.
YEAH, BUT...!
IF YOU REALLY NEED IT, THEN YOU HAVE NO CHOICE!
IF THERE WAS NO OTHER WAY, THEN--
THEN WHAT ABOUT YOU?!
SLAM

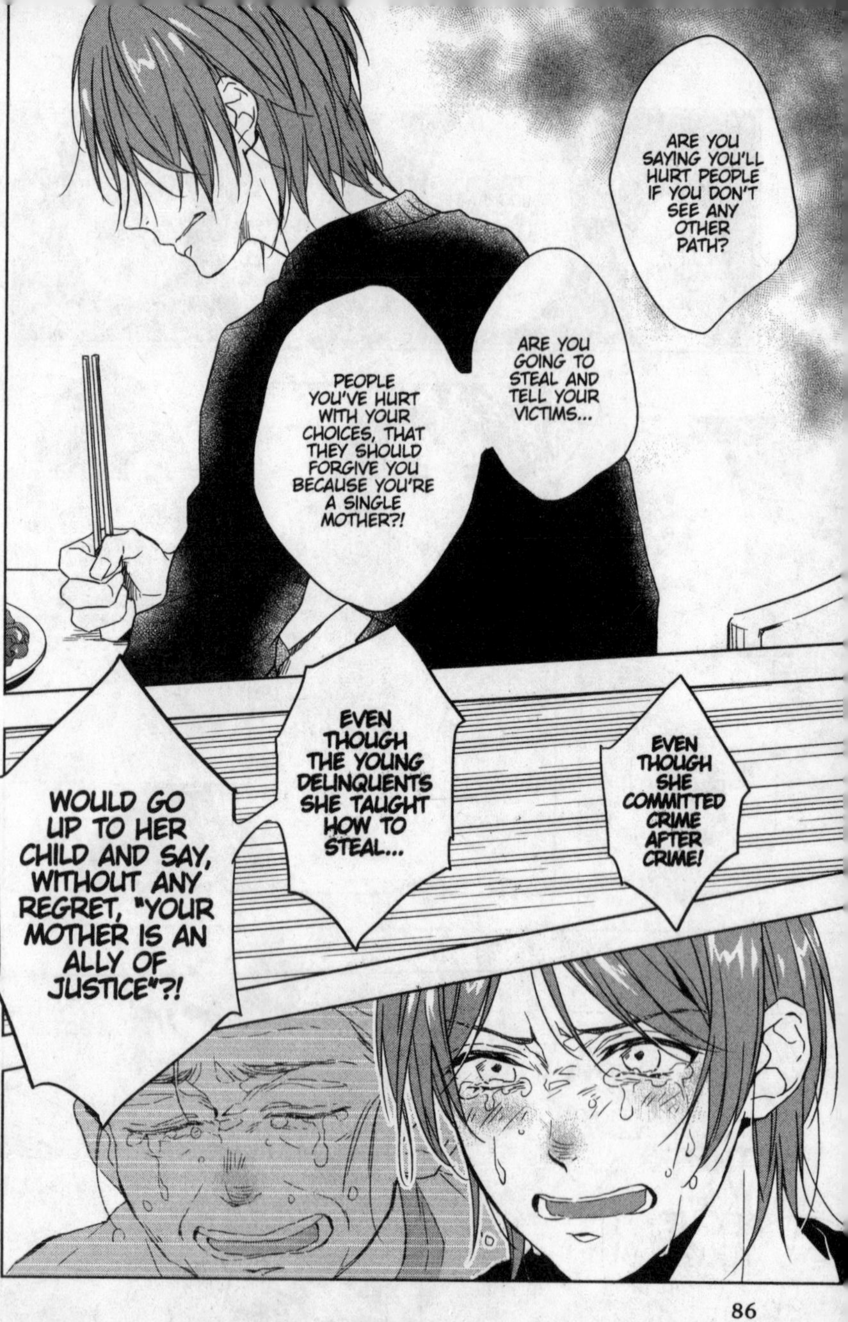
ARE YOU SAYING YOU'LL HURT PEOPLE IF YOU DON'T SEE ANY OTHER PATH?
ARE YOU GOING TO STEAL AND TELL YOUR VICTIMS...
PEOPLE YOU'VE HURT WITH YOUR CHOICES, THAT THEY SHOULD FORGIVE YOU BECAUSE YOU'RE A SINGLE MOTHER?!
EVEN THOUGH SHE COMMITTED CRIME AFTER CRIME!
EVEN THOUGH THE YOUNG DELINQUENTS SHE TAUGHT HOW TO STEAL...
WOULD GO UP TO HER CHILD AND SAY, WITHOUT ANY REGRET, "YOUR MOTHER IS AN ALLY OF JUSTICE"?!

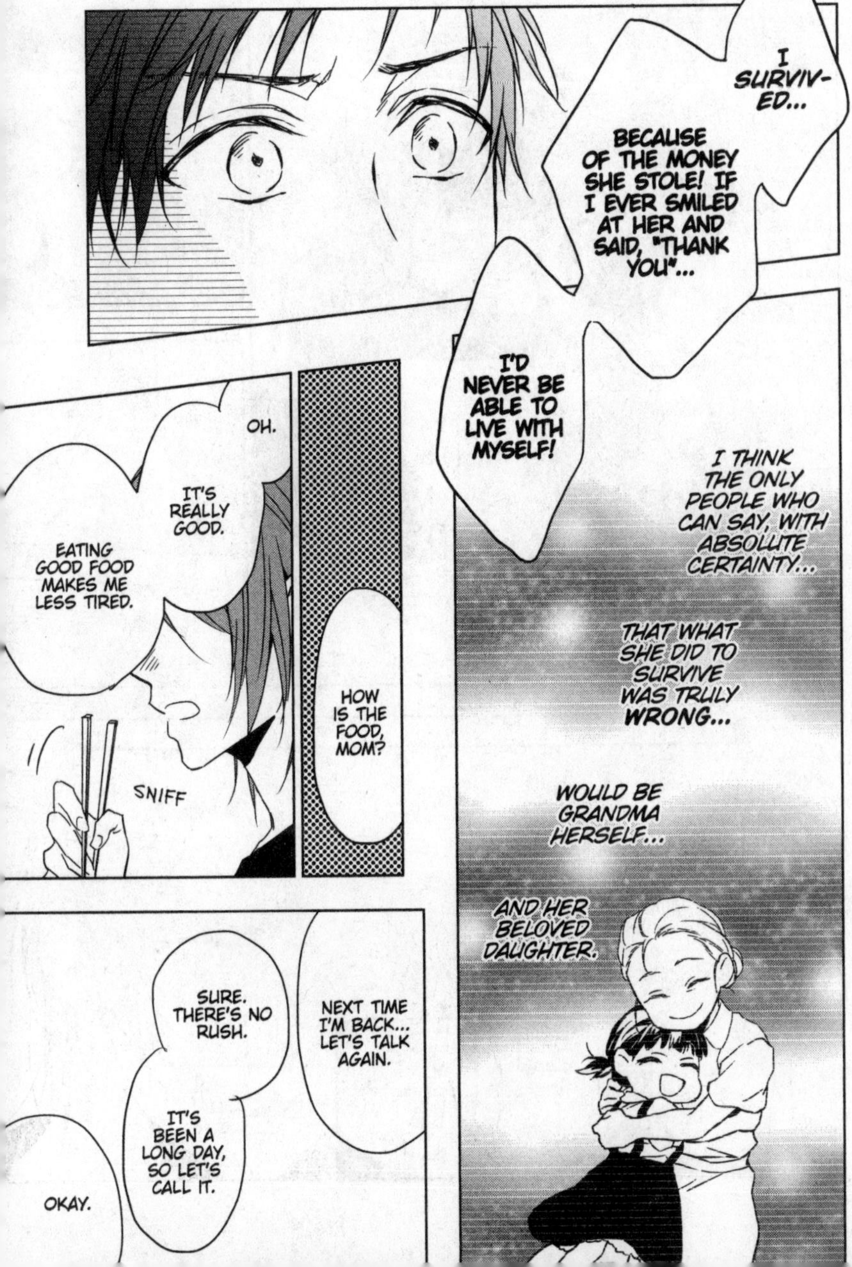
I SURVIVED...
BECAUSE OF THE MONEY SHE STOLE! IF I EVER SMILED AT HER AND SAID, "THANK YOU"...
I'D NEVER BE ABLE TO LIVE WITH MYSELF!
I THINK THE ONLY PEOPLE WHO CAN SAY, WITH ABSOLUTE CERTAINTY...
THAT WHAT SHE DID TO SURVIVE WAS TRULY **WRONG...**
WOULD BE GRANDMA HERSELF...
AND HER BELOVED DAUGHTER.
HOW IS THE FOOD, MOM?
OH.
IT'S REALLY GOOD.
EATING GOOD FOOD MAKES ME LESS TIRED.
SNIFF
NEXT TIME I'M BACK... LET'S TALK AGAIN.
SURE. THERE'S NO RUSH.
IT'S BEEN A LONG DAY, SO LET'S CALL IT.
OKAY.

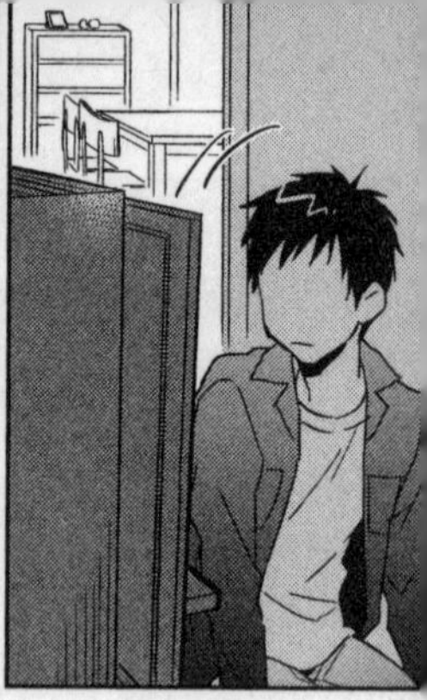

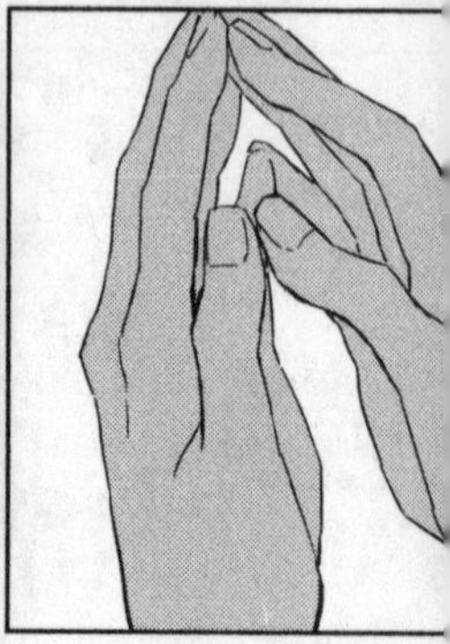

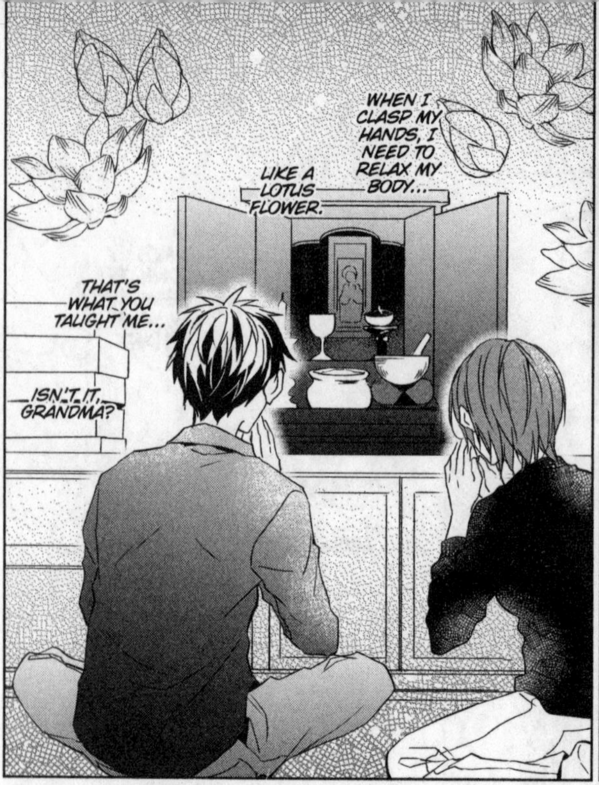
WHEN I CLASP MY HANDS, I NEED TO RELAX MY BODY...
LIKE A LOTUS FLOWER.
THAT'S WHAT YOU TAUGHT ME...
ISN'T IT, GRANDMA?

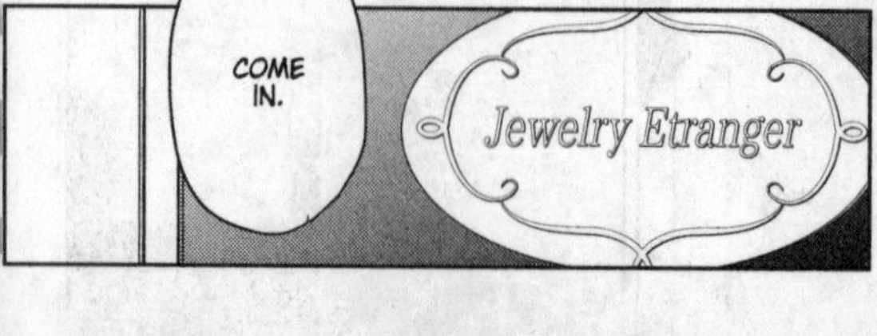
Jewelry Etranger
COME IN.

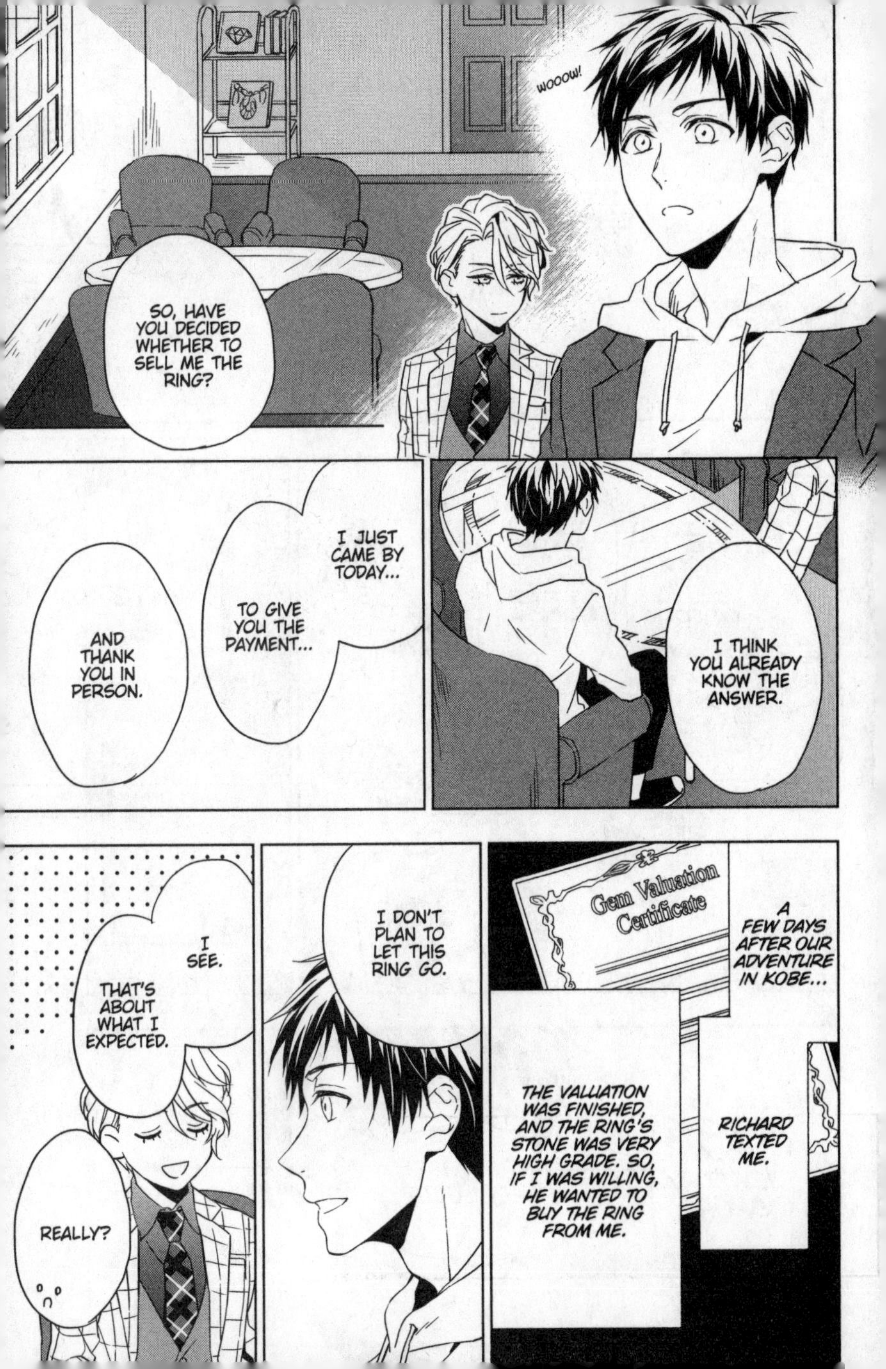
WOOOW!
SO, HAVE YOU DECIDED WHETHER TO SELL ME THE RING?
I THINK YOU ALREADY KNOW THE ANSWER.
I JUST CAME BY TODAY...
TO GIVE YOU THE PAYMENT...
AND THANK YOU IN PERSON.
A FEW DAYS AFTER OUR ADVENTURE IN KOBE...
Gem Valuation Certificate
RICHARD TEXTED ME.
THE VALUATION WAS FINISHED, AND THE RING'S STONE WAS VERY HIGH GRADE. SO, IF I WAS WILLING, HE WANTED TO BUY THE RING FROM ME.
I DON'T PLAN TO LET THIS RING GO.
I SEE.
THAT'S ABOUT WHAT I EXPECTED.
REALLY?

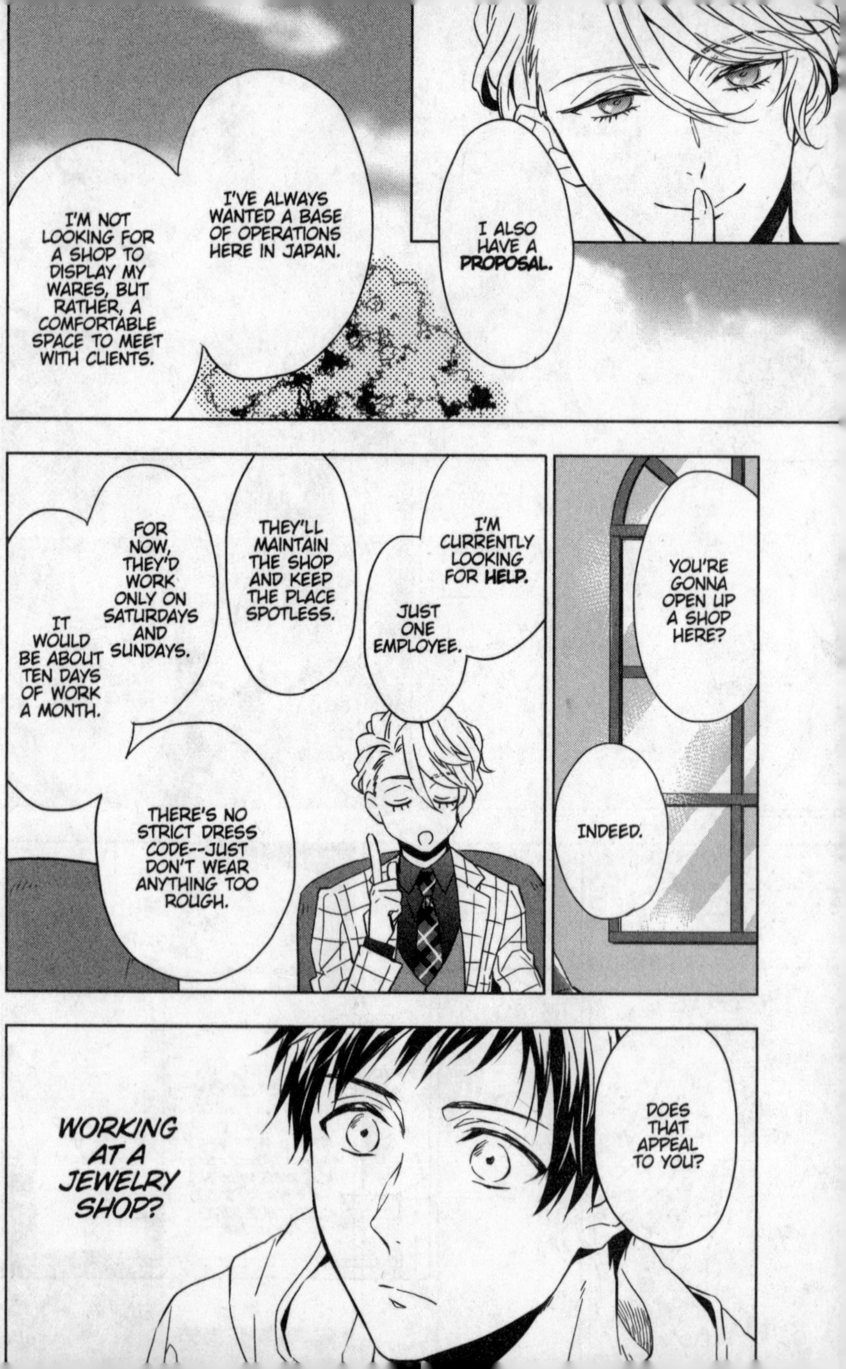
I ALSO HAVE A **PROPOSAL.**
I'VE ALWAYS WANTED A BASE OF OPERATIONS HERE IN JAPAN.
I'M NOT LOOKING FOR A SHOP TO DISPLAY MY WARES, BUT RATHER, A COMFORTABLE SPACE TO MEET WITH CLIENTS.
YOU'RE GONNA OPEN UP A SHOP HERE?
INDEED.
I'M CURRENTLY LOOKING FOR **HELP.**
JUST ONE EMPLOYEE.
THEY'LL MAINTAIN THE SHOP AND KEEP THE PLACE SPOTLESS.
FOR NOW, THEY'D WORK ONLY ON SATURDAYS AND SUNDAYS.
IT WOULD BE ABOUT TEN DAYS OF WORK A MONTH.
THERE'S NO STRICT DRESS CODE--JUST DON'T WEAR ANYTHING TOO ROUGH.
DOES THAT APPEAL TO YOU?
WORKING AT A JEWELRY SHOP?

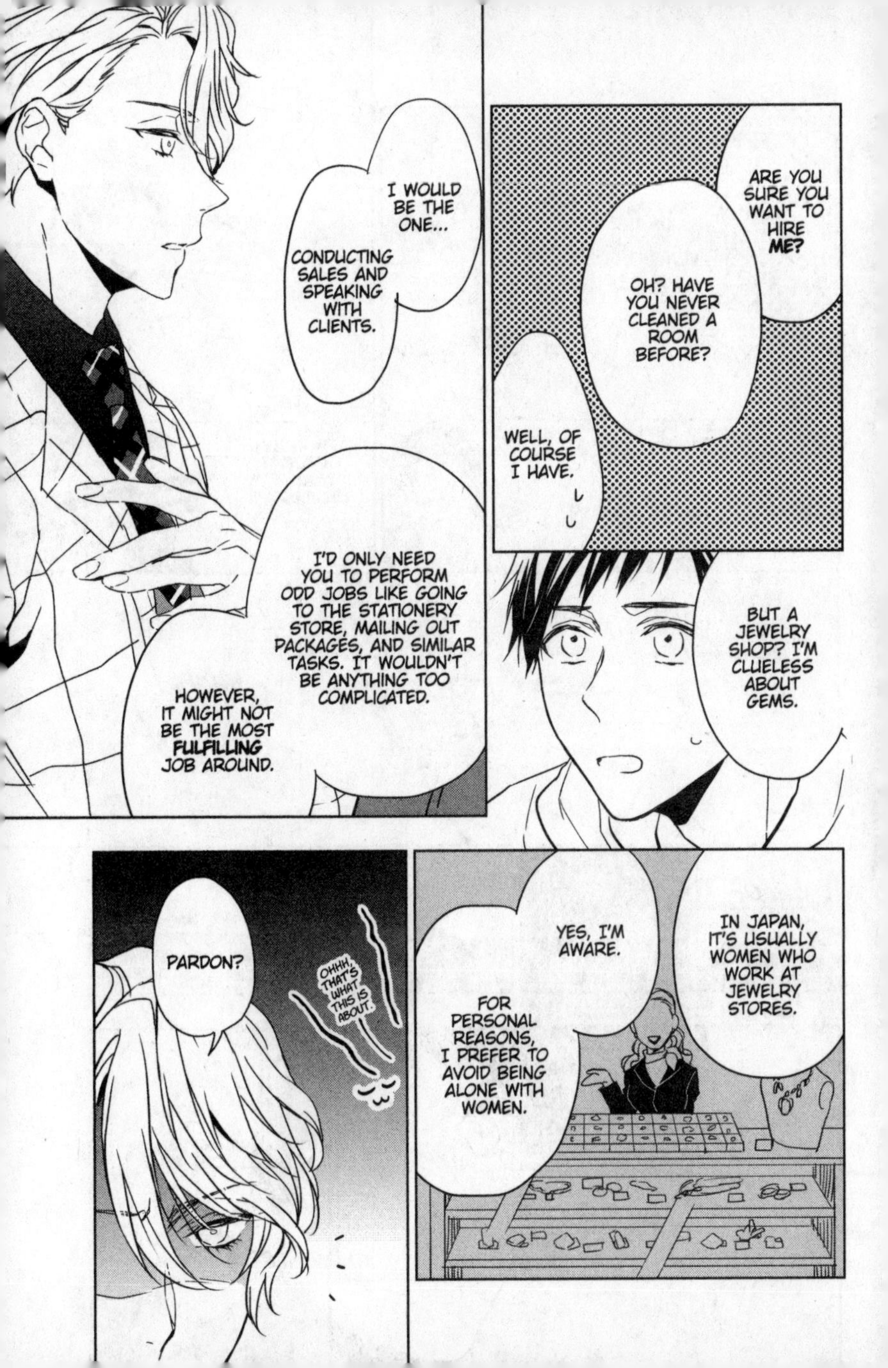
ARE YOU SURE YOU WANT TO HIRE **ME?**
OH? HAVE YOU NEVER CLEANED A ROOM BEFORE?
WELL, OF COURSE I HAVE.
BUT A JEWELRY SHOP? I'M CLUELESS ABOUT GEMS.
I WOULD BE THE ONE...
CONDUCTING SALES AND SPEAKING WITH CLIENTS.
I'D ONLY NEED YOU TO PERFORM ODD JOBS LIKE GOING TO THE STATIONERY STORE, MAILING OUT PACKAGES, AND SIMILAR TASKS. IT WOULDN'T BE ANYTHING TOO COMPLICATED.
HOWEVER, IT MIGHT NOT BE THE MOST **FULFILLING** JOB AROUND.
IN JAPAN, IT'S USUALLY WOMEN WHO WORK AT JEWELRY STORES.
YES, I'M AWARE.
FOR PERSONAL REASONS, I PREFER TO AVOID BEING ALONE WITH WOMEN.
PARDON?
OHHH, THAT'S WHAT THIS IS ABOUT.

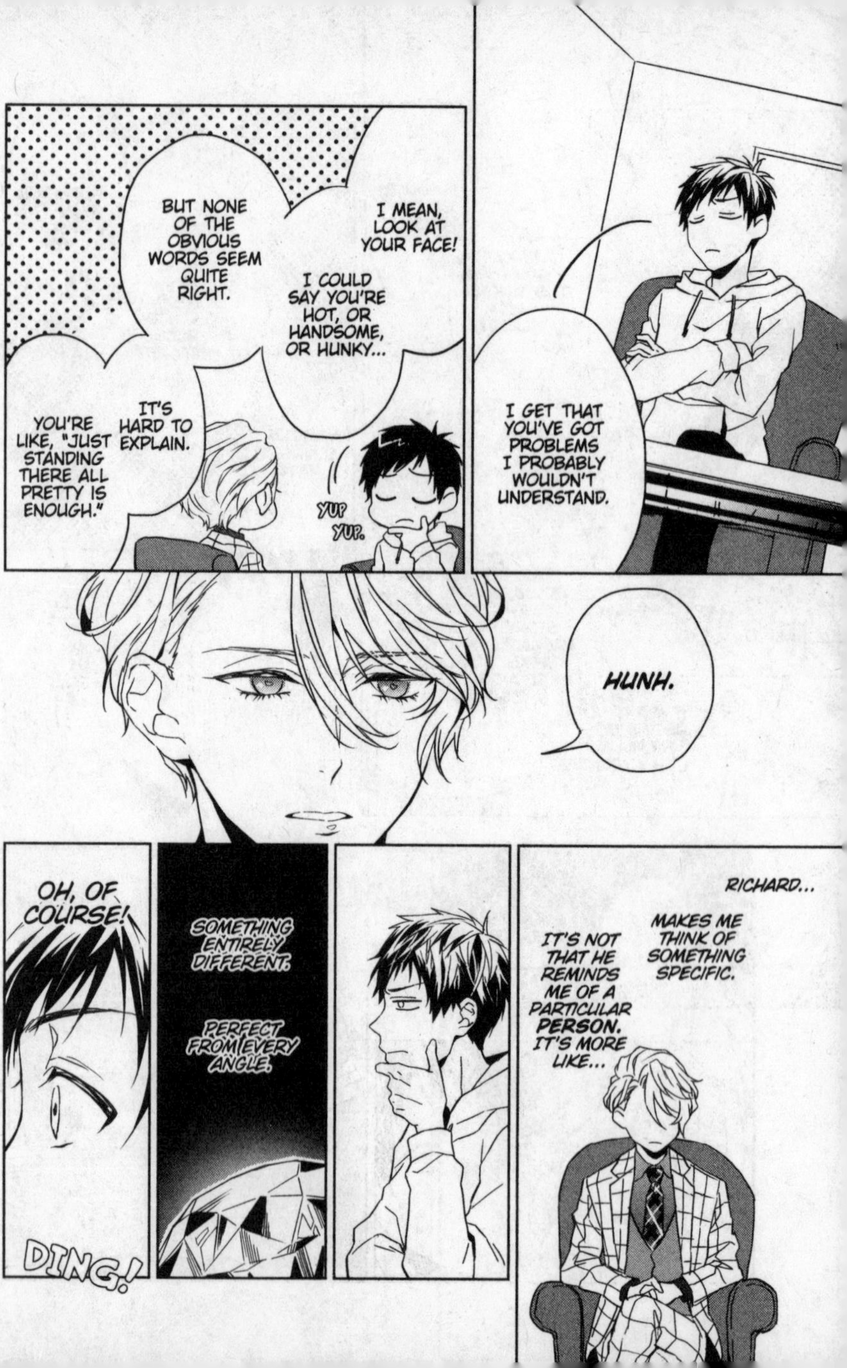
I GET THAT YOU'VE GOT PROBLEMS I PROBABLY WOULDN'T UNDERSTAND.
I MEAN, LOOK AT YOUR FACE!
I COULD SAY YOU'RE HOT, OR HANDSOME, OR HUNKY...
BUT NONE OF THE OBVIOUS WORDS SEEM QUITE RIGHT.
IT'S HARD TO EXPLAIN.
YUP YUP.
YOU'RE LIKE, "JUST STANDING THERE ALL PRETTY IS ENOUGH."
HUNH.
RICHARD...
MAKES ME THINK OF SOMETHING SPECIFIC.
IT'S NOT THAT HE REMINDS ME OF A PARTICULAR PERSON. IT'S MORE LIKE...
SOMETHING ENTIRELY DIFFERENT.
PERFECT FROM EVERY ANGLE.
OH, OF COURSE!
DING!

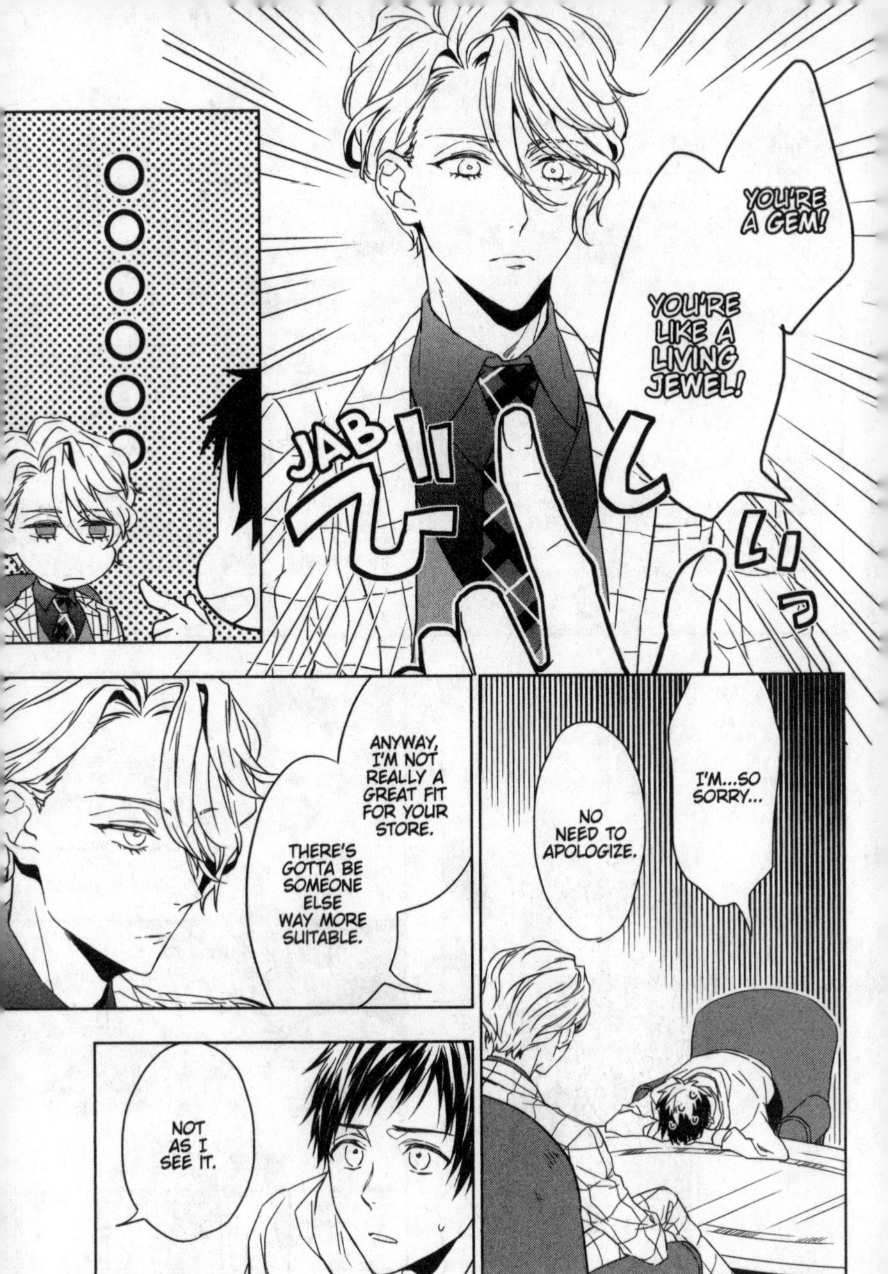
YOU'RE A GEM!
YOU'RE LIKE A LIVING JEWEL!
JAB
I'M...SO SORRY...
NO NEED TO APOLOGIZE.
ANYWAY, I'M NOT REALLY A GREAT FIT FOR YOUR STORE.
THERE'S GOTTA BE SOMEONE ELSE WAY MORE SUITABLE.
NOT AS I SEE IT.

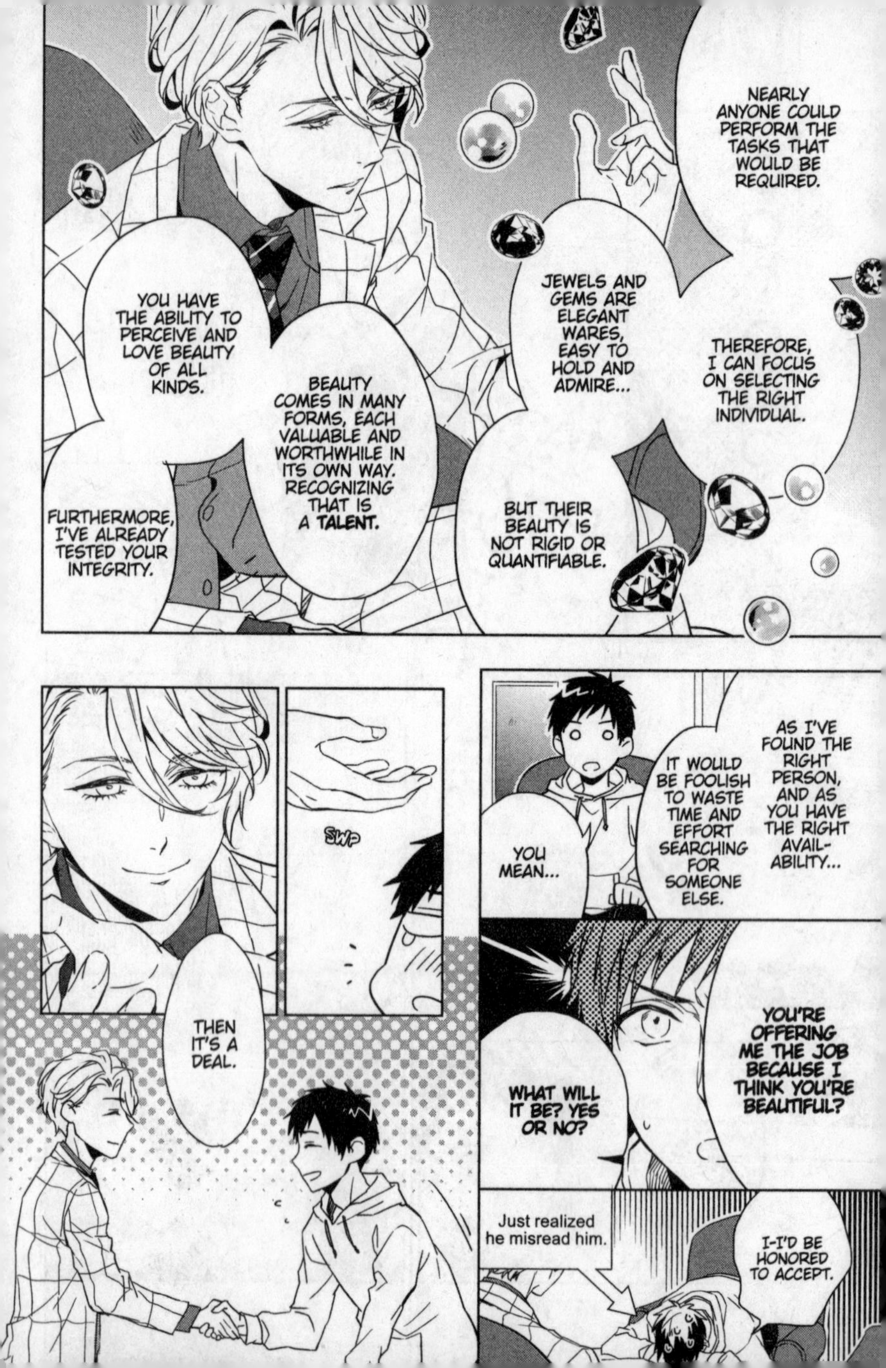
NEARLY ANYONE COULD PERFORM THE TASKS THAT WOULD BE REQUIRED.
THEREFORE, I CAN FOCUS ON SELECTING THE RIGHT INDIVIDUAL.
JEWELS AND GEMS ARE ELEGANT WARES, EASY TO HOLD AND ADMIRE...
BUT THEIR BEAUTY IS NOT RIGID OR QUANTIFIABLE.
BEAUTY COMES IN MANY FORMS, EACH VALUABLE AND WORTHWHILE IN ITS OWN WAY. RECOGNIZING THAT IS A TALENT.
YOU HAVE THE ABILITY TO PERCEIVE AND LOVE BEAUTY OF ALL KINDS.
FURTHERMORE, I'VE ALREADY TESTED YOUR INTEGRITY.
AS I'VE FOUND THE RIGHT PERSON, AND AS YOU HAVE THE RIGHT AVAIL-ABILITY...
IT WOULD BE FOOLISH TO WASTE TIME AND EFFORT SEARCHING FOR SOMEONE ELSE.
YOU MEAN...
YOU'RE OFFERING ME THE JOB BECAUSE I THINK YOU'RE BEAUTIFUL?
WHAT WILL IT BE? YES OR NO?
I-I'D BE HONORED TO ACCEPT.
Just realized he misread him.
SWP
THEN IT'S A DEAL.

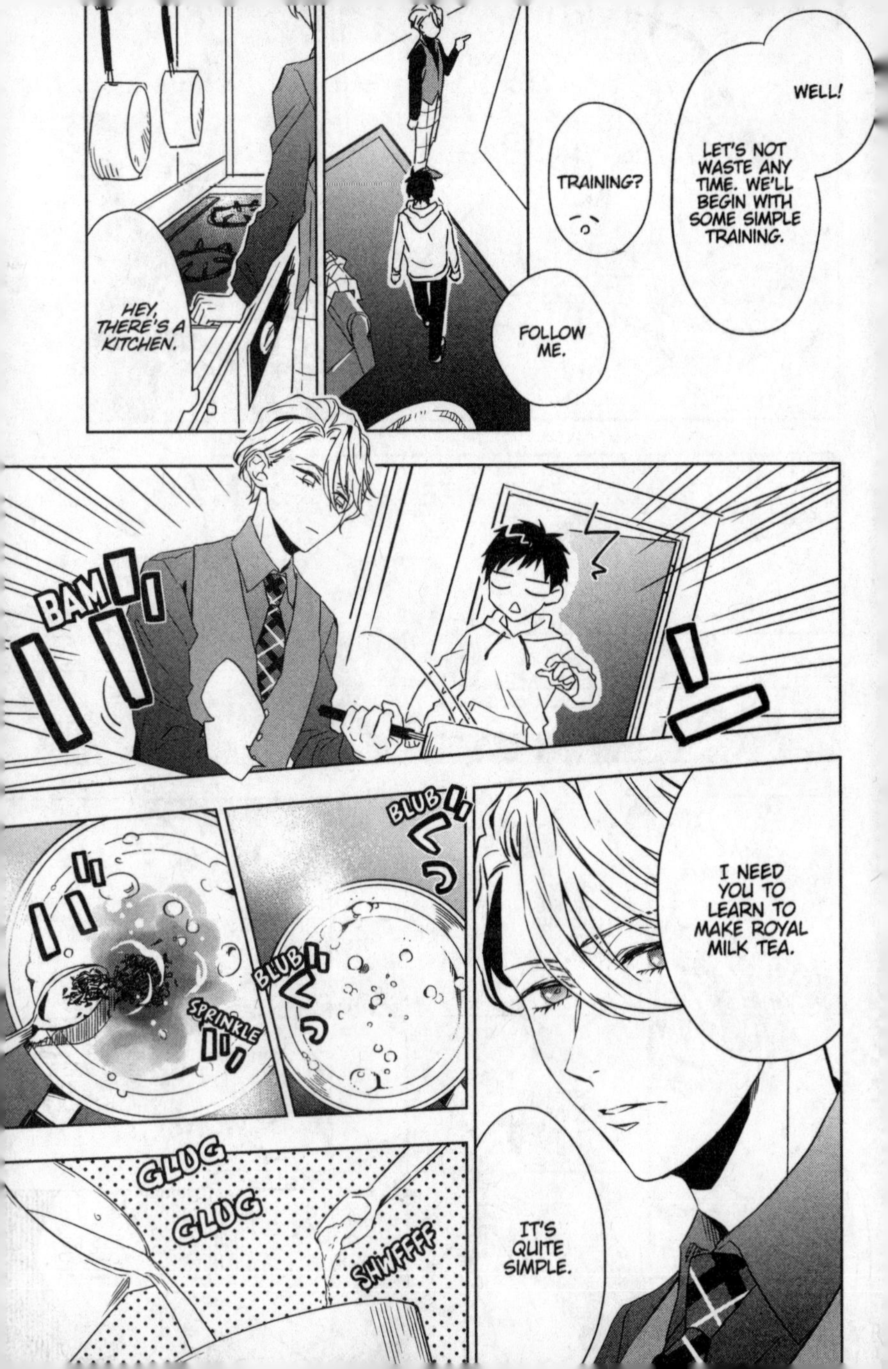
WELL!
LET'S NOT WASTE ANY TIME. WE'LL BEGIN WITH SOME SIMPLE TRAINING.
TRAINING?
FOLLOW ME.
HEY, THERE'S A KITCHEN.
BAM
I NEED YOU TO LEARN TO MAKE ROYAL MILK TEA.
IT'S QUITE SIMPLE.
BLUB
BLUB
SPRINKLE
GLUG
GLUG
SHWFFFF

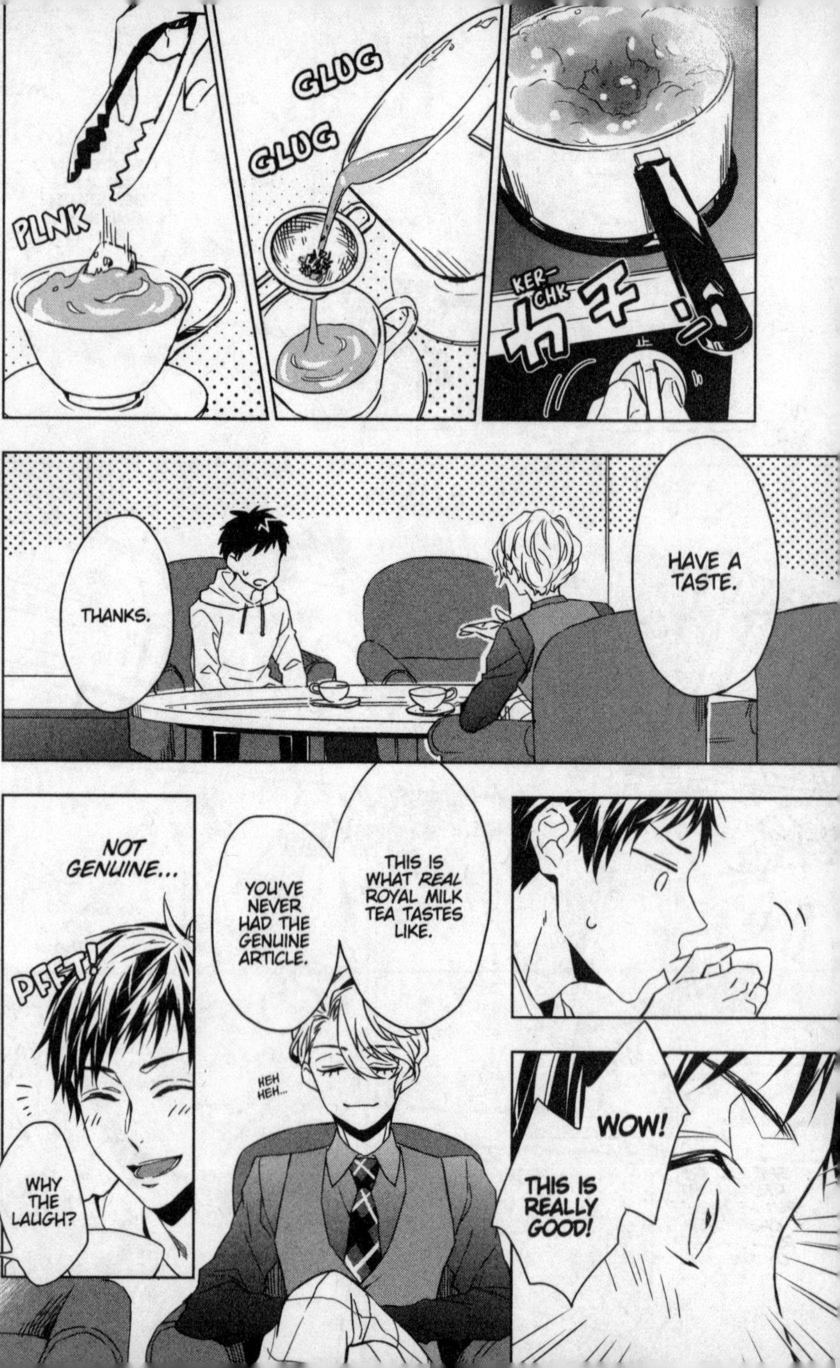
KER-CHK
カチッ
GLUG
GLUG
PLNK
HAVE A TASTE.
THANKS.
WOW!
THIS IS REALLY GOOD!
THIS IS WHAT *REAL* ROYAL MILK TEA TASTES LIKE.
YOU'VE NEVER HAD THE GENUINE ARTICLE.
HEH HEH...
NOT GENUINE...
PFFT!
WHY THE LAUGH?

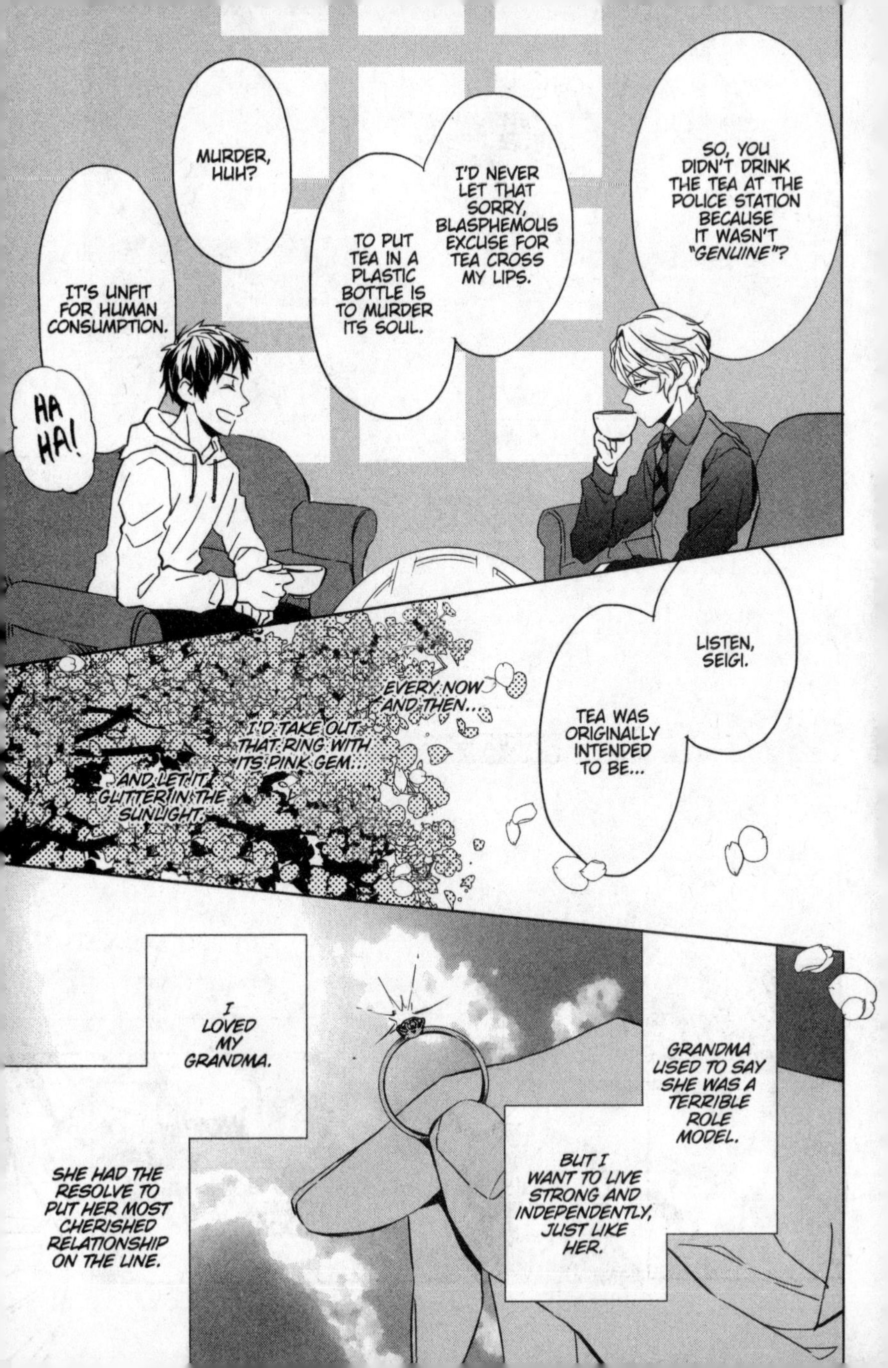
SO, YOU DIDN'T DRINK THE TEA AT THE POLICE STATION BECAUSE IT WASN'T "GENUINE"?
I'D NEVER LET THAT SORRY, BLASPHEMOUS EXCUSE FOR TEA CROSS MY LIPS.
TO PUT TEA IN A PLASTIC BOTTLE IS TO MURDER ITS SOUL.
MURDER, HUH?
IT'S UNFIT FOR HUMAN CONSUMPTION.
HA HA!
LISTEN, SEIGI.
TEA WAS ORIGINALLY INTENDED TO BE...
EVERY NOW AND THEN...
I'D TAKE OUT THAT RING WITH ITS PINK GEM...
AND LET IT GLITTER IN THE SUNLIGHT.
GRANDMA USED TO SAY SHE WAS A TERRIBLE ROLE MODEL.
BUT I WANT TO LIVE STRONG AND INDEPENDENTLY, JUST LIKE HER.
I LOVED MY GRANDMA.
SHE HAD THE RESOLVE TO PUT HER MOST CHERISHED RELATIONSHIP ON THE LINE.

EVEN IF HER DECISIONS WEREN'T CONSIDERED "RIGHT"...

I STILL FOUND HER AND HER RESOLVE SO TRAGICALLY BEAUTIFUL.

HEY!

NAKATA!

I HEARD YOU DROPPED SOME SHIFTS AT...

THE STATION ...?

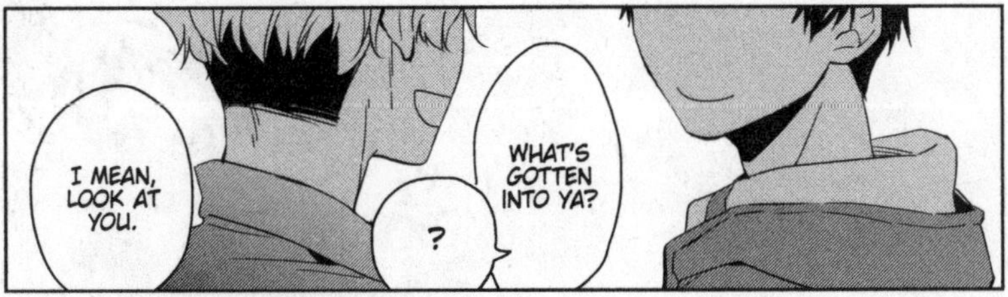
WHAT'S GOTTEN INTO YA?
?
I MEAN, LOOK AT YOU.

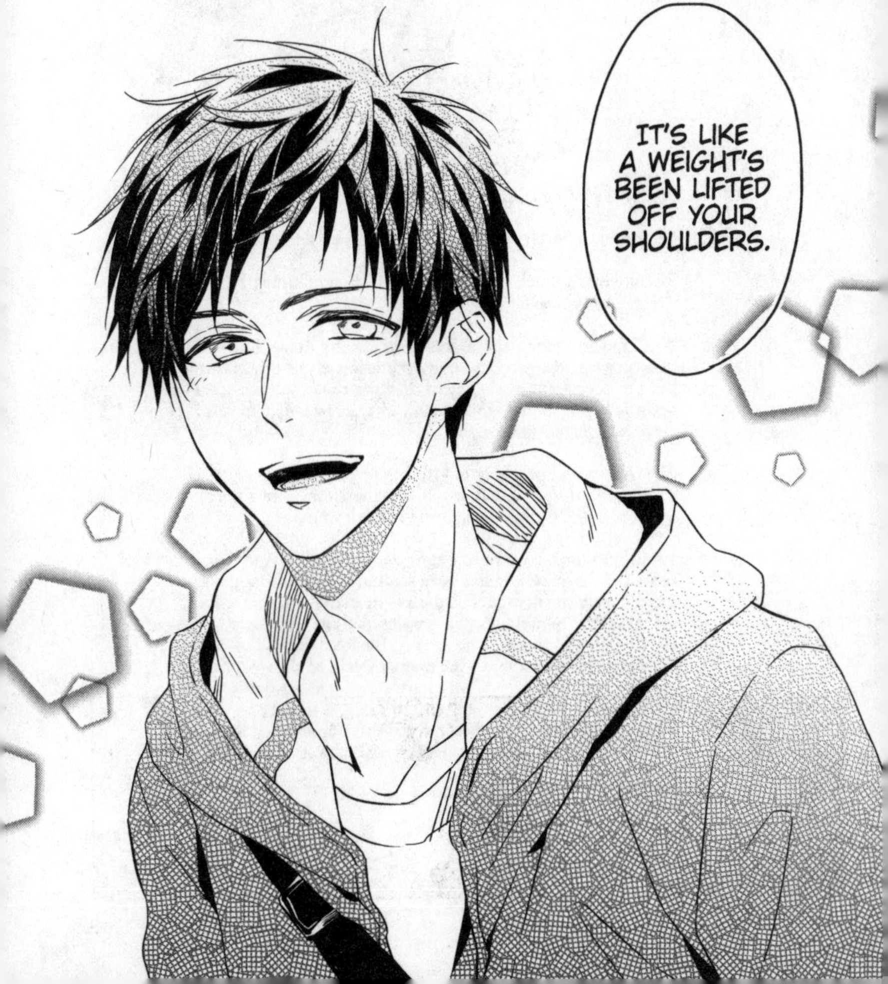
IT'S LIKE A WEIGHT'S BEEN LIFTED OFF YOUR SHOULDERS.

Hello! My name is **Akatsuki.**

Welcome to Jewelry Etranger! (I've always wanted to say that.)

Thank you so much for picking up the first volume of *The Case Files of Jeweler Richard*.

Not knowing much about gems and jewelry made it quite difficult for me to create a manga adaptation of the original story, but I'm enamored by the joy of drawing those beloved scenes and the expressions of these lovely characters. My pen just flies across the paper on its own.

The manga will probably progress at its own unique pace compared to the original novels and the anime, but I'd be overjoyed if you'd keep watching the story bloom.

I want to thank my editor, I-san, who loves the original work more than anyone and has been working hand-in-hand with me to create the manga. I also want to thank Tsujimura-sensei and Yukihiro-sensei, who have welcomed me with open arms; the designer, Dan-san, who created the lovely logo and design that gave life and color to the manga world of the story; and all of my family and friends who have supported me daily.

From the bottom of my heart, I want to thank every single person who's supported me in the serialization of this manga.

I hope I can write to all of you again soon.

THE CASE FILES OF JEWELER RICHARD

THE CASE FILES
OF
JEWELER
RICHARD

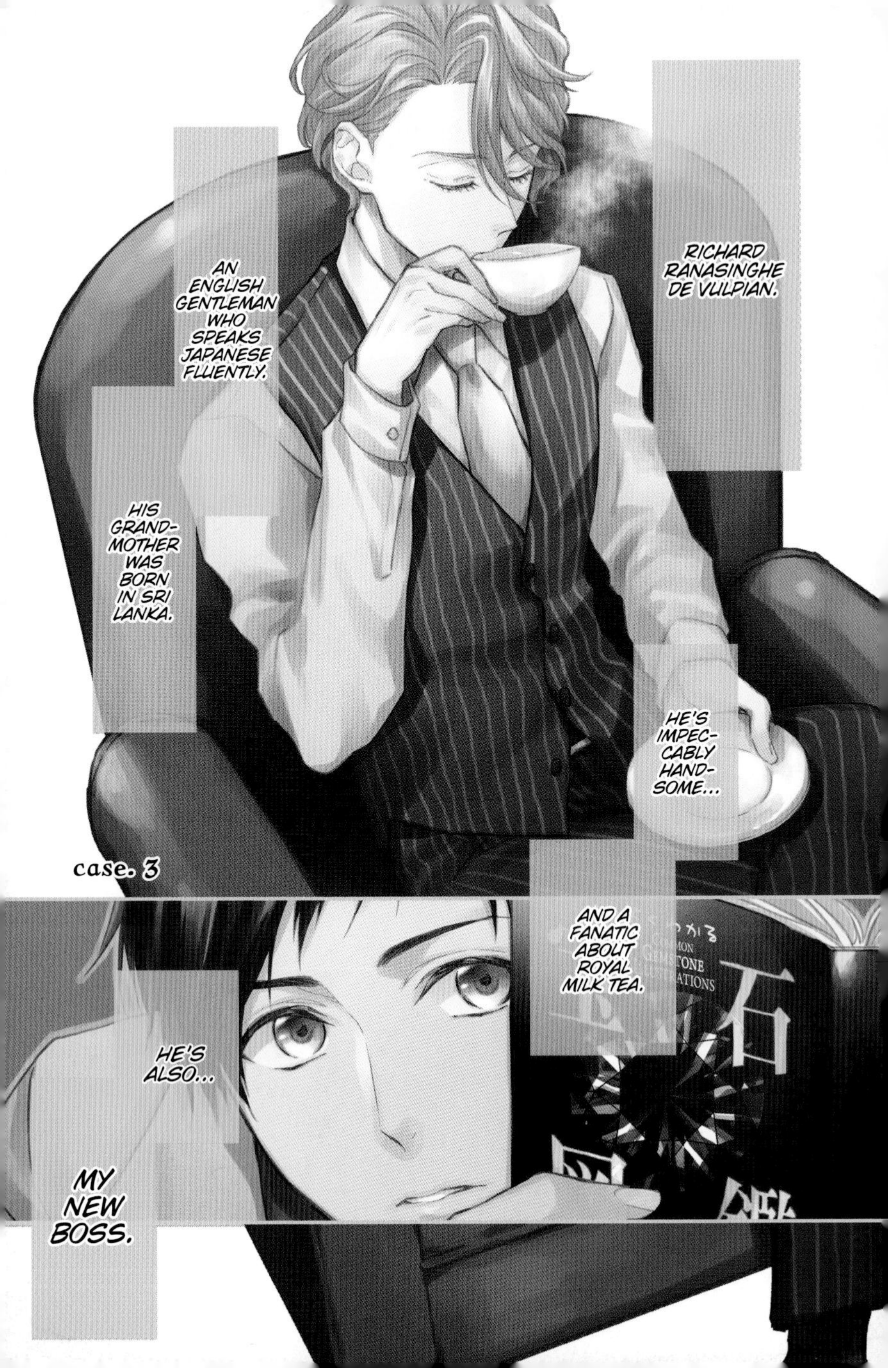
RICHARD RANASINGHE DE VULPIAN.
AN ENGLISH GENTLEMAN WHO SPEAKS JAPANESE FLUENTLY.
HIS GRAND-MOTHER WAS BORN IN SRI LANKA.
HE'S IMPEC-CABLY HAND-SOME...
case. 3
AND A FANATIC ABOUT ROYAL MILK TEA.
HE'S ALSO...
MY NEW BOSS.

case. 3
Truth of the Ruby
Part 1

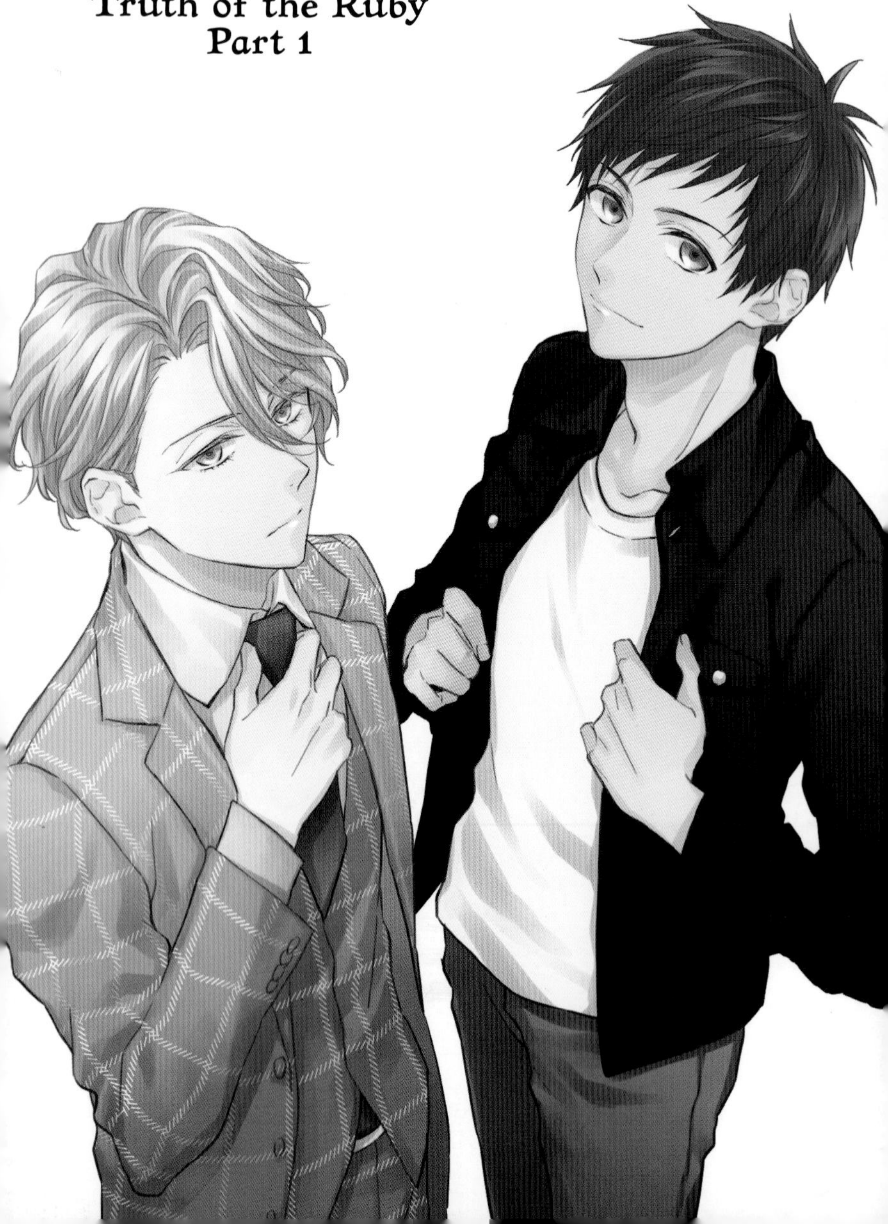

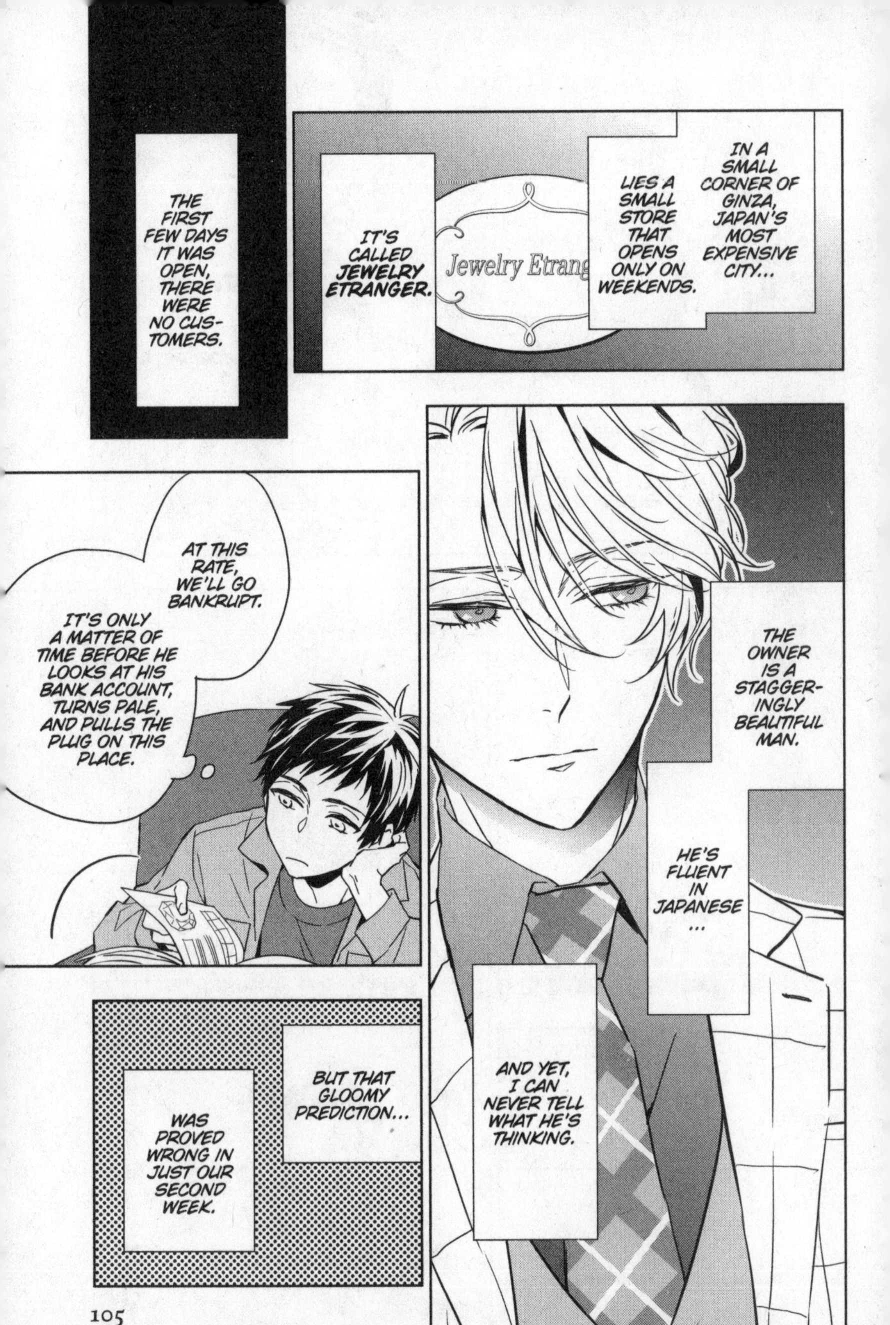
IN A SMALL CORNER OF GINZA, JAPAN'S MOST EXPENSIVE CITY...
LIES A SMALL STORE THAT OPENS ONLY ON WEEKENDS.
Jewelry Etrang
IT'S CALLED JEWELRY ETRANGER.
THE FIRST FEW DAYS IT WAS OPEN, THERE WERE NO CUS-TOMERS.
THE OWNER IS A STAGGER-INGLY BEAUTIFUL MAN.
HE'S FLUENT IN JAPANESE...
AND YET, I CAN NEVER TELL WHAT HE'S THINKING.
AT THIS RATE, WE'LL GO BANKRUPT.
IT'S ONLY A MATTER OF TIME BEFORE HE LOOKS AT HIS BANK ACCOUNT, TURNS PALE, AND PULLS THE PLUG ON THIS PLACE.
BUT THAT GLOOMY PREDICTION...
WAS PROVED WRONG IN JUST OUR SECOND WEEK.

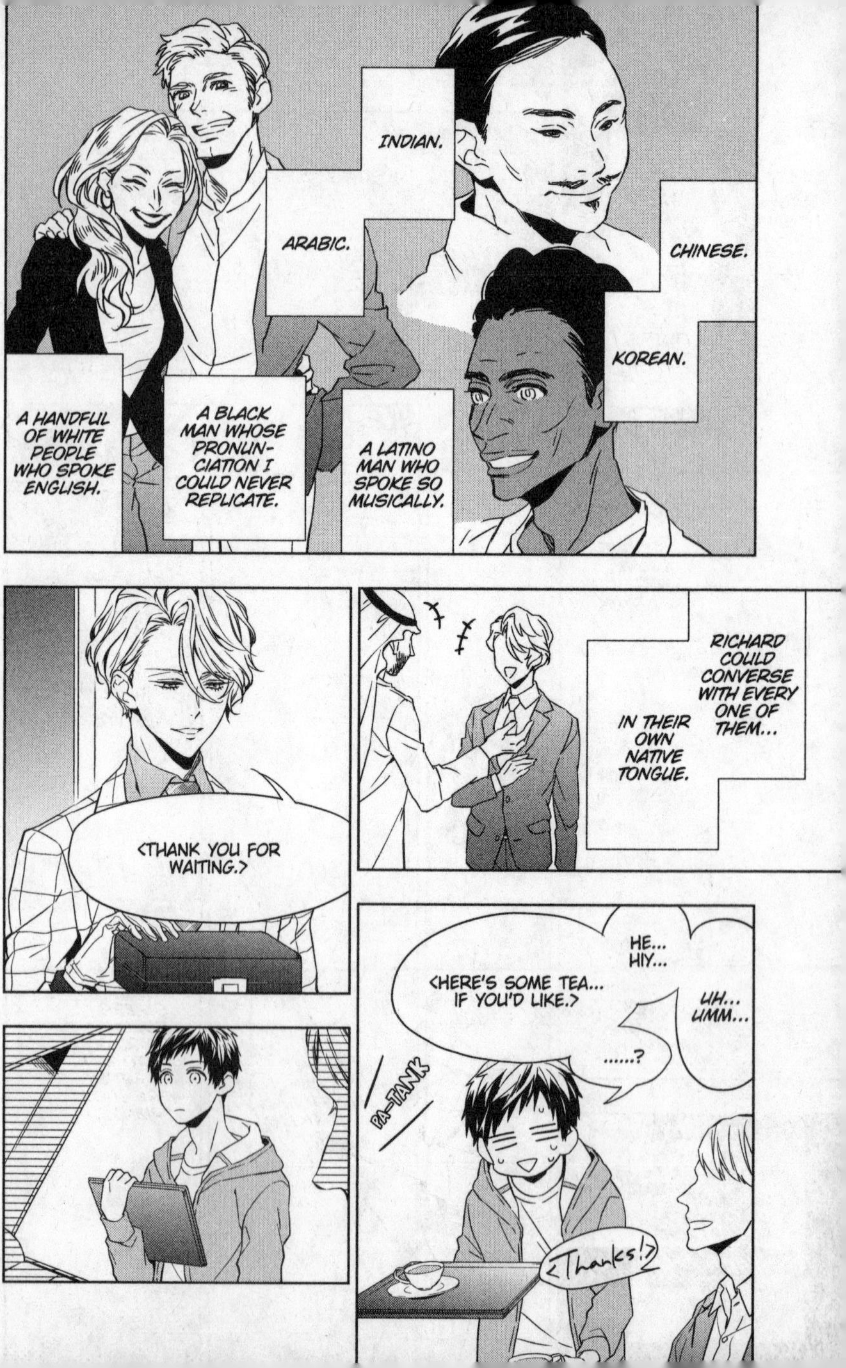
CHINESE.
KOREAN.
INDIAN.
ARABIC.
A LATINO MAN WHO SPOKE SO MUSICALLY.
A BLACK MAN WHOSE PRONUNCIATION I COULD NEVER REPLICATE.
A HANDFUL OF WHITE PEOPLE WHO SPOKE ENGLISH.
RICHARD COULD CONVERSE WITH EVERY ONE OF THEM...
IN THEIR OWN NATIVE TONGUE.
<THANK YOU FOR WAITING.>
HE... HIY...
UH... UMM...
<HERE'S SOME TEA... IF YOU'D LIKE.>
......?
PA-TANK
<Thanks!>

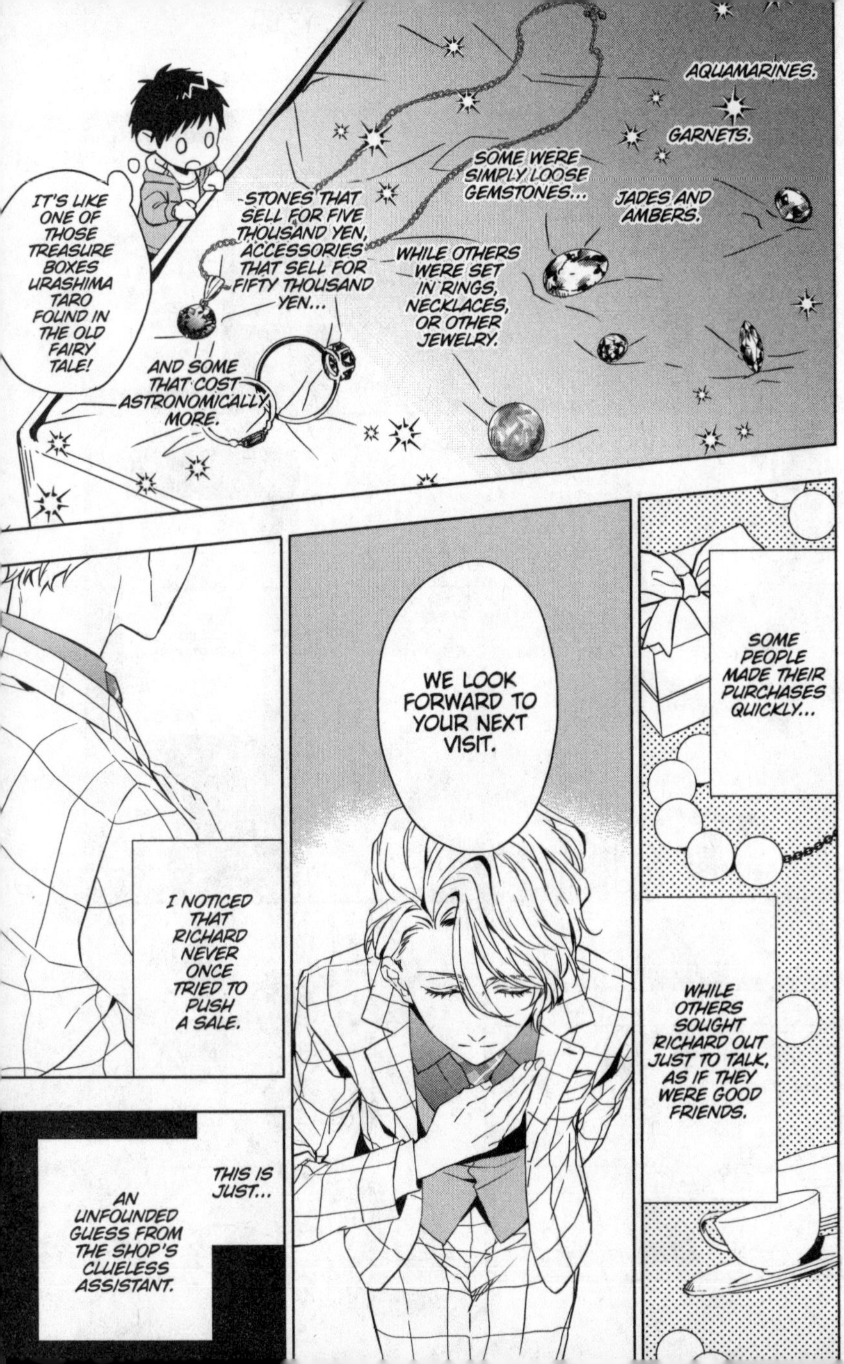
AQUAMARINES.
GARNETS.
JADES AND AMBERS.
SOME WERE SIMPLY LOOSE GEMSTONES...
WHILE OTHERS WERE SET IN RINGS, NECKLACES, OR OTHER JEWELRY.
-STONES THAT SELL FOR FIVE THOUSAND YEN, ACCESSORIES THAT SELL FOR FIFTY THOUSAND YEN...
AND SOME THAT COST ASTRONOMICALLY MORE.
IT'S LIKE ONE OF THOSE TREASURE BOXES URASHIMA TARO FOUND IN THE OLD FAIRY TALE!
SOME PEOPLE MADE THEIR PURCHASES QUICKLY...
WHILE OTHERS SOUGHT RICHARD OUT JUST TO TALK, AS IF THEY WERE GOOD FRIENDS.
WE LOOK FORWARD TO YOUR NEXT VISIT.
I NOTICED THAT RICHARD NEVER ONCE TRIED TO PUSH A SALE.
THIS IS JUST...
AN UNFOUNDED GUESS FROM THE SHOP'S CLUELESS ASSISTANT.

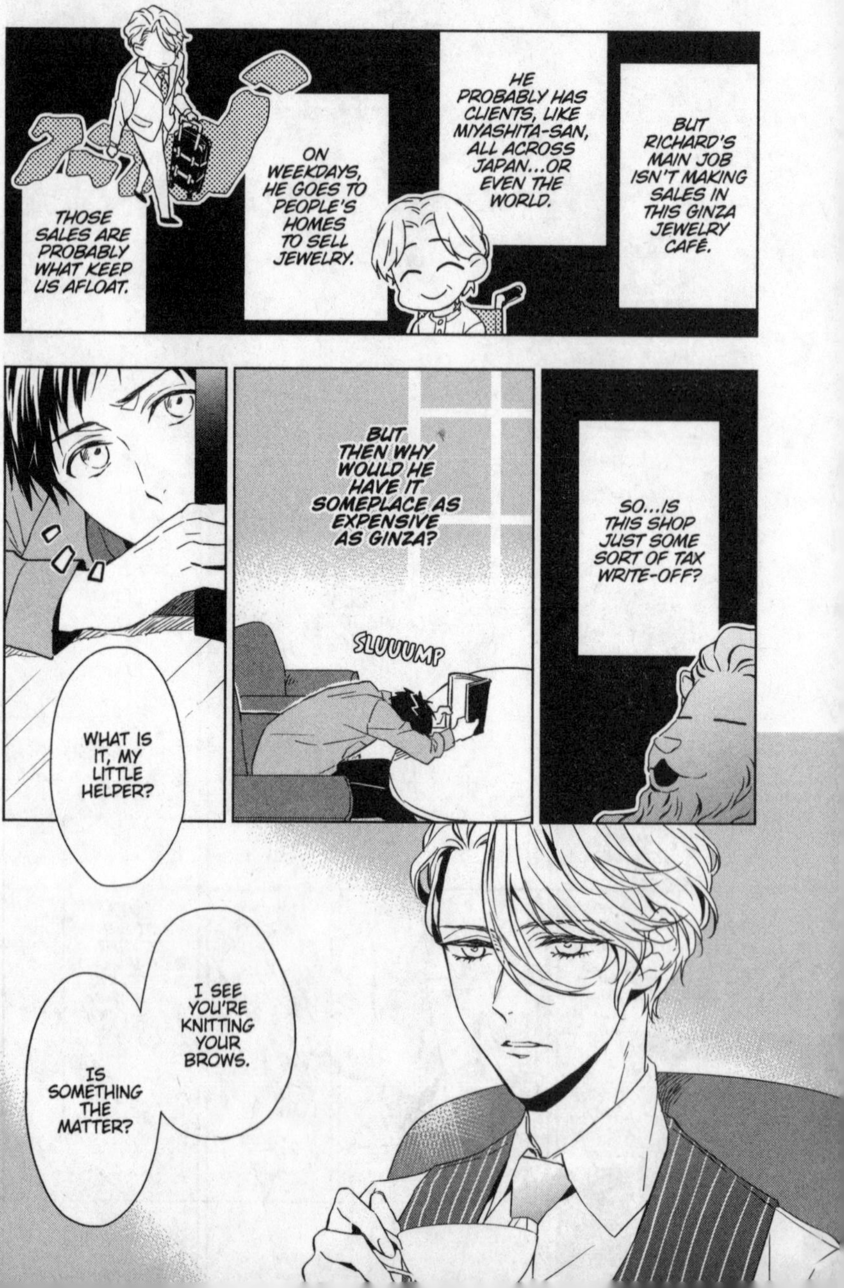

BUT RICHARD'S MAIN JOB ISN'T MAKING SALES IN THIS GINZA JEWELRY CAFÉ.
HE PROBABLY HAS CLIENTS, LIKE MIYASHITA-SAN, ALL ACROSS JAPAN...OR EVEN THE WORLD.
ON WEEKDAYS, HE GOES TO PEOPLE'S HOMES TO SELL JEWELRY.
THOSE SALES ARE PROBABLY WHAT KEEP US AFLOAT.
SO...IS THIS SHOP JUST SOME SORT OF TAX WRITE-OFF?
BUT THEN WHY WOULD HE HAVE IT SOMEPLACE AS EXPENSIVE AS GINZA?
SLUUUMP
WHAT IS IT, MY LITTLE HELPER?
I SEE YOU'RE KNITTING YOUR BROWS.
IS SOMETHING THE MATTER?

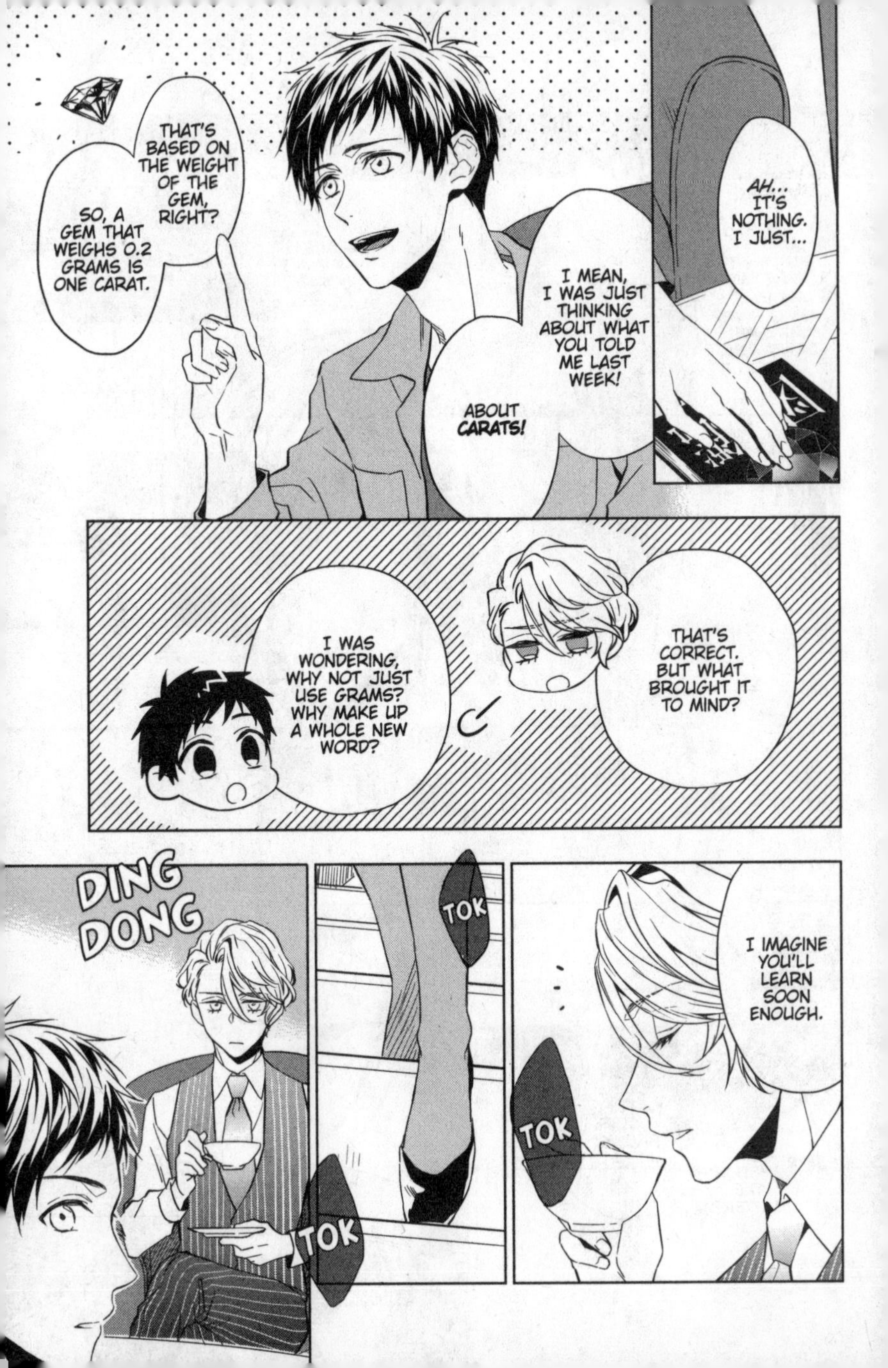

AH... IT'S NOTHING. I JUST...
I MEAN, I WAS JUST THINKING ABOUT WHAT YOU TOLD ME LAST WEEK!
ABOUT CARATS!
THAT'S BASED ON THE WEIGHT OF THE GEM, RIGHT?
SO, A GEM THAT WEIGHS 0.2 GRAMS IS ONE CARAT.
THAT'S CORRECT. BUT WHAT BROUGHT IT TO MIND?
I WAS WONDERING, WHY NOT JUST USE GRAMS? WHY MAKE UP A WHOLE NEW WORD?
I IMAGINE YOU'LL LEARN SOON ENOUGH.
TOK
TOK
TOK
DING DONG
TOK

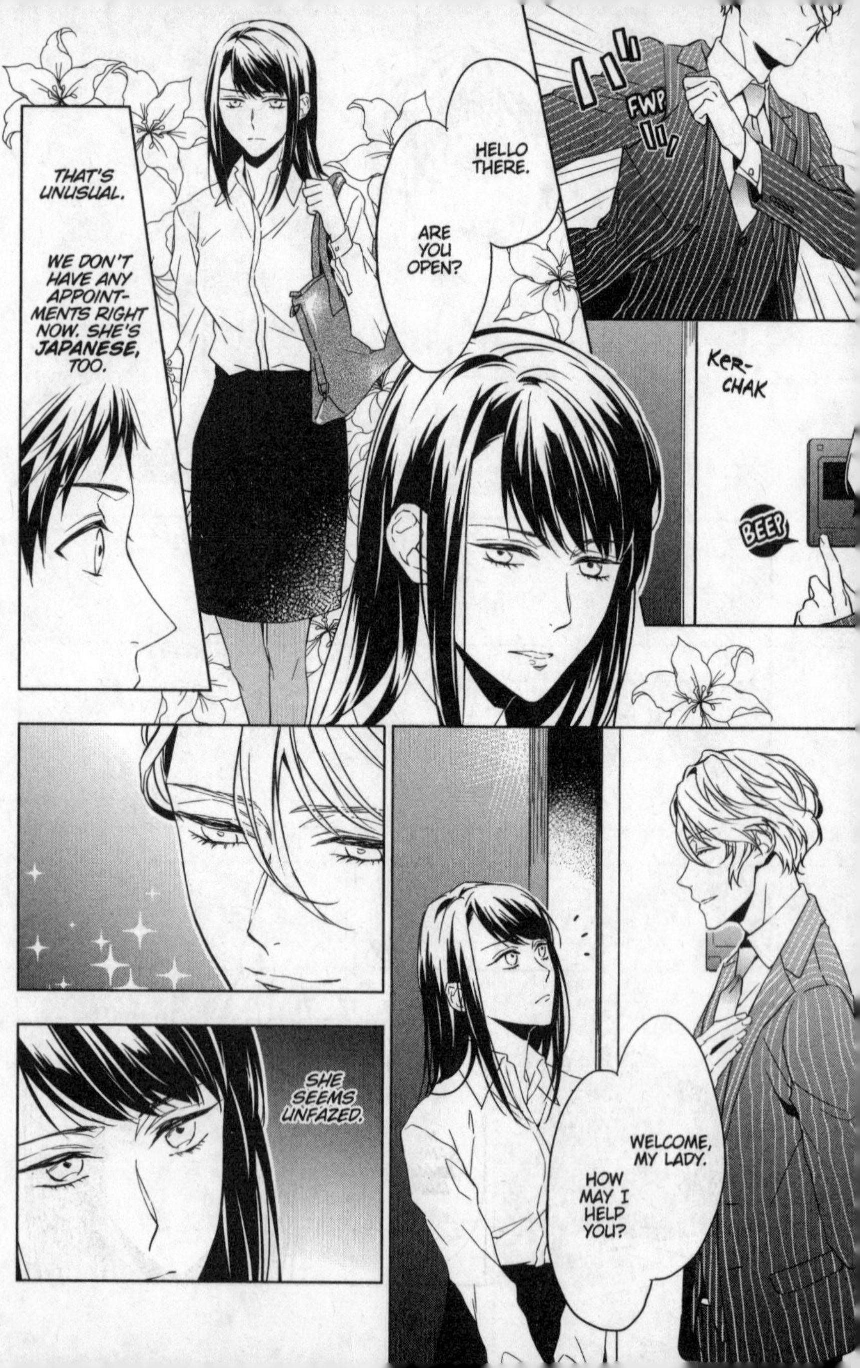
FWP
Ker-CHAK
BEEP
HELLO THERE.
ARE YOU OPEN?
THAT'S UNUSUAL.
WE DON'T HAVE ANY APPOINT-MENTS RIGHT NOW. SHE'S JAPANESE, TOO.
WELCOME, MY LADY.
HOW MAY I HELP YOU?
SHE SEEMS UNFAZED.

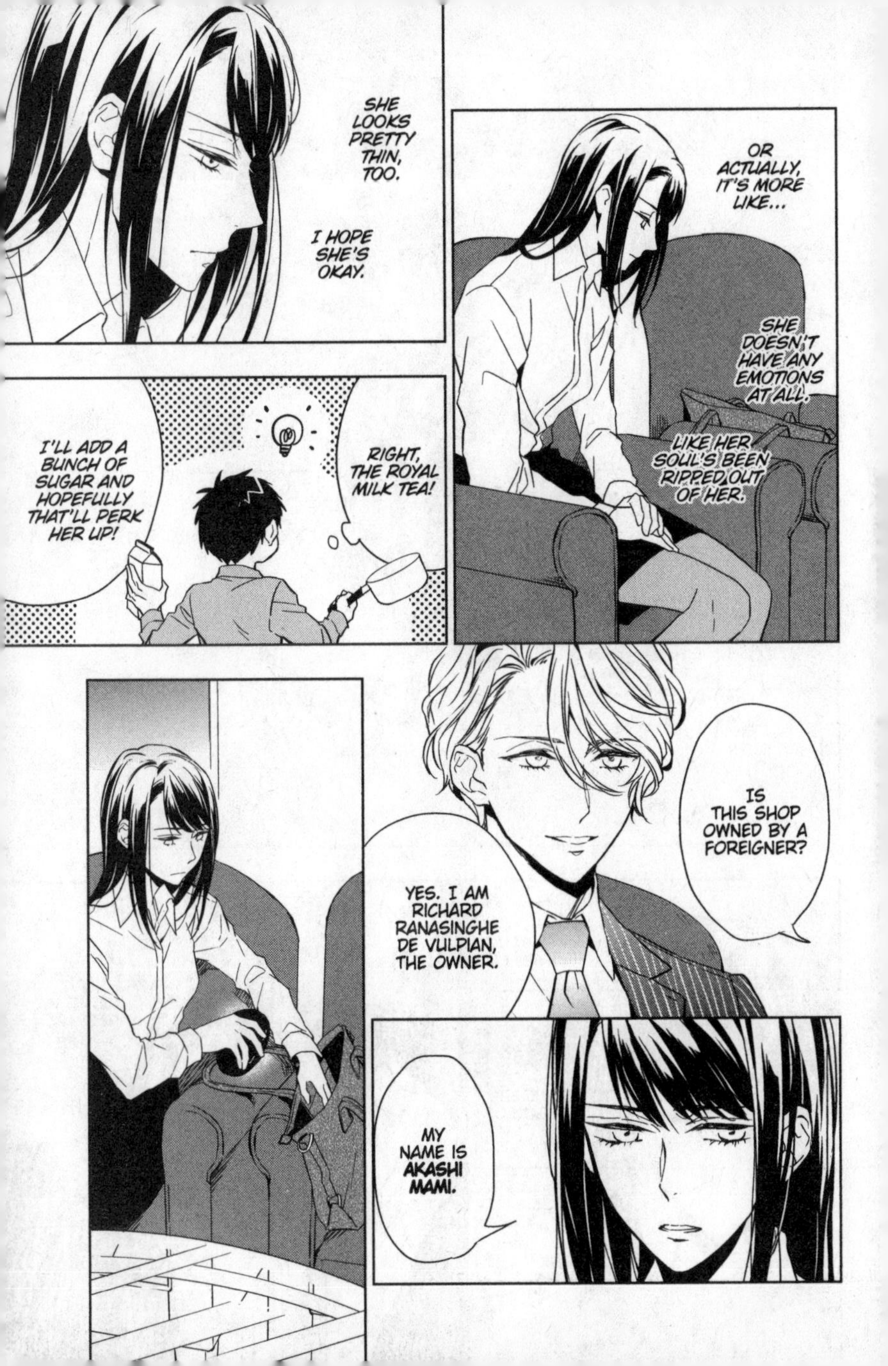
OR ACTUALLY, IT'S MORE LIKE...
SHE DOESN'T HAVE ANY EMOTIONS AT ALL.
LIKE HER SOUL'S BEEN RIPPED OUT OF HER.
SHE LOOKS PRETTY THIN, TOO.
I HOPE SHE'S OKAY.
RIGHT, THE ROYAL MILK TEA!
I'LL ADD A BUNCH OF SUGAR AND HOPEFULLY THAT'LL PERK HER UP!
IS THIS SHOP OWNED BY A FOREIGNER?
YES. I AM RICHARD RANASINGHE DE VULPIAN, THE OWNER.
MY NAME IS AKASHI MAMI.

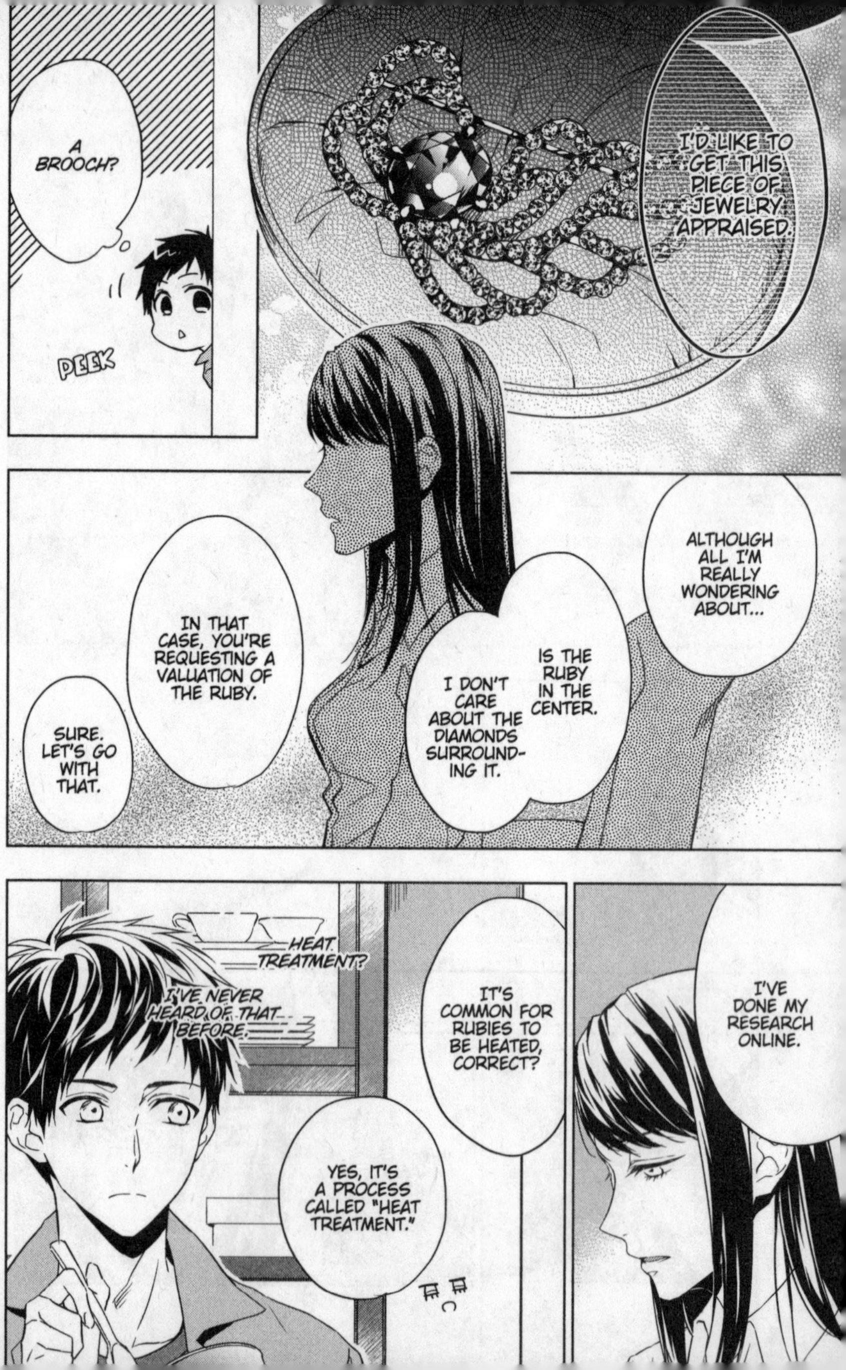
I'D LIKE TO GET THIS PIECE OF JEWELRY APPRAISED.
A BROOCH?
PEEK
ALTHOUGH ALL I'M REALLY WONDERING ABOUT...
IS THE RUBY IN THE CENTER.
I DON'T CARE ABOUT THE DIAMONDS SURROUNDING IT.
IN THAT CASE, YOU'RE REQUESTING A VALUATION OF THE RUBY.
SURE. LET'S GO WITH THAT.
I'VE DONE MY RESEARCH ONLINE.
IT'S COMMON FOR RUBIES TO BE HEATED, CORRECT?
HEAT TREATMENT?
I'VE NEVER HEARD OF THAT BEFORE.
YES, IT'S A PROCESS CALLED "HEAT TREATMENT."

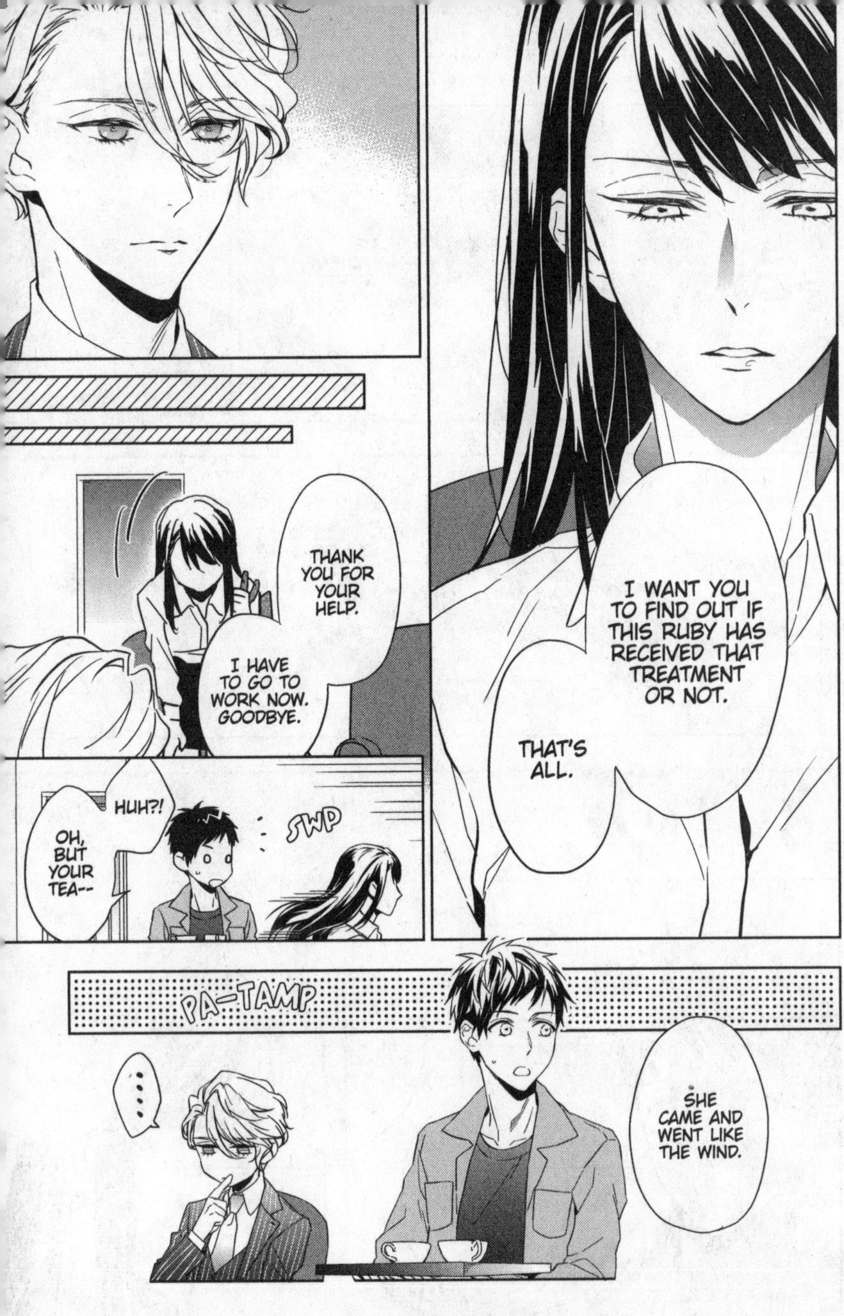
I WANT YOU TO FIND OUT IF THIS RUBY HAS RECEIVED THAT TREATMENT OR NOT.
THAT'S ALL.
THANK YOU FOR YOUR HELP.
I HAVE TO GO TO WORK NOW. GOODBYE.
SWP
HUH?!
OH, BUT YOUR TEA--
PA-TAMP
SHE CAME AND WENT LIKE THE WIND.
....

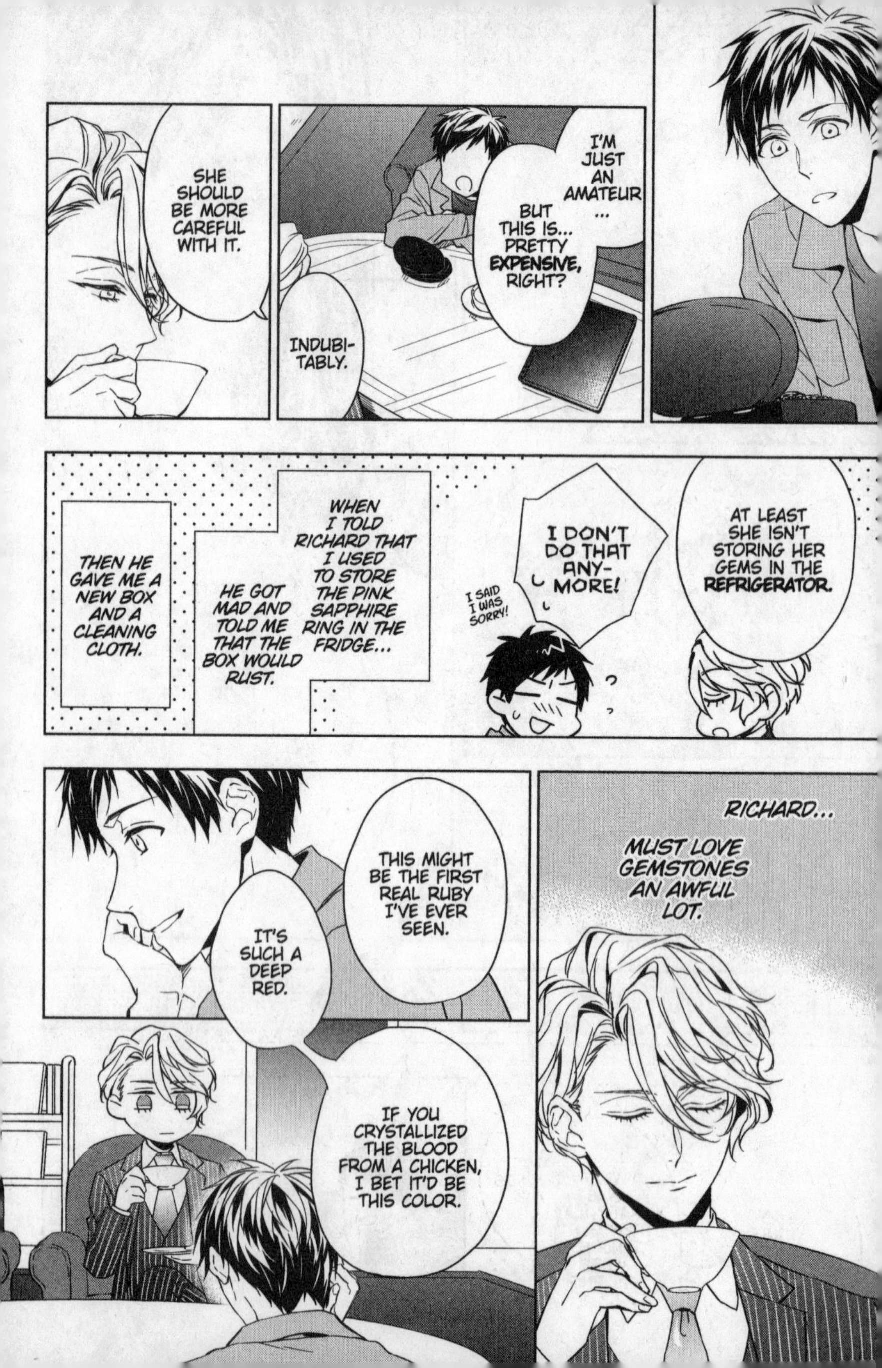
I'M JUST AN AMATEUR ... BUT THIS IS... PRETTY EXPENSIVE, RIGHT?
INDUBI-TABLY.
SHE SHOULD BE MORE CAREFUL WITH IT.
AT LEAST SHE ISN'T STORING HER GEMS IN THE REFRIGERATOR.
I DON'T DO THAT ANY-MORE!
I SAID I WAS SORRY!
WHEN I TOLD RICHARD THAT I USED TO STORE THE PINK SAPPHIRE RING IN THE FRIDGE...
HE GOT MAD AND TOLD ME THAT THE BOX WOULD RUST.
THEN HE GAVE ME A NEW BOX AND A CLEANING CLOTH.
RICHARD...
MUST LOVE GEMSTONES AN AWFUL LOT.
THIS MIGHT BE THE FIRST REAL RUBY I'VE EVER SEEN.
IT'S SUCH A DEEP RED.
IF YOU CRYSTALLIZED THE BLOOD FROM A CHICKEN, I BET IT'D BE THIS COLOR.

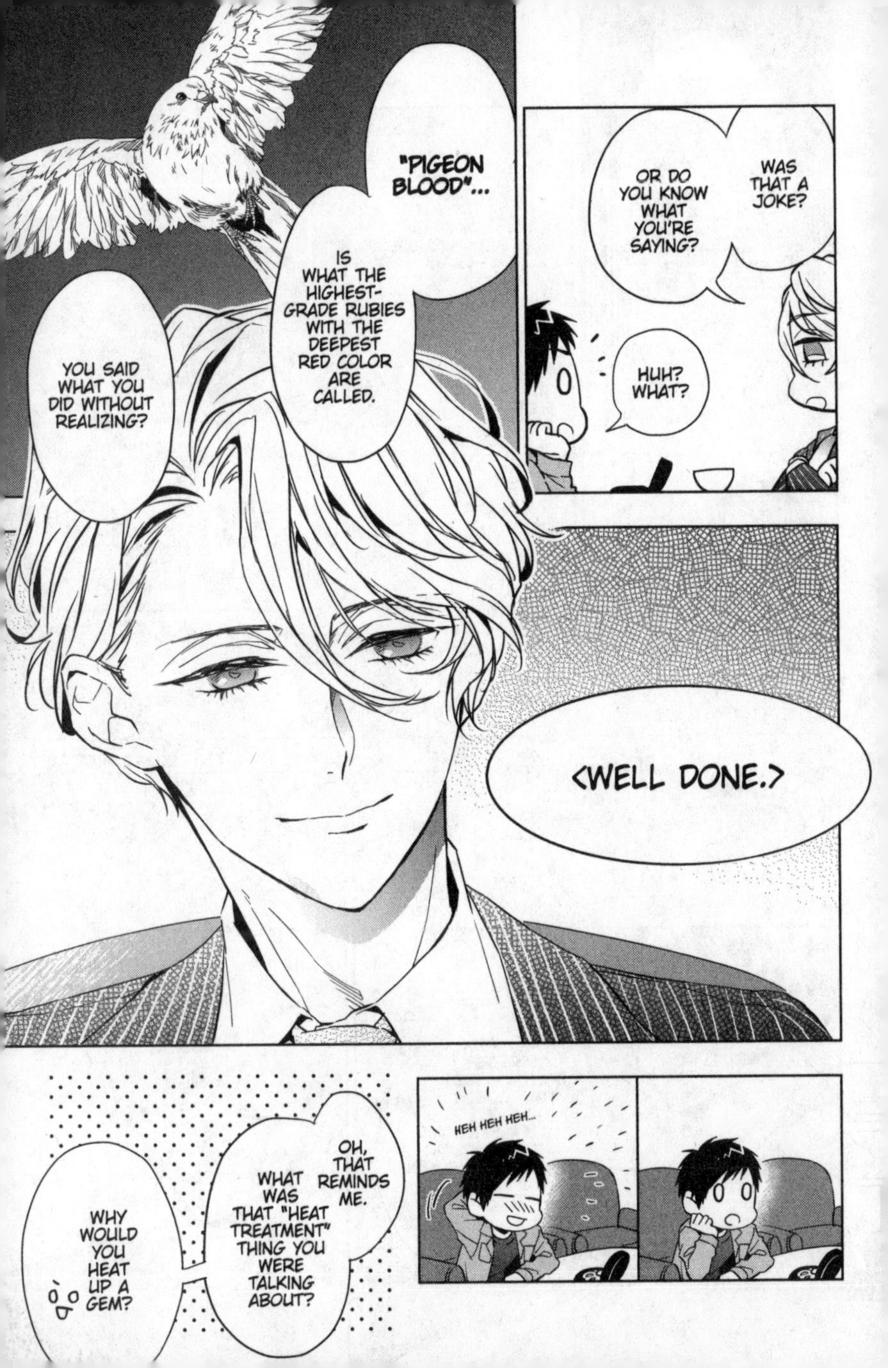
"PIGEON BLOOD"...
IS WHAT THE HIGHEST-GRADE RUBIES WITH THE DEEPEST RED COLOR ARE CALLED.
YOU SAID WHAT YOU DID WITHOUT REALIZING?
WAS THAT A JOKE?
OR DO YOU KNOW WHAT YOU'RE SAYING?
HUH? WHAT?
<WELL DONE.>
HEH HEH HEH...
OH, THAT REMINDS ME.
WHAT WAS THAT "HEAT TREATMENT" THING YOU WERE TALKING ABOUT?
WHY WOULD YOU HEAT UP A GEM?

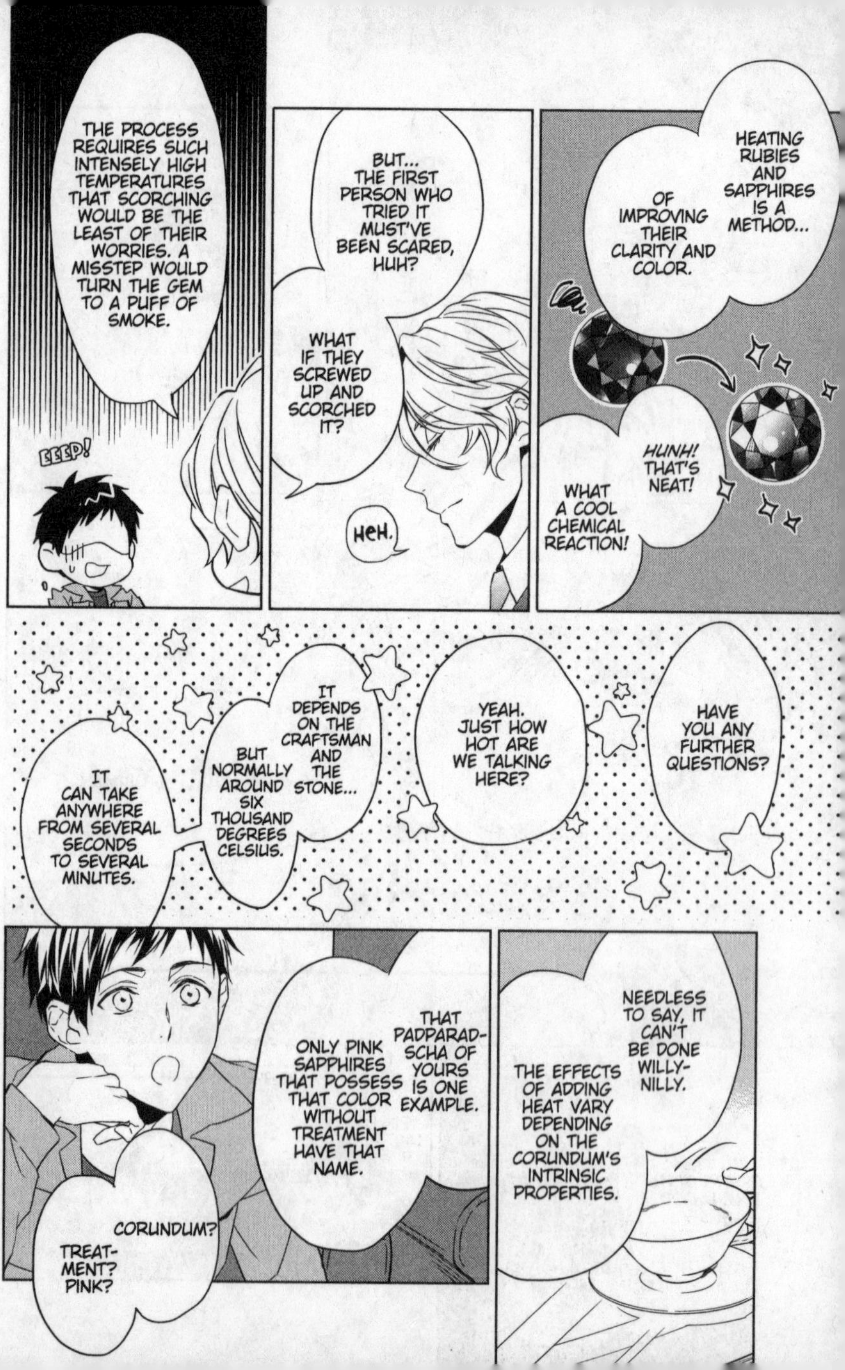
HEATING RUBIES AND SAPPHIRES IS A METHOD...
OF IMPROVING THEIR CLARITY AND COLOR.
HUNH! THAT'S NEAT!
WHAT A COOL CHEMICAL REACTION!
BUT... THE FIRST PERSON WHO TRIED IT MUST'VE BEEN SCARED, HUH?
WHAT IF THEY SCREWED UP AND SCORCHED IT?
HEH.
THE PROCESS REQUIRES SUCH INTENSELY HIGH TEMPERATURES THAT SCORCHING WOULD BE THE LEAST OF THEIR WORRIES. A MISSTEP WOULD TURN THE GEM TO A PUFF OF SMOKE.
EEEP!
HAVE YOU ANY FURTHER QUESTIONS?
YEAH. JUST HOW HOT ARE WE TALKING HERE?
IT DEPENDS ON THE CRAFTSMAN AND THE STONE...
BUT NORMALLY AROUND SIX THOUSAND DEGREES CELSIUS.
IT CAN TAKE ANYWHERE FROM SEVERAL SECONDS TO SEVERAL MINUTES.
NEEDLESS TO SAY, IT CAN'T BE DONE WILLY-NILLY.
THE EFFECTS OF ADDING HEAT VARY DEPENDING ON THE CORUNDUM'S INTRINSIC PROPERTIES.
THAT PADPARAD-SCHA OF YOURS IS ONE EXAMPLE.
ONLY PINK SAPPHIRES THAT POSSESS THAT COLOR WITHOUT TREATMENT HAVE THAT NAME.
CORUNDUM?
TREAT-MENT? PINK?

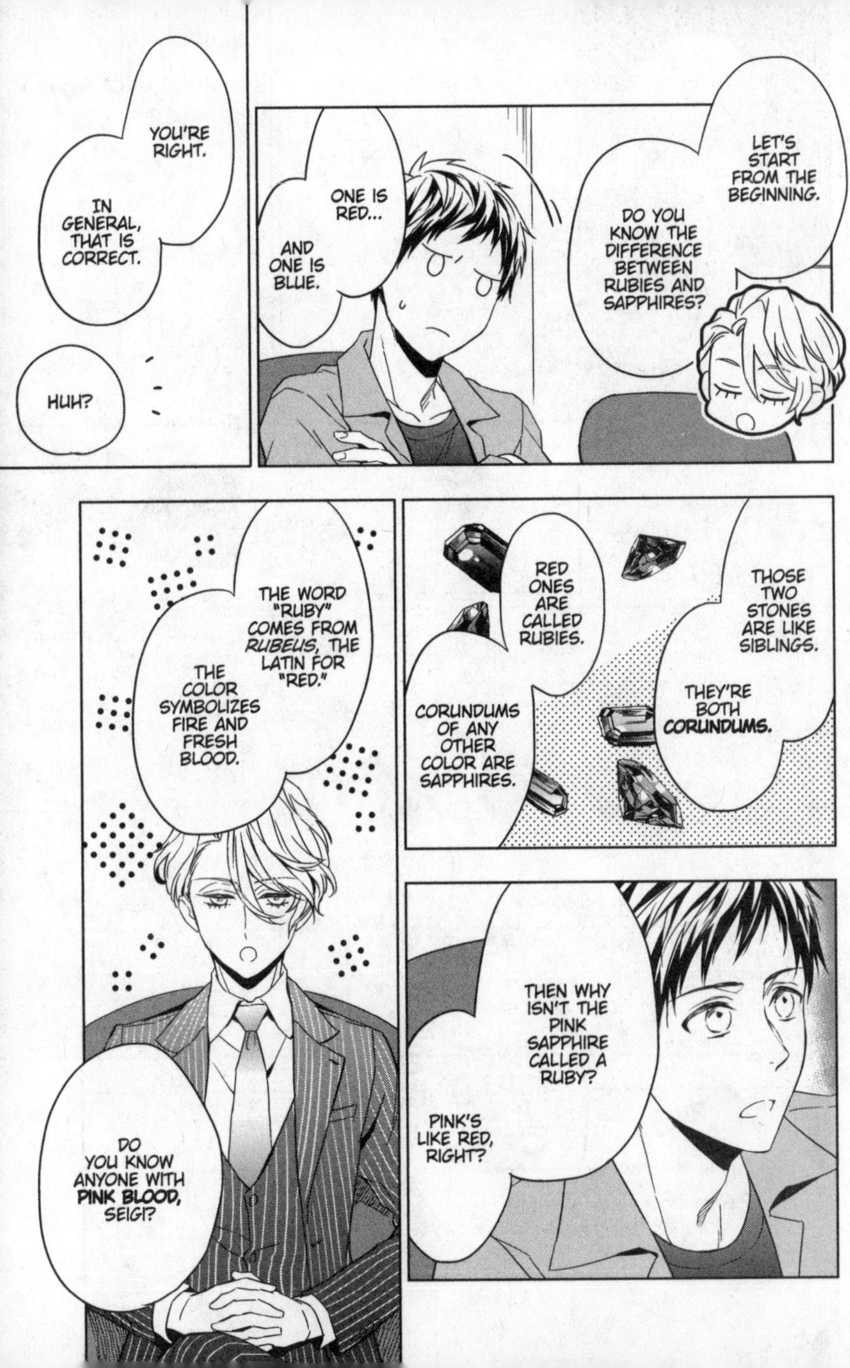
LET'S START FROM THE BEGINNING.
DO YOU KNOW THE DIFFERENCE BETWEEN RUBIES AND SAPPHIRES?
ONE IS RED...
AND ONE IS BLUE.
YOU'RE RIGHT.
IN GENERAL, THAT IS CORRECT.
HUH?
THOSE TWO STONES ARE LIKE SIBLINGS.
THEY'RE BOTH **CORUNDUMS.**
RED ONES ARE CALLED RUBIES.
CORUNDUMS OF ANY OTHER COLOR ARE SAPPHIRES.
THEN WHY ISN'T THE PINK SAPPHIRE CALLED A RUBY?
PINK'S LIKE RED, RIGHT?
THE WORD "RUBY" COMES FROM *RUBEUS*, THE LATIN FOR "RED."
THE COLOR SYMBOLIZES FIRE AND FRESH BLOOD.
DO YOU KNOW ANYONE WITH **PINK BLOOD,** SEIGI?

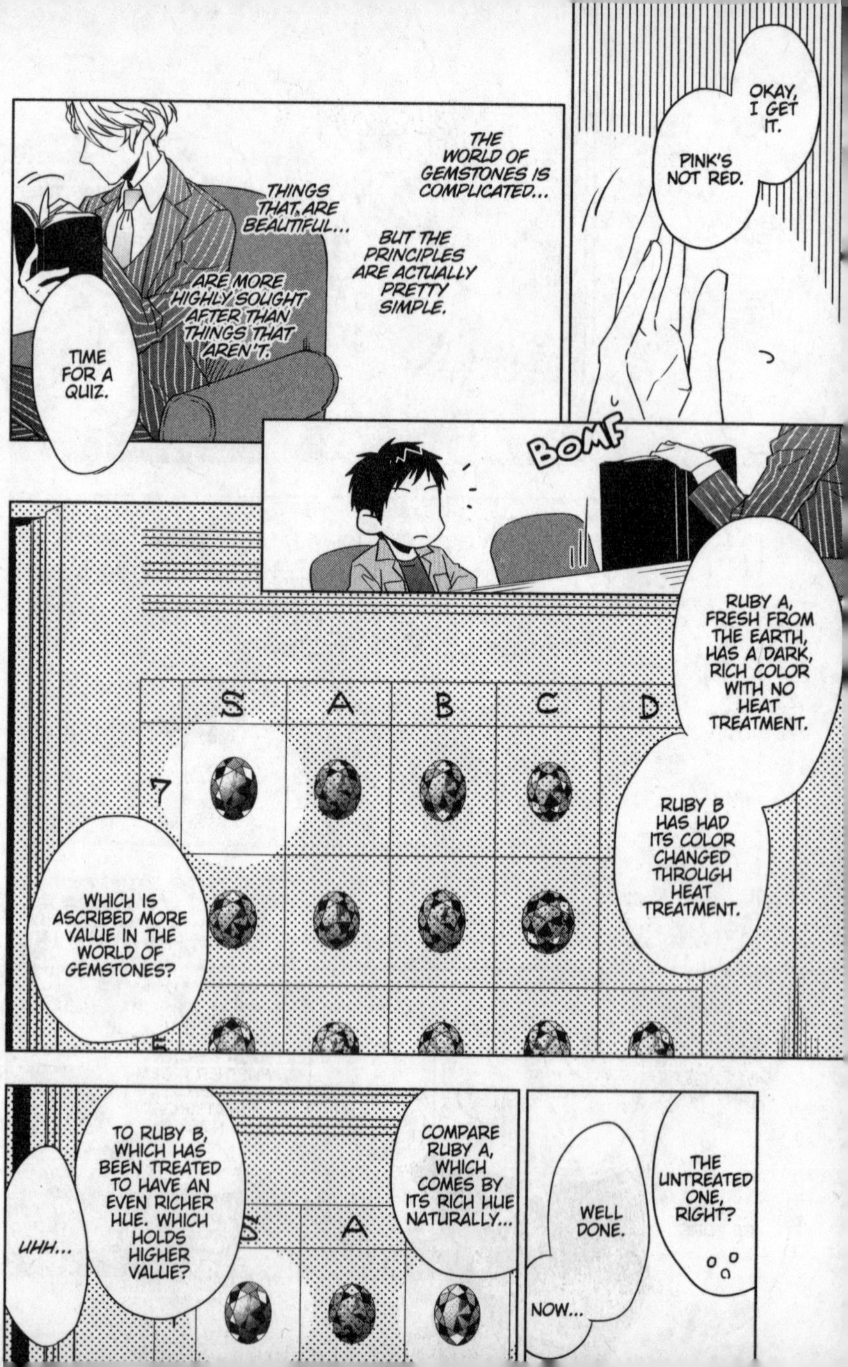
OKAY, I GET IT.
PINK'S NOT RED.
THE WORLD OF GEMSTONES IS COMPLICATED...
BUT THE PRINCIPLES ARE ACTUALLY PRETTY SIMPLE.
THINGS THAT ARE BEAUTIFUL...
ARE MORE HIGHLY SOUGHT AFTER THAN THINGS THAT AREN'T.
TIME FOR A QUIZ.
BOMF
RUBY A, FRESH FROM THE EARTH, HAS A DARK, RICH COLOR WITH NO HEAT TREATMENT.
RUBY B HAS HAD ITS COLOR CHANGED THROUGH HEAT TREATMENT.
S A B C D
7
WHICH IS ASCRIBED MORE VALUE IN THE WORLD OF GEMSTONES?
THE UNTREATED ONE, RIGHT?
WELL DONE.
NOW...
COMPARE RUBY A, WHICH COMES BY ITS RICH HUE NATURALLY...
TO RUBY B, WHICH HAS BEEN TREATED TO HAVE AN EVEN RICHER HUE. WHICH HOLDS HIGHER VALUE?
UHH...

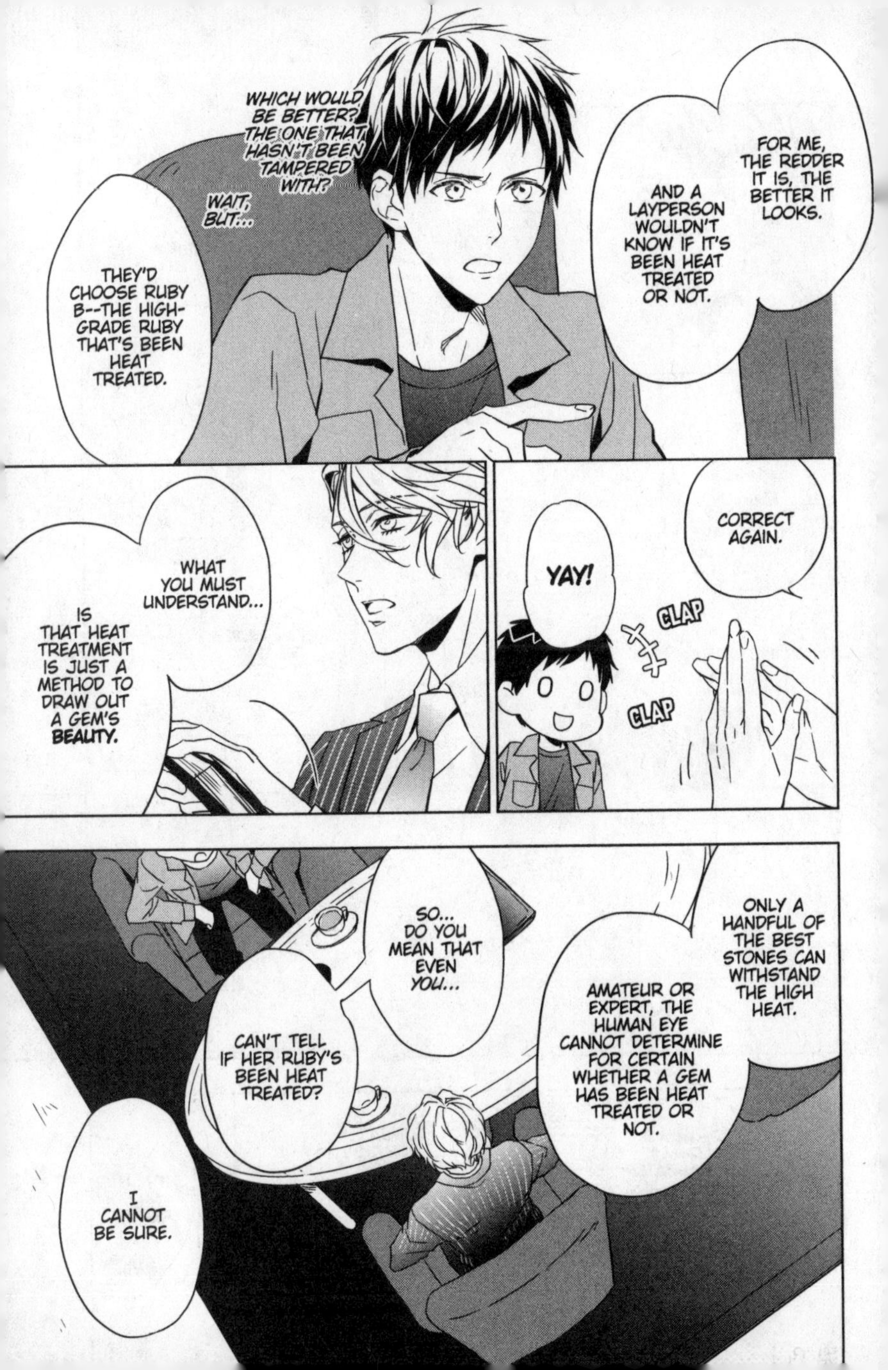
FOR ME, THE REDDER IT IS, THE BETTER IT LOOKS.
AND A LAYPERSON WOULDN'T KNOW IF IT'S BEEN HEAT TREATED OR NOT.
WHICH WOULD BE BETTER? THE ONE THAT HASN'T BEEN TAMPERED WITH?
WAIT, BUT...
THEY'D CHOOSE RUBY B--THE HIGH-GRADE RUBY THAT'S BEEN HEAT TREATED.
CORRECT AGAIN.
YAY!
CLAP
CLAP
WHAT YOU MUST UNDERSTAND...
IS THAT HEAT TREATMENT IS JUST A METHOD TO DRAW OUT A GEM'S **BEAUTY**.
ONLY A HANDFUL OF THE BEST STONES CAN WITHSTAND THE HIGH HEAT.
AMATEUR OR EXPERT, THE HUMAN EYE CANNOT DETERMINE FOR CERTAIN WHETHER A GEM HAS BEEN HEAT TREATED OR NOT.
SO... DO YOU MEAN THAT EVEN *YOU*...
CAN'T TELL IF HER RUBY'S BEEN HEAT TREATED?
I CANNOT BE SURE.

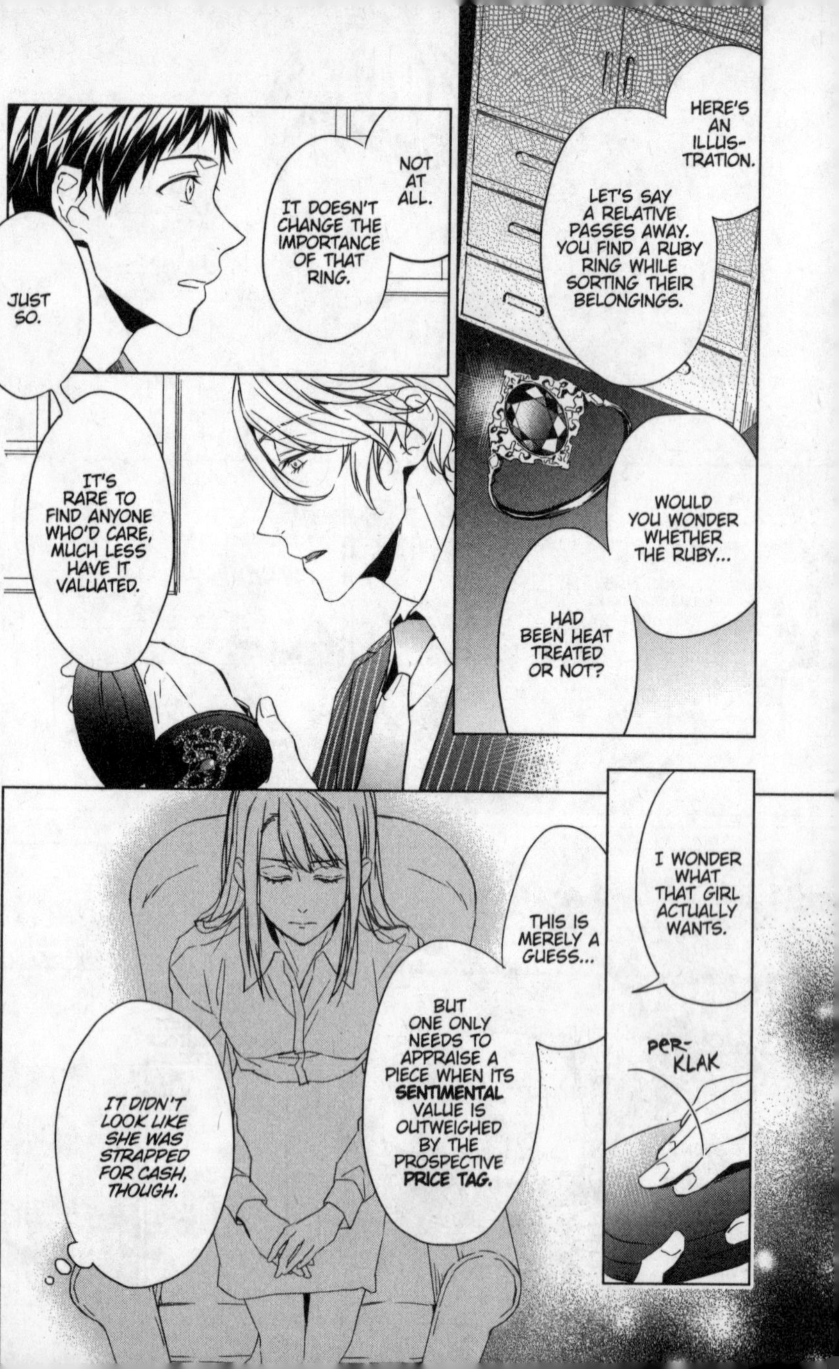
HERE'S AN ILLUSTRATION.
LET'S SAY A RELATIVE PASSES AWAY. YOU FIND A RUBY RING WHILE SORTING THEIR BELONGINGS.
WOULD YOU WONDER WHETHER THE RUBY...
HAD BEEN HEAT TREATED OR NOT?
NOT AT ALL.
IT DOESN'T CHANGE THE IMPORTANCE OF THAT RING.
JUST SO.
IT'S RARE TO FIND ANYONE WHO'D CARE, MUCH LESS HAVE IT VALUATED.
I WONDER WHAT THAT GIRL ACTUALLY WANTS.
PER-KLAK
THIS IS MERELY A GUESS...
BUT ONE ONLY NEEDS TO APPRAISE A PIECE WHEN ITS **SENTIMENTAL** VALUE IS OUTWEIGHED BY THE PROSPECTIVE **PRICE TAG.**
IT DIDN'T LOOK LIKE SHE WAS STRAPPED FOR CASH, THOUGH.

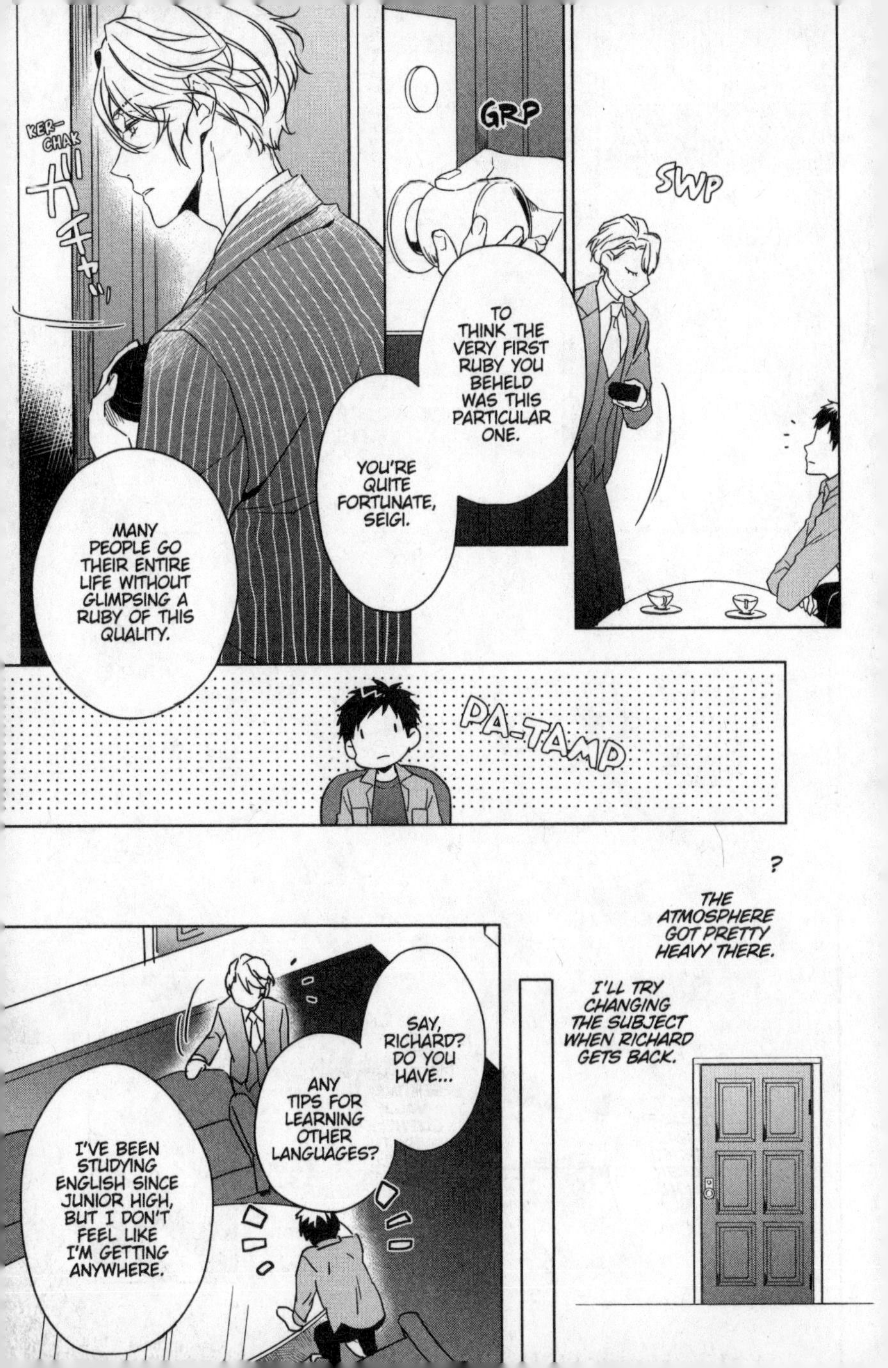
SWP
GRP
TO THINK THE VERY FIRST RUBY YOU BEHELD WAS THIS PARTICULAR ONE.
YOU'RE QUITE FORTUNATE, SEIGI.
KER-CHAK
MANY PEOPLE GO THEIR ENTIRE LIFE WITHOUT GLIMPSING A RUBY OF THIS QUALITY.
PA-TAMP
?
THE ATMOSPHERE GOT PRETTY HEAVY THERE.
I'LL TRY CHANGING THE SUBJECT WHEN RICHARD GETS BACK.
SAY, RICHARD? DO YOU HAVE...
ANY TIPS FOR LEARNING OTHER LANGUAGES?
I'VE BEEN STUDYING ENGLISH SINCE JUNIOR HIGH, BUT I DON'T FEEL LIKE I'M GETTING ANYWHERE.

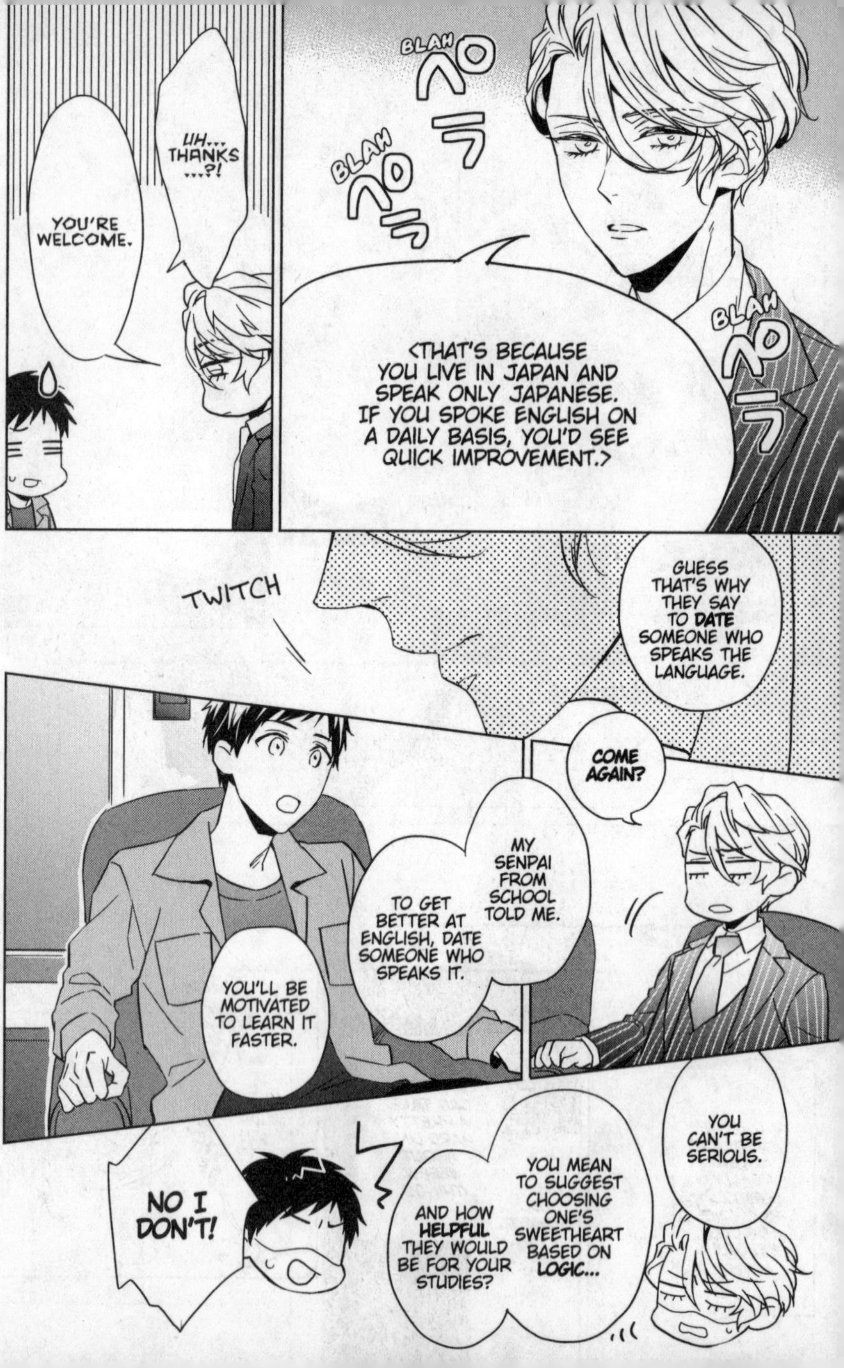
BLAH ヘラ
BLAH ヘラ
BLAH ヘラ
<THAT'S BECAUSE YOU LIVE IN JAPAN AND SPEAK ONLY JAPANESE. IF YOU SPOKE ENGLISH ON A DAILY BASIS, YOU'D SEE QUICK IMPROVEMENT.>
UH... THANKS ...?!
YOU'RE WELCOME.
GUESS THAT'S WHY THEY SAY TO **DATE** SOMEONE WHO SPEAKS THE LANGUAGE.
TWITCH
COME AGAIN?
MY SENPAI FROM SCHOOL TOLD ME.
TO GET BETTER AT ENGLISH, DATE SOMEONE WHO SPEAKS IT.
YOU'LL BE MOTIVATED TO LEARN IT FASTER.
YOU CAN'T BE SERIOUS.
YOU MEAN TO SUGGEST CHOOSING ONE'S SWEETHEART BASED ON **LOGIC...**
AND HOW **HELPFUL** THEY WOULD BE FOR YOUR STUDIES?
NO I DON'T!

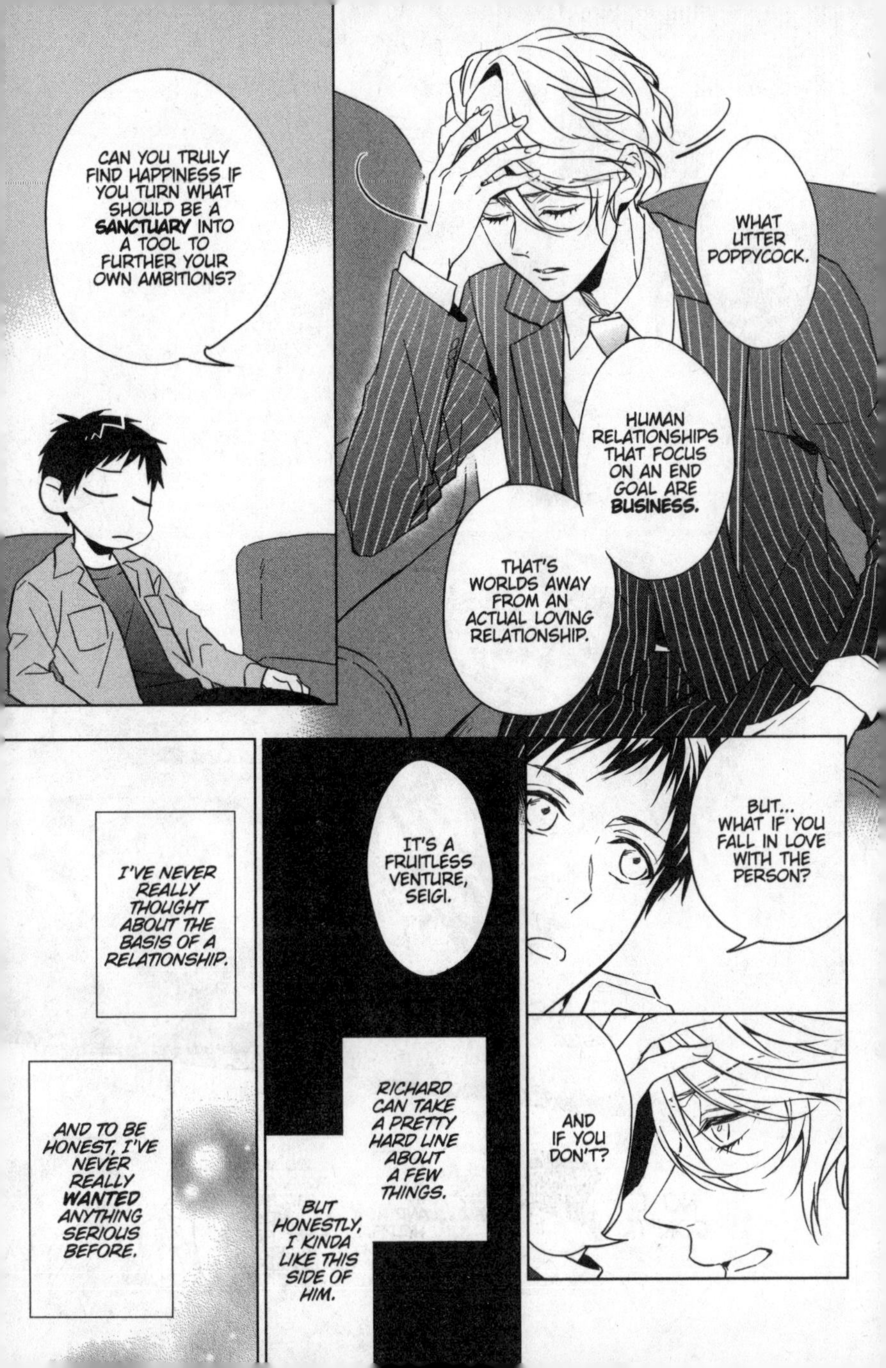
WHAT UTTER POPPYCOCK.
HUMAN RELATIONSHIPS THAT FOCUS ON AN END GOAL ARE **BUSINESS.**
THAT'S WORLDS AWAY FROM AN ACTUAL LOVING RELATIONSHIP.
CAN YOU TRULY FIND HAPPINESS IF YOU TURN WHAT SHOULD BE A **SANCTUARY** INTO A TOOL TO FURTHER YOUR OWN AMBITIONS?
BUT... WHAT IF YOU FALL IN LOVE WITH THE PERSON?
AND IF YOU DON'T?
IT'S A FRUITLESS VENTURE, SEIGI.
RICHARD CAN TAKE A PRETTY HARD LINE ABOUT A FEW THINGS.
BUT HONESTLY, I KINDA LIKE THIS SIDE OF HIM.
I'VE NEVER REALLY THOUGHT ABOUT THE BASIS OF A RELATIONSHIP.
*AND TO BE HONEST, I'VE NEVER REALLY **WANTED** ANYTHING SERIOUS BEFORE.*

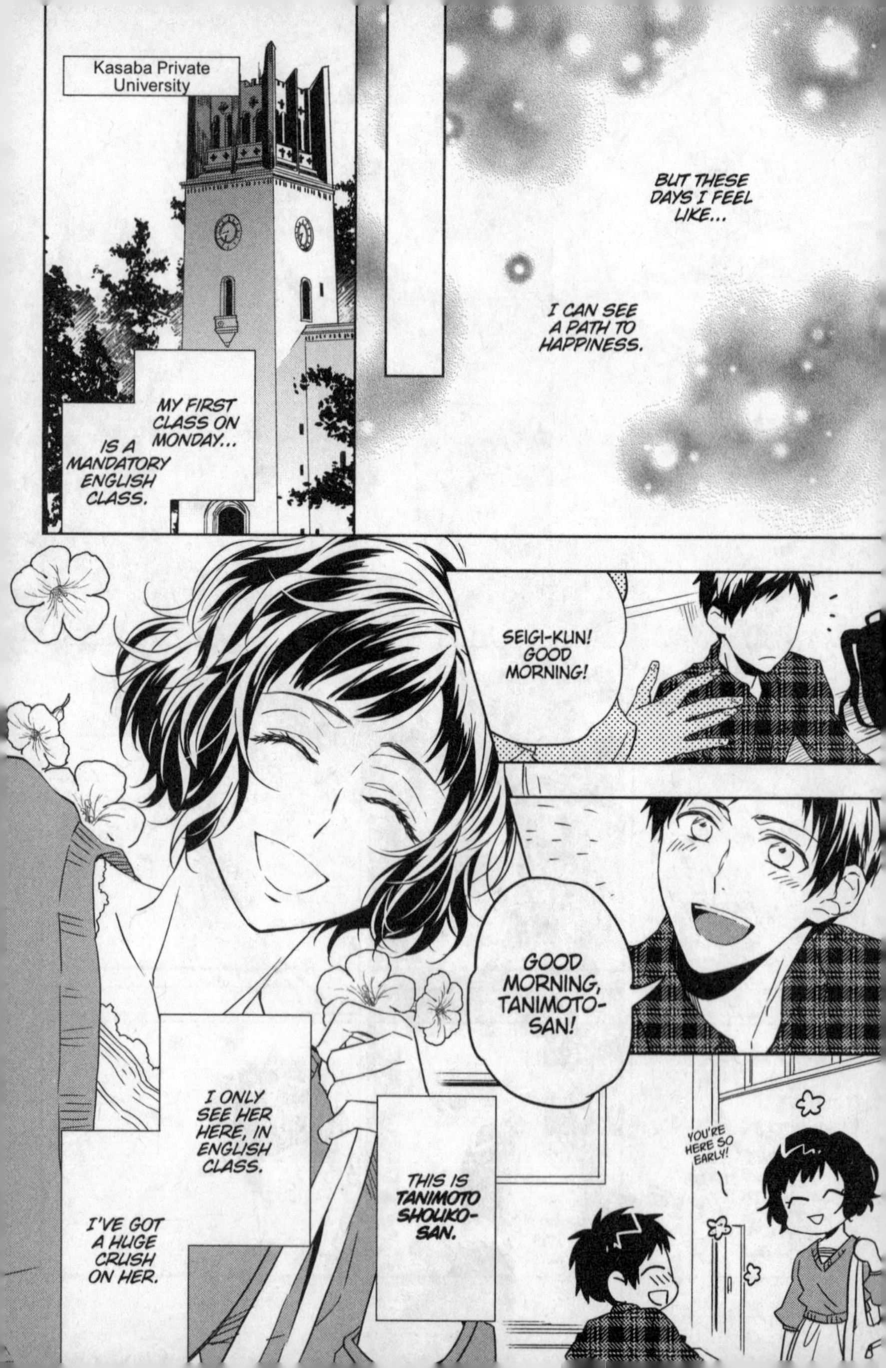
BUT THESE DAYS I FEEL LIKE...
I CAN SEE A PATH TO HAPPINESS.
Kasaba Private University
MY FIRST CLASS ON MONDAY...
IS A MANDATORY ENGLISH CLASS.
SEIGI-KUN! GOOD MORNING!
GOOD MORNING, TANIMOTO-SAN!
YOU'RE HERE SO EARLY!
THIS IS TANIMOTO SHOUKO-SAN.
I ONLY SEE HER HERE, IN ENGLISH CLASS.
I'VE GOT A HUGE CRUSH ON HER.

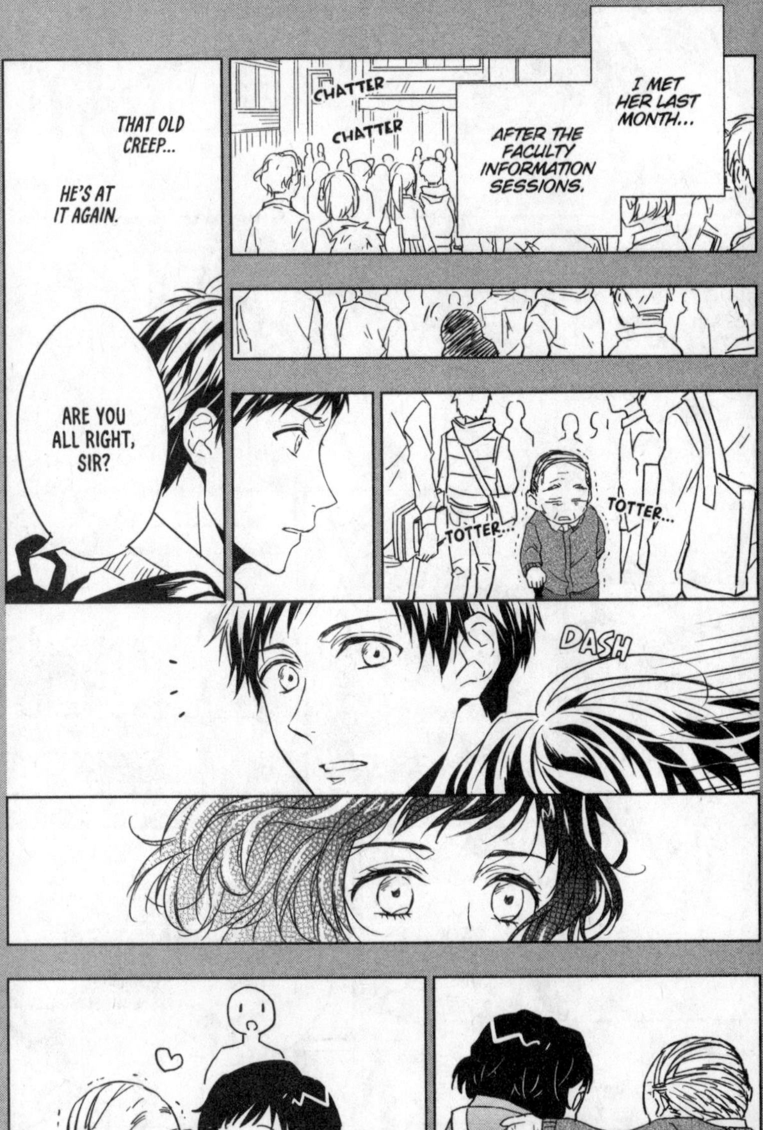
I MET HER LAST MONTH...
AFTER THE FACULTY INFORMATION SESSIONS.
CHATTER
CHATTER
TOTTER...
TOTTER...
THAT OLD CREEP...
HE'S AT IT AGAIN.
ARE YOU ALL RIGHT, SIR?
DASH

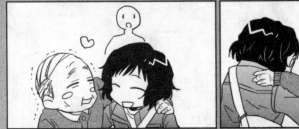

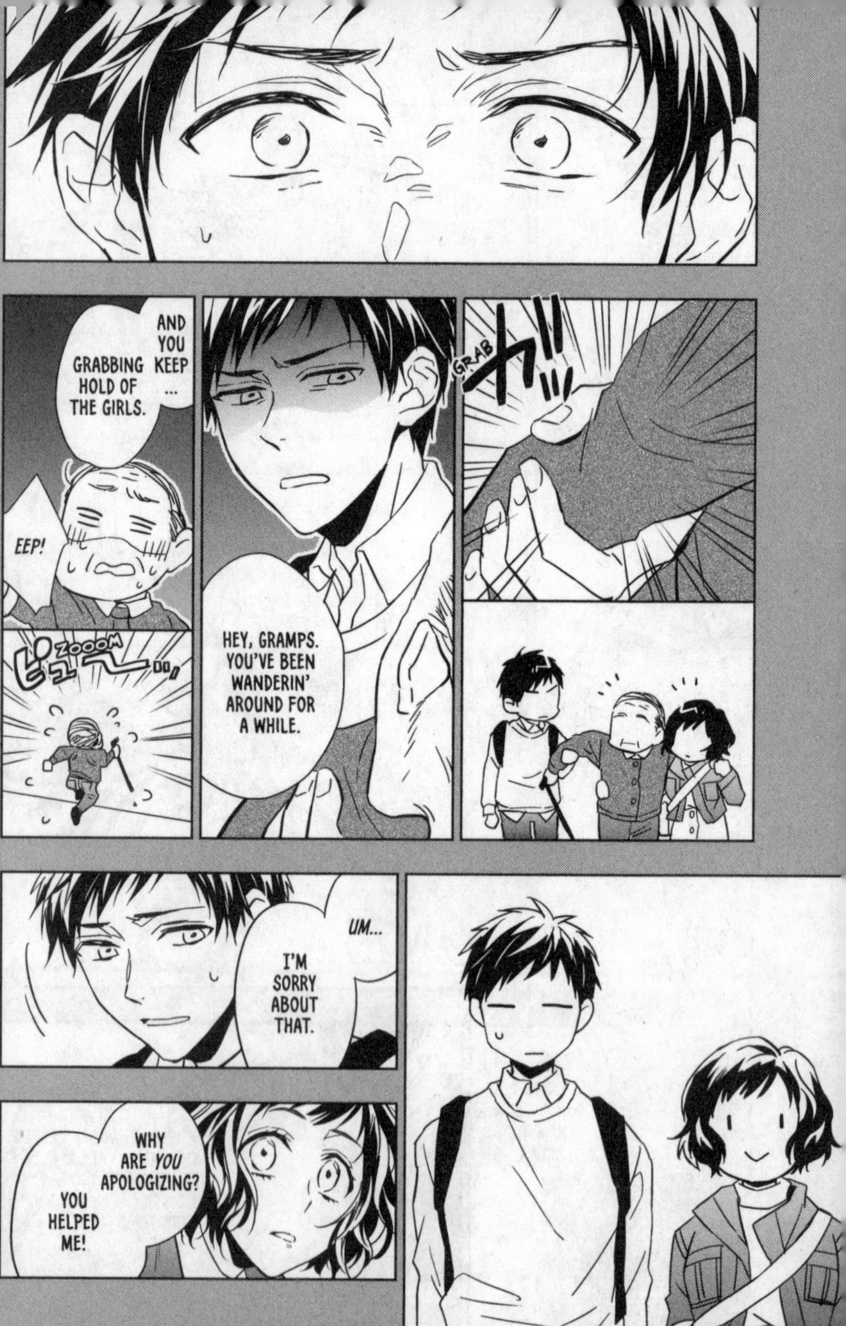
GRAB
HEY, GRAMPS. YOU'VE BEEN WANDERIN' AROUND FOR A WHILE.
AND YOU KEEP... GRABBING HOLD OF THE GIRLS.
EEP!
ZOOOM
UM...
I'M SORRY ABOUT THAT.
WHY ARE *YOU* APOLOGIZING?
YOU HELPED ME!

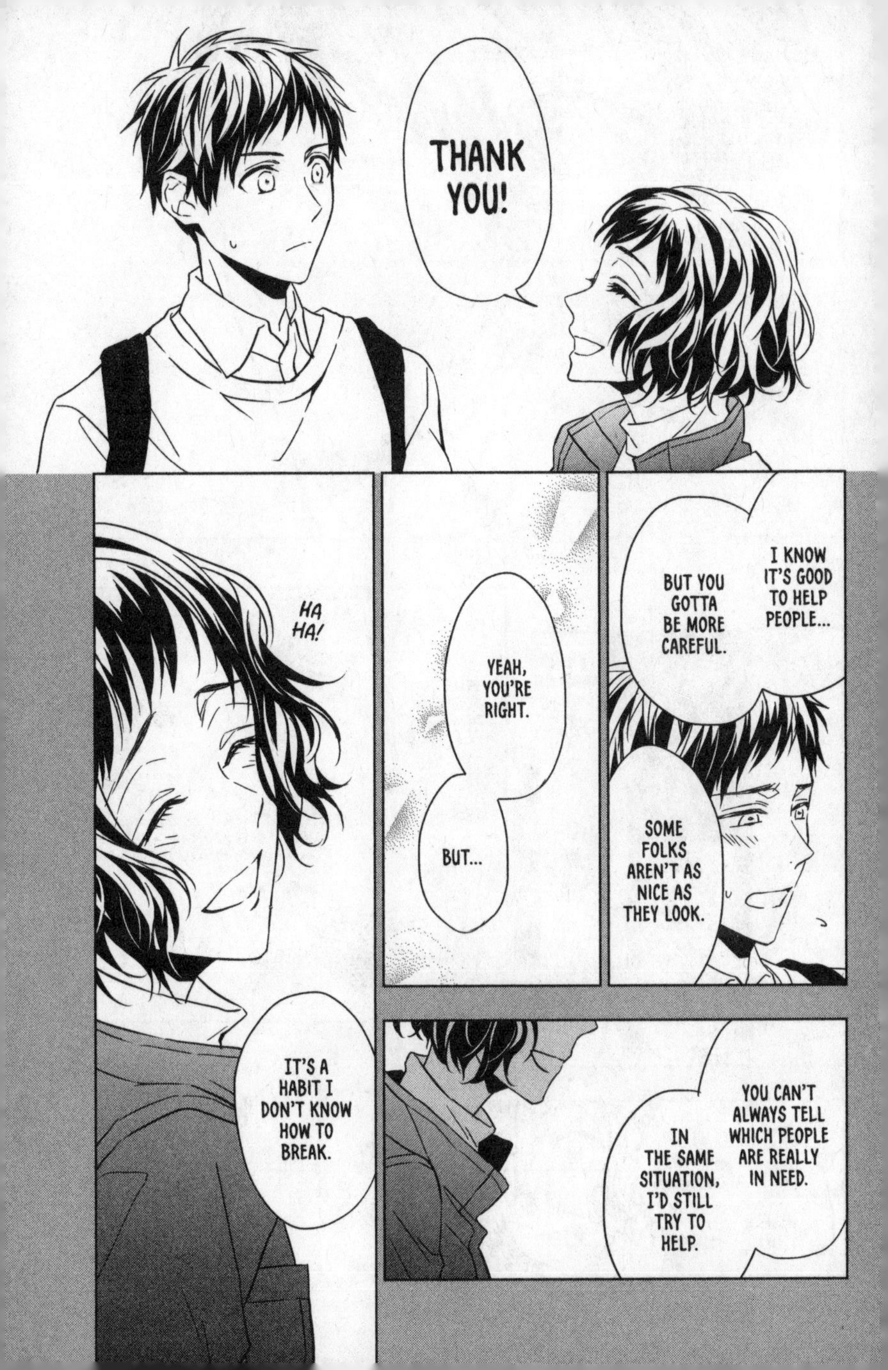
THANK YOU!
I KNOW IT'S GOOD TO HELP PEOPLE...
BUT YOU GOTTA BE MORE CAREFUL.
SOME FOLKS AREN'T AS NICE AS THEY LOOK.
YEAH, YOU'RE RIGHT.
BUT...
YOU CAN'T ALWAYS TELL WHICH PEOPLE ARE REALLY IN NEED.
IN THE SAME SITUATION, I'D STILL TRY TO HELP.
HA HA!
IT'S A HABIT I DON'T KNOW HOW TO BREAK.

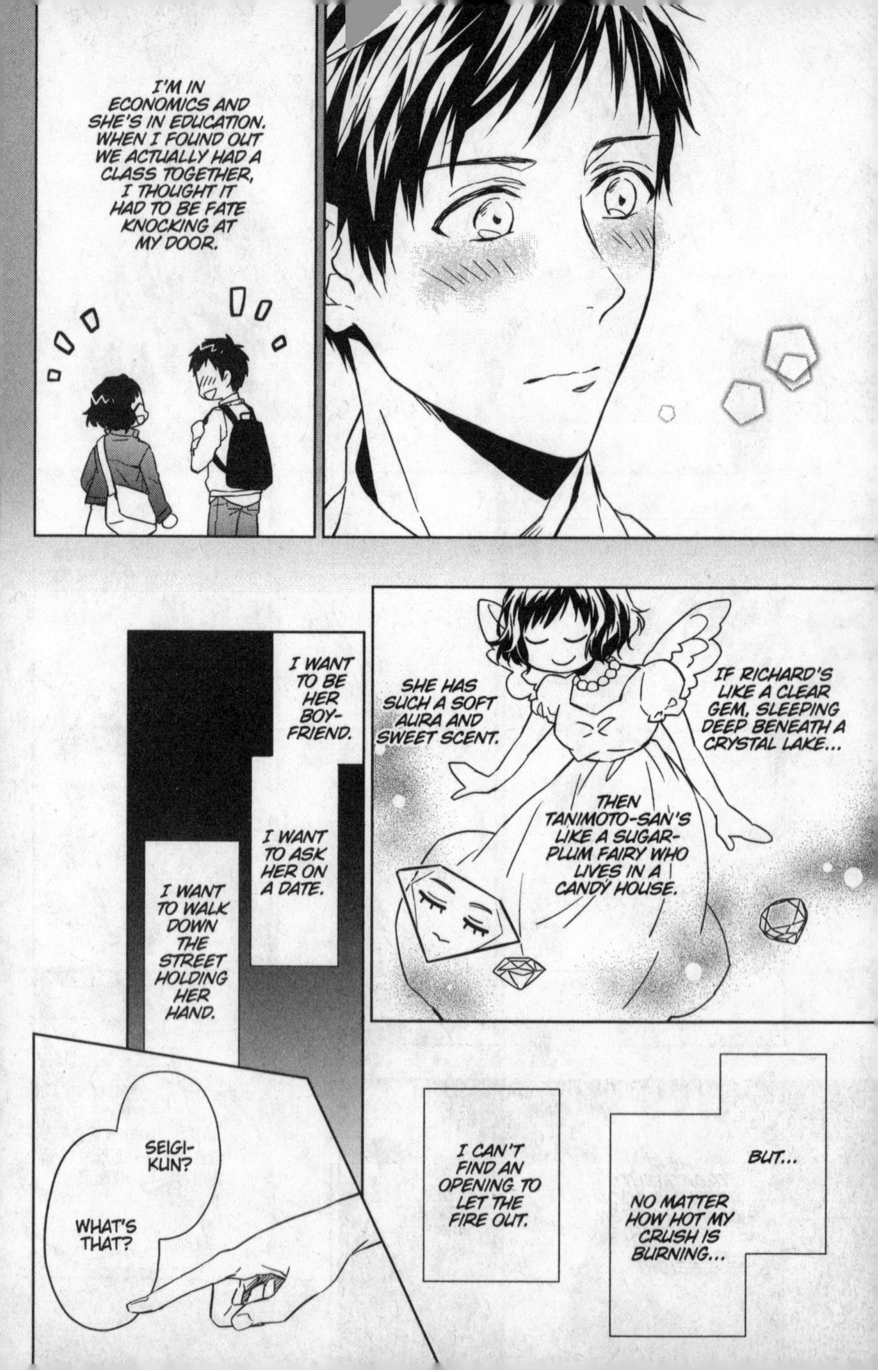
I'M IN ECONOMICS AND SHE'S IN EDUCATION. WHEN I FOUND OUT WE ACTUALLY HAD A CLASS TOGETHER, I THOUGHT IT HAD TO BE FATE KNOCKING AT MY DOOR.
IF RICHARD'S LIKE A CLEAR GEM, SLEEPING DEEP BENEATH A CRYSTAL LAKE...
SHE HAS SUCH A SOFT AURA AND SWEET SCENT.
THEN TANIMOTO-SAN'S LIKE A SUGAR-PLUM FAIRY WHO LIVES IN A CANDY HOUSE.
I WANT TO BE HER BOY-FRIEND.
I WANT TO ASK HER ON A DATE.
I WANT TO WALK DOWN THE STREET HOLDING HER HAND.
BUT...
NO MATTER HOW HOT MY CRUSH IS BURNING...
I CAN'T FIND AN OPENING TO LET THE FIRE OUT.
SEIGI-KUN?
WHAT'S THAT?

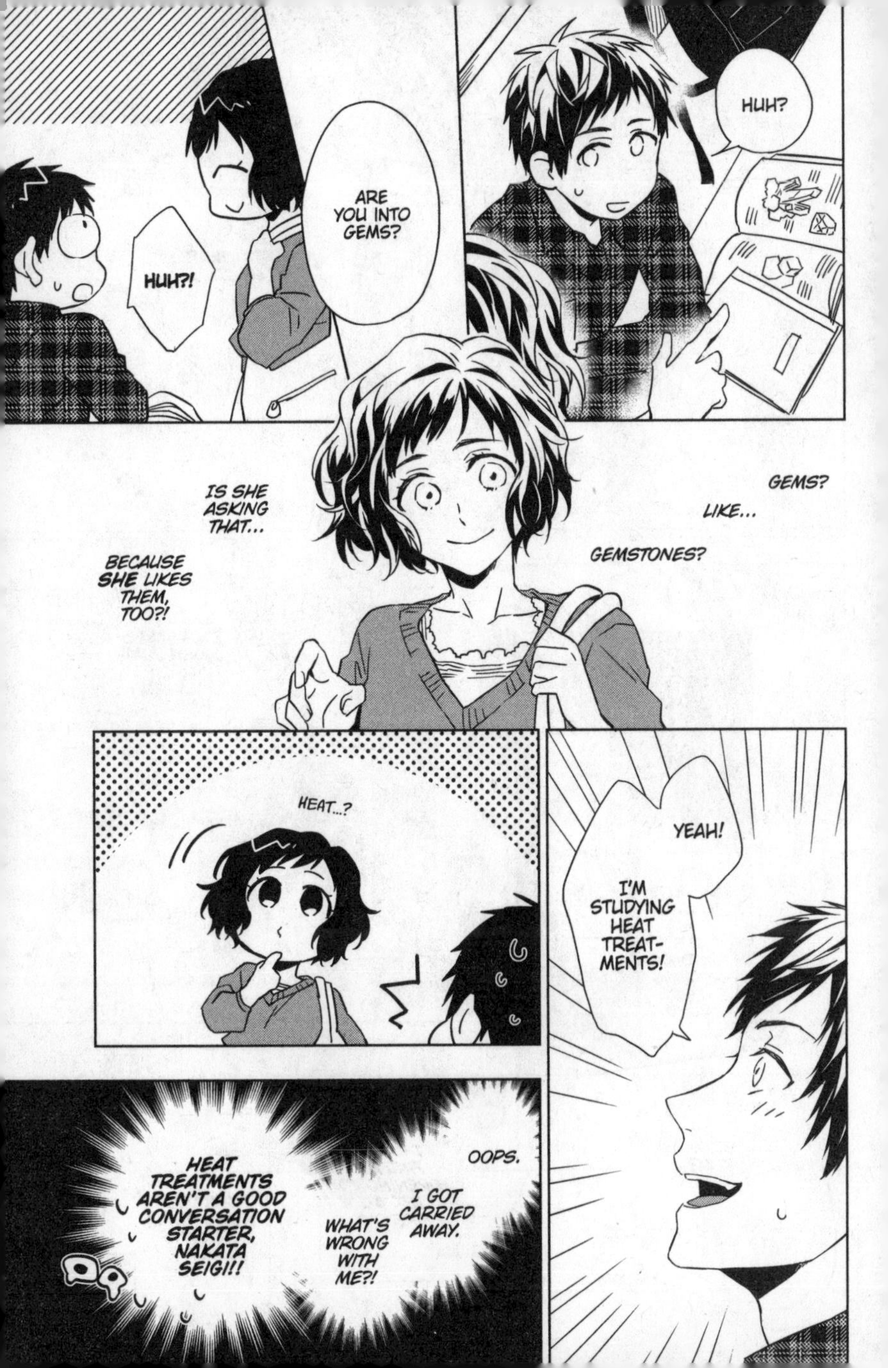
HUH?
ARE YOU INTO GEMS?
HUH?!
GEMS?
LIKE...
GEMSTONES?
IS SHE ASKING THAT...
BECAUSE SHE LIKES THEM, TOO?!
YEAH!
I'M STUDYING HEAT TREAT-MENTS!
HEAT...?
OOPS.
I GOT CARRIED AWAY.
WHAT'S WRONG WITH ME?!
HEAT TREATMENTS AREN'T A GOOD CONVERSATION STARTER, NAKATA SEIGI!!

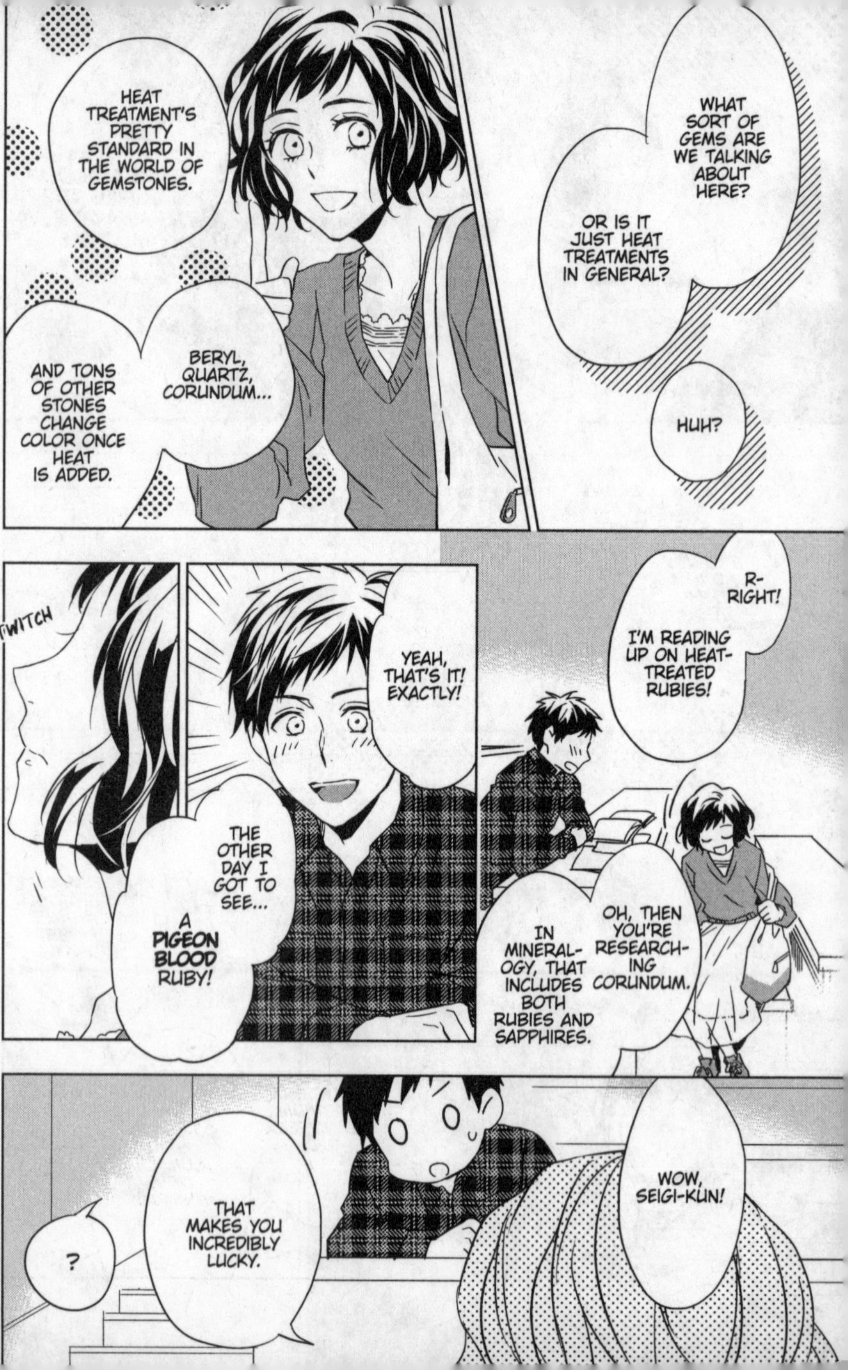
WHAT SORT OF GEMS ARE WE TALKING ABOUT HERE?
OR IS IT JUST HEAT TREATMENTS IN GENERAL?
HUH?
HEAT TREATMENT'S PRETTY STANDARD IN THE WORLD OF GEMSTONES.
BERYL, QUARTZ, CORUNDUM...
AND TONS OF OTHER STONES CHANGE COLOR ONCE HEAT IS ADDED.
R- RIGHT!
I'M READING UP ON HEAT-TREATED RUBIES!
OH, THEN YOU'RE RESEARCHING CORUNDUM.
IN MINERALOGY, THAT INCLUDES BOTH RUBIES AND SAPPHIRES.
YEAH, THAT'S IT! EXACTLY!
THE OTHER DAY I GOT TO SEE...
A **PIGEON BLOOD** RUBY!
TWITCH
WOW, SEIGI-KUN!
THAT MAKES YOU INCREDIBLY LUCKY.
?

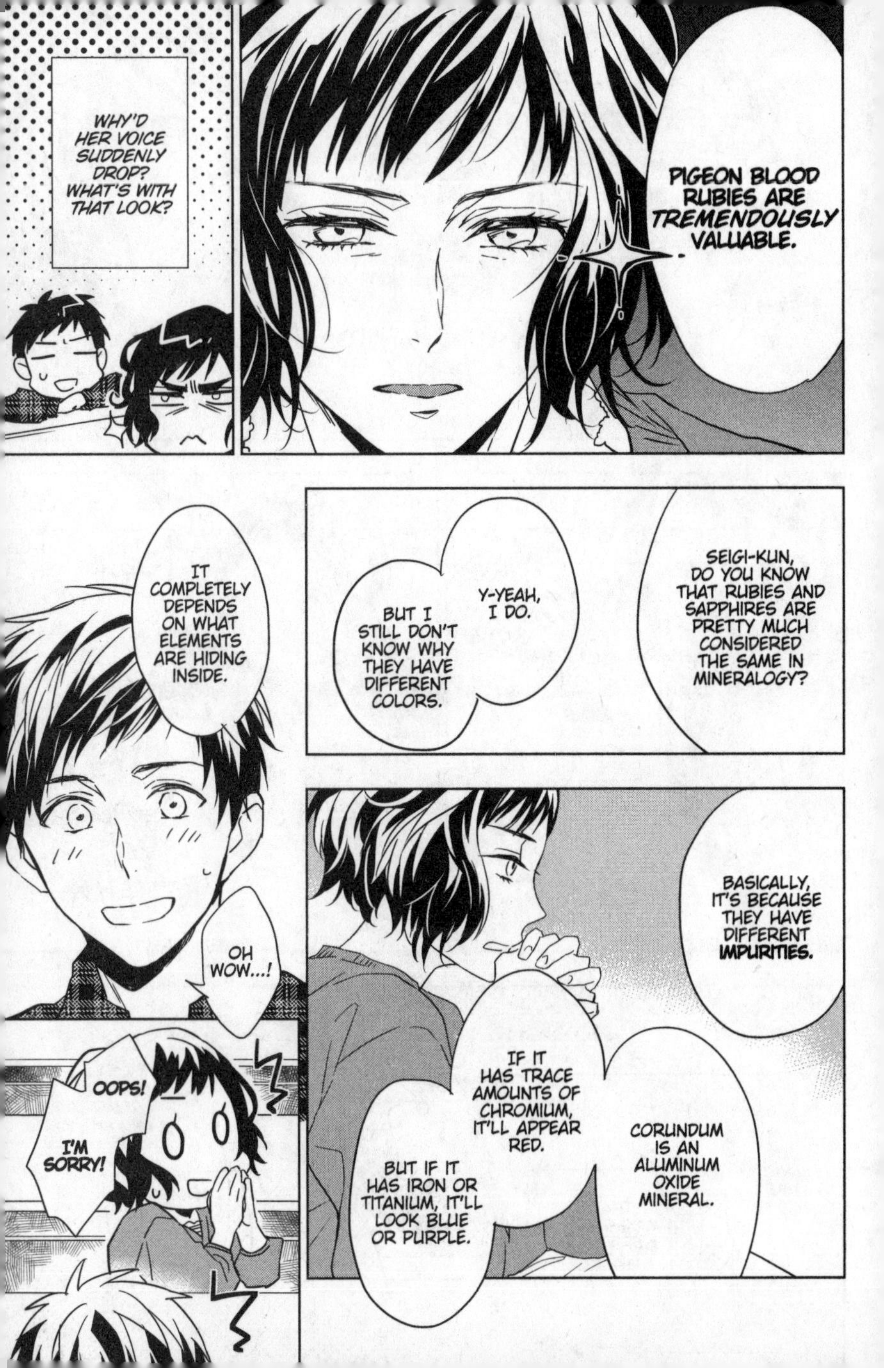
PIGEON BLOOD RUBIES ARE TREMENDOUSLY VALUABLE.
WHY'D HER VOICE SUDDENLY DROP? WHAT'S WITH THAT LOOK?
SEIGI-KUN, DO YOU KNOW THAT RUBIES AND SAPPHIRES ARE PRETTY MUCH CONSIDERED THE SAME IN MINERALOGY?
Y-YEAH, I DO.
BUT I STILL DON'T KNOW WHY THEY HAVE DIFFERENT COLORS.
BASICALLY, IT'S BECAUSE THEY HAVE DIFFERENT IMPURITIES.
CORUNDUM IS AN ALUMINUM OXIDE MINERAL.
IF IT HAS TRACE AMOUNTS OF CHROMIUM, IT'LL APPEAR RED.
BUT IF IT HAS IRON OR TITANIUM, IT'LL LOOK BLUE OR PURPLE.
IT COMPLETELY DEPENDS ON WHAT ELEMENTS ARE HIDING INSIDE.
OH WOW...!
OOPS!
I'M SORRY!

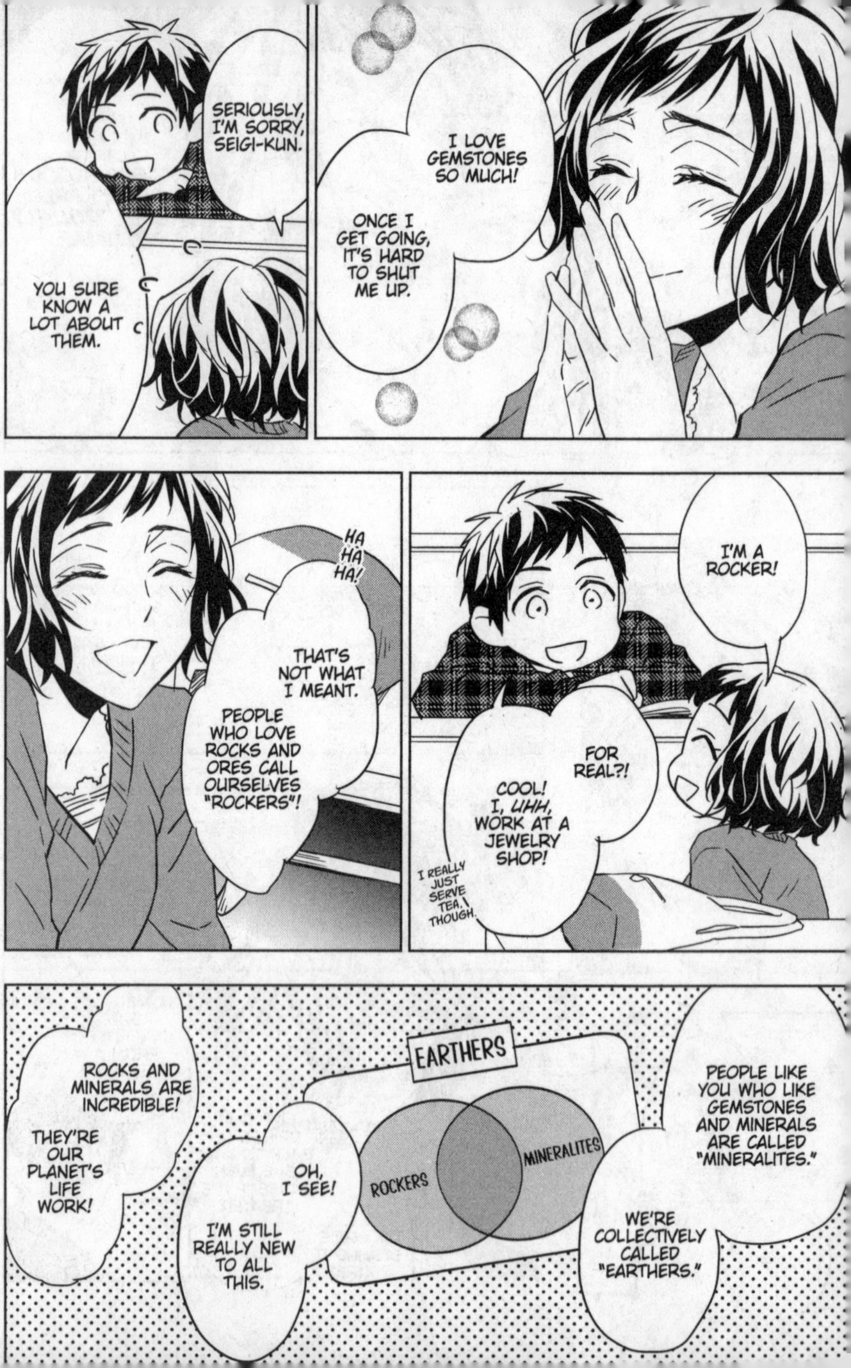
I LOVE GEMSTONES SO MUCH!
ONCE I GET GOING, IT'S HARD TO SHUT ME UP.
SERIOUSLY, I'M SORRY, SEIGI-KUN.
YOU SURE KNOW A LOT ABOUT THEM.
I'M A ROCKER!
FOR REAL?!
COOL! I, *UHH*, WORK AT A JEWELRY SHOP!
I REALLY JUST SERVE TEA, THOUGH.
HA HA HA!
THAT'S NOT WHAT I MEANT.
PEOPLE WHO LOVE ROCKS AND ORES CALL OURSELVES "ROCKERS"!
PEOPLE LIKE YOU WHO LIKE GEMSTONES AND MINERALS ARE CALLED "MINERALITES."
WE'RE COLLECTIVELY CALLED "EARTHERS."
EARTHERS
MINERALITES
ROCKERS
OH, I SEE!
I'M STILL REALLY NEW TO ALL THIS.
ROCKS AND MINERALS ARE INCREDIBLE!
THEY'RE OUR PLANET'S LIFE WORK!

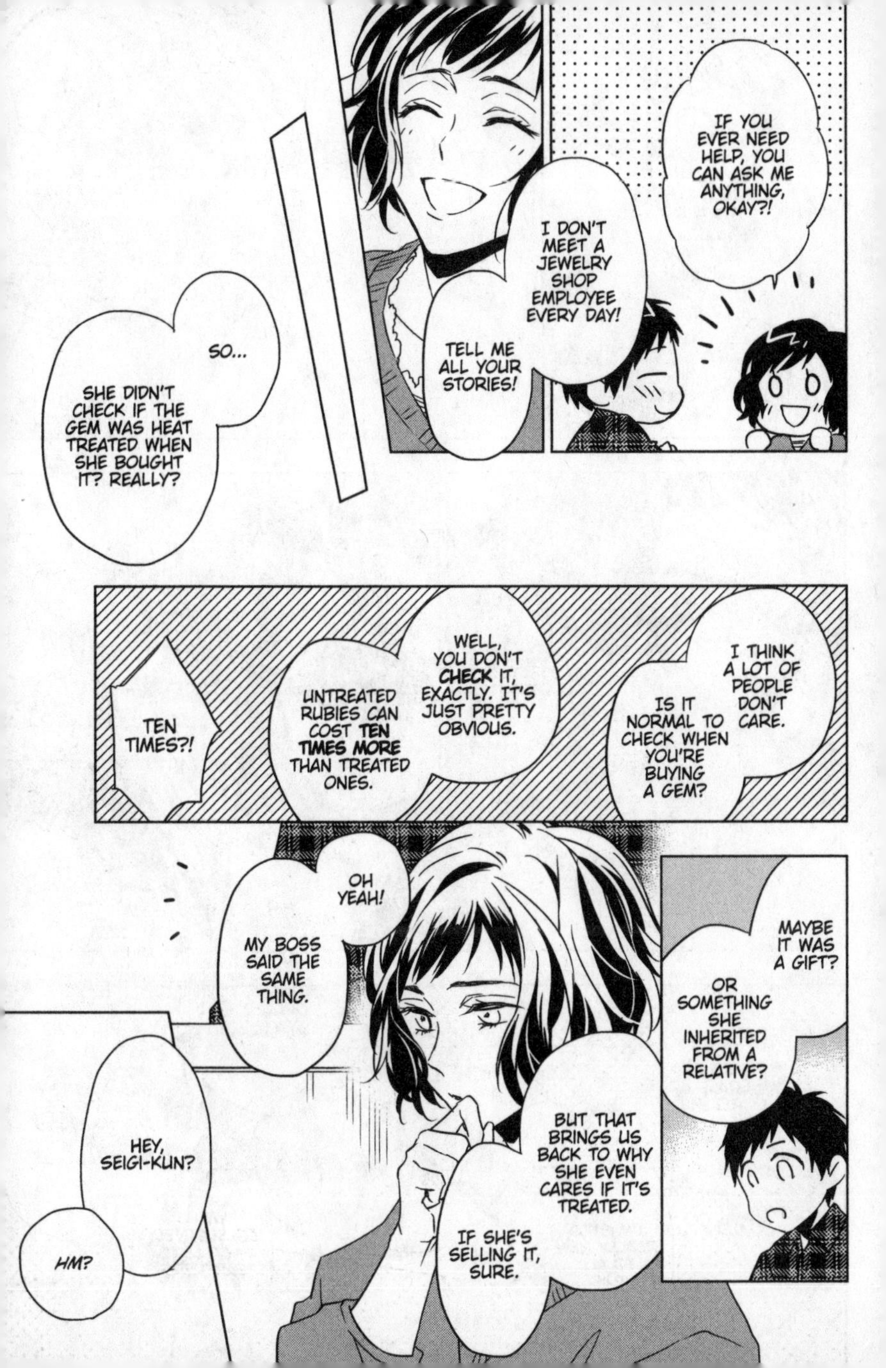
IF YOU EVER NEED HELP, YOU CAN ASK ME ANYTHING, OKAY?!
I DON'T MEET A JEWELRY SHOP EMPLOYEE EVERY DAY!
TELL ME ALL YOUR STORIES!
SO...
SHE DIDN'T CHECK IF THE GEM WAS HEAT TREATED WHEN SHE BOUGHT IT? REALLY?
I THINK A LOT OF PEOPLE DON'T CARE.
IS IT NORMAL TO CHECK WHEN YOU'RE BUYING A GEM?
WELL, YOU DON'T **CHECK** IT, EXACTLY. IT'S JUST PRETTY OBVIOUS.
UNTREATED RUBIES CAN COST **TEN TIMES MORE** THAN TREATED ONES.
TEN TIMES?!
MAYBE IT WAS A GIFT?
OR SOMETHING SHE INHERITED FROM A RELATIVE?
BUT THAT BRINGS US BACK TO WHY SHE EVEN CARES IF IT'S TREATED.
IF SHE'S SELLING IT, SURE.
OH YEAH!
MY BOSS SAID THE SAME THING.
HEY, SEIGI-KUN?
HM?

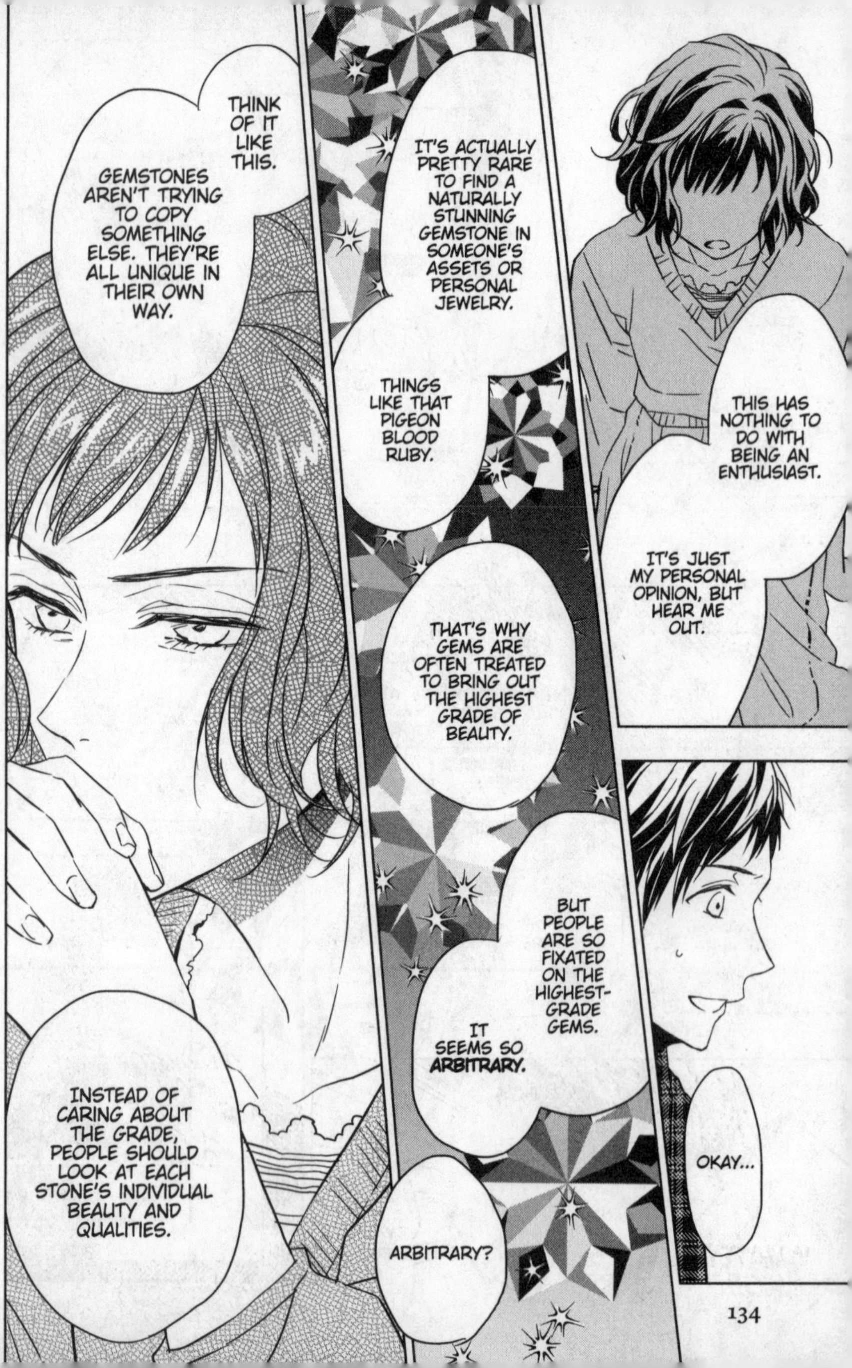

THIS HAS NOTHING TO DO WITH BEING AN ENTHUSIAST.
IT'S JUST MY PERSONAL OPINION, BUT HEAR ME OUT.
OKAY...
IT'S ACTUALLY PRETTY RARE TO FIND A NATURALLY STUNNING GEMSTONE IN SOMEONE'S ASSETS OR PERSONAL JEWELRY.
THINGS LIKE THAT PIGEON BLOOD RUBY.
THAT'S WHY GEMS ARE OFTEN TREATED TO BRING OUT THE HIGHEST GRADE OF BEAUTY.
BUT PEOPLE ARE SO FIXATED ON THE HIGHEST-GRADE GEMS.
IT SEEMS SO **ARBITRARY.**
ARBITRARY?
THINK OF IT LIKE THIS.
GEMSTONES AREN'T TRYING TO COPY SOMETHING ELSE. THEY'RE ALL UNIQUE IN THEIR OWN WAY.
INSTEAD OF CARING ABOUT THE GRADE, PEOPLE SHOULD LOOK AT EACH STONE'S INDIVIDUAL BEAUTY AND QUALITIES.

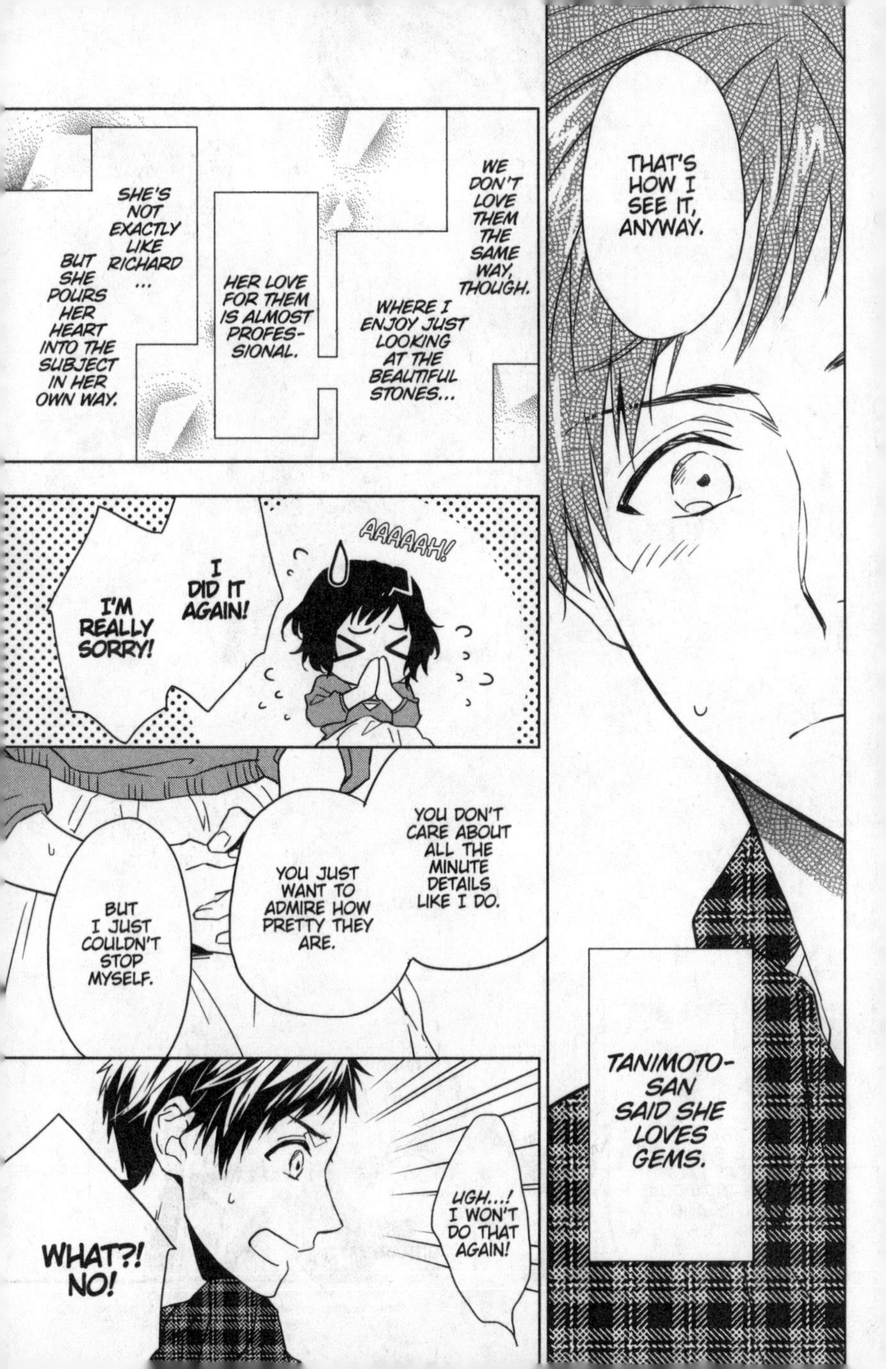
THAT'S HOW I SEE IT, ANYWAY.
TANIMOTO-SAN SAID SHE LOVES GEMS.
WE DON'T LOVE THEM THE SAME WAY, THOUGH.
WHERE I ENJOY JUST LOOKING AT THE BEAUTIFUL STONES...
HER LOVE FOR THEM IS ALMOST PROFESSIONAL.
SHE'S NOT EXACTLY LIKE RICHARD...
BUT SHE POURS HER HEART INTO THE SUBJECT IN HER OWN WAY.
AAAAAH!
I DID IT AGAIN!
I'M REALLY SORRY!
YOU DON'T CARE ABOUT ALL THE MINUTE DETAILS LIKE I DO.
YOU JUST WANT TO ADMIRE HOW PRETTY THEY ARE.
BUT I JUST COULDN'T STOP MYSELF.
UGH...! I WON'T DO THAT AGAIN!
WHAT?! NO!

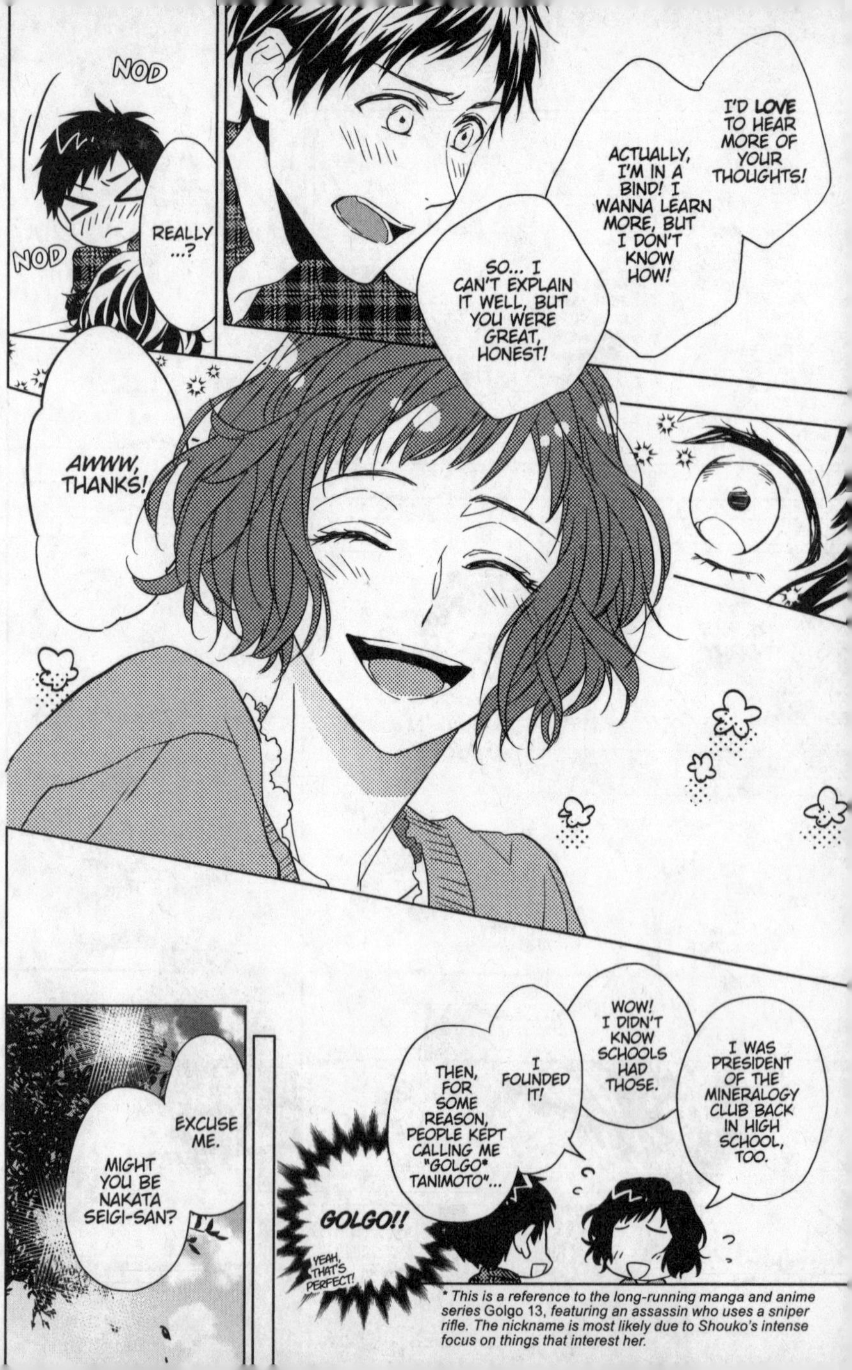
I'D LOVE TO HEAR MORE OF YOUR THOUGHTS!
ACTUALLY, I'M IN A BIND! I WANNA LEARN MORE, BUT I DON'T KNOW HOW!
SO... I CAN'T EXPLAIN IT WELL, BUT YOU WERE GREAT, HONEST!
NOD
REALLY ...?
NOD
AWWW, THANKS!
I WAS PRESIDENT OF THE MINERALOGY CLUB BACK IN HIGH SCHOOL, TOO.
WOW! I DIDN'T KNOW SCHOOLS HAD THOSE.
I FOUNDED IT!
THEN, FOR SOME REASON, PEOPLE KEPT CALLING ME "GOLGO* TANIMOTO"...
GOLGO!!
YEAH, THAT'S PERFECT!
EXCUSE ME.
MIGHT YOU BE NAKATA SEIGI-SAN?

** This is a reference to the long-running manga and anime series* Golgo 13*, featuring an assassin who uses a sniper rifle. The nickname is most likely due to Shouko's intense focus on things that interest her.*

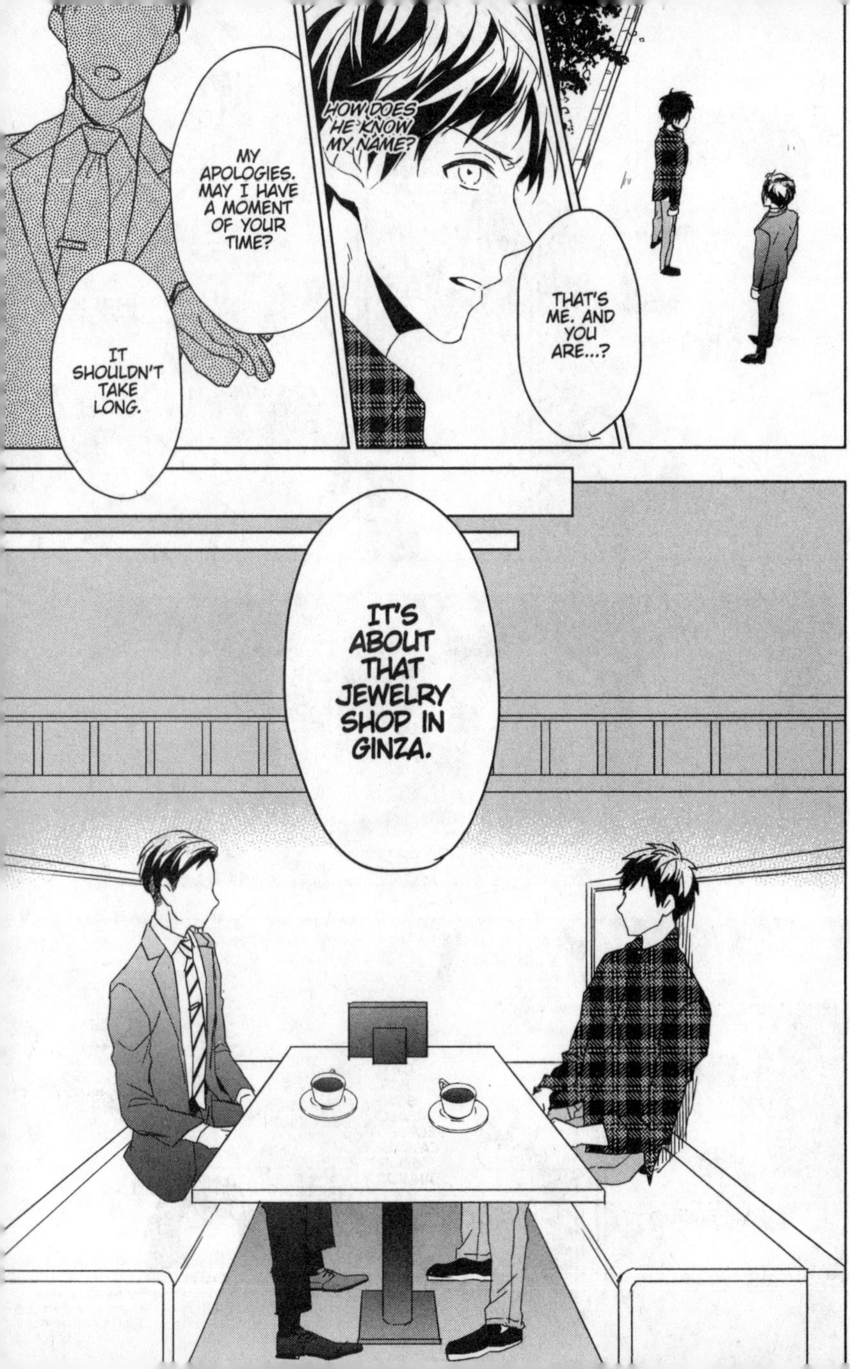
HOW DOES HE KNOW MY NAME?
THAT'S ME. AND YOU ARE...?
MY APOLOGIES. MAY I HAVE A MOMENT OF YOUR TIME?
IT SHOULDN'T TAKE LONG.
IT'S ABOUT THAT JEWELRY SHOP IN GINZA.

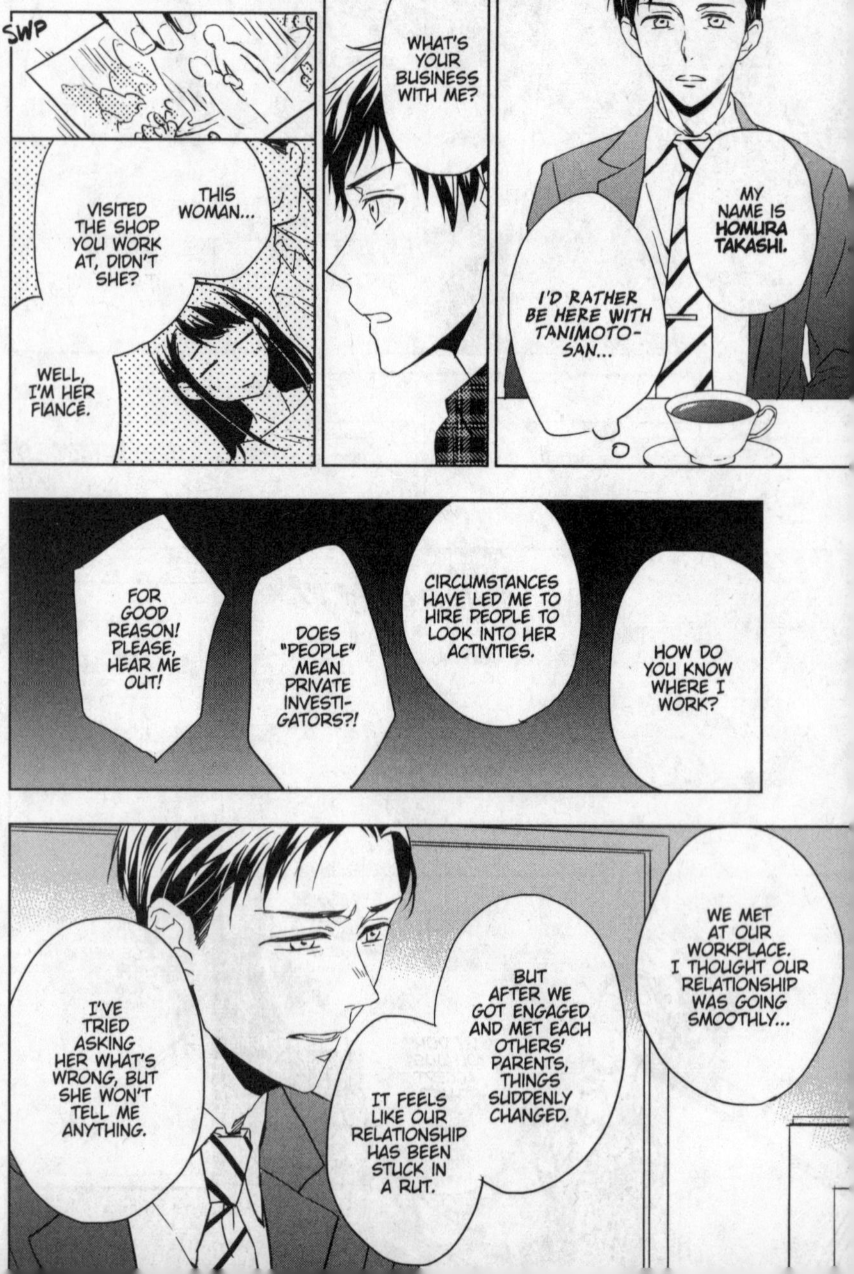
MY NAME IS HOMURA TAKASHI.
I'D RATHER BE HERE WITH TANIMOTO-SAN...
WHAT'S YOUR BUSINESS WITH ME?
SWP
THIS WOMAN...
VISITED THE SHOP YOU WORK AT, DIDN'T SHE?
WELL, I'M HER FIANCÉ.
HOW DO YOU KNOW WHERE I WORK?
CIRCUMSTANCES HAVE LED ME TO HIRE PEOPLE TO LOOK INTO HER ACTIVITIES.
DOES "PEOPLE" MEAN PRIVATE INVESTI-GATORS?!
FOR GOOD REASON! PLEASE, HEAR ME OUT!
WE MET AT OUR WORKPLACE. I THOUGHT OUR RELATIONSHIP WAS GOING SMOOTHLY...
BUT AFTER WE GOT ENGAGED AND MET EACH OTHERS' PARENTS, THINGS SUDDENLY CHANGED.
IT FEELS LIKE OUR RELATIONSHIP HAS BEEN STUCK IN A RUT.
I'VE TRIED ASKING HER WHAT'S WRONG, BUT SHE WON'T TELL ME ANYTHING.

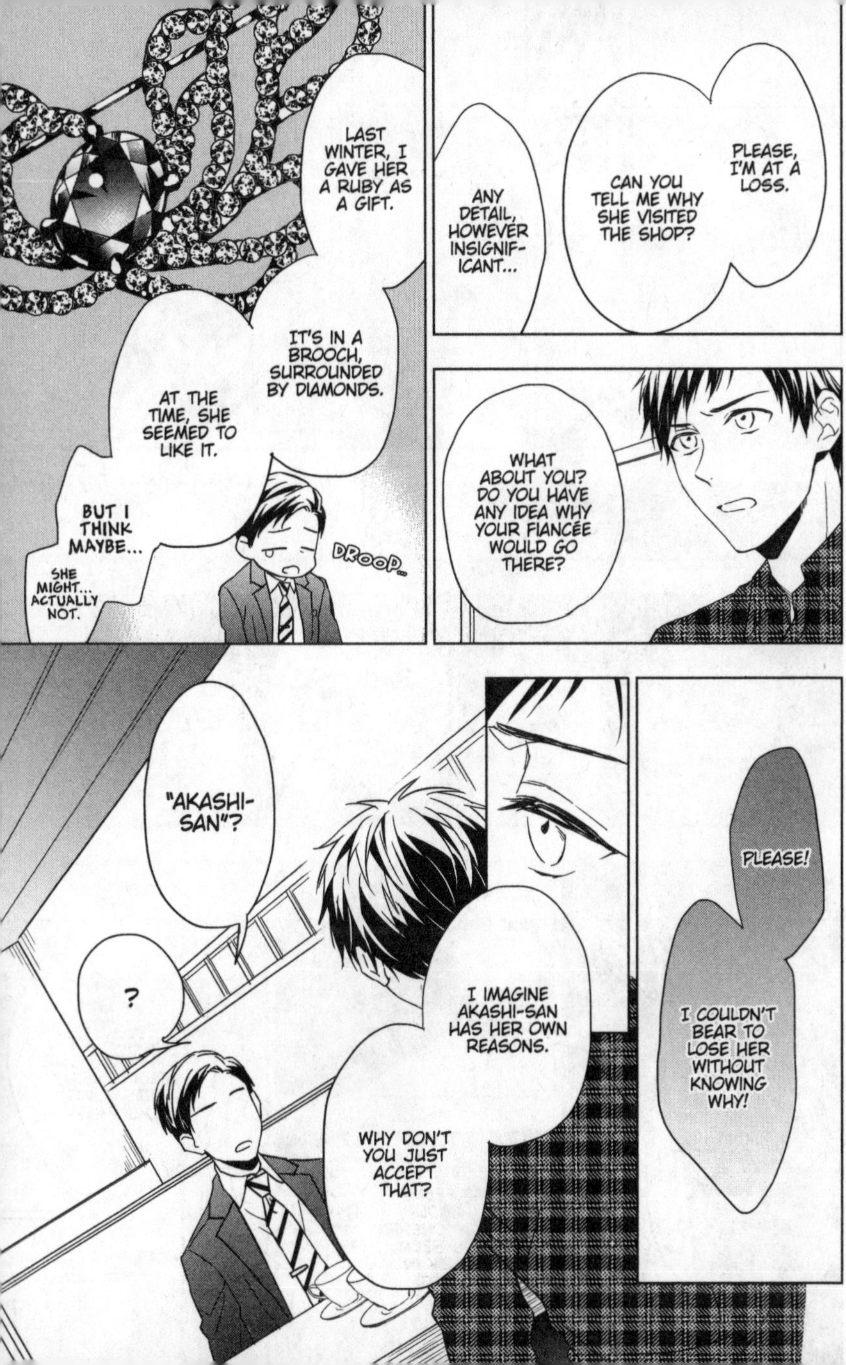
PLEASE, I'M AT A LOSS.
CAN YOU TELL ME WHY SHE VISITED THE SHOP?
ANY DETAIL, HOWEVER INSIGNIFICANT...
WHAT ABOUT YOU? DO YOU HAVE ANY IDEA WHY YOUR FIANCÉE WOULD GO THERE?
LAST WINTER, I GAVE HER A RUBY AS A GIFT.
IT'S IN A BROOCH, SURROUNDED BY DIAMONDS.
AT THE TIME, SHE SEEMED TO LIKE IT.
BUT I THINK MAYBE...
SHE MIGHT... ACTUALLY NOT.
DROOP...
PLEASE!
I COULDN'T BEAR TO LOSE HER WITHOUT KNOWING WHY!
I IMAGINE AKASHI-SAN HAS HER OWN REASONS.
WHY DON'T YOU JUST ACCEPT THAT?
"AKASHI-SAN"?
?

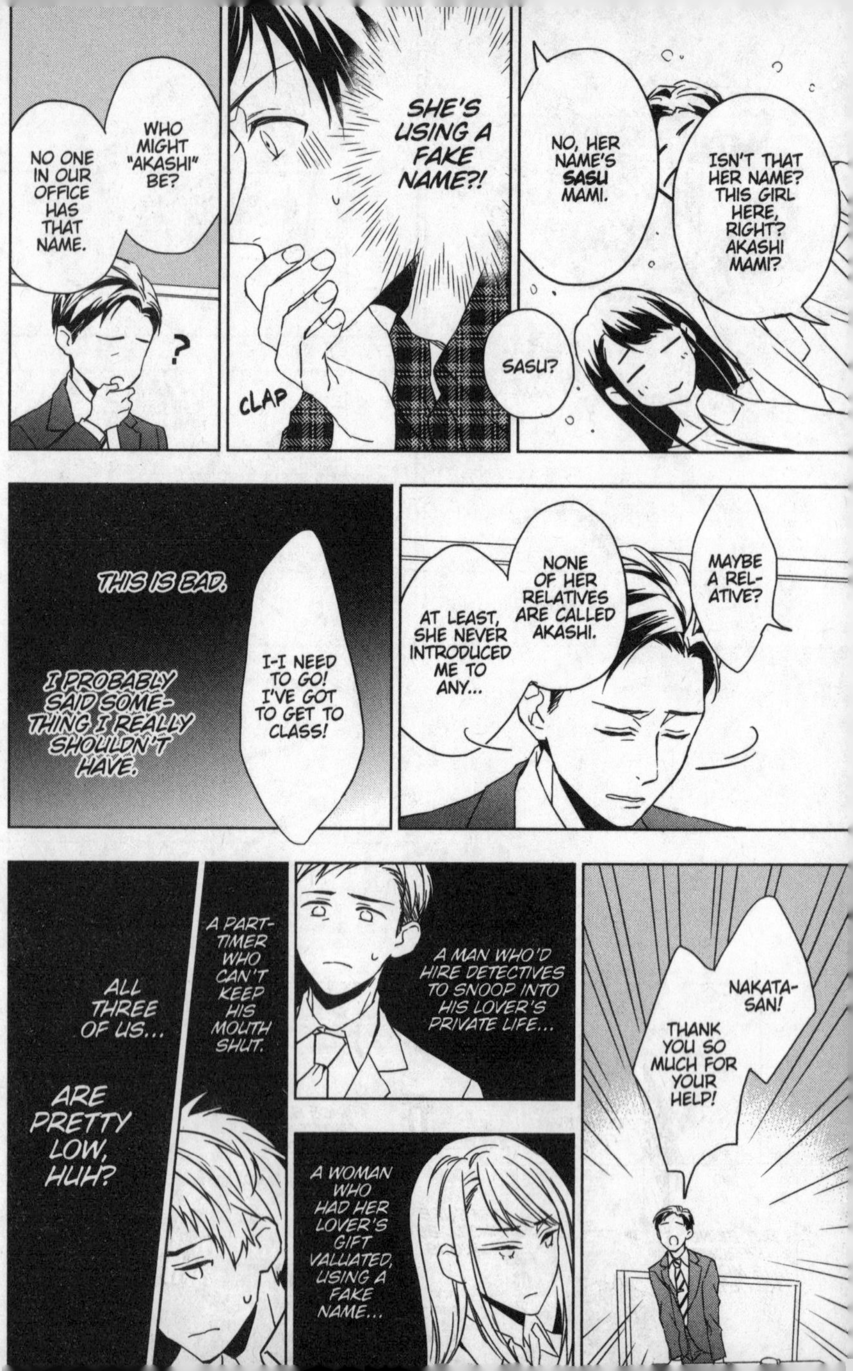
ISN'T THAT HER NAME? THIS GIRL HERE, RIGHT? AKASHI MAMI?
NO, HER NAME'S SASU MAMI.
SASU?
SHE'S USING A FAKE NAME?!
CLAP
WHO MIGHT "AKASHI" BE?
NO ONE IN OUR OFFICE HAS THAT NAME.
?
MAYBE A RELATIVE?
NONE OF HER RELATIVES ARE CALLED AKASHI.
AT LEAST, SHE NEVER INTRODUCED ME TO ANY...
I-I NEED TO GO! I'VE GOT TO GET TO CLASS!
THIS IS BAD.
I PROBABLY SAID SOMETHING I REALLY SHOULDN'T HAVE.
NAKATA-SAN!
THANK YOU SO MUCH FOR YOUR HELP!
A MAN WHO'D HIRE DETECTIVES TO SNOOP INTO HIS LOVER'S PRIVATE LIFE...
A WOMAN WHO HAD HER LOVER'S GIFT VALUATED, USING A FAKE NAME...
A PART-TIMER WHO CAN'T KEEP HIS MOUTH SHUT.
ALL THREE OF US...
ARE PRETTY LOW, HUH?

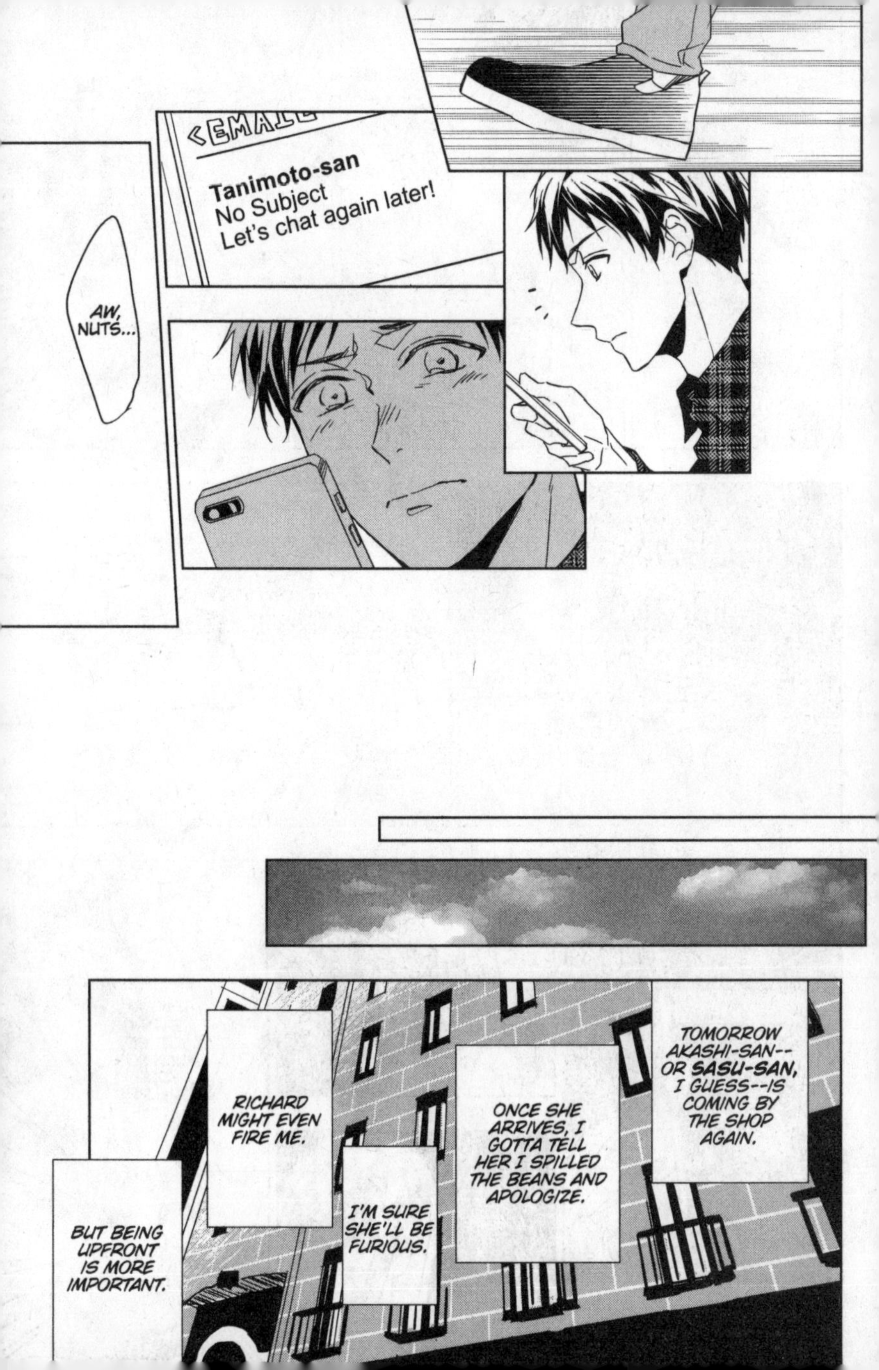
<EMAIL
Tanimoto-san
No Subject
Let's chat again later!
AW, NUTS...
TOMORROW AKASHI-SAN--OR SASU-SAN, I GUESS--IS COMING BY THE SHOP AGAIN.
ONCE SHE ARRIVES, I GOTTA TELL HER I SPILLED THE BEANS AND APOLOGIZE.
RICHARD MIGHT EVEN FIRE ME.
I'M SURE SHE'LL BE FURIOUS.
BUT BEING UPFRONT IS MORE IMPORTANT.

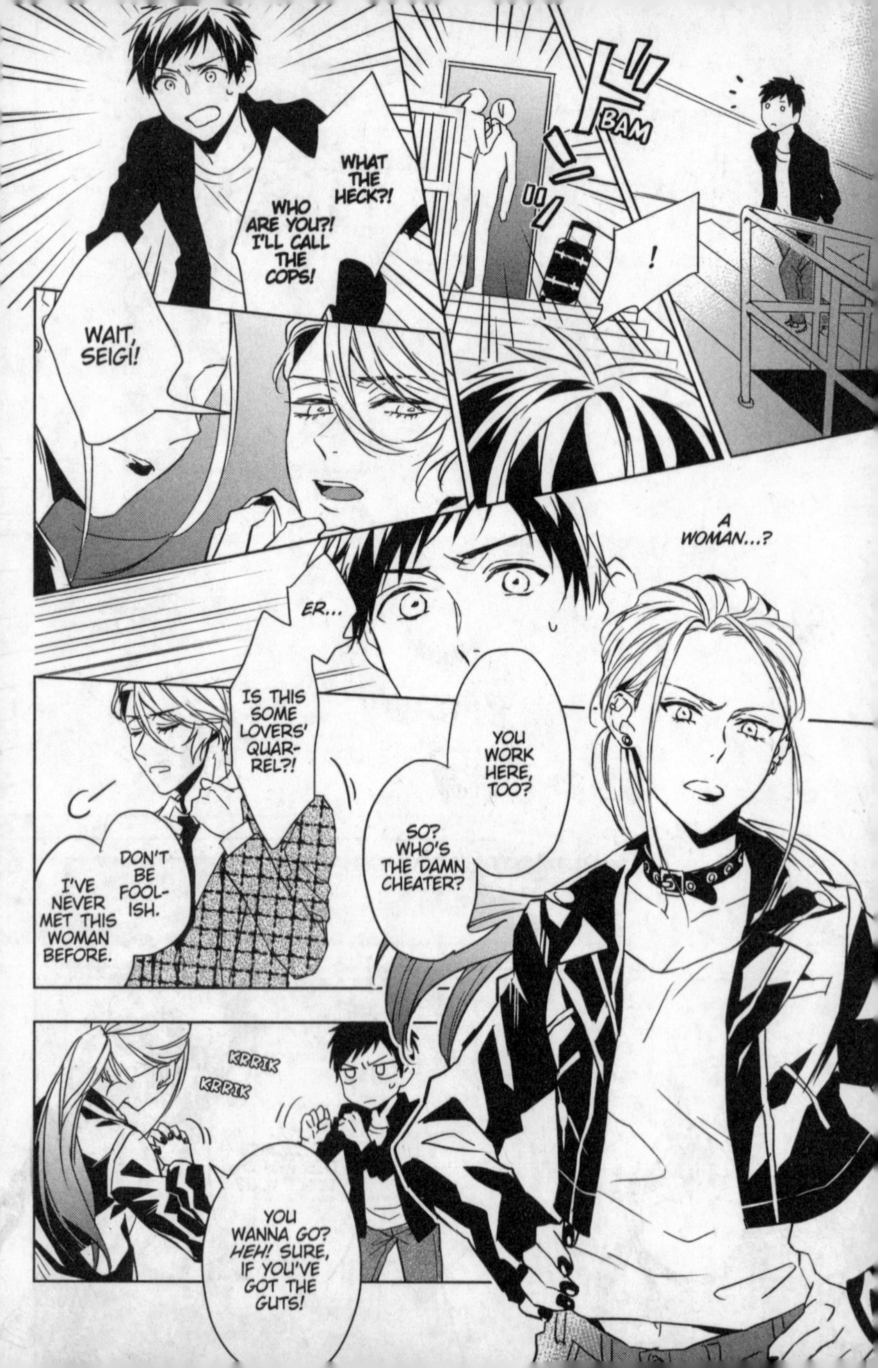
BAM
!
WHAT THE HECK?!
WHO ARE YOU?! I'LL CALL THE COPS!
WAIT, SEIGI!
A WOMAN...?
ER...
YOU WORK HERE, TOO?
SO? WHO'S THE DAMN CHEATER?
IS THIS SOME LOVERS' QUAR-REL?!
DON'T BE FOOL-ISH.
I'VE NEVER MET THIS WOMAN BEFORE.
KRRIK
KRRIK
YOU WANNA GO? *HEH!* SURE, IF YOU'VE GOT THE GUTS!

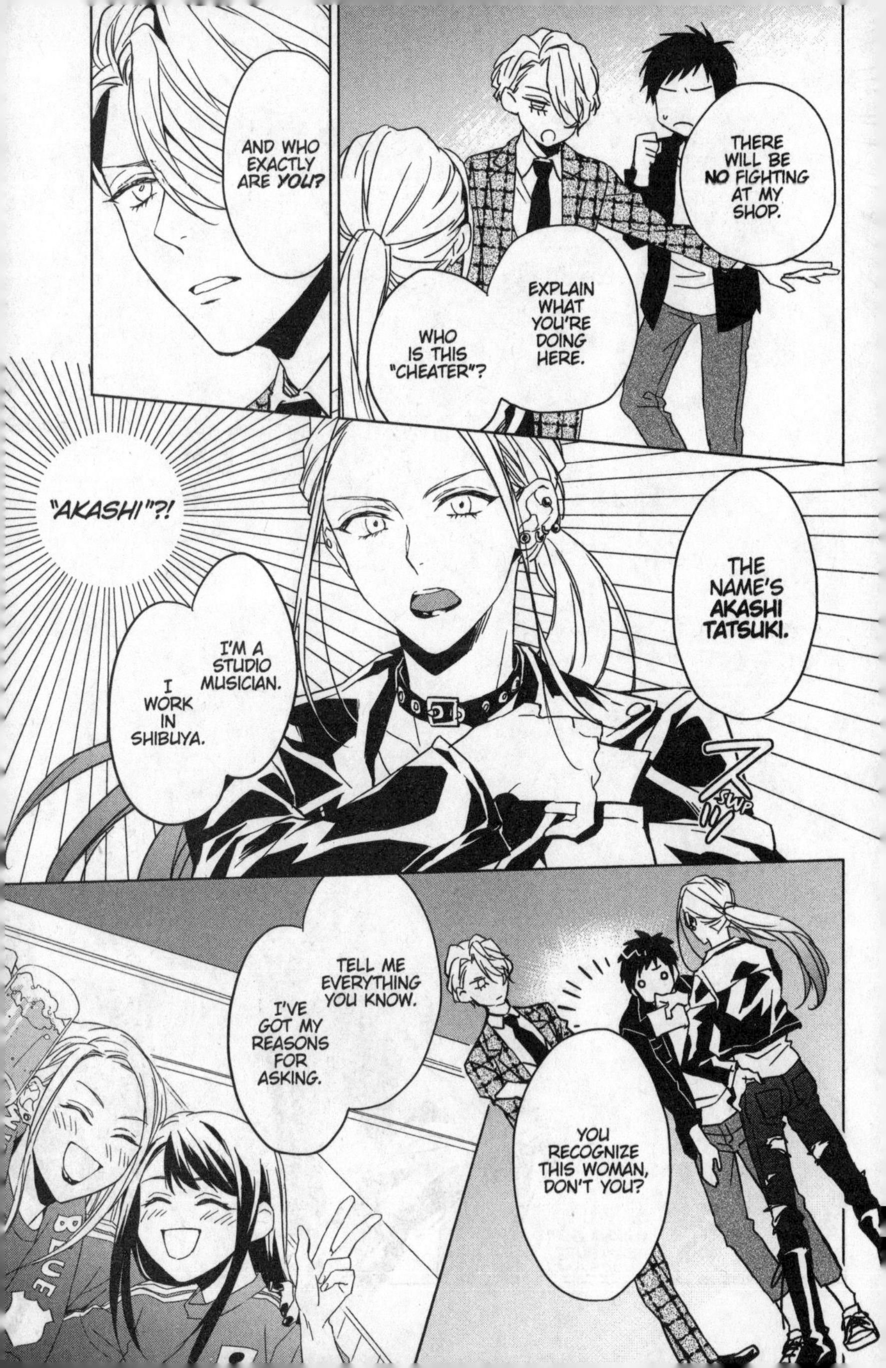
THERE WILL BE NO FIGHTING AT MY SHOP.
EXPLAIN WHAT YOU'RE DOING HERE.
WHO IS THIS "CHEATER"?
AND WHO EXACTLY ARE YOU?
THE NAME'S AKASHI TATSUKI.
SWP
I'M A STUDIO MUSICIAN.
I WORK IN SHIBUYA.
"AKASHI"?!
YOU RECOGNIZE THIS WOMAN, DON'T YOU?
TELL ME EVERYTHING YOU KNOW.
I'VE GOT MY REASONS FOR ASKING.
BLUE

THE CASE FILES OF JEWELER RICHARD

case. 4
Truth of the Ruby
Part 2

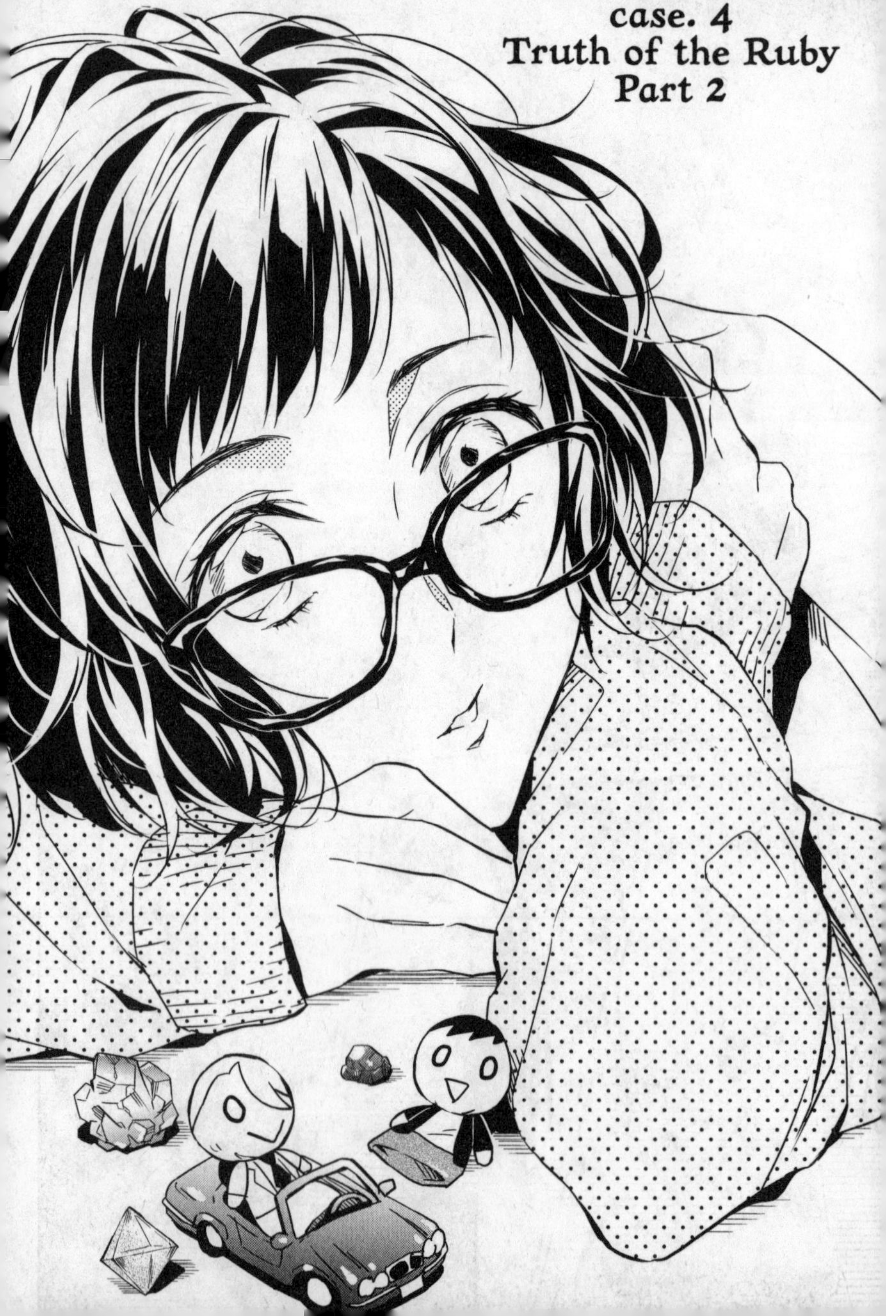

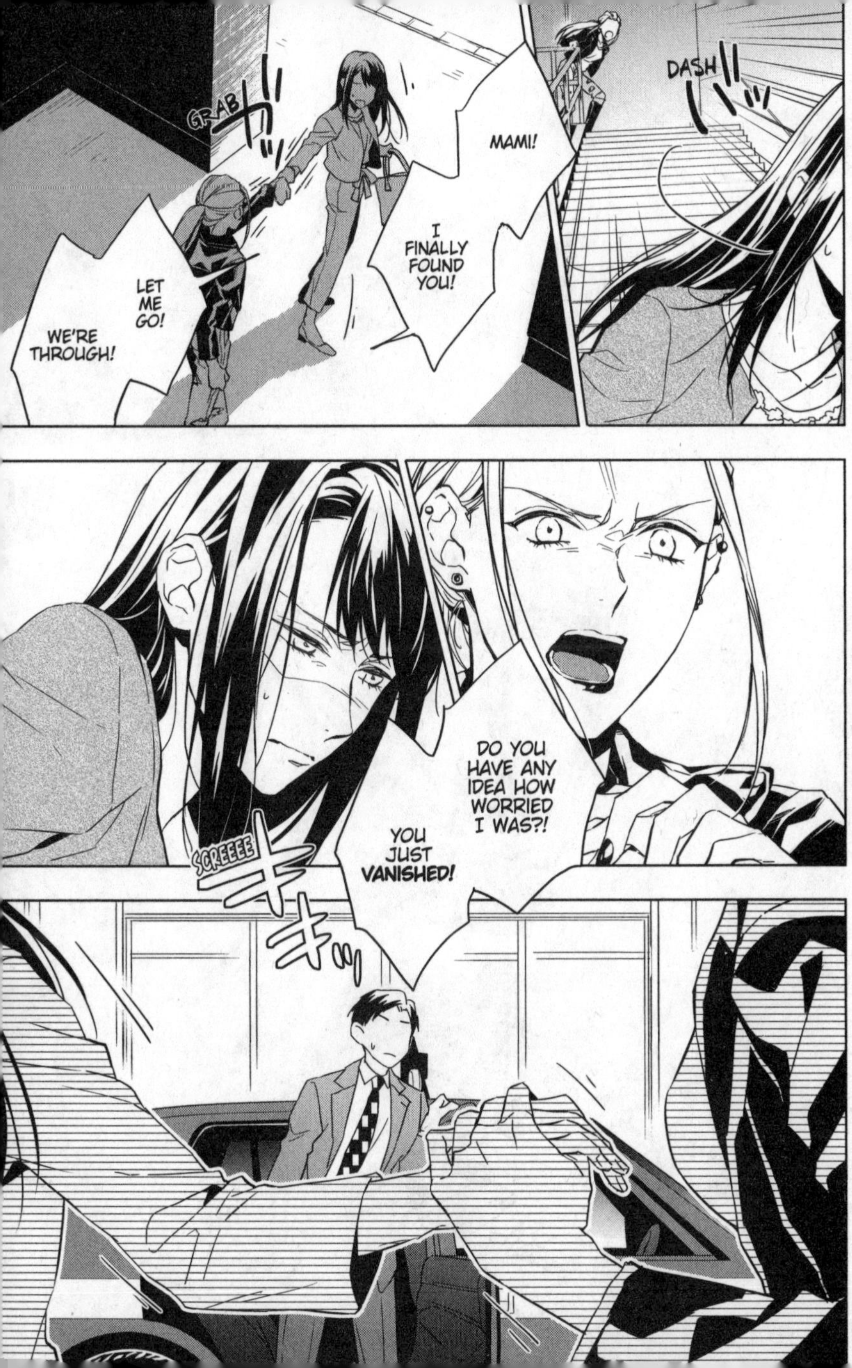
DASH
MAMI!
I FINALLY FOUND YOU!
GRAB
LET ME GO!
WE'RE THROUGH!
DO YOU HAVE ANY IDEA HOW WORRIED I WAS?!
YOU JUST **VANISHED!**
SCREEEEE

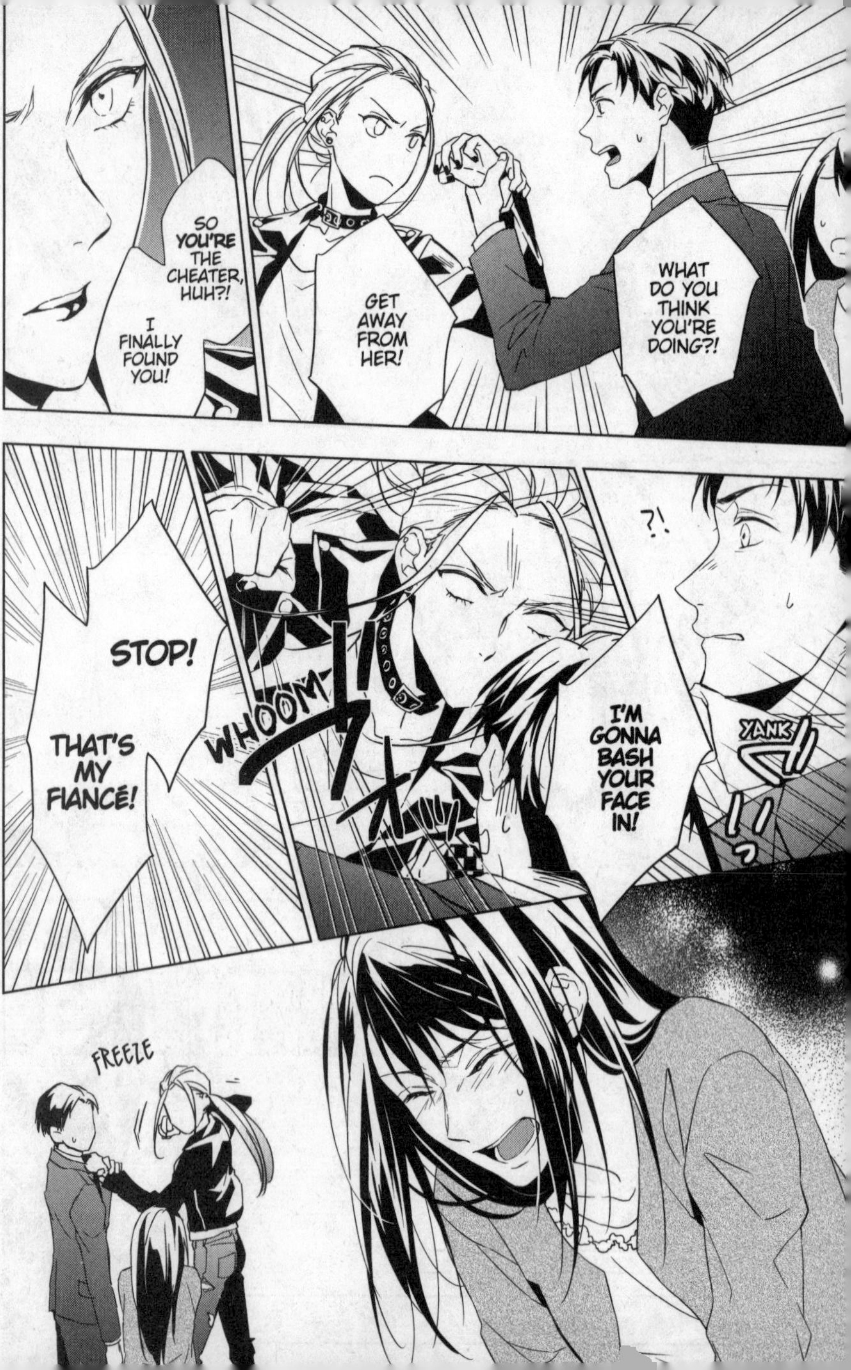
WHAT DO YOU THINK YOU'RE DOING?!
GET AWAY FROM HER!
SO YOU'RE THE CHEATER, HUH?!
I FINALLY FOUND YOU!
?!
YANK
I'M GONNA BASH YOUR FACE IN!
WHOOM
STOP!
THAT'S MY FIANCÉ!
FREEZE

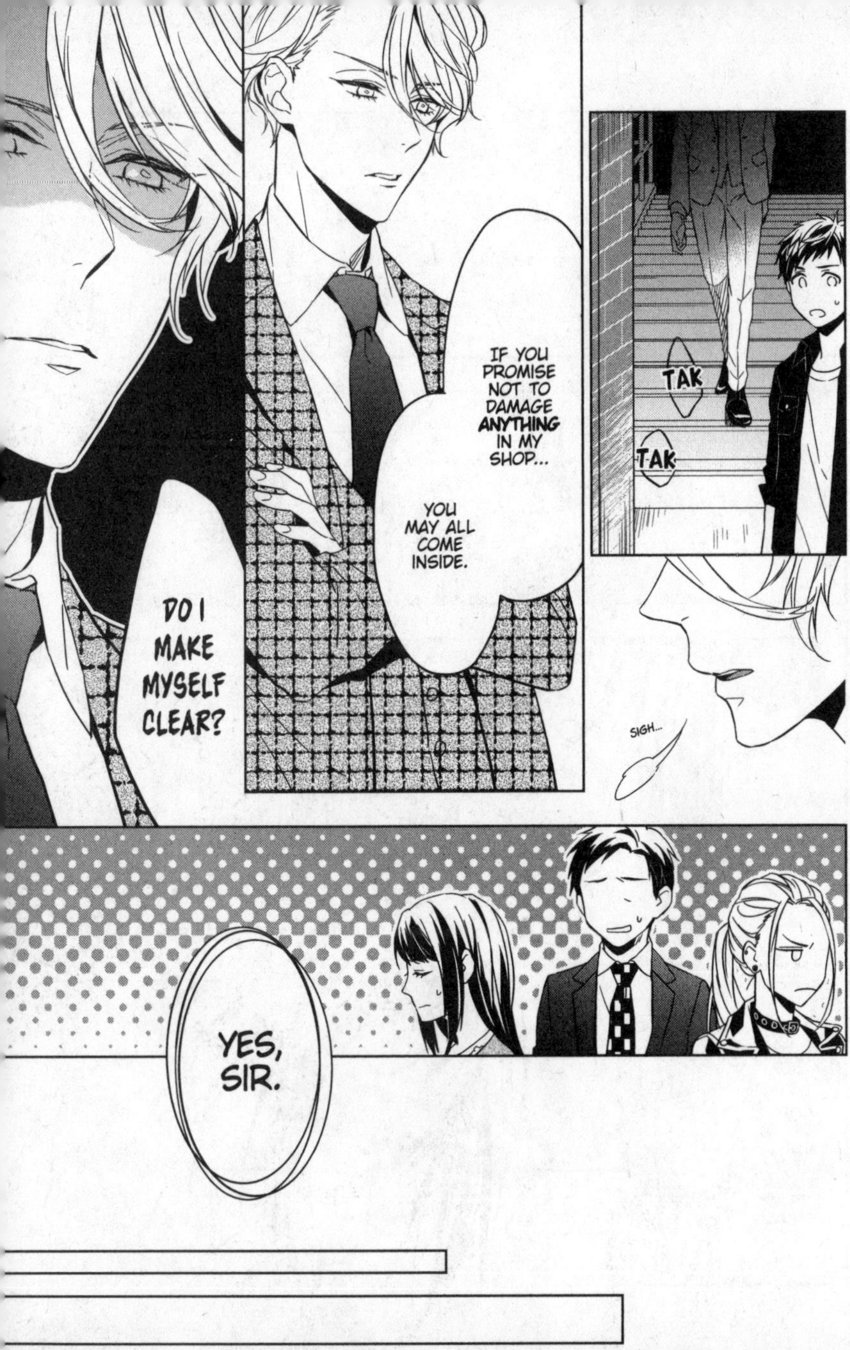
TAK
TAK
SIGH...
IF YOU PROMISE NOT TO DAMAGE **ANYTHING** IN MY SHOP...
YOU MAY ALL COME INSIDE.
DO I MAKE MYSELF CLEAR?
YES, SIR.

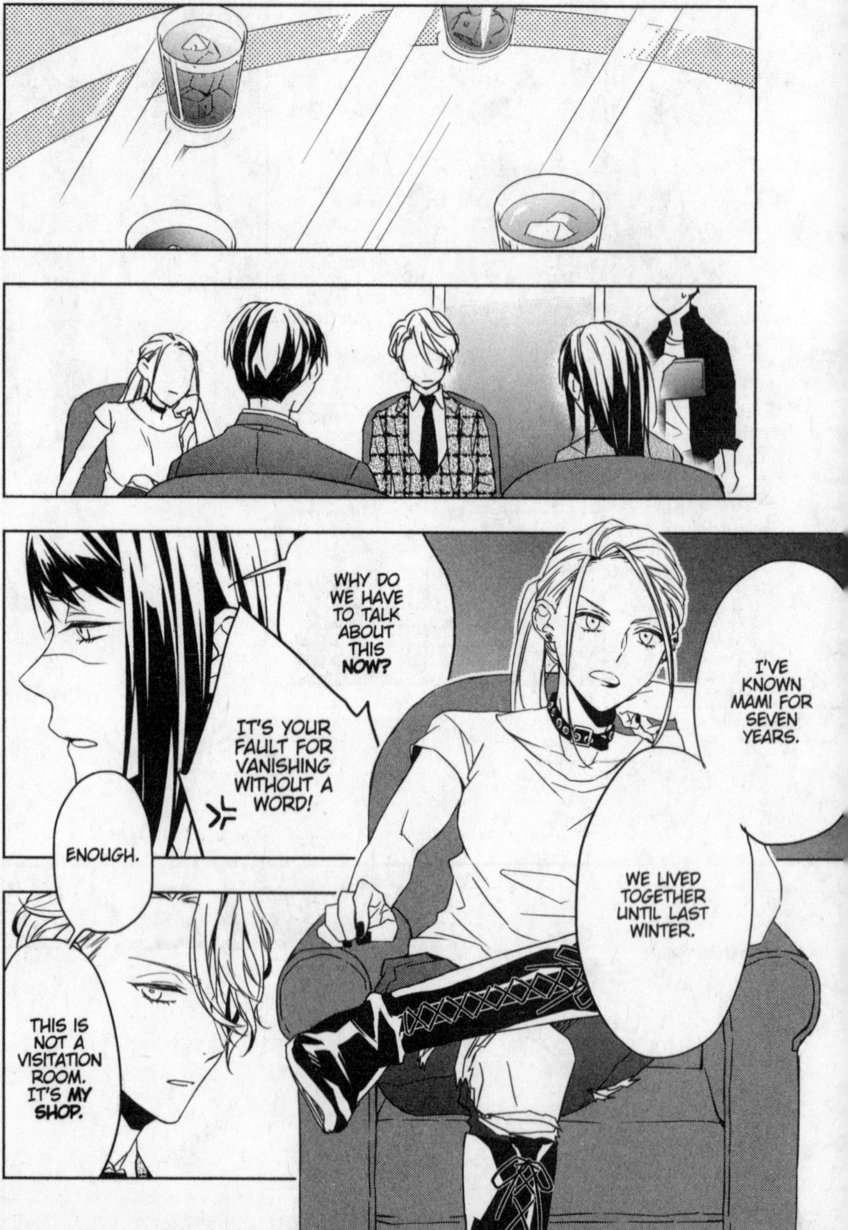
I'VE KNOWN MAMI FOR SEVEN YEARS.
WE LIVED TOGETHER UNTIL LAST WINTER.
WHY DO WE HAVE TO TALK ABOUT THIS **NOW?**
IT'S YOUR FAULT FOR VANISHING WITHOUT A WORD!
ENOUGH.
THIS IS NOT A VISITATION ROOM. IT'S **MY SHOP.**

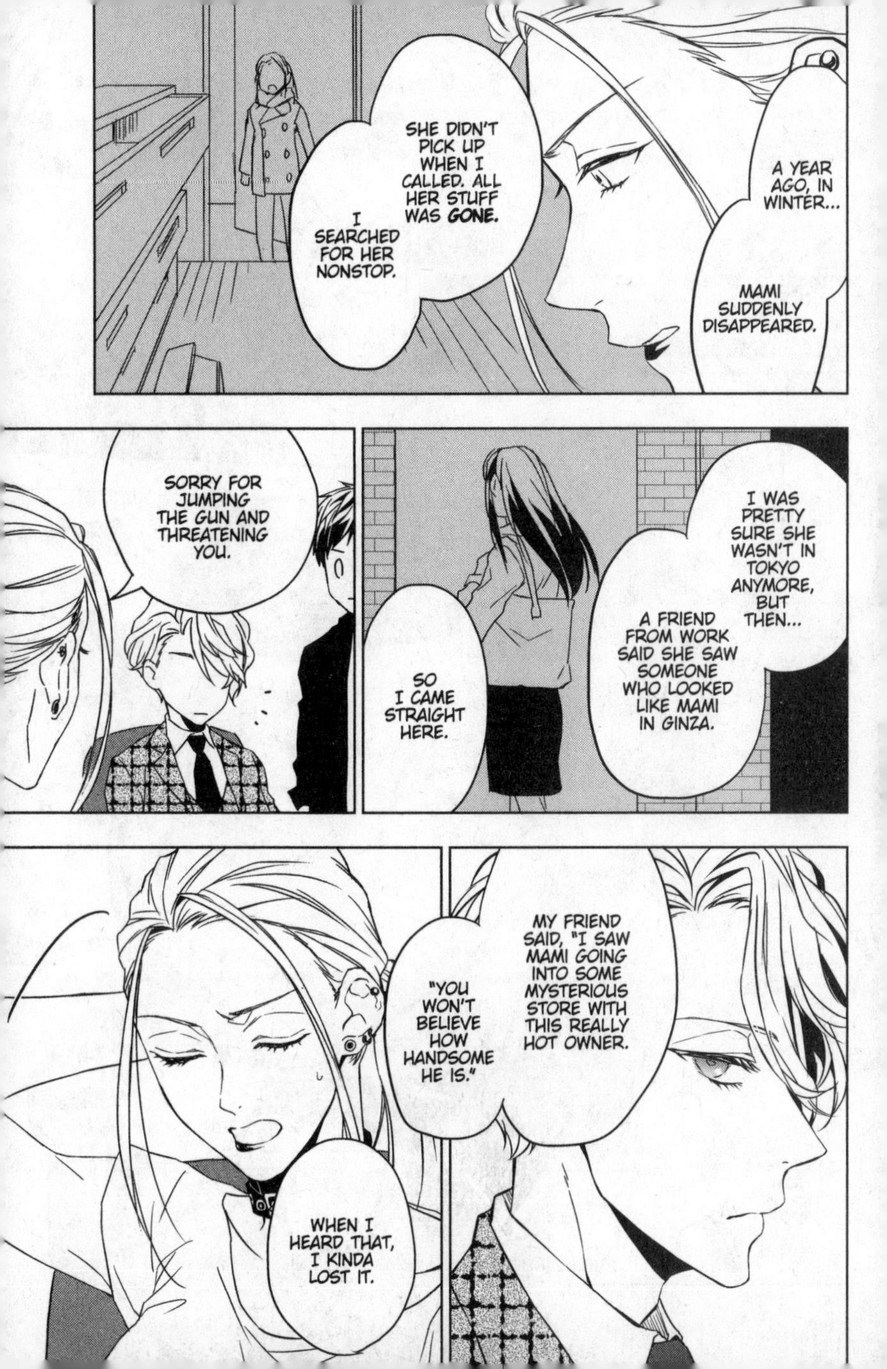
A YEAR AGO, IN WINTER...
MAMI SUDDENLY DISAPPEARED.
SHE DIDN'T PICK UP WHEN I CALLED. ALL HER STUFF WAS **GONE.**
I SEARCHED FOR HER NONSTOP.
I WAS PRETTY SURE SHE WASN'T IN TOKYO ANYMORE, BUT THEN...
A FRIEND FROM WORK SAID SHE SAW SOMEONE WHO LOOKED LIKE MAMI IN GINZA.
SO I CAME STRAIGHT HERE.
SORRY FOR JUMPING THE GUN AND THREATENING YOU.
MY FRIEND SAID, "I SAW MAMI GOING INTO SOME MYSTERIOUS STORE WITH THIS REALLY HOT OWNER.
"YOU WON'T BELIEVE HOW HANDSOME HE IS."
WHEN I HEARD THAT, I KINDA LOST IT.

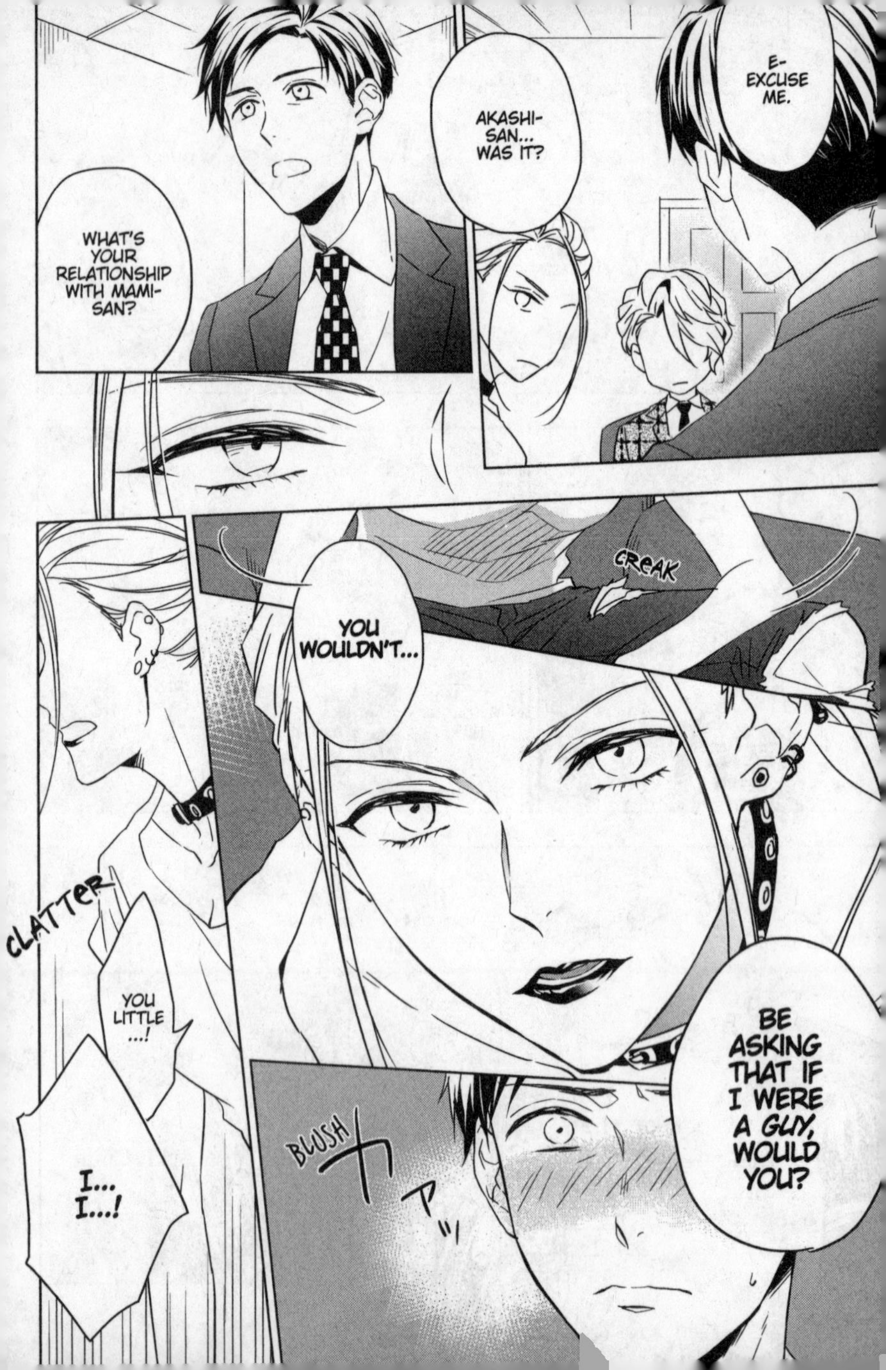
E-EXCUSE ME.
AKASHI-SAN... WAS IT?
WHAT'S YOUR RELATIONSHIP WITH MAMI-SAN?
CREAK
YOU WOULDN'T...
BE ASKING THAT IF I WERE A GUY, WOULD YOU?
BLUSH
CLATTER
YOU LITTLE ...!
I... I...!

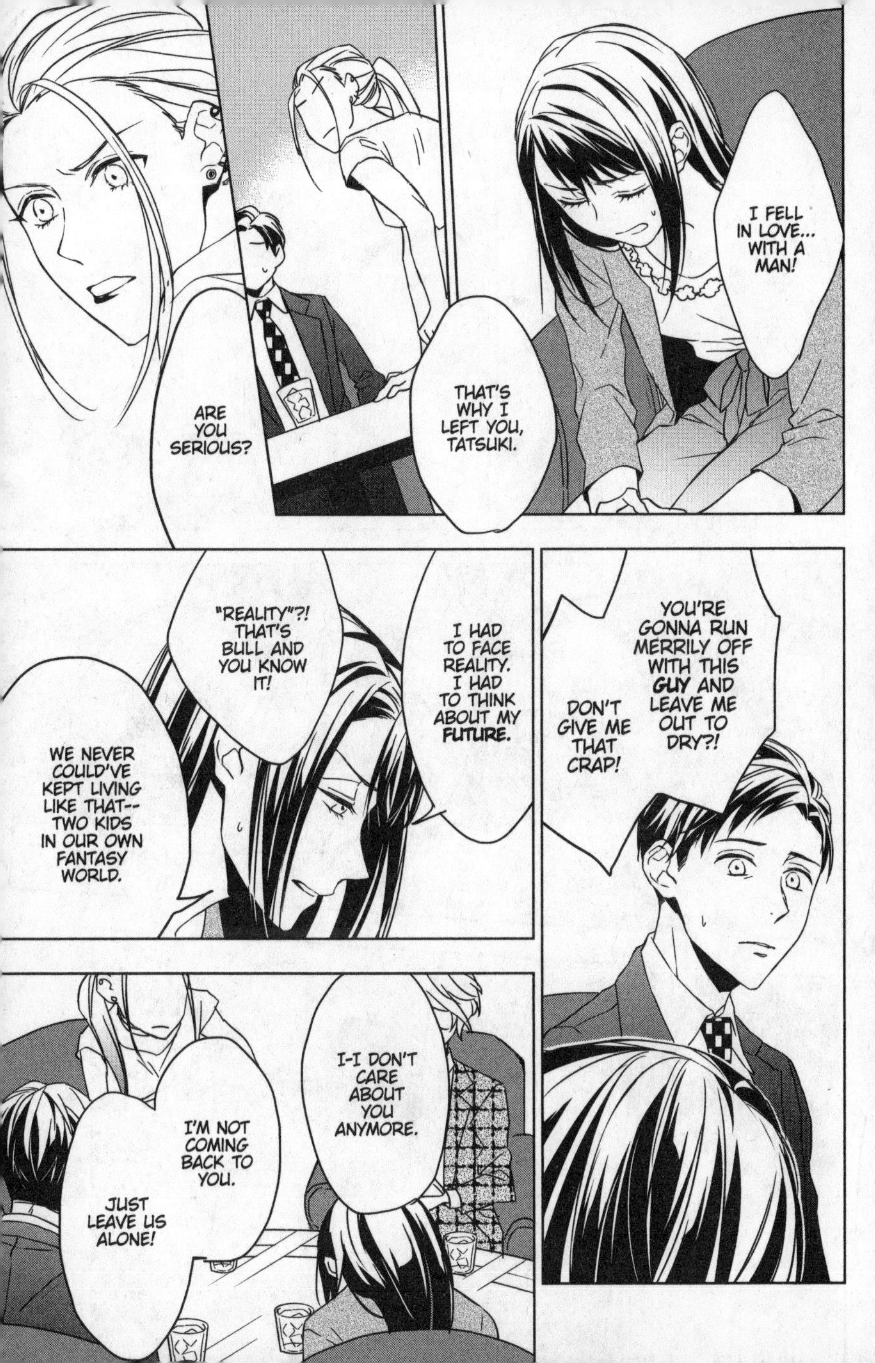
I FELL IN LOVE... WITH A MAN!
THAT'S WHY I LEFT YOU, TATSUKI.
ARE YOU SERIOUS?
YOU'RE GONNA RUN MERRILY OFF WITH THIS **GUY** AND LEAVE ME OUT TO DRY?!
DON'T GIVE ME THAT CRAP!
I HAD TO FACE REALITY. I HAD TO THINK ABOUT MY **FUTURE**.
"REALITY"?! THAT'S BULL AND YOU KNOW IT!
WE NEVER COULD'VE KEPT LIVING LIKE THAT-- TWO KIDS IN OUR OWN FANTASY WORLD.
I-I DON'T CARE ABOUT YOU ANYMORE.
I'M NOT COMING BACK TO YOU.
JUST LEAVE US ALONE!

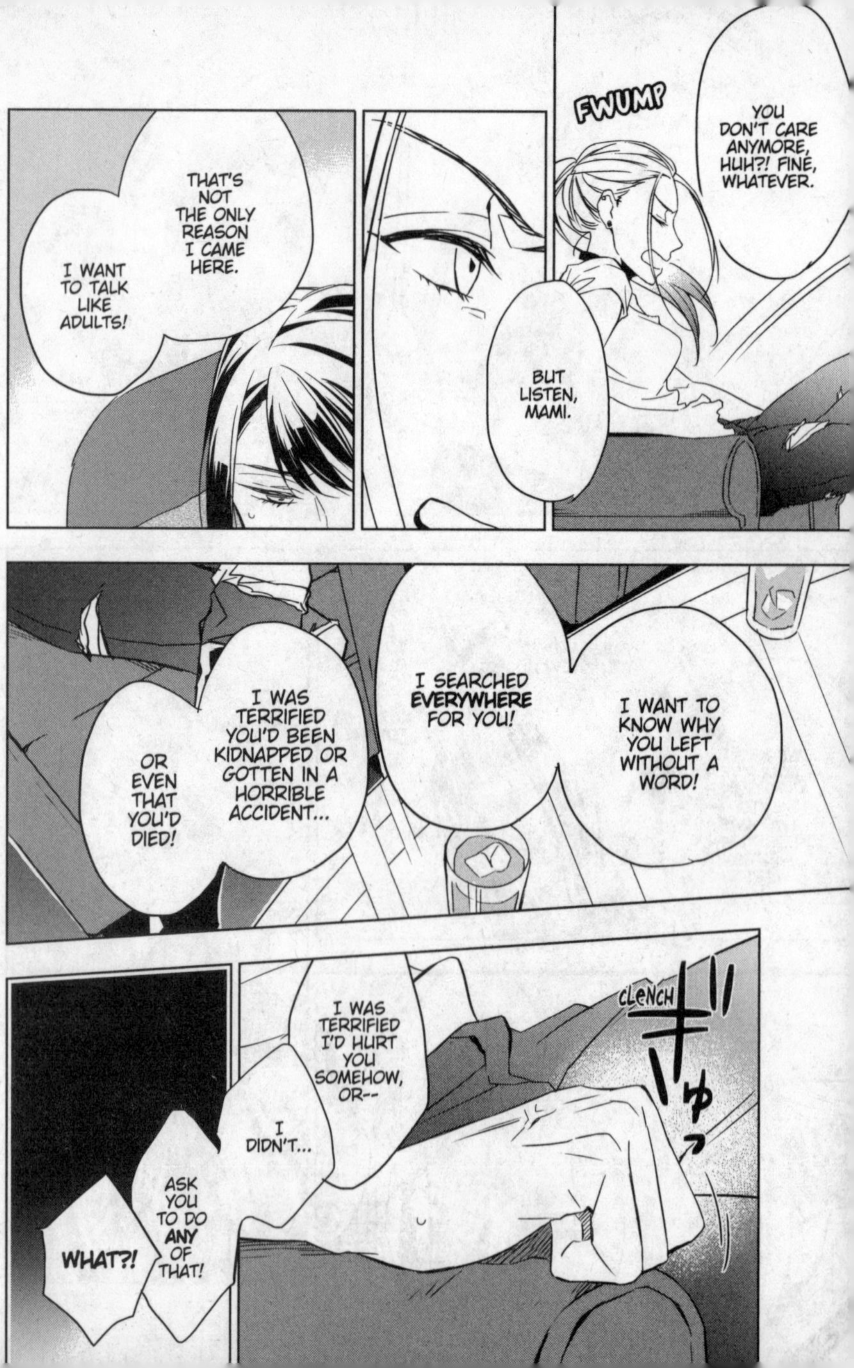
YOU DON'T CARE ANYMORE, HUH?! FINE, WHATEVER.
FWUMP
BUT LISTEN, MAMI.
THAT'S NOT THE ONLY REASON I CAME HERE.
I WANT TO TALK LIKE ADULTS!
I WANT TO KNOW WHY YOU LEFT WITHOUT A WORD!
I SEARCHED **EVERYWHERE** FOR YOU!
I WAS TERRIFIED YOU'D BEEN KIDNAPPED OR GOTTEN IN A HORRIBLE ACCIDENT...
OR EVEN THAT YOU'D DIED!
CLENCH
ぎゅっ
I WAS TERRIFIED I'D HURT YOU SOMEHOW, OR--
I DIDN'T...
ASK YOU TO DO **ANY** OF THAT!
WHAT?!

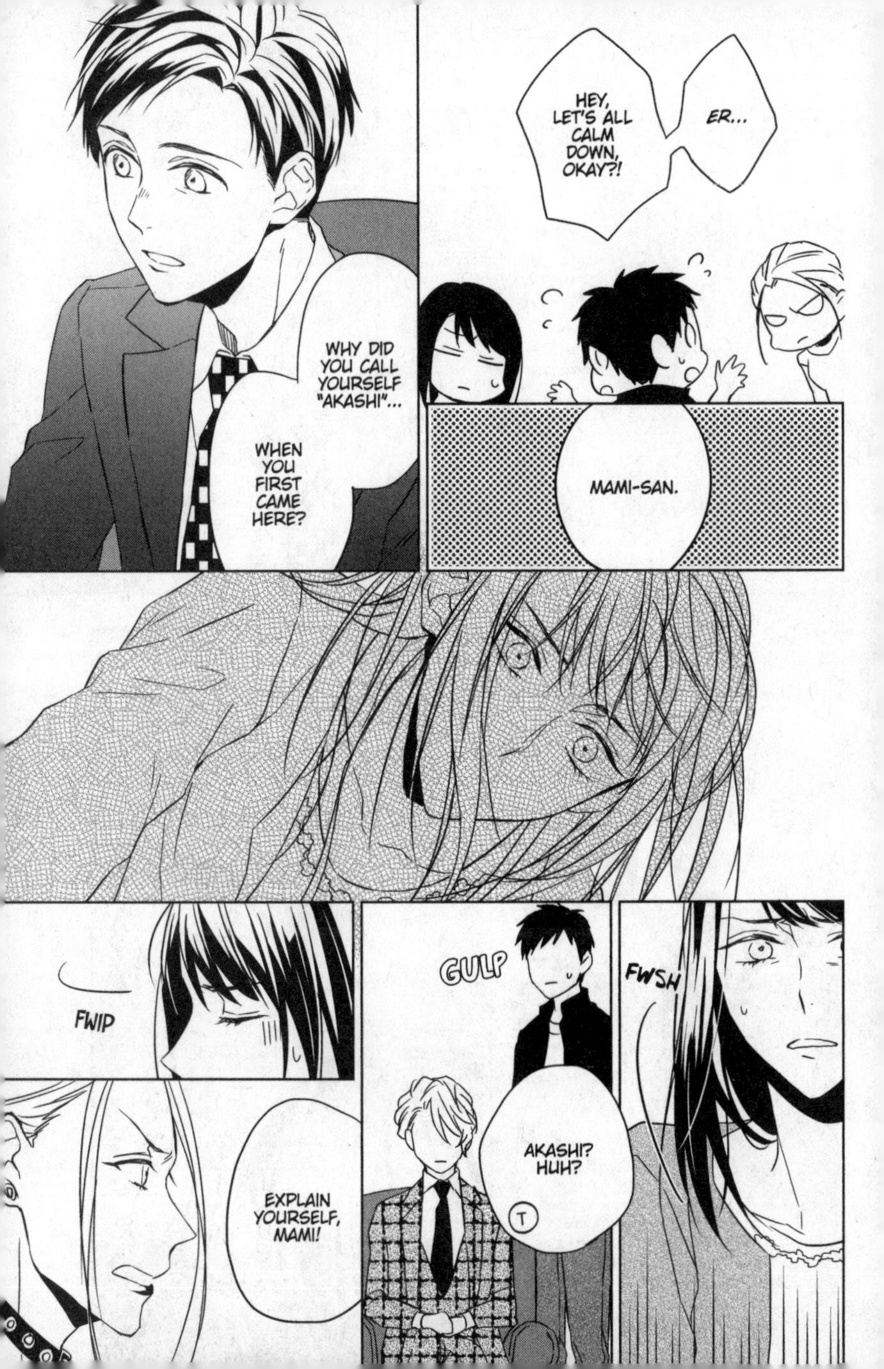
ER...
HEY, LET'S ALL CALM DOWN, OKAY?!
MAMI-SAN.
WHY DID YOU CALL YOURSELF "AKASHI"...
WHEN YOU FIRST CAME HERE?
FWSH
GULP
AKASHI? HUH?
T
FWIP
EXPLAIN YOURSELF, MAMI!

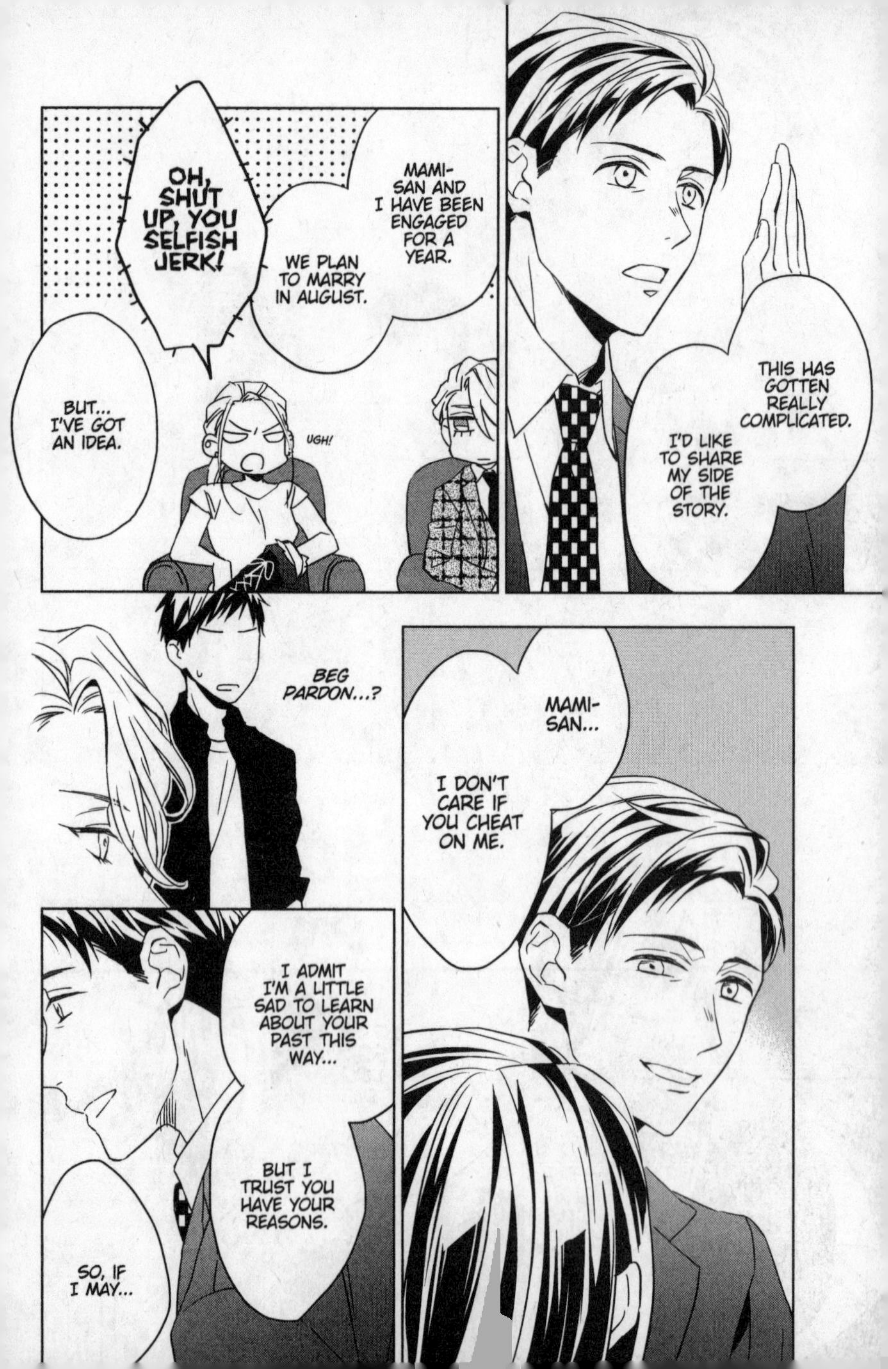
THIS HAS GOTTEN REALLY COMPLICATED.
I'D LIKE TO SHARE MY SIDE OF THE STORY.
MAMI-SAN AND I HAVE BEEN ENGAGED FOR A YEAR.
WE PLAN TO MARRY IN AUGUST.
OH, SHUT UP, YOU SELFISH JERK!
UGH!
BUT... I'VE GOT AN IDEA.
MAMI-SAN...
I DON'T CARE IF YOU CHEAT ON ME.
BEG PARDON...?
I ADMIT I'M A LITTLE SAD TO LEARN ABOUT YOUR PAST THIS WAY...
BUT I TRUST YOU HAVE YOUR REASONS.
SO, IF I MAY...

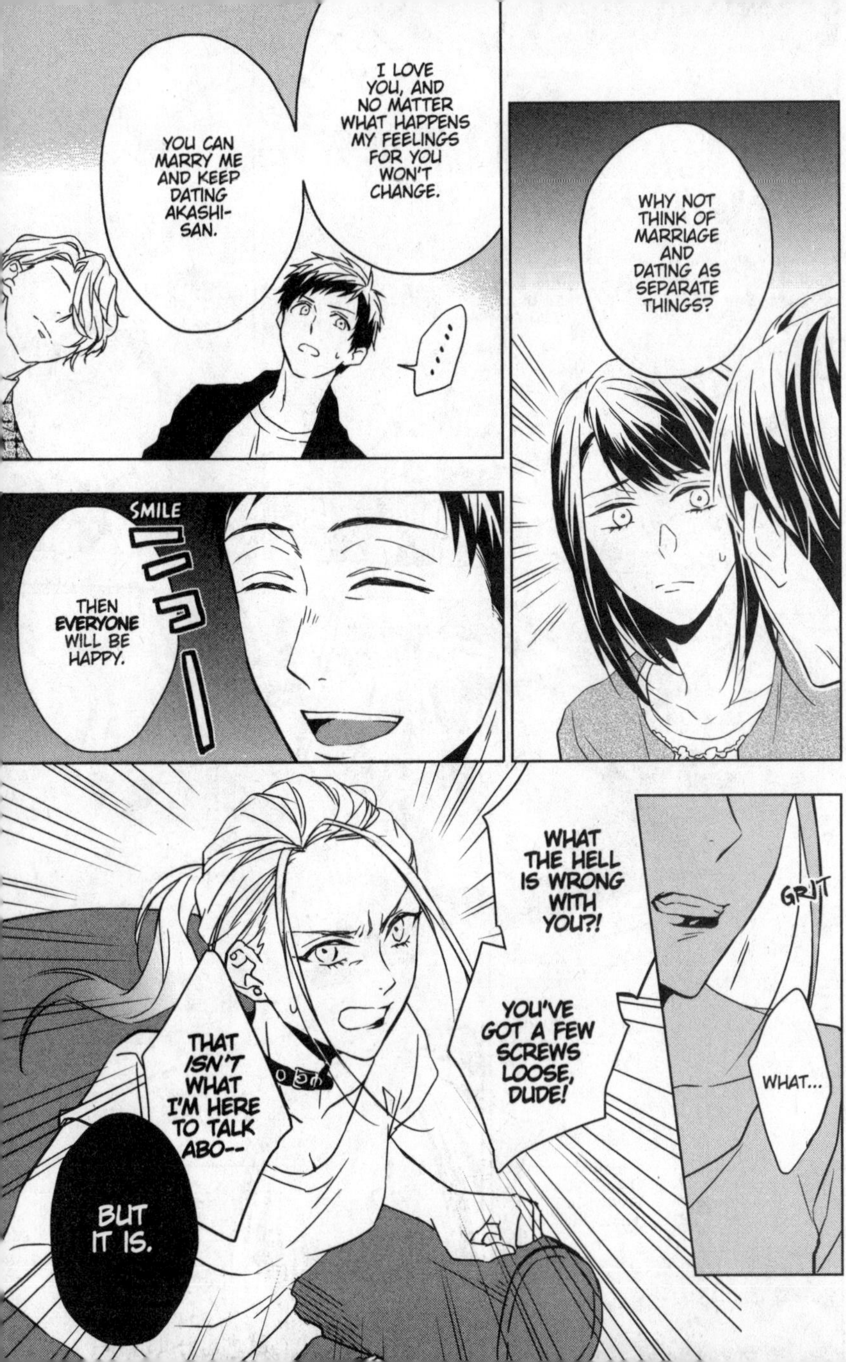
WHY NOT THINK OF MARRIAGE AND DATING AS SEPARATE THINGS?
I LOVE YOU, AND NO MATTER WHAT HAPPENS MY FEELINGS FOR YOU WON'T CHANGE.
YOU CAN MARRY ME AND KEEP DATING AKASHI-SAN.
......
SMILE
THEN EVERYONE WILL BE HAPPY.
GRIT
WHAT...
WHAT THE HELL IS WRONG WITH YOU?!
YOU'VE GOT A FEW SCREWS LOOSE, DUDE!
THAT *ISN'T* WHAT I'M HERE TO TALK ABO--
BUT IT IS.

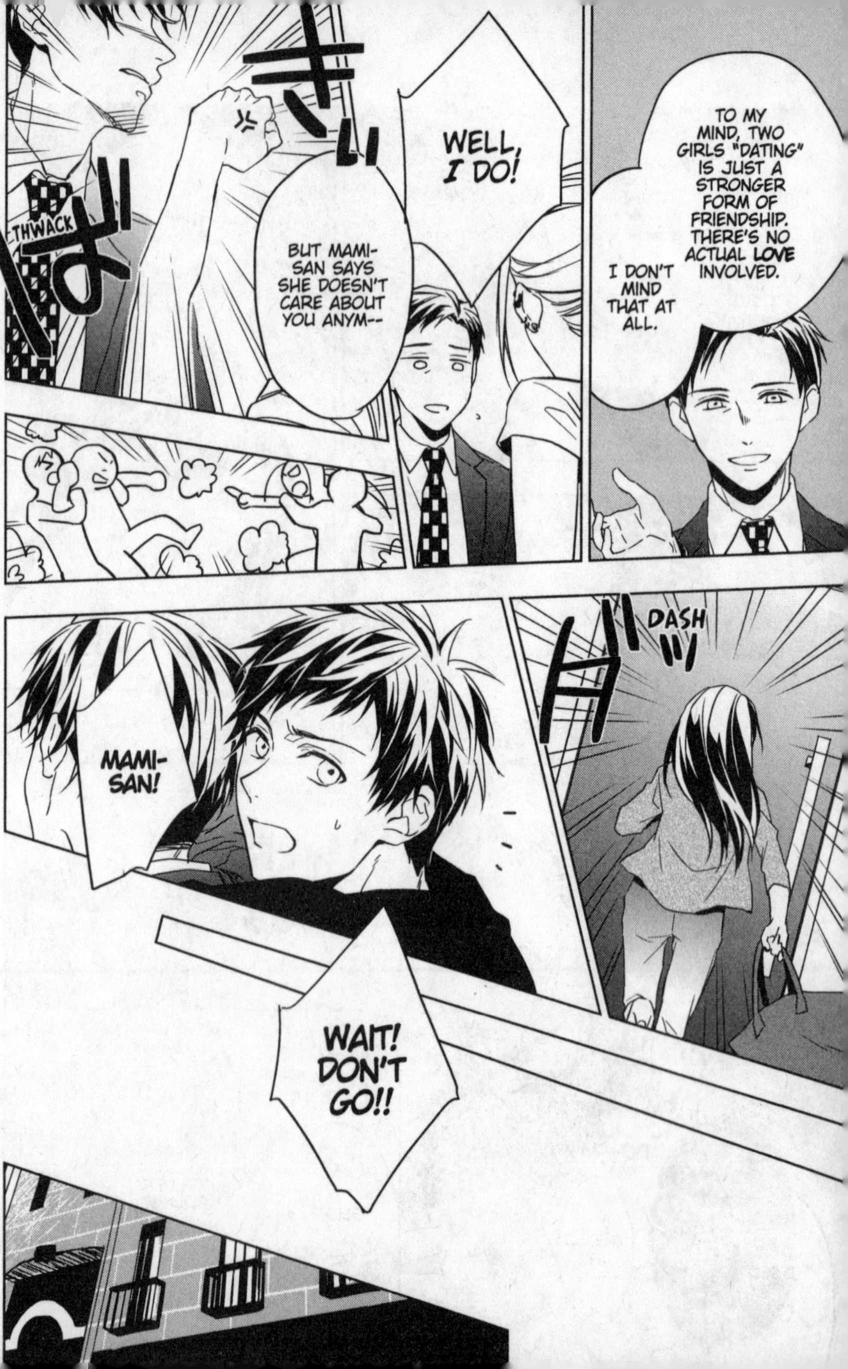
TO MY MIND, TWO GIRLS "DATING" IS JUST A STRONGER FORM OF FRIENDSHIP. THERE'S NO ACTUAL LOVE INVOLVED.
I DON'T MIND THAT AT ALL.
WELL, I DO!
BUT MAMI-SAN SAYS SHE DOESN'T CARE ABOUT YOU ANYM--
THWACK
DASH
MAMI-SAN!
WAIT! DON'T GO!!

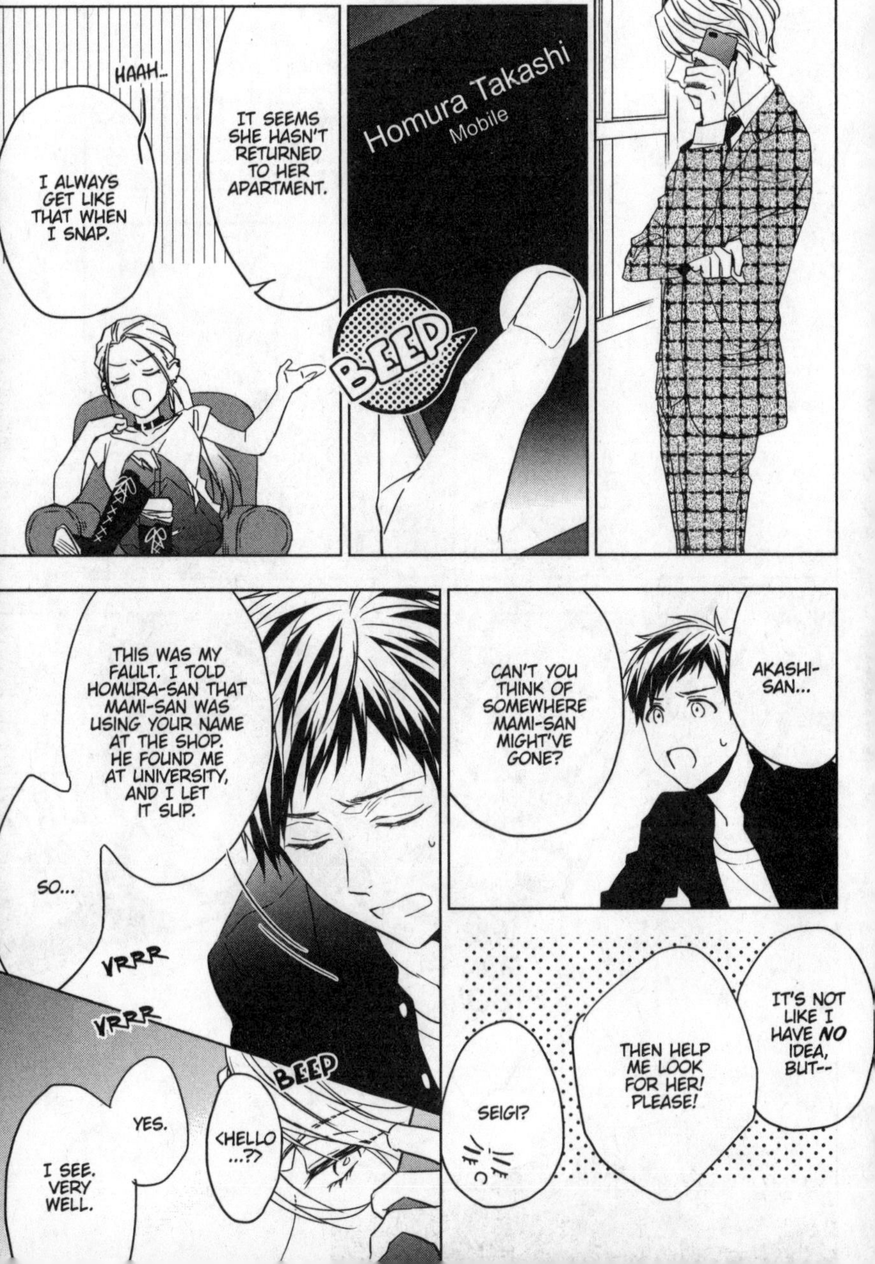
Homura Takashi
Mobile
BEEP
IT SEEMS SHE HASN'T RETURNED TO HER APARTMENT.
HAAH..
I ALWAYS GET LIKE THAT WHEN I SNAP.
AKASHI-SAN...
CAN'T YOU THINK OF SOMEWHERE MAMI-SAN MIGHT'VE GONE?
IT'S NOT LIKE I HAVE *NO* IDEA, BUT--
THEN HELP ME LOOK FOR HER! PLEASE!
SEIGI?
THIS WAS MY FAULT. I TOLD HOMURA-SAN THAT MAMI-SAN WAS USING YOUR NAME AT THE SHOP. HE FOUND ME AT UNIVERSITY, AND I LET IT SLIP.
SO...
VRRR
VRRR
BEEP
<HELLO ...?>
YES.
I SEE. VERY WELL.

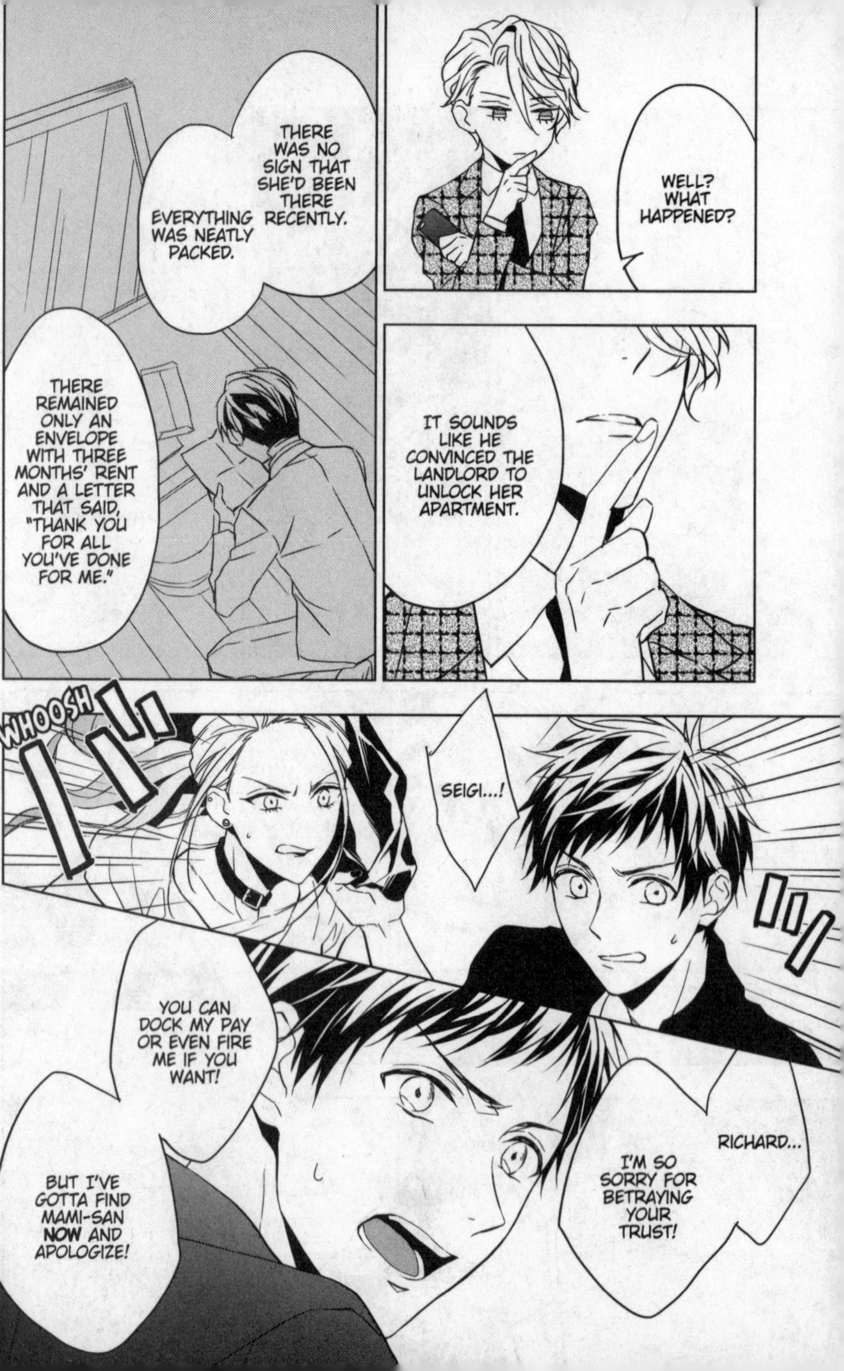
WELL? WHAT HAPPENED?
IT SOUNDS LIKE HE CONVINCED THE LANDLORD TO UNLOCK HER APARTMENT.
THERE WAS NO SIGN THAT SHE'D BEEN THERE RECENTLY.
EVERYTHING WAS NEATLY PACKED.
THERE REMAINED ONLY AN ENVELOPE WITH THREE MONTHS' RENT AND A LETTER THAT SAID, "THANK YOU FOR ALL YOU'VE DONE FOR ME."
SEIGI...!
WHOOSH
RICHARD...
I'M SO SORRY FOR BETRAYING YOUR TRUST!
YOU CAN DOCK MY PAY OR EVEN FIRE ME IF YOU WANT!
BUT I'VE GOTTA FIND MAMI-SAN NOW AND APOLOGIZE!

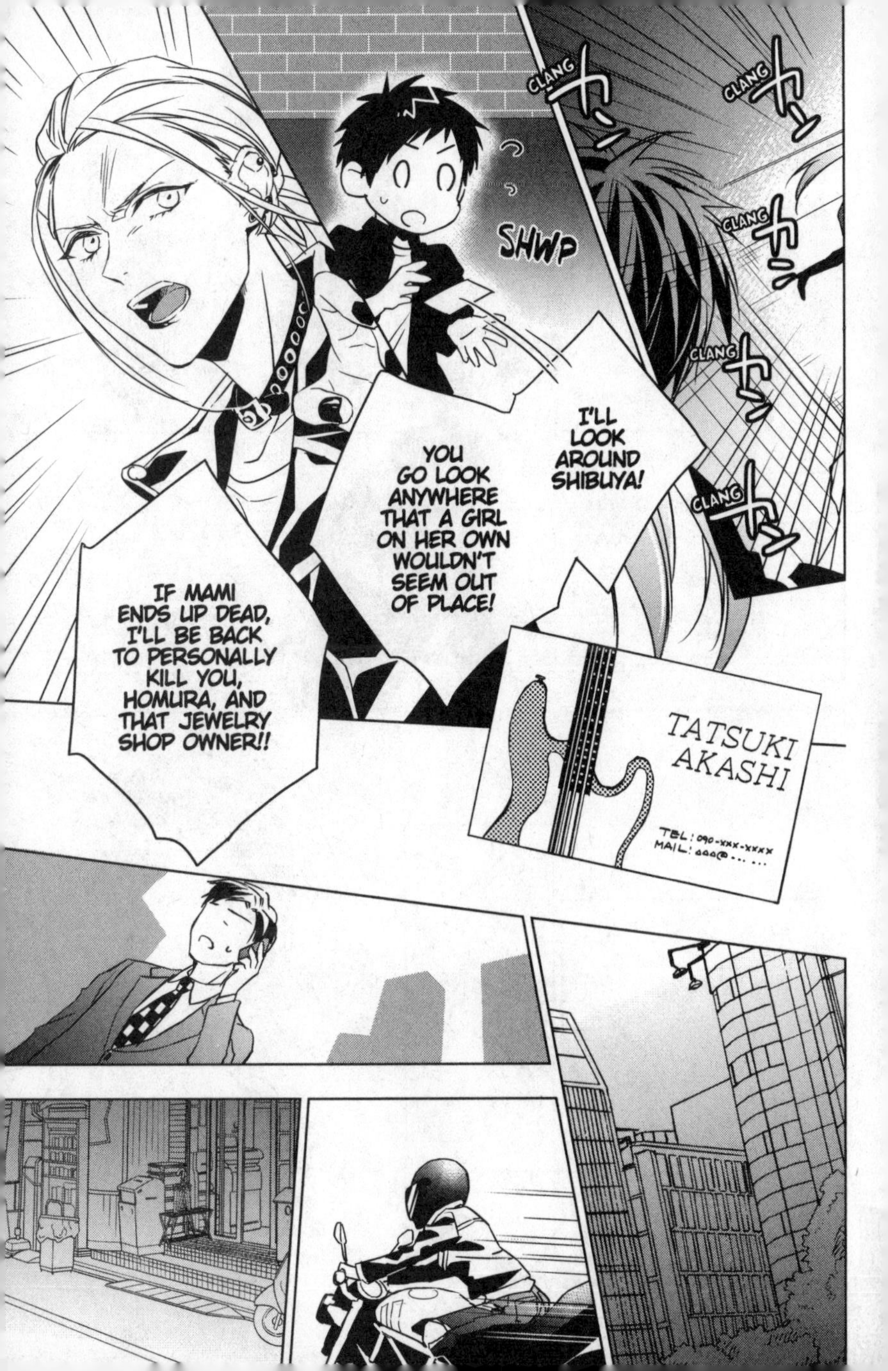
CLANG
CLANG
CLANG
CLANG
CLANG
SHWP
I'LL LOOK AROUND SHIBUYA!
YOU GO LOOK ANYWHERE THAT A GIRL ON HER OWN WOULDN'T SEEM OUT OF PLACE!
IF MAMI ENDS UP DEAD, I'LL BE BACK TO PERSONALLY KILL YOU, HOMURA, AND THAT JEWELRY SHOP OWNER!!
TATSUKI AKASHI
TEL: 090-XXX-XXXX

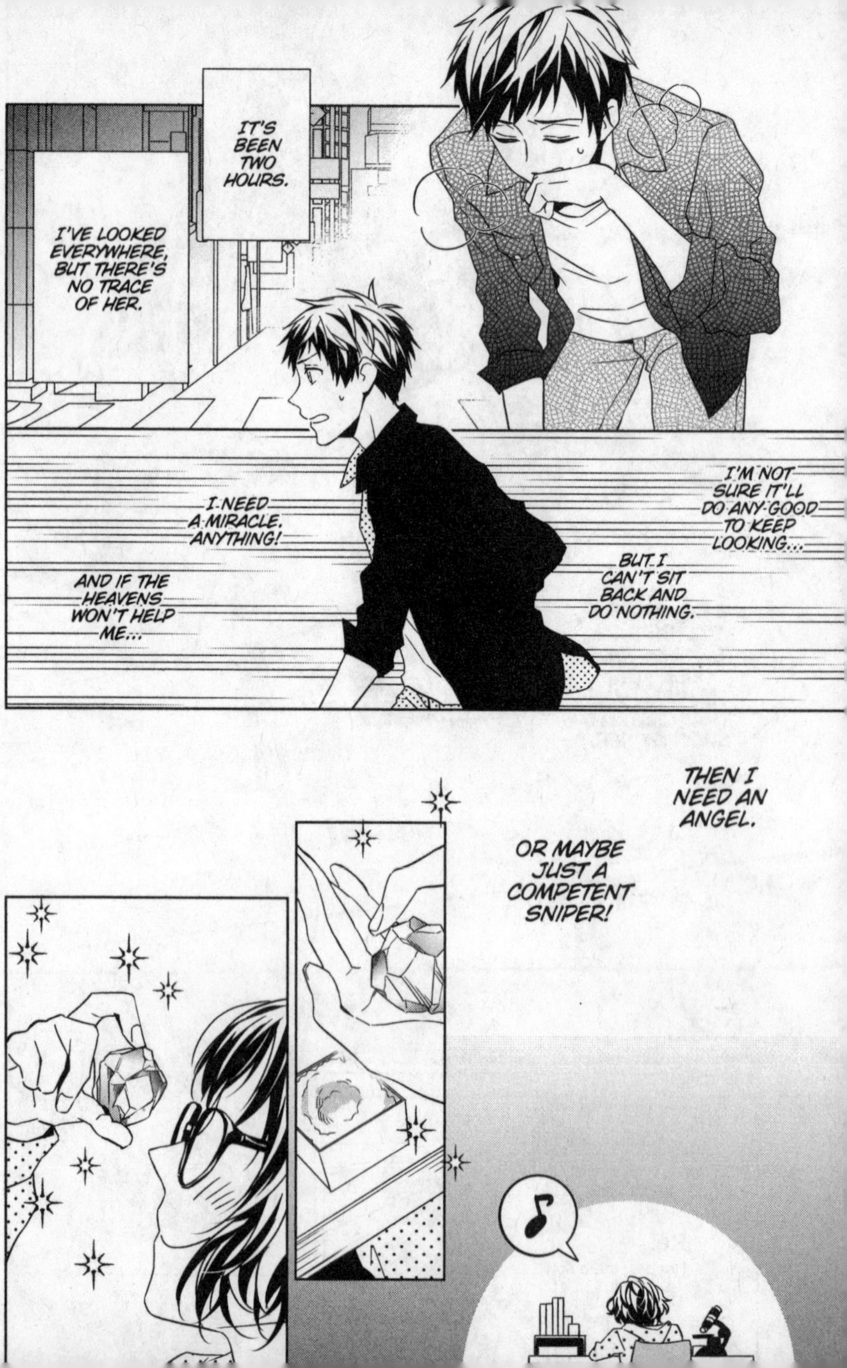
IT'S BEEN TWO HOURS.
I'VE LOOKED EVERYWHERE, BUT THERE'S NO TRACE OF HER.
I'M NOT SURE IT'LL DO ANY GOOD TO KEEP LOOKING...
BUT I CAN'T SIT BACK AND DO NOTHING.
I NEED A MIRACLE. ANYTHING!
AND IF THE HEAVENS WON'T HELP ME...
THEN I NEED AN ANGEL.
OR MAYBE JUST A COMPETENT SNIPER!

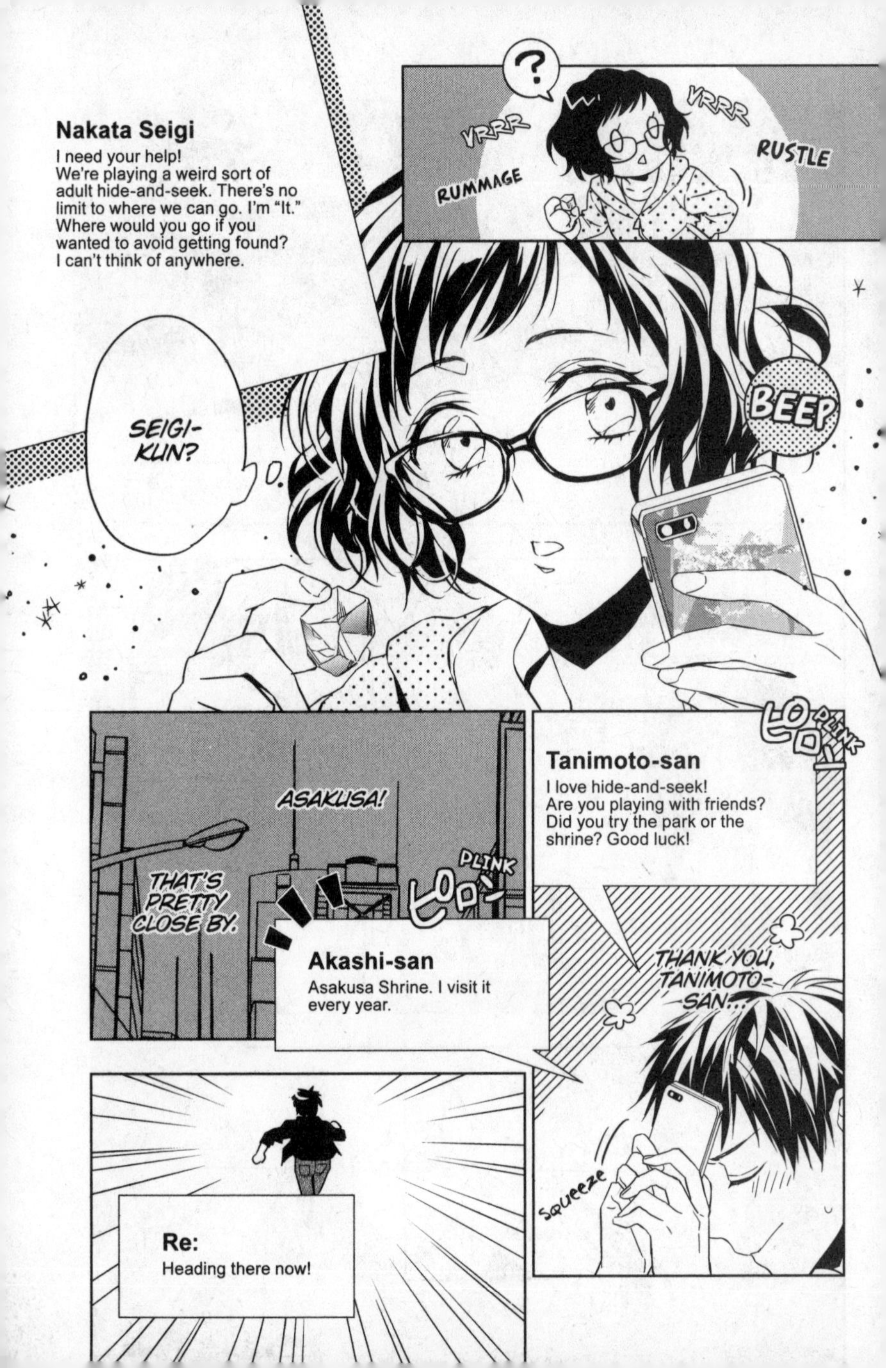
?
YRRR
YRRR
RUSTLE
RUMMAGE
Nakata Seigi
I need your help!
We're playing a weird sort of adult hide-and-seek. There's no limit to where we can go. I'm "It."
Where would you go if you wanted to avoid getting found?
I can't think of anywhere.
BEEP
SEIGI-KUN?
PLINK
Tanimoto-san
I love hide-and-seek!
Are you playing with friends?
Did you try the park or the shrine? Good luck!
THANK YOU, TANIMOTO-SAN...
Squeeze
ASAKUSA!
PLINK
THAT'S PRETTY CLOSE BY.
Akashi-san
Asakusa Shrine. I visit it every year.
Re:
Heading there now!

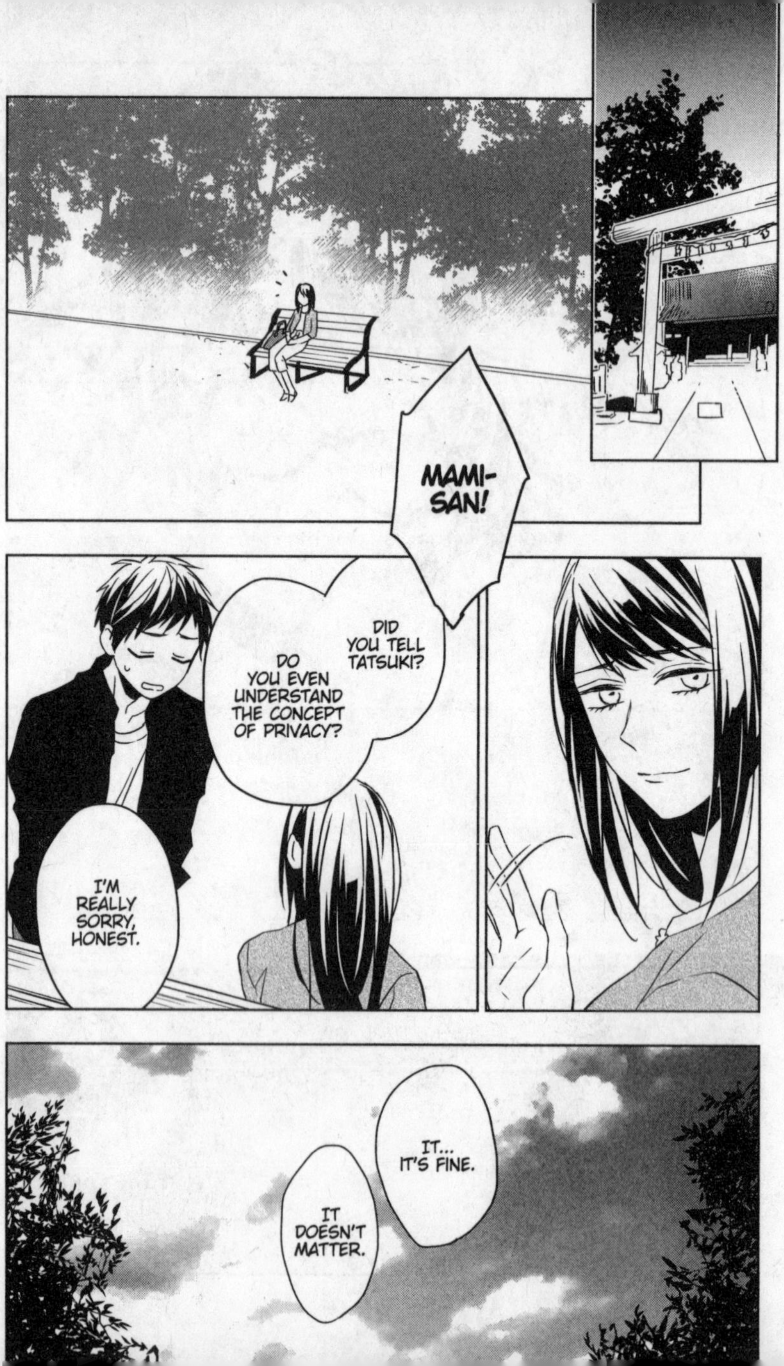
MAMI-SAN!
DID YOU TELL TATSUKI? DO YOU EVEN UNDERSTAND THE CONCEPT OF PRIVACY?
I'M REALLY SORRY, HONEST.
IT... IT'S FINE.
IT DOESN'T MATTER.

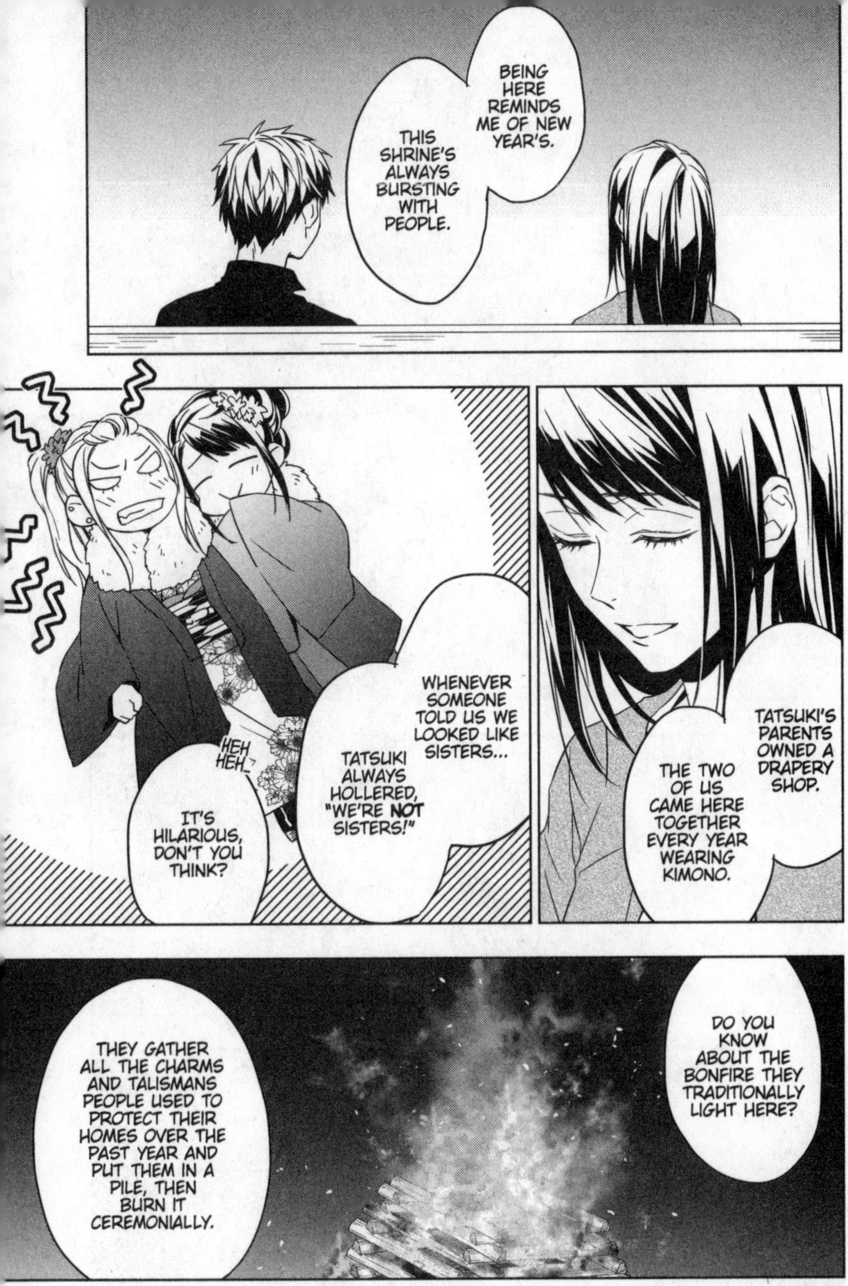
BEING HERE REMINDS ME OF NEW YEAR'S.
THIS SHRINE'S ALWAYS BURSTING WITH PEOPLE.
TATSUKI'S PARENTS OWNED A DRAPERY SHOP.
THE TWO OF US CAME HERE TOGETHER EVERY YEAR WEARING KIMONO.
WHENEVER SOMEONE TOLD US WE LOOKED LIKE SISTERS...
TATSUKI ALWAYS HOLLERED, "WE'RE **NOT** SISTERS!"
HEH HEH...
IT'S HILARIOUS, DON'T YOU THINK?
DO YOU KNOW ABOUT THE BONFIRE THEY TRADITIONALLY LIGHT HERE?
THEY GATHER ALL THE CHARMS AND TALISMANS PEOPLE USED TO PROTECT THEIR HOMES OVER THE PAST YEAR AND PUT THEM IN A PILE, THEN BURN IT CEREMONIALLY.

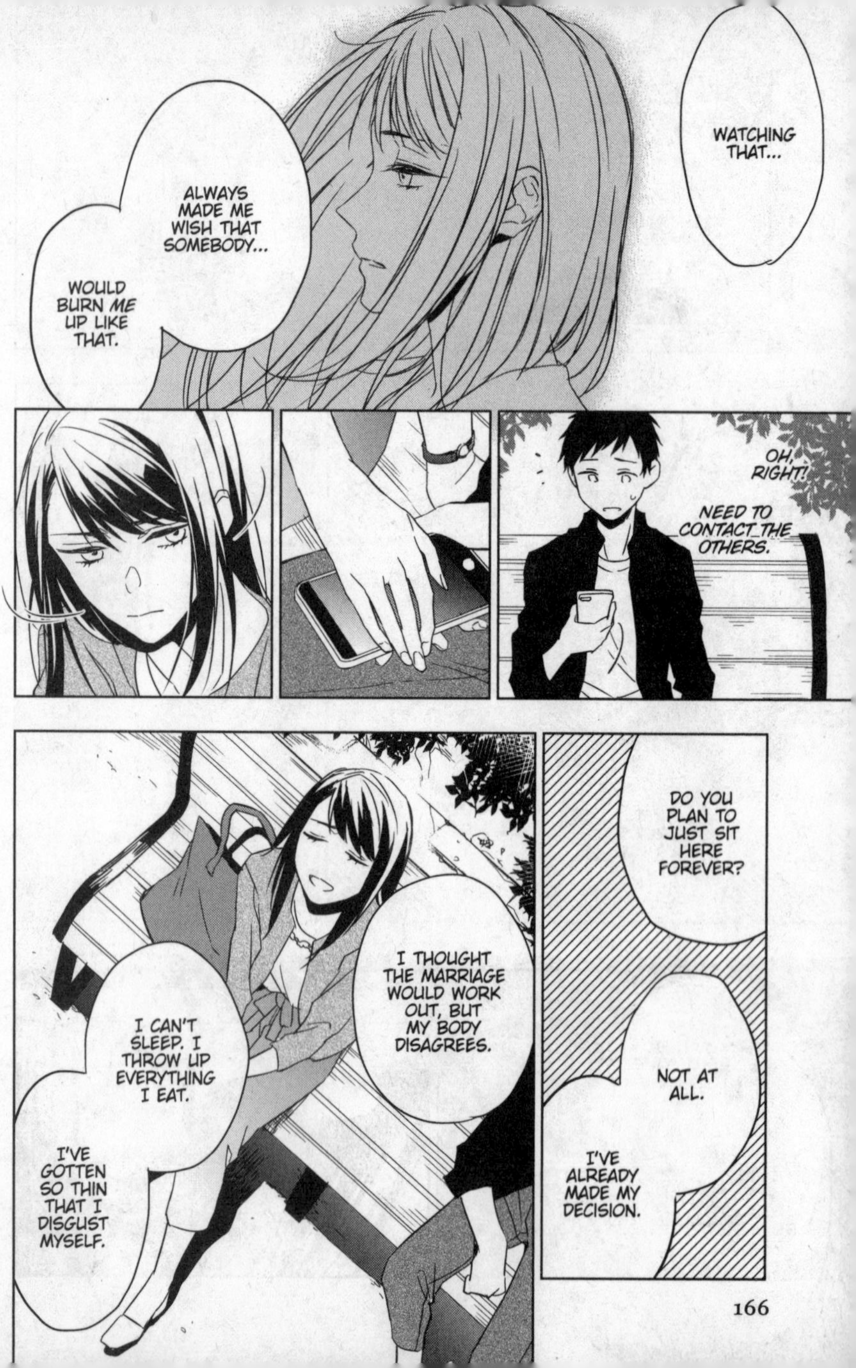

WATCHING THAT...
ALWAYS MADE ME WISH THAT SOMEBODY...
WOULD BURN *ME* UP LIKE THAT.
OH, RIGHT!
NEED TO CONTACT THE OTHERS.
DO YOU PLAN TO JUST SIT HERE FOREVER?
NOT AT ALL.
I'VE ALREADY MADE MY DECISION.
I THOUGHT THE MARRIAGE WOULD WORK OUT, BUT MY BODY DISAGREES.
I CAN'T SLEEP. I THROW UP EVERYTHING I EAT.
I'VE GOTTEN SO THIN THAT I DISGUST MYSELF.

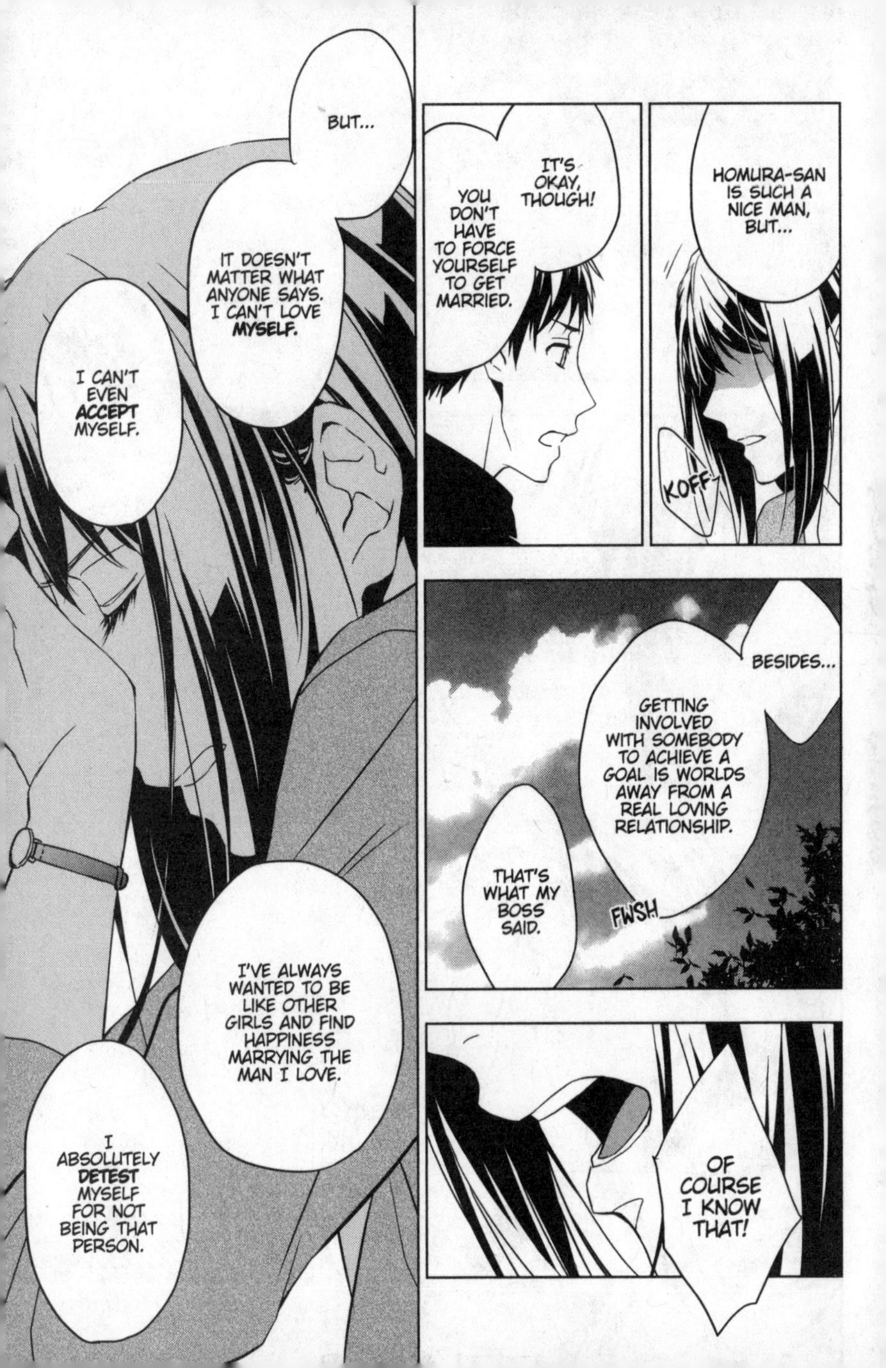
HOMURA-SAN IS SUCH A NICE MAN, BUT...
KOFF
IT'S OKAY, THOUGH!
YOU DON'T HAVE TO FORCE YOURSELF TO GET MARRIED.
BESIDES...
GETTING INVOLVED WITH SOMEBODY TO ACHIEVE A GOAL IS WORLDS AWAY FROM A REAL LOVING RELATIONSHIP.
THAT'S WHAT MY BOSS SAID.
FWSH
OF COURSE I KNOW THAT!
BUT...
IT DOESN'T MATTER WHAT ANYONE SAYS. I CAN'T LOVE MYSELF.
I CAN'T EVEN ACCEPT MYSELF.
I'VE ALWAYS WANTED TO BE LIKE OTHER GIRLS AND FIND HAPPINESS MARRYING THE MAN I LOVE.
I ABSOLUTELY DETEST MYSELF FOR NOT BEING THAT PERSON.

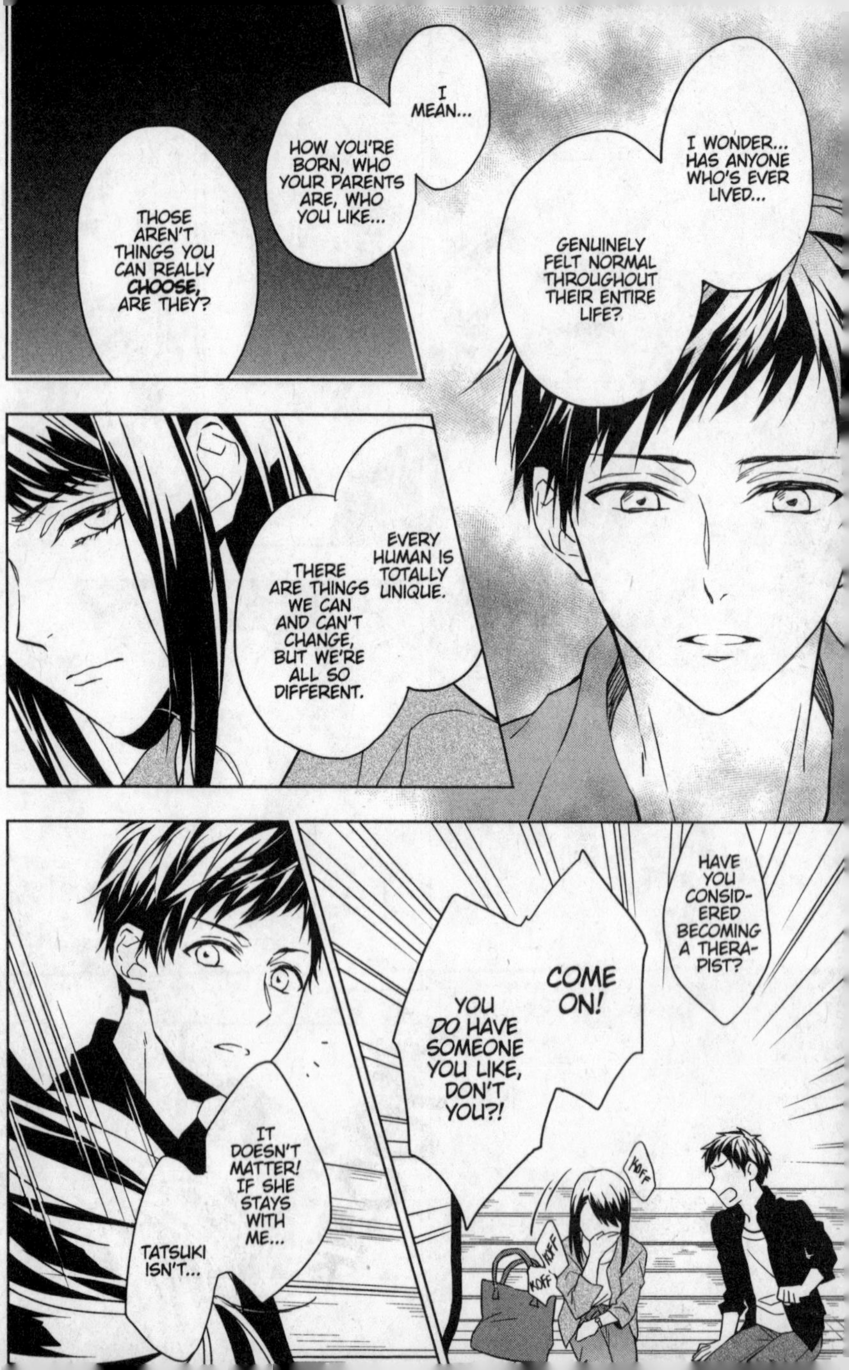
I WONDER... HAS ANYONE WHO'S EVER LIVED...
GENUINELY FELT NORMAL THROUGHOUT THEIR ENTIRE LIFE?
I MEAN...
HOW YOU'RE BORN, WHO YOUR PARENTS ARE, WHO YOU LIKE...
THOSE AREN'T THINGS YOU CAN REALLY **CHOOSE,** ARE THEY?
EVERY HUMAN IS TOTALLY UNIQUE.
THERE ARE THINGS WE CAN AND CAN'T CHANGE, BUT WE'RE ALL SO DIFFERENT.
HAVE YOU CONSID-ERED BECOMING A THERA-PIST?
COME ON!
YOU DO HAVE SOMEONE YOU LIKE, DON'T YOU?!
KOFF
KOFF
KOFF
IT DOESN'T MATTER! IF SHE STAYS WITH ME...
TATSUKI ISN'T...

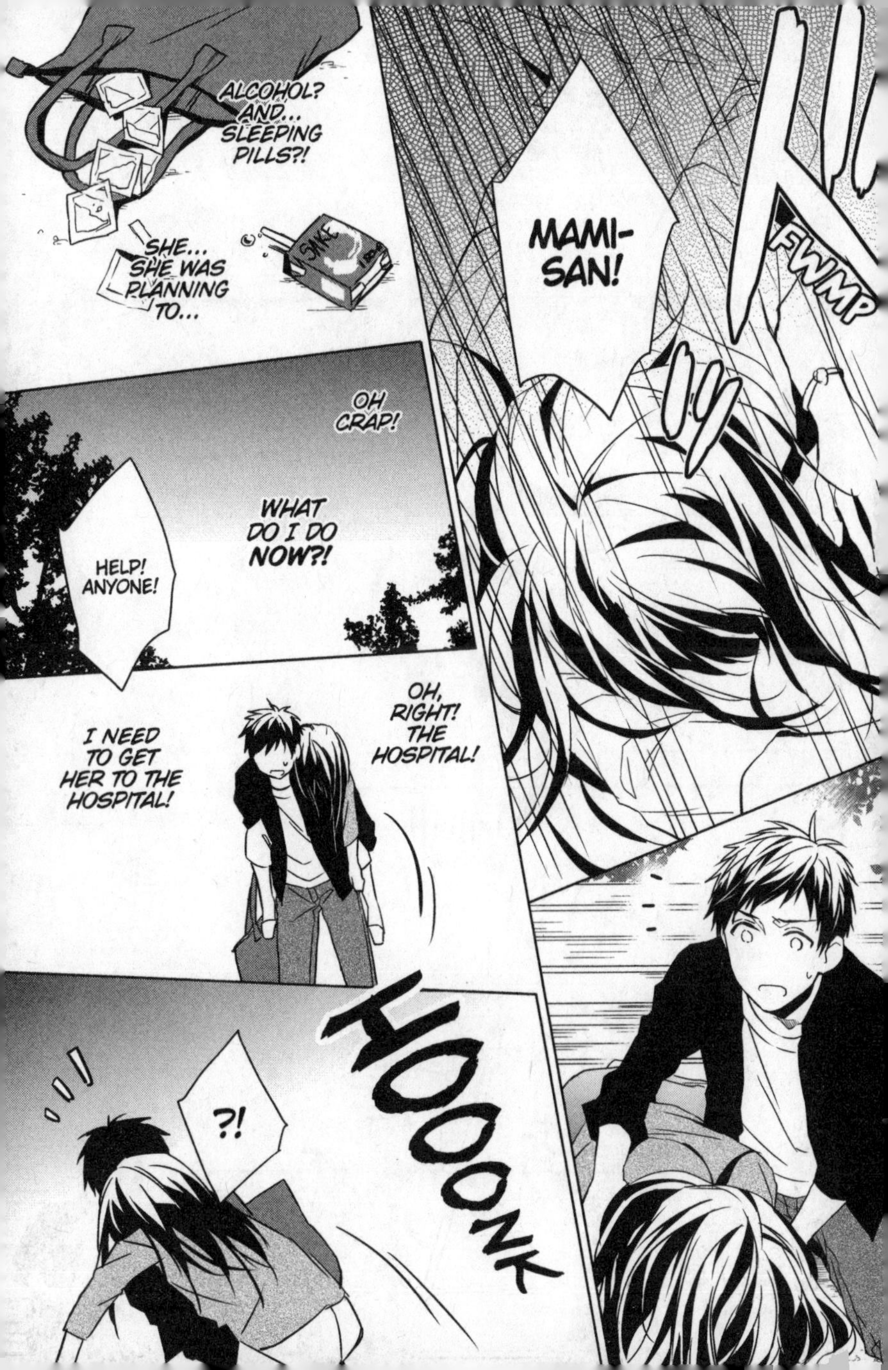
FWMP
MAMI-SAN!
ALCOHOL? AND... SLEEPING PILLS?!
SAKE
SHE... SHE WAS PLANNING TO...
OH CRAP!
WHAT DO I DO NOW?!
HELP! ANYONE!
OH, RIGHT! THE HOSPITAL!
I NEED TO GET HER TO THE HOSPITAL!
HOOONK
?!

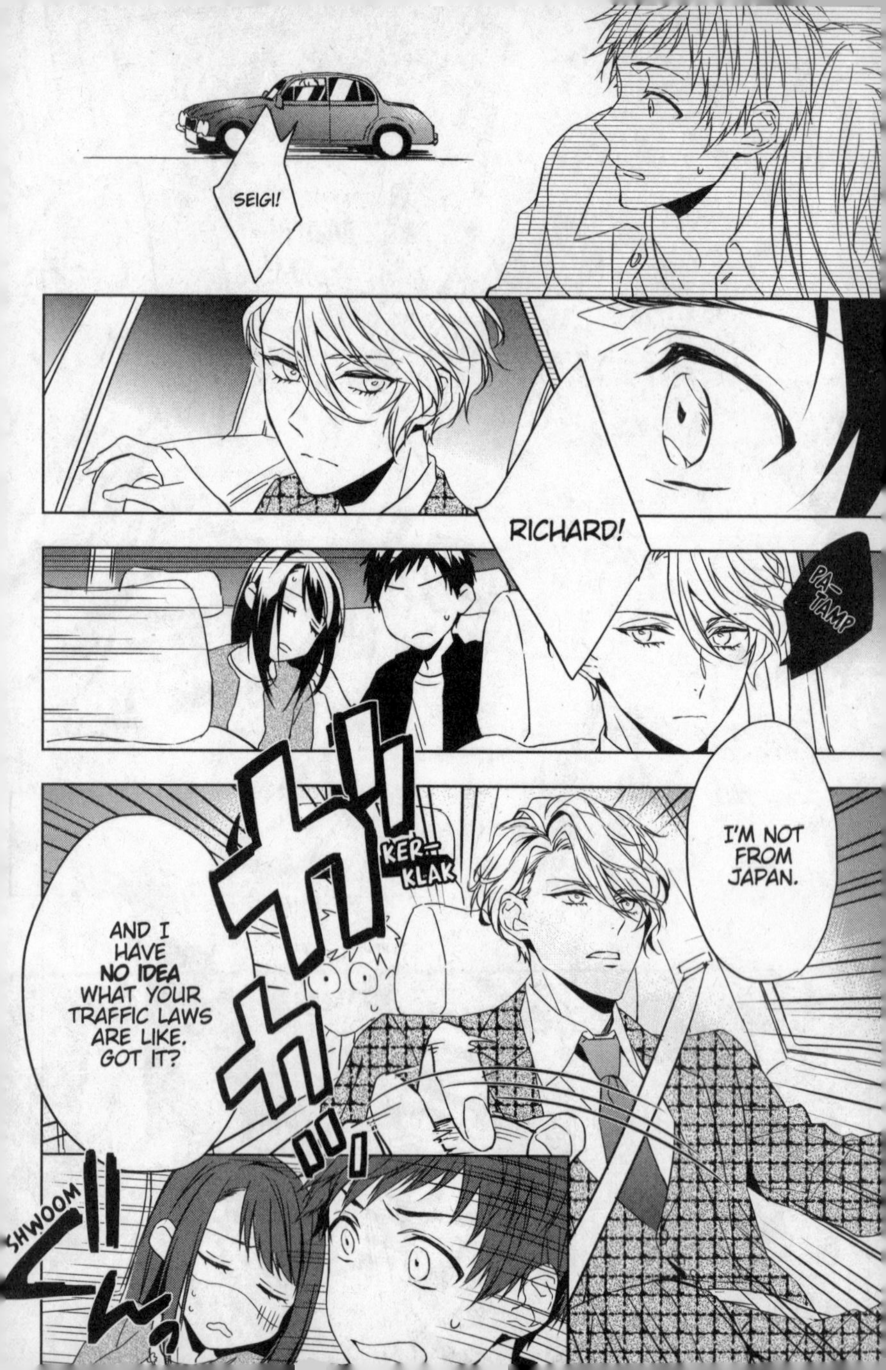
SEIGI!
RICHARD!
PA-TAMP
I'M NOT FROM JAPAN.
KER-KLAK
AND I HAVE NO IDEA WHAT YOUR TRAFFIC LAWS ARE LIKE. GOT IT?
SHWOOM

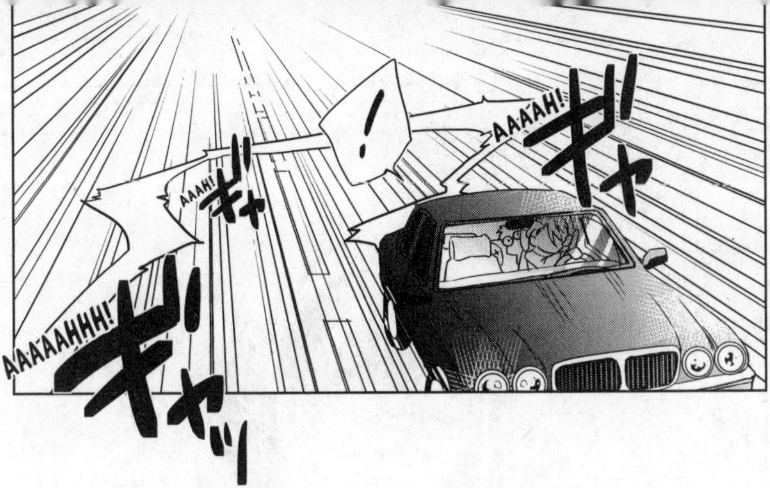
!
AAAAH!
ギャ
AAAH!
ギャ
AAAAAHHH!
ギャッ

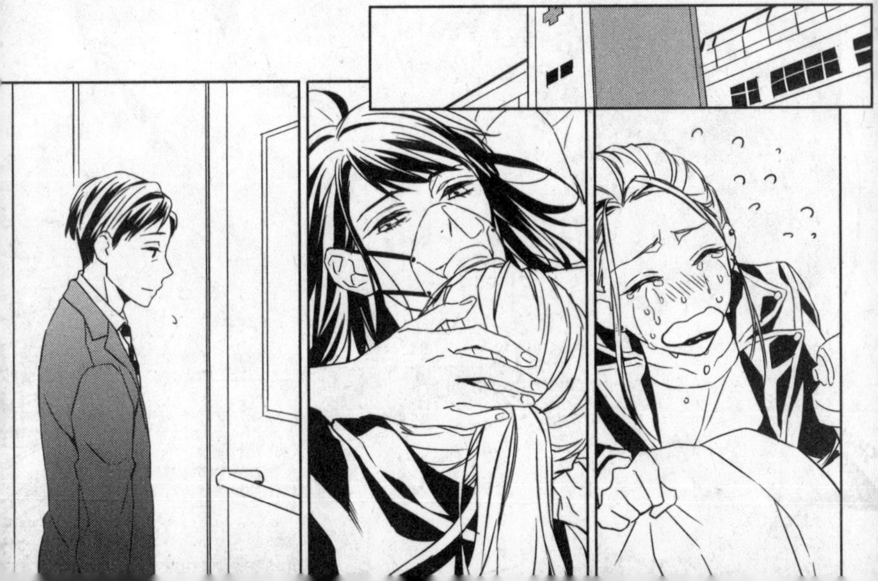

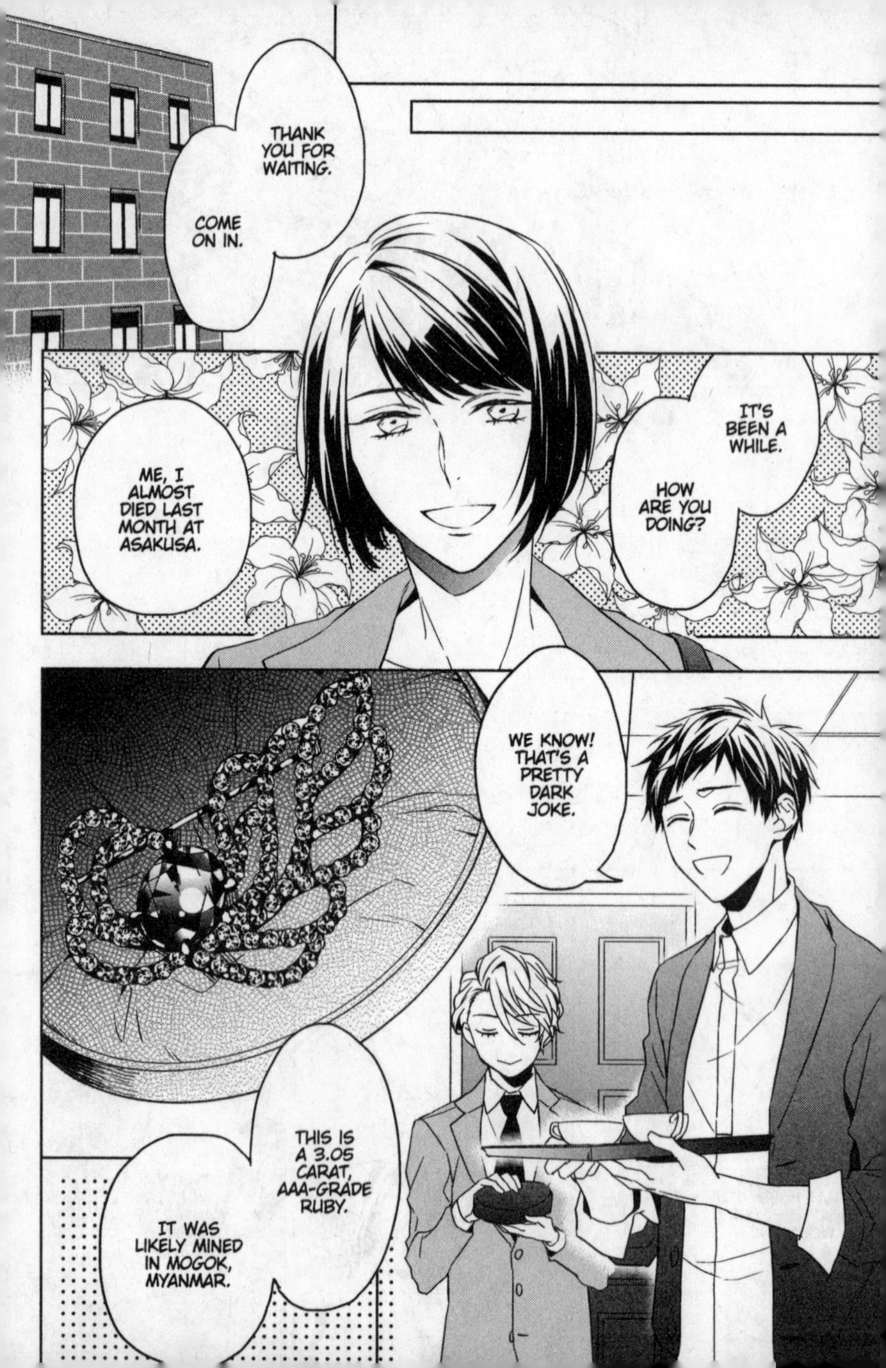
THANK YOU FOR WAITING.
COME ON IN.
IT'S BEEN A WHILE.
HOW ARE YOU DOING?
ME, I ALMOST DIED LAST MONTH AT ASAKUSA.
WE KNOW! THAT'S A PRETTY DARK JOKE.
THIS IS A 3.05 CARAT, AAA-GRADE RUBY.
IT WAS LIKELY MINED IN MOGOK, MYANMAR.

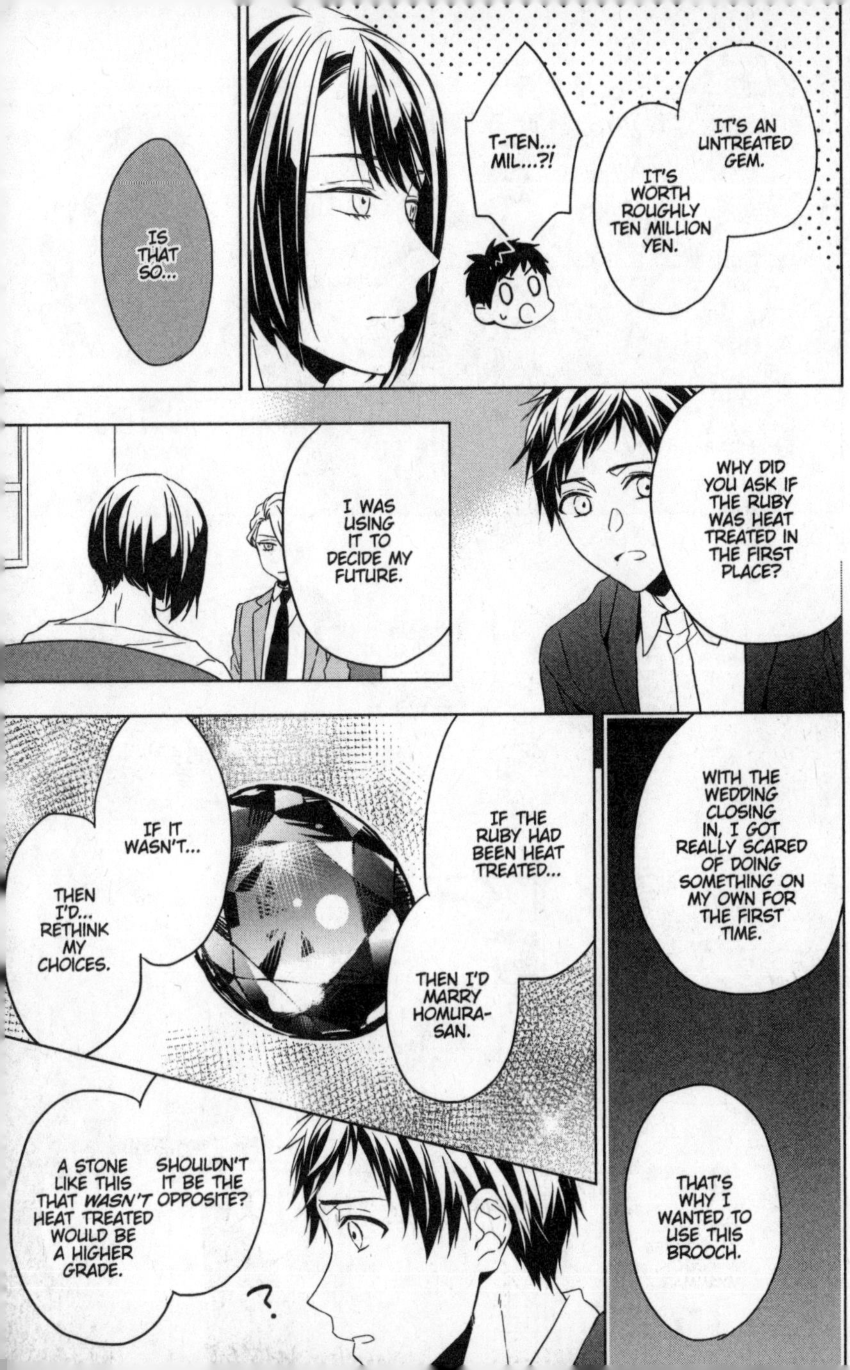
IT'S AN UNTREATED GEM.
IT'S WORTH ROUGHLY TEN MILLION YEN.
T-TEN... MIL...?!
IS THAT SO...
WHY DID YOU ASK IF THE RUBY WAS HEAT TREATED IN THE FIRST PLACE?
I WAS USING IT TO DECIDE MY FUTURE.
WITH THE WEDDING CLOSING IN, I GOT REALLY SCARED OF DOING SOMETHING ON MY OWN FOR THE FIRST TIME.
THAT'S WHY I WANTED TO USE THIS BROOCH.
IF THE RUBY HAD BEEN HEAT TREATED...
THEN I'D MARRY HOMURA-SAN.
IF IT WASN'T...
THEN I'D... RETHINK MY CHOICES.
SHOULDN'T IT BE THE OPPOSITE?
A STONE LIKE THIS THAT *WASN'T* HEAT TREATED WOULD BE A HIGHER GRADE.
?

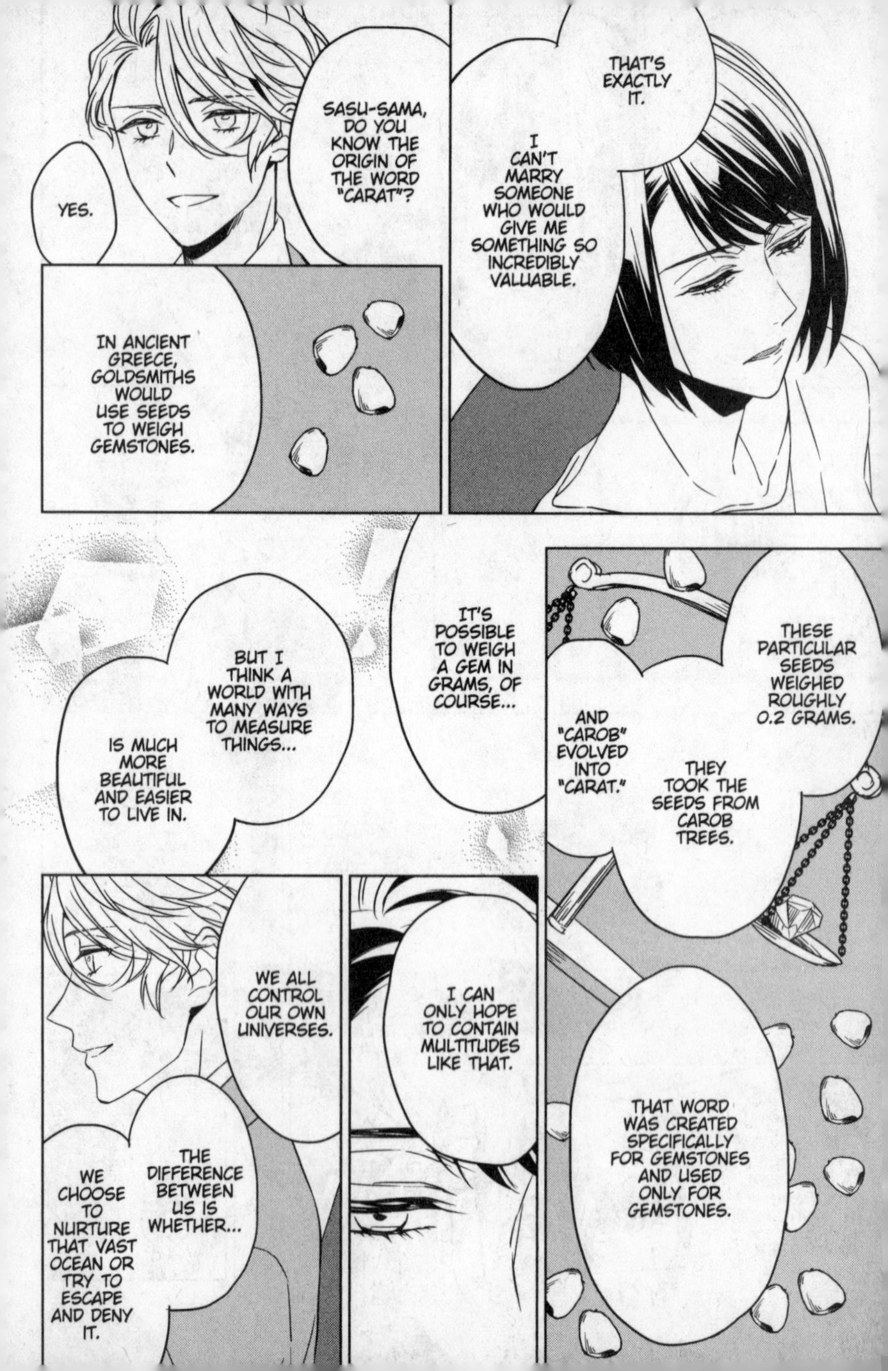
THAT'S EXACTLY IT.
I CAN'T MARRY SOMEONE WHO WOULD GIVE ME SOMETHING SO INCREDIBLY VALUABLE.
SASU-SAMA, DO YOU KNOW THE ORIGIN OF THE WORD "CARAT"?
YES.
IN ANCIENT GREECE, GOLDSMITHS WOULD USE SEEDS TO WEIGH GEMSTONES.
THESE PARTICULAR SEEDS WEIGHED ROUGHLY 0.2 GRAMS.
THEY TOOK THE SEEDS FROM CAROB TREES.
AND "CAROB" EVOLVED INTO "CARAT."
THAT WORD WAS CREATED SPECIFICALLY FOR GEMSTONES AND USED ONLY FOR GEMSTONES.
IT'S POSSIBLE TO WEIGH A GEM IN GRAMS, OF COURSE...
BUT I THINK A WORLD WITH MANY WAYS TO MEASURE THINGS...
IS MUCH MORE BEAUTIFUL AND EASIER TO LIVE IN.
I CAN ONLY HOPE TO CONTAIN MULTITUDES LIKE THAT.
WE ALL CONTROL OUR OWN UNIVERSES.
THE DIFFERENCE BETWEEN US IS WHETHER...
WE CHOOSE TO NURTURE THAT VAST OCEAN OR TRY TO ESCAPE AND DENY IT.

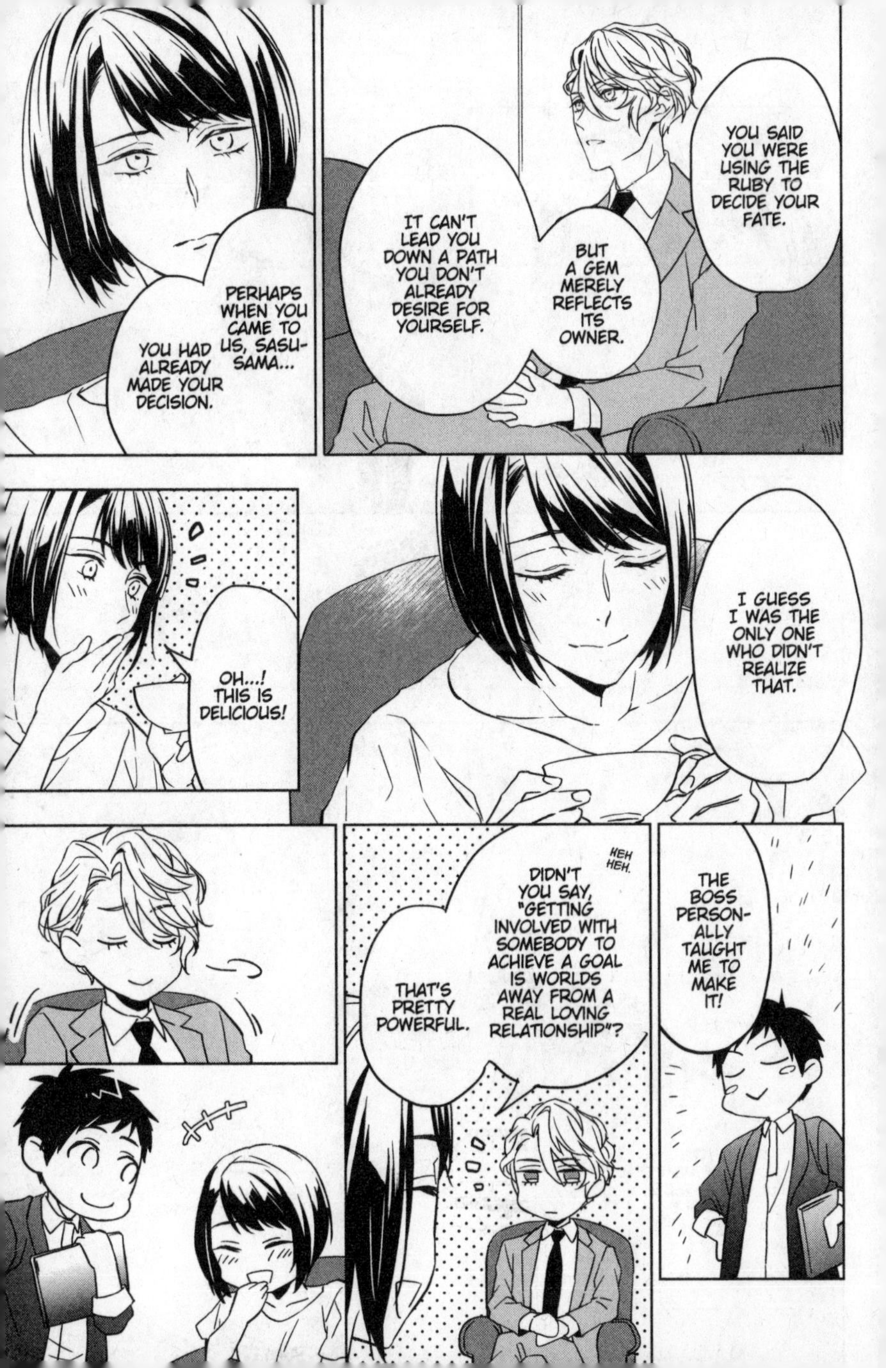
YOU SAID YOU WERE USING THE RUBY TO DECIDE YOUR FATE.
BUT A GEM MERELY REFLECTS ITS OWNER.
IT CAN'T LEAD YOU DOWN A PATH YOU DON'T ALREADY DESIRE FOR YOURSELF.
PERHAPS WHEN YOU CAME TO US, SASU-SAMA...
YOU HAD ALREADY MADE YOUR DECISION.
I GUESS I WAS THE ONLY ONE WHO DIDN'T REALIZE THAT.
OH...! THIS IS DELICIOUS!
THE BOSS PERSONALLY TAUGHT ME TO MAKE IT!
HEH HEH.
DIDN'T YOU SAY, "GETTING INVOLVED WITH SOMEBODY TO ACHIEVE A GOAL IS WORLDS AWAY FROM A REAL LOVING RELATIONSHIP"?
THAT'S PRETTY POWERFUL.

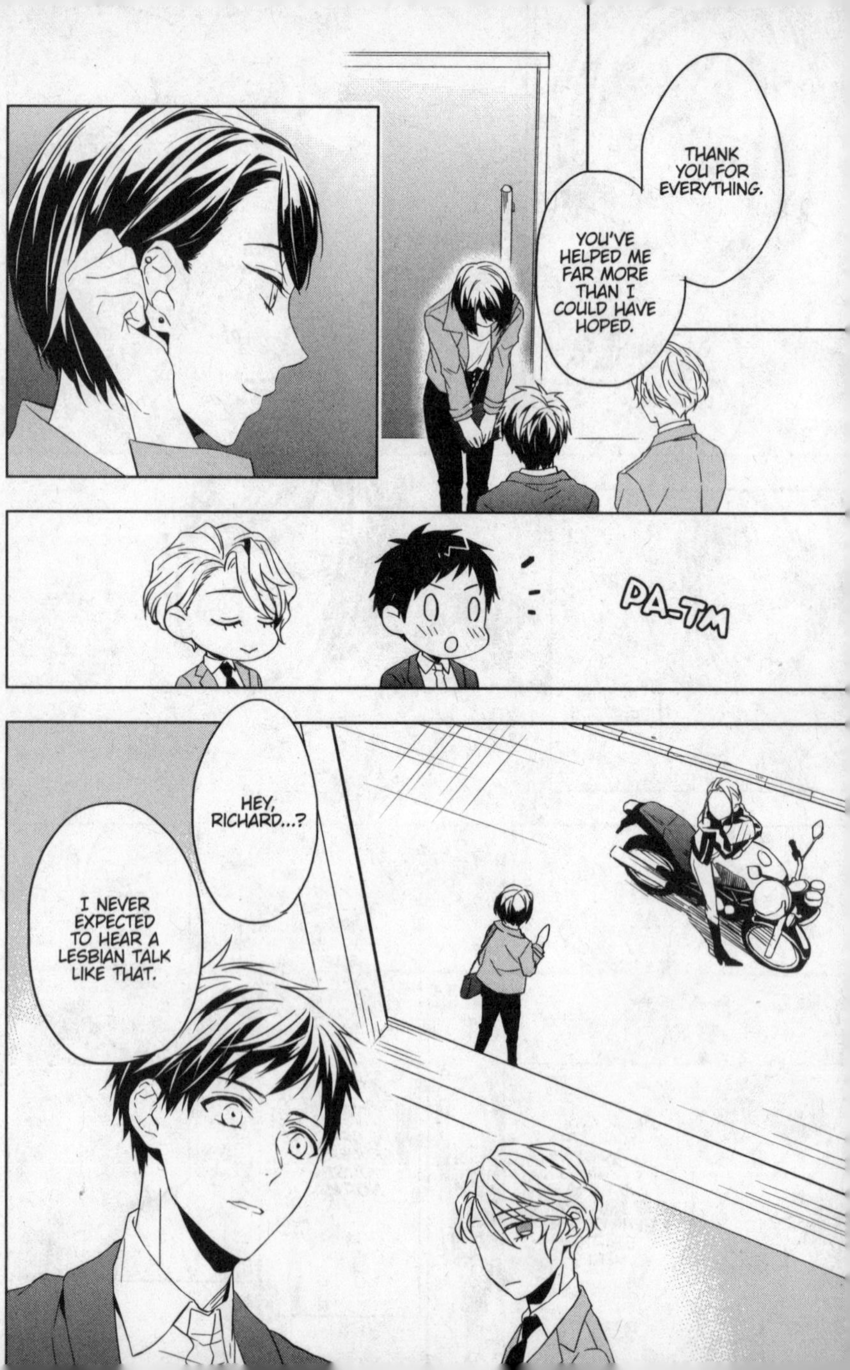
THANK YOU FOR EVERYTHING.
YOU'VE HELPED ME FAR MORE THAN I COULD HAVE HOPED.
PA-TM
HEY, RICHARD...?
I NEVER EXPECTED TO HEAR A LESBIAN TALK LIKE THAT.

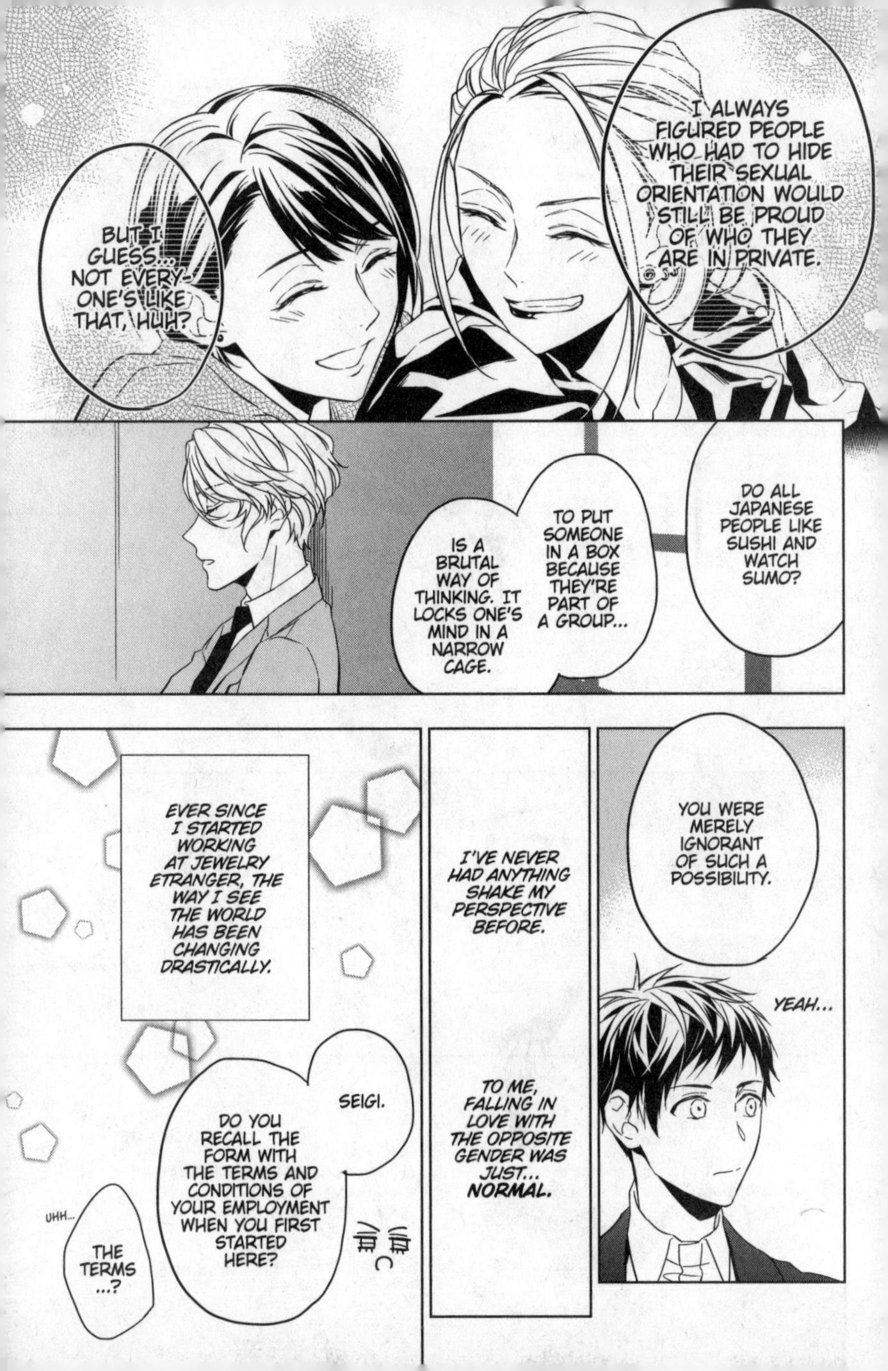
I ALWAYS FIGURED PEOPLE WHO HAD TO HIDE THEIR SEXUAL ORIENTATION WOULD STILL BE PROUD OF WHO THEY ARE IN PRIVATE.
BUT I GUESS... NOT EVERY-ONE'S LIKE THAT, HUH?
DO ALL JAPANESE PEOPLE LIKE SUSHI AND WATCH SUMO?
TO PUT SOMEONE IN A BOX BECAUSE THEY'RE PART OF A GROUP...
IS A BRUTAL WAY OF THINKING. IT LOCKS ONE'S MIND IN A NARROW CAGE.
YOU WERE MERELY IGNORANT OF SUCH A POSSIBILITY.
YEAH...
I'VE NEVER HAD ANYTHING SHAKE MY PERSPECTIVE BEFORE.
TO ME, FALLING IN LOVE WITH THE OPPOSITE GENDER WAS JUST... **NORMAL.**
EVER SINCE I STARTED WORKING AT JEWELRY ETRANGER, THE WAY I SEE THE WORLD HAS BEEN CHANGING DRASTICALLY.
SEIGI.
DO YOU RECALL THE FORM WITH THE TERMS AND CONDITIONS OF YOUR EMPLOYMENT WHEN YOU FIRST STARTED HERE?
UHH...
THE TERMS ...?

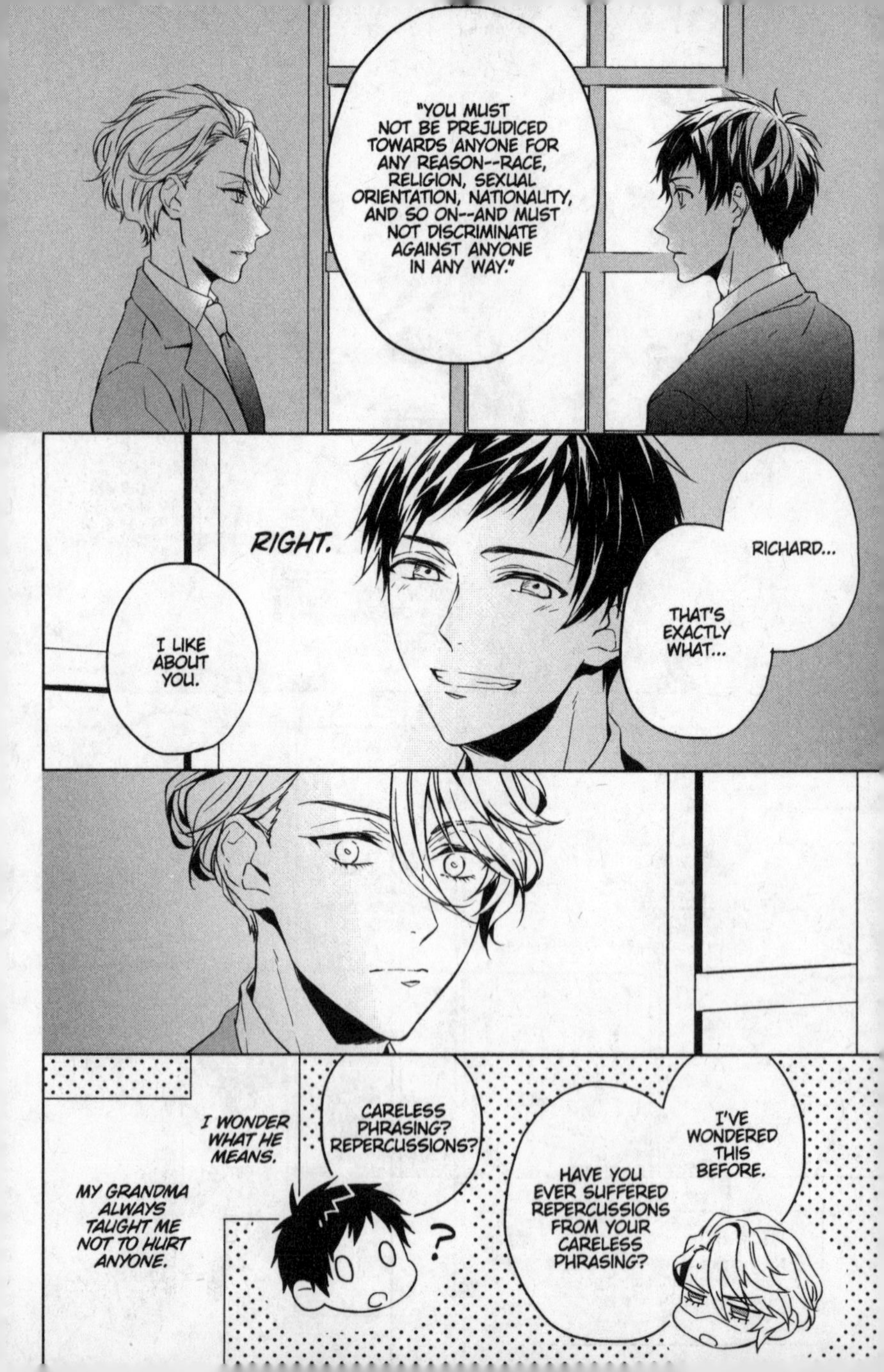
"YOU MUST NOT BE PREJUDICED TOWARDS ANYONE FOR ANY REASON--RACE, RELIGION, SEXUAL ORIENTATION, NATIONALITY, AND SO ON--AND MUST NOT DISCRIMINATE AGAINST ANYONE IN ANY WAY."
RICHARD...
THAT'S EXACTLY WHAT...
RIGHT.
I LIKE ABOUT YOU.
I'VE WONDERED THIS BEFORE.
HAVE YOU EVER SUFFERED REPERCUSSIONS FROM YOUR CARELESS PHRASING?
CARELESS PHRASING? REPERCUSSIONS?
?
I WONDER WHAT HE MEANS.
MY GRANDMA ALWAYS TAUGHT ME NOT TO HURT ANYONE.

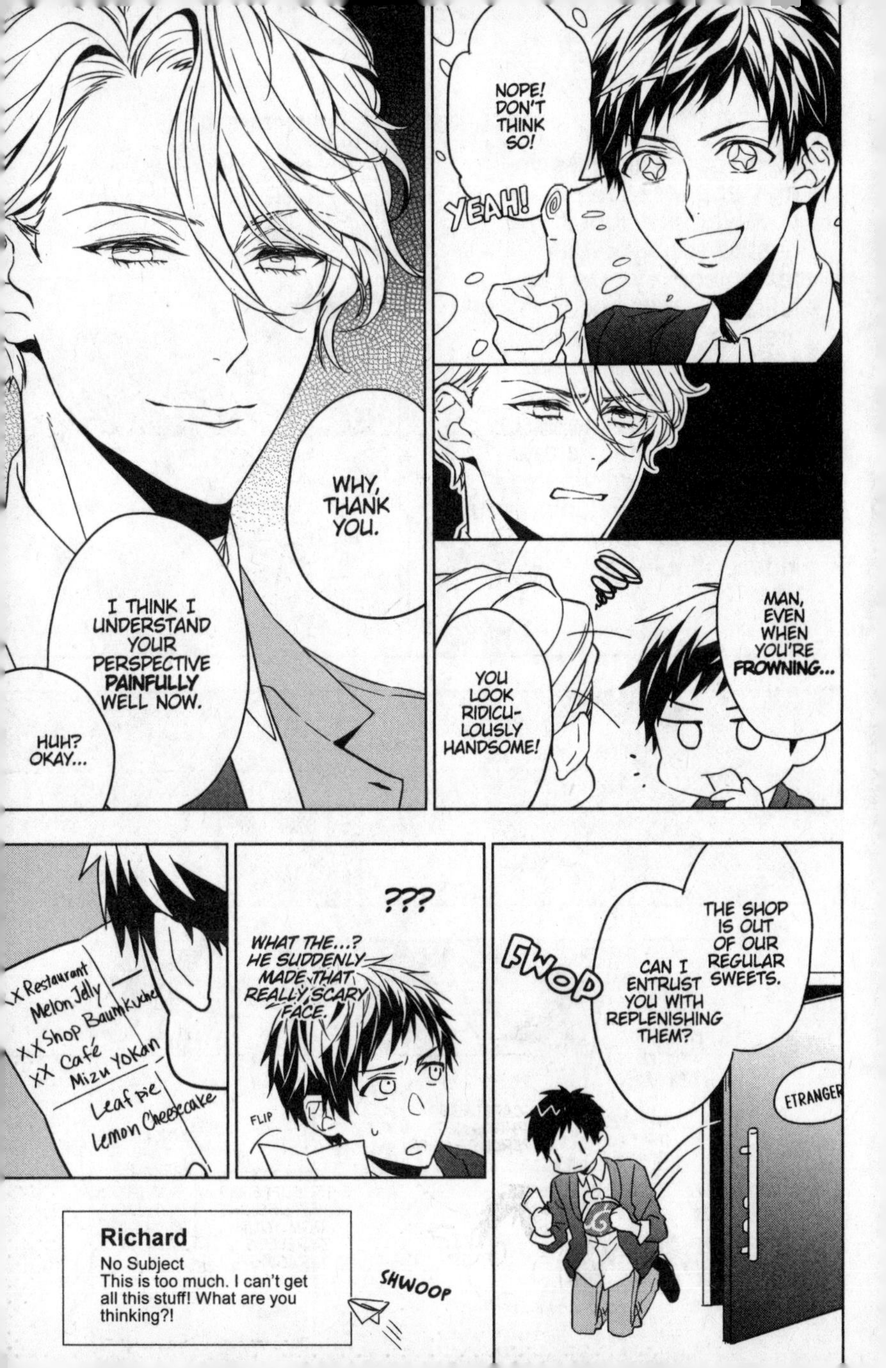
NOPE! DON'T THINK SO!
YEAH!
MAN, EVEN WHEN YOU'RE **FROWNING...**
YOU LOOK RIDICU-LOUSLY HANDSOME!
WHY, THANK YOU.
I THINK I UNDERSTAND YOUR PERSPECTIVE **PAINFULLY** WELL NOW.
HUH? OKAY...
FWOP
THE SHOP IS OUT OF OUR REGULAR SWEETS.
CAN I ENTRUST YOU WITH REPLENISHING THEM?
ETRANGER
???
WHAT THE...? HE SUDDENLY MADE THAT REALLY SCARY FACE.
FLIP
XX Restaurant Melon Jelly
XX Shop Baumkuchen
XX Café Mizu Yokan
Leaf pie
Lemon Cheesecake
SHWOOP
Richard
No Subject
This is too much. I can't get all this stuff! What are you thinking?!

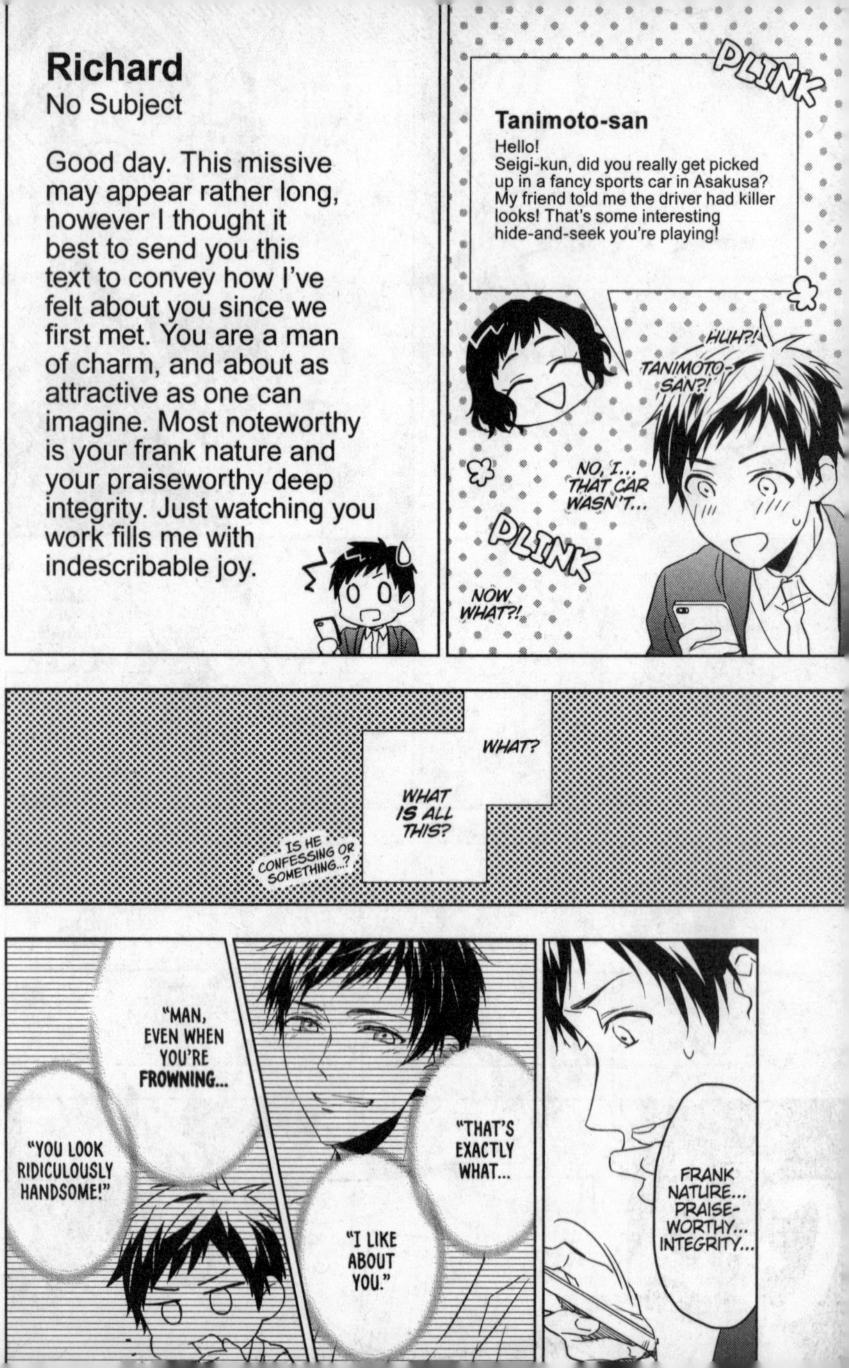
PLINK
Tanimoto-san
Hello!
Seigi-kun, did you really get picked up in a fancy sports car in Asakusa? My friend told me the driver had killer looks! That's some interesting hide-and-seek you're playing!
HUH?!
TANIMOTO-SAN?!
NO, I... THAT CAR WASN'T...
PLINK
NOW WHAT?!
Richard
No Subject
Good day. This missive may appear rather long, however I thought it best to send you this text to convey how I've felt about you since we first met. You are a man of charm, and about as attractive as one can imagine. Most noteworthy is your frank nature and your praiseworthy deep integrity. Just watching you work fills me with indescribable joy.
WHAT?
WHAT IS ALL THIS?
IS HE CONFESSING OR SOMETHING...?
FRANK NATURE... PRAISE-WORTHY... INTEGRITY...
"THAT'S EXACTLY WHAT...
"I LIKE ABOUT YOU."
"MAN, EVEN WHEN YOU'RE FROWNING...
"YOU LOOK RIDICULOUSLY HANDSOME!"

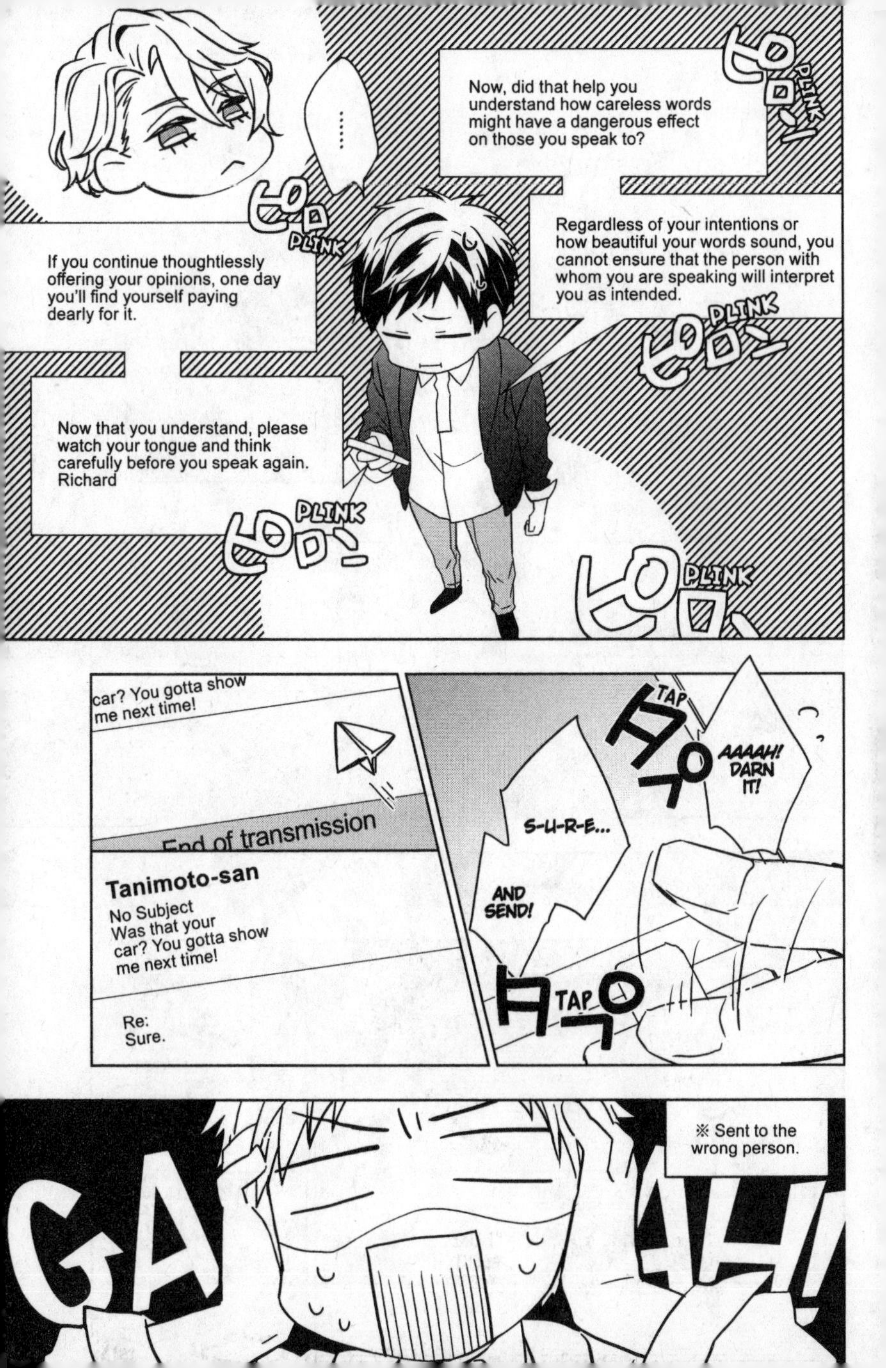

PLINK
Now, did that help you understand how careless words might have a dangerous effect on those you speak to?
......
PLINK
Regardless of your intentions or how beautiful your words sound, you cannot ensure that the person with whom you are speaking will interpret you as intended.
PLINK
If you continue thoughtlessly offering your opinions, one day you'll find yourself paying dearly for it.
PLINK
Now that you understand, please watch your tongue and think carefully before you speak again.
Richard
PLINK
TAP
AAAAH! DARN IT!
S-U-R-E...
AND SEND!
TAP
car? You gotta show me next time!
End of transmission
Tanimoto-san
No Subject
Was that your car? You gotta show me next time!
Re:
Sure.
※ Sent to the wrong person.
GAAH!

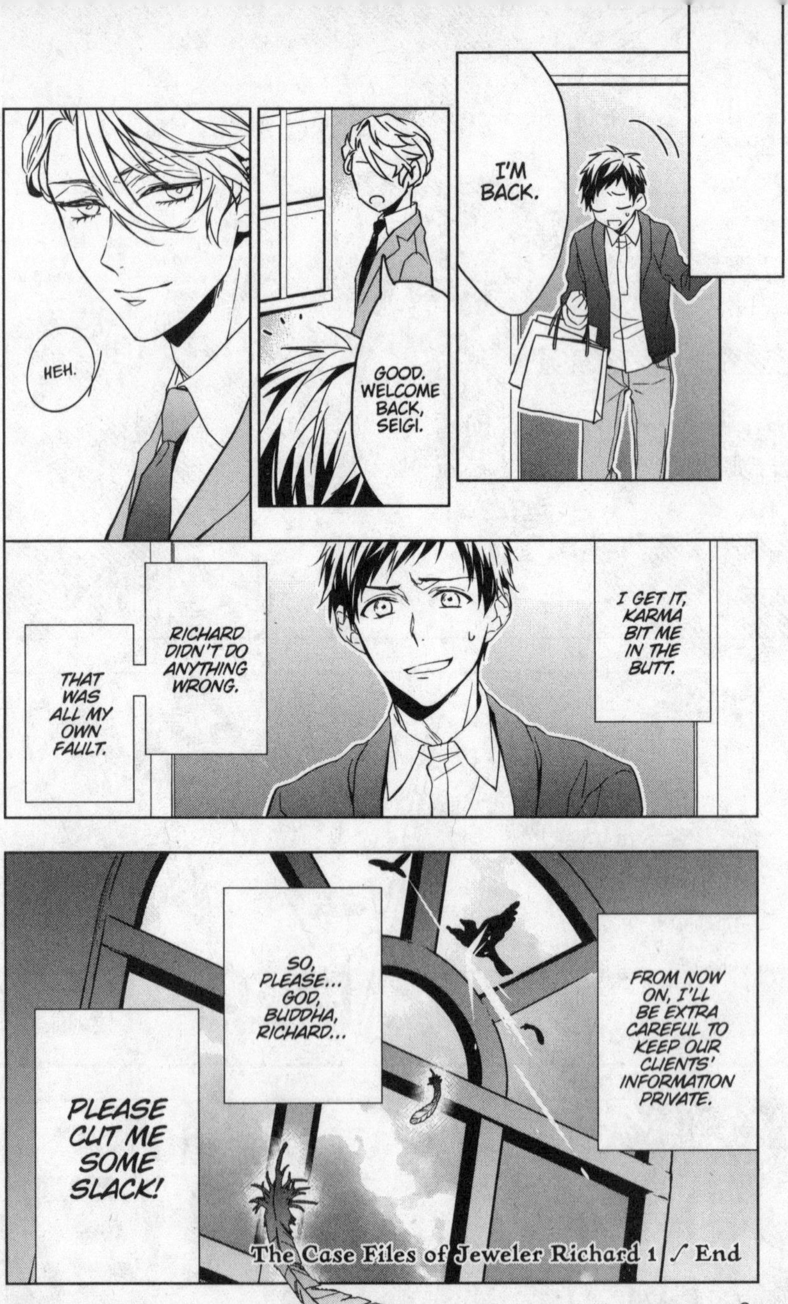
I'M BACK.
GOOD. WELCOME BACK, SEIGI.
HEH.
I GET IT, KARMA BIT ME IN THE BUTT.
RICHARD DIDN'T DO ANYTHING WRONG.
THAT WAS ALL MY OWN FAULT.
FROM NOW ON, I'LL BE EXTRA CAREFUL TO KEEP OUR CLIENTS' INFORMATION PRIVATE.
SO, PLEASE... GOD, BUDDHA, RICHARD...
PLEASE CUT ME SOME SLACK!
The Case Files of Jeweler Richard 1 / End

THE CASE FILES OF JEWELER RICHARD

THE CASE FILES OF JEWELER RICHARD

Hello! I'm **Nanako Tsujimura,** the original creator of this series.

Congratulations on the release of the manga version of *The Case Files of Jeweler Richard*!

Light novels are a world of text. Manga is a world of text *and* art. It can craft a world of *Jeweler Richard* that's entirely unique, and reconstruct that world within a new medium. Watching this world bloom is so intriguing and beautiful, every time.

Every month, I'm touched by the clean, beautiful, and sometimes comedic manga version. As a fan who truly enjoys this luxurious jewelry box world, I am overjoyed from the bottom of my heart to see this book. Now it'll be that much easier to reread all of the chapters!

Akatsuki-sensei, truly, thank you for what you've created. Please get some proper rest. I look forward to working with you in our shared future! I love this world that you have created!

I hope you readers will continue to enjoy the manga world of *Jeweler Richard*, too!

It's a pleasure
to meet you.
My name is Mikka
Akatsuki. *The Case
Files of Jeweler
Richard* manga has
finally been serialized
and released in book
form. I hope you
enjoyed the jewel-like,
colorful, shining
story in its new
manga form!

©

The white gloves and gemstones were decided from the start. I thought it might be better if it looked even shinier, so that's how we decided on the ultimate cover.

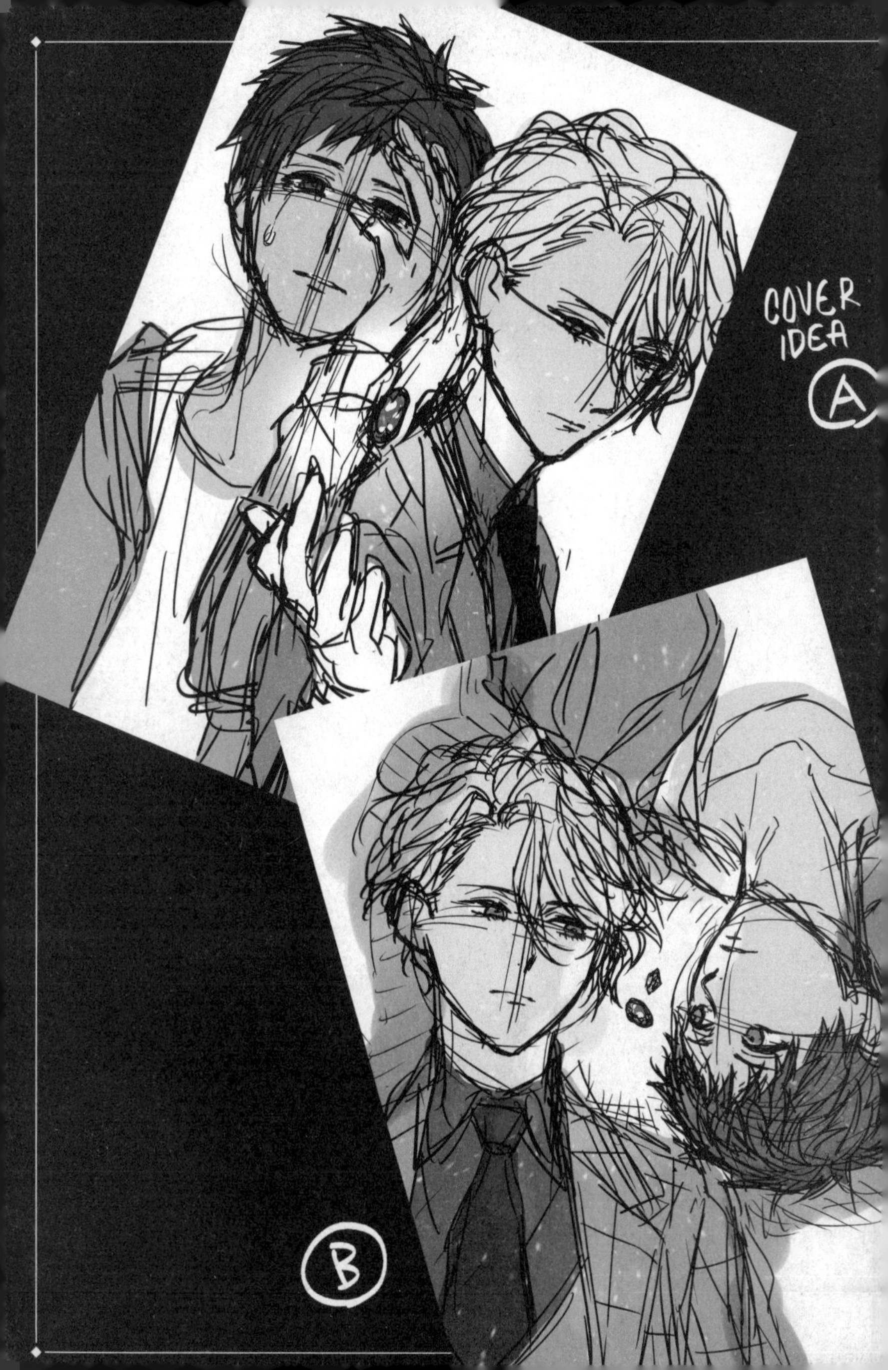
COVER IDEA
A
B

THE CASE FILES
OF
JEWELER
RICHARD

SEVEN SEAS ENTERTAINMENT PRESENTS

The Case Files of Jeweler Richard

Vol. 1

art by **MIKA AKATSUKI** story by **NANAKO TSUJIMURA** character design by **UTAKO YUKIHIRO**

TRANSLATION
Jacqueline Fung

ADAPTATION
Ysabet Reinhardt MacFarlane

LETTERING
Danya Shevchenko

COVER DESIGN
Hanase Qi

PROOFREADER
Kurestin Armada

EDITOR
Shanti Whitesides

PRODUCTION MANAGER
Lissa Pattillo

PREPRESS TECHNICIAN
Melanie Ujimori

PRINT MANAGER
hiannon Rasmussen-Silverstein

EDITOR-IN-CHIEF
Julie Davis

ASSOCIATE PUBLISHER
Adam Arnold

PUBLISHER
Jason DeAngelis

HOUSEKISHOU RICHARD-SHI NO NAZOKANTEI VOL. 1

First published in Japan in 2020 by Ichijinsha Inc., Tokyo.
Publication rights for this English edition arranged through Kodansha Ltd., Tokyo.

Seven Seas press and purchase enquiries can be sent to Marketing Manager Lianne Sentar at press@gomanga.com. Information regarding the distribution and purchase of digital editions is available from Digital Manager CK Russell at digital@gomanga.com.

ISBN: 978-1-64827-837-2
Printed in Canada
First Printing: February 2022
10 9 8 7 6 5 4 3 2 1

READING DIRECTIONS

This book reads from ***right to left***, Japanese style. If this is your first time reading manga, you start reading from the top right panel on each page and take it from there. If you get lost, just follow the numbered diagram here. It may seem backwards at first, but you'll get the hang of it! Have fun!!

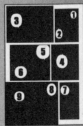

1
2
3
4
5
6
7
8
9